38·39.

# The Network Press Administrator's Handbook to NetWare 4.11/ IntranetWare

D1759418

# The Network Press Administrator's Handbook to NetWare® 4.11/IntranetWare™

Michael G. Moncur

NETWORK PRESS
SYBEX

San Francisco ■ Paris ■ Düsseldorf ■ Soest

Associate Publisher: Steve Sayre
Acquisitions Manager: Kristine Plachy
Acquisitions & Developmental Editor: Guy Hart-Davis
Editor: Dusty Bernard
Project Editor: Shelby Zimmerman
Technical Editor: David Kearns
Book Designer: London Road Design
Graphic Illustrator: Inbar Berman
Electronic Publishing Specialists: Bill Gibson, Bob Bihlmayer
Production Coordinator: Kimberley Askew-Qasem
Indexer: Lynnzee Elze Spence
Cover Designer: Archer Design
Cover Photographer: Ron Thomas (FPG International)

Library of Congress Card Number: 96-69288
ISBN: 0-7821-1949-2

Manufactured in the United States of America

10 9 8 7 6 5 4 3 2

*This book is dedicated to my wife, Laura Moncur.*
*I couldn't have done it without your support.*

# Acknowledgments

PRODUCING A GOOD book requires a team effort, and I'm thankful to the other members of the team. Guy Hart-Davis at Sybex got things started and has lent a hand throughout the project. Shelby Zimmerman and Barbara Gordon kept things running smoothly. Kristine Plachy helped with the business side of things. Thanks also go to the many other members of the Sybex team who helped put together this book.

Dusty Bernard edited the text and provided many useful suggestions; the clarity of this book's explanations owes a great deal to her watchful eye. Dave Kearns was extremely helpful in fine-tuning the technical details that make up each chapter and also provided helpful feedback. Thanks also to Carl Montgomery for his help with the cover text.

I'd like to thank my previous employers—Cummins Intermountain, Call-Ware Technologies, and Reliant Data Systems. My time there gave me much needed real-world experience with NetWare. I'd also like to thank Novell for continued innovation and for providing helpful beta copies of the latest versions. Thanks also to John Jenkins at Computerland in Salt Lake City for the use of his network.

On the personal side, I'd like to thank my wife, Laura, and my family—Mom, Dad, Kristen, Matt and Melanie, and their upcoming addition to the family. I'd also like to thank my friends, including Dylan and Joan, Chuck, Cory and Kathleen, Matt and Kristy, Robert, Curt, and James. Thanks for your friendship and support.

# Contents at a Glance

# Table of Contents

# Introduction

ETWARE HAS BEEN the premier network operating system for years, and with the latest versions, NetWare 4.11 and IntranetWare, it's been improved again. Although easy to work with in most cases, NetWare 4 has many complex features.

NetWare can be confusing—and downright frustrating—at times, but keeping a network running smoothly can be a rewarding experience, and an enjoyable career. I hope you find this book a helpful addition to your administrator's toolkit.

## Who Should Read This Book?

This book is a helpful guide to the most important—and the most confusing—features of NetWare 4. It has been designed for the network administrator. Whether you're an experienced NetWare administrator upgrading to NetWare 4 or a beginner at NetWare administration, this book is for you. However, we have made a few assumptions:

- You should have a basic knowledge of computers and networking. This book does not explain computing basics, but it does cover DOS and Windows operating systems, which are required to run NetWare 4 utilities.

- You'll need a network with at least one workstation and one NetWare 4 server in order to follow along with the examples. A workstation running DOS or Windows is required for most NetWare 4 utilities.

- This book includes a chapter on NetWare 3.1x administration since many networks still include this version. If your network is composed entirely of NetWare 3.1x servers, this book won't be very useful—unless you plan to upgrade.

Whether you're experienced with DOS, Windows, Macintosh, or UNIX, you'll have no trouble understanding this book. Where appropriate, I've included comparisons between NetWare 4's features and their counterparts in these operating systems.

## How This Book Is Organized

While you may enjoy reading this book cover to cover, if you're a typical Net-Ware 4 administrator you probably don't have time. To accommodate the sometimes hectic schedule of network administration, this book has been designed to be read in any order.

For example, if you need to configure or troubleshoot NetWare 4 printing, you can turn directly to Chapter 8, "NetWare 4 Printing." Ample cross-references are provided for information in other chapters and the comprehensive appendices.

This book has been designed to cover the essentials of NetWare 4 administration without unnecessary academic details. You may wish to refer to the NetWare 4 manuals or electronic documentation for additional information.

## Conventions Used in This Book

This book has been designed to cover NetWare 4.1, including the latest versions, NetWare 4.11 and IntranetWare. To avoid confusion, we have used the following conventions:

- Items that refer to *NetWare 4.11*, *NetWare 4.1*, or another exact number are specific to those versions.

- *NetWare 4* refers in general to NetWare 4.1 or 4.11. Most of these items should also apply to NetWare 4.0 through 4.02, but there may be minor differences.

- *NetWare 3.1*x refers to NetWare 3.11 or 3.12; the versions are similar.

- *IntranetWare,* as described in Chapter 17, is the new product from Novell that includes NetWare 4.11 along with Internet-related products.

## How to Contact the Author

I'd love to receive your comments about this book and hear about interesting problems and solutions you've discovered with your network. I'll also try my best to answer any questions you may have—but be patient, since I'm usually about two weeks behind on my e-mail.

You can reach me at the following address:

- Internet e-mail: nwadmin@starlingtech.com

- CompuServe: 102516,224

- World Wide Web: http://www.starlingtech.com/books/

# The NetWare 4 Network

W HEN IBM FIRST introduced the PC, it wasn't really intended to compete with the mainframe computers most large businesses used. It was a small, simple computer with its own disk storage. It had only one screen and one keyboard, and it didn't allow multiple users. Now, however, almost every business uses PCs, and there are few mainframe vendors left. The reason, of course, is networking.

The definition of a network can be very simple: two or more computers that communicate in some fashion. It can also be very complex, involving such buzzwords as *client-server* and *resource sharing*. In this chapter we'll discuss the basics of networking from a NetWare 4 perspective, including a network's purpose, its components, and the wires that keep it connected.

# Components of a Network

A NY TWO COMPUTERS with a connection between them can be a network. However, NetWare 4 is used with a specific kind of network called *client-server*. This simply means that there are two kinds of computers on the network:

- *Servers* provide services, and users share them on the network.

- *Clients* are the users' machines that share the resources of the server.

Typically, in a NetWare network, the client and server machines are both ordinary, IBM-compatible PCs, although just about any machine can be used as a client. The difference between them lies in how they are used and in the software that runs on them.

*The alternative to a client-server network is a peer-to-peer network, in which all machines may act as both clients and servers. LANtastic, Windows 95, and OS/2 Warp Connect are examples of peer-to-peer systems.*

The components of a typical network are shown in Figure 1.1. We'll discuss each of them in the following sections.

**FIGURE 1.1**

Components of a typical network

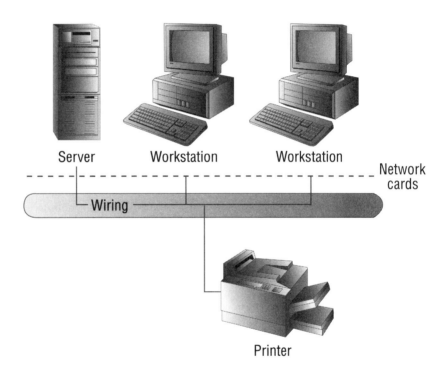

## The Server

The most important piece of hardware in a NetWare 4 network is the server. The server's storage devices, memory, and peripherals, such as printers, are shared by users on the network.

A NetWare 4 server is a *dedicated* server; this means it spends all its time acting as a server for other users. It isn't used to run end-user applications.

Typically, the server is locked in a secure room (or even a closet) and isn't accessed except to manage and maintain the network.

While a typical computer uses DOS, Windows, or another operating system, the server runs a *network operating system,* or *NOS.* The NOS is a piece of software that manages client connections, security, and resource sharing. As you might have guessed, the NOS that runs on a NetWare 4 server is NetWare 4.

Although several companies sell computers that are specifically designed to be servers, any PC can be used as a NetWare server if it meets certain requirements:

- **Memory:** At least 12MB. 16MB is a much more practical minimum.

- **Disk storage:** This depends on the number of users and the data they will store on the server. A typical small company (five or fewer users) server uses about 1GB of disk storage.

- **Processor:** NetWare 4 requires a 386 or newer processor. Because a busy server does a lot of thinking, a fast 486 or Pentium is a practical minimum.

You'll find more details on the type of machine you'll need for a NetWare 4 server in Chapter 13.

A typical small NetWare 4 network has only one server. A larger network might use many servers; in fact, NetWare 4 has features that make it as easy to manage the network on many servers as on a single server.

## Workstations

Although a server is important to the network, it isn't much use by itself. You can't run your favorite word processor, database, or spreadsheet on the server, because it's dedicated to networking. As a matter of fact, you can't even create a new user using the server itself. That's where workstations come in.

A *workstation* (also called a client) is a computer that connects to the network and uses the resources of the network. There are usually many more workstations than servers on the network because one workstation is needed for each currently active user.

*The word* workstation *has several meanings in the computer field, including a dumb terminal, a high-powered graphics workstation, and even a type of furniture. Throughout this book we refer to the NetWare definition of a workstation: a computer (client) that connects to the network.*

Client workstations run typical software, such as word processors, spreadsheets, and databases. This is the same software a stand-alone machine might use, and it does not even have to be aware that the network exists. (Some advanced applications do have special functions for networks; for example, WordPerfect allows you to print directly to a printer on the network.)

Before the workstation can use the network's resources, it must run the *network client software.* For DOS, Windows, and Windows 95 machines on a NetWare 4 network, the software is called the NetWare 32-Bit Client. (Some networks still use an older version—the NetWare DOS Requester). The software functions as a TSR (terminate-and-stay-resident) program; this means it runs once, usually automatically, to attach to the network, and a portion of it stays in memory to maintain the network connection.

The reason you can use non-network applications and still take full advantage of the network is that the NetWare client offers *redirection;* this means that accesses to a local device are redirected to a network device. For example, after loading the NetWare client, you can save files on a network disk drive as though it were a local one and print files to a network printer as easily as to a local printer.

A workstation is typically an ordinary computer, and in fact, you can use just about any computer as a workstation on a NetWare 4 network. The following platforms are supported, each with its own version of the NetWare client:

- MS-DOS (Microsoft Disk Operating System), running on PC-compatible computers. Anything from an 8088 to the latest Pentium Pro can be used, although a 386 or better is required to run the latest and most versatile client software. Other versions of DOS, such as IBM DOS and Novell DOS, can also be used.

- Microsoft Windows (version 3.1 or Windows for Workgroups), running on 386 or better PC-compatibles. Since these versions of Windows run on top of DOS, the DOS client can be used with special add-ons for Windows functionality. The latest client, Client 32 for DOS/Windows 3.*x,* supports both DOS and Windows.

- Microsoft Windows 95, using the latest 32-bit client (Client 32 for Windows 95).

- Microsoft Windows NT. Although Windows NT was previously not well supported, new client software allows it full NetWare connectivity.

- NetWare for Macintosh supports Macintosh computers. Almost any Macintosh can be used, but the latest client software requires system 7.0 or above as the operating system.

- UNIX workstations and servers, using software available separately from Novell or from the UNIX vendor.

We'll discuss the various types of client software and how to install them in Chapter 3. In addition, Chapter 16 covers the Macintosh features in detail.

## Network Cards and Wiring

Data has to travel from the workstation to the server and back, and this is accomplished through network wiring. Wiring comes in various sizes and shapes, and some networks even connect through wireless radio or infrared links. We'll look at the various common types of wiring in detail in the section "Networking Standards" later in this chapter.

Most computers don't have a network connection of any kind built in. This is where *network cards* come in. Also called network boards or network interface cards (NICs), these devices provide the interface between the computer and the network wiring.

*Some computers, such as high-end models made by Dell, IBM, and Compaq, include network functionality. In this case the circuitry of a network card is built into the motherboard but functions similarly to an external network card.*

For PC-compatible machines, a network card is typically inserted into one of the slots (ISA, EISA, PCI, or VESA) inside the computer. In the case of portable computers, this may be a credit card–sized PC-card adapter. Macintosh computers usually come with a network connection, but they sometimes use internal cards or an external network adapter instead.

Novell doesn't include network boards with NetWare. Although some of the newer computers include a network card, you must usually purchase one separately. A wide variety of network boards is available from hundreds of manufacturers. Common ones include Intel, 3COM, and SMC.

In a NetWare 4 network, both workstations and servers use a network card. A busy server might have several different cards. A piece of software called the *network driver* allows the computer to communicate with the card. This driver is included with the network card and is usually different for each manufacturer.

*You can imagine the confusion that would result from having 100 different computers with as many different network cards and drivers. For this reason many administrators find it convenient to standardize on a single type of card for the machines in a company.*

## Peripherals

You'll also find non-computer devices on a typical network; these are referred to as *peripherals*. The most common peripheral is a printer. Any user can use these devices from any workstation on the network. Peripherals fall into three main categories:

- Output devices, such as printers and plotters

- Storage devices, such as disk drives, tape drives, and optical storage

- Communications devices, such as modems, used to link to other networks, mainframes, or the Internet

These peripherals may be attached to the server, to a workstation, to a special dedicated server, or in some cases, directly to the network. NetWare fully supports printing; for other devices, special drivers and client software may be required.

## The Network Administrator

Anything but the simplest network can be complicated—much more so than a simple stand-alone computer with a printer attached. Because of this, typical network users don't have the knowledge to configure new devices, manage access, or solve problems when they occur.

That's where you come in. As a network administrator, your job is to keep the network, and the various machines on it, running efficiently and available to users. This can be a daunting task at times, particularly when everything goes wrong at once. However, with the help of this book, you should be able to do a great job with any NetWare 4 network.

Beyond the technical aspects, a network administrator has a responsibility for communication. You'll need to show the users the proper way to access the network and their computers and how to know when something goes wrong. You'll also need to inform them, in nontechnical terms, when there is a problem and what you are doing to fix it; this can often be the hardest part of the job.

# Network Uses and Services

OBVIOUSLY, COMPANIES WOULDN'T spend thousands of dollars putting together a network if it didn't offer a significant benefit. In this section we look at the benefits a NetWare 4 network can provide.

The benefits a network provides to its users are called *network services*. The following services are provided as part of NetWare 4:

- File sharing

- Printer sharing

- Directory services

- Security

- Data integrity

- Messaging

- Communications services

We'll look at each of these services, and how they are implemented in NetWare 4, in the following sections.

# File Sharing

File sharing is, simply, the ability to allow more than one user to access the same file. In fact, these accesses can happen at the same time. File sharing is an integral part of NetWare 4 and its most important service. For this reason a NetWare server is often referred to as a *file server*.

The files that are shared on a NetWare 4 network are stored on a disk drive (or volume, in NetWare terms) on a server. Any user who is attached to the network and allowed access to the file can use it as easily as a local file.

If you're familiar with the DOS file system and file-naming conventions, you'll be relieved to know that NetWare uses a very similar system. Chapter 4 discusses the NetWare file system in detail.

If all files in a company are shared, you can easily imagine the problems that might be created; a secretary might be working on a document, for example, and the manager might load the same file, change it, and save it, erasing the hours of work the secretary put into it. NetWare protects against this through *file-locking* mechanisms. When one user opens a file, it is locked, so other users can't modify it at the same time. (Unfortunately, the specific application must also support file-locking; if it doesn't, you can still have problems.)

Database applications use a more complex kind of locking called *record locking.* When a user edits a record in the database file, it is locked so that other users can't modify it at the same time. Other users can, however, use other records in the database and can often even read the record that is being modified. NetWare doesn't specifically handle this type of locking; a network-aware database application usually provides it.

# Printer Sharing

Although file sharing allows great increases in productivity for a network's users, most employees like to provide evidence of their productivity in the form of printouts scattered around the office. That's where *printer sharing*—the second most important network service—comes in.

You would be surprised at the number of companies that buy a new printer for each new employee. With a network, this is not necessary. A single printer (or, more often, many printers) can be made available to all the employees in a room, a building, or an entire multinational organization. There's a limit to the usefulness of printer sharing, of course—most users would rather not travel to a foreign country to pick up their printouts. However, this ability can be an advantage when a user needs to get a hard copy of a document quickly to users in several locations.

You can connect a printer to the network in several ways: through the server, through a workstation, or directly to the network cable. Which method you choose will depend on the hardware and the printer's physical location. Regardless of the hookup, NetWare treats all network printers the same way.

With so many users attached to a single printer, at some point two or more of them will try to print at the same time. NetWare manages this situation through the use of a *print queue*. When you print a document to a network printer, the document is stored in a special directory on the server before it is printed. All the documents that need to be printed—called *print jobs*—are stored in this queue. NetWare then sends the documents from the queue to the printer, usually in the order in which they were sent.

In addition to preventing two print jobs from sharing the same piece of paper, print queues offer a versatile array of options. You can assign priorities so that certain jobs (or certain users' jobs) will be printed first. You can also configure several printers to print from the same queue; many companies use this arrangement for invoice printers so a customer isn't kept waiting while other customers' invoices are printed. An administrator or a user can stop and resume printing, restart a printout, and perform other management tasks.

Although it sounds simple, printing is actually one of the more complicated aspects of NetWare 4 and can be one of the most frustrating to get working. For this reason we've devoted all of Chapter 8 to the ins and outs of printing.

## Directory Services

NetWare refers to the servers, printers, users, and other components of the network as *objects*. A large network might incorporate thousands of these objects. One of the most important jobs of a networking system is to keep track of these objects—who or what they are, what they can do, and what they're doing at the moment.

NetWare 4 stores information about all these objects in a database called the *Directory*. (Note the capital *D*; we'll use a capital throughout this book to distinguish this Directory from the directories in the file system.) You manage

the Directory through a service called *NetWare Directory Services,* or *NDS.*
The objects in the Directory are organized in a tree-like structure, as shown in
Figure 1.2.

**FIGURE I.2**

NDS organizes objects
into a tree-like structure.

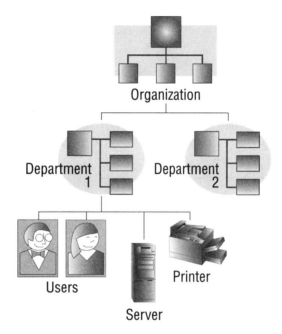

NDS is the most significant feature NetWare 4 provides over NetWare 3.
NetWare 3 uses a database called the bindery to store the same information;
however, each server requires a separate bindery, and on a large network
this can be difficult to manage. NDS solves this problem by keeping the
Directory—a global, distributed database. You can access the Directory from
anywhere on the network, and it is stored on multiple servers.

*You'll probably run into NetWare 3 at times during your career as a NetWare 4 adminis-
trator. Chapter 15 covers the differences between NetWare 3 and NetWare 4 and the
utilities you'll use to manage NetWare 3.*

Along with internally managing the objects that make up the network,
NDS provides a network service: applications can access NDS information to
determine information about users and other objects. The most obvious

example of this is an e-mail application. If you use an NDS-enabled e-mail application, you won't have to reenter information for each user.

NDS is the foundation of NetWare 4, and you can't do much to manage NetWare 4 without understanding it. It's also one of the more complicated features of NetWare 4, so we've devoted Chapters 5 and 6 to the subject of NDS. You'll also run into it in just about every other chapter.

## Security

Thanks to file sharing, users from any location on a huge network can access the same file—but that doesn't mean all of them should. Leaving files accessible across the entire network can be as bad as leaving the doors unlocked when you leave the building. That's why *network security* is an important feature of NetWare.

Although you might think of security as something used by top-secret government organizations and criminals, even the smallest companies can lose data or valuable information because of an insecure network. Small-time criminals, bitter ex-employees, and even bitter current employees may try to read or destroy data they shouldn't be messing with.

Even more important, you must protect the data from the worst enemy of all: users who don't know what they're doing. By properly configuring security, you can prevent most disasters a well-meaning user could cause.

NetWare 4 provides several types of security:

- **Login security:** To access the network, the user needs to enter a username and password. This process is called *logging in* to the network. This information is stored in the NDS Directory. As the network administrator, one of your primary jobs is to create accounts for new users; this process is explained in detail in Chapter 5.

- **Console security:** Someone who gains access to the NetWare server console can do very dangerous things, such as taking the server down or destroying data. For this reason NetWare allows you to lock the console with a password.

- **File system security:** This is the type of security you'll use most frequently. It controls access to files on the server. By using these features you make sure unauthorized users won't use or abuse data.

- **NDS security:** This type of security controls access to objects in the NDS Directory: users, printers, file servers, and any other resource on the network.

- **Communication security:** The data in the network cables can sometimes be vulnerable to unauthorized snooping. NetWare features such as encryption and packet signature ensure that nobody can read your passwords or data in this manner.

- **Network auditing:** NetWare 4 includes a versatile auditing system. The server can keep a log of files and NDS objects that are accessed, created, deleted, or changed. This allows an auditor to be sure there is no unauthorized access and to keep statistics on authorized access.

- **Physical security:** All the security features listed above will do you no good if someone walks up to the file server, turns it off, and takes it home. That's why physical security is important. It is you, not NetWare, who must provide this type of security. A locked room is the first step.

NetWare 4 is known for its powerful security. Everyone from the smallest company to the most secretive government will find the security they need in NetWare 4. The simplest types of security are automatic and require a minimal effort on your part; there are also advanced features complicated enough to write an entire book about. You'll find all the security information you need for most purposes in Chapter 7.

## Data Integrity

All users on the network can store data on the file server. A server in a large company might have several gigabytes of storage, comprising thousands of hours of work by as many users. If you think this sounds a bit like putting all your eggs in one basket, you're right—if the hard drive on the server crashes, all the data from all users can be lost. This would be frustrating, not to mention expensive.

Thankfully, in a well-managed network it's almost impossible to lose a significant amount of data. This is due to the *data integrity* features of NetWare 4. There are many facets to the data protection NetWare offers:

- First and foremost, you should use a *backup system* regularly to copy the data on the network to a more permanent form of storage—usually a tape. NetWare 4 includes a simple backup system.

- In an environment where data is critical, you can use the disk mirroring and disk duplexing features of NetWare 4 to keep multiple copies of the data. When one copy fails, the other is still available. As an extreme case, you can use SFT III to establish multiple servers.

■ NetWare offers *transaction tracking* features that make it easy to protect the integrity of a database. For example, if the server goes down in the middle of writing a record, the transaction-tracking system will know whether the record was finished and can remove a partial record when the server restarts.

The backup system included with NetWare 4 is called SBACKUP. It's a simple program but will work for most purposes. This utility, and the techniques you can use to ensure reliable backups, are discussed in Chapter 11.

## Messaging

We mentioned earlier in the chapter that e-mail is one of the applications that can take advantage of NDS. NetWare provides such an e-mail package, called *MHS,* for *message-handling services.* This service is included with NetWare 4 and can be installed on the NetWare 4 server.

The e-mail in MHS is handled by the MHS utilities, which run on the Net-Ware server. In addition, an actual e-mail application is needed to allow users to send and receive mail. NetWare provides a simple mail client called First-Mail that can be used for this purpose.

MHS also provides services more sophisticated e-mail applications can use. MHS-compatible e-mail applications are available from several companies. The latest release of NetWare 4 also includes a "lite" version of Novell's GroupWise e-mail system, formerly known as WordPerfect Office. Although not an MHS-based system, it is a sophisticated, scaleable mail package.

## Communications Services

Many networks are simply the combination of a server and a few workstations. However, in a large company, much more complicated arrangements exist. Connectivity may be required with other types of networks, such as the IBM OS/2 Warp Server, Banyan VINES, or Microsoft Windows NT; to mainframe computers; and to larger networks, such as the Internet.

These *communications services* are another important NetWare feature. They are handled by several different components of NetWare 4:

■ NetWare provides the Multiprotocol Router (MPR) to allow connectivity to other types of networks. This is referred to as internetworking.

- Mainframe connectivity is provided by separate modules; for example, NetWare for SAA is used to connect with IBM mainframes.

- UNIX networks and the Internet can connect with NetWare through the use of the TCP/IP protocol, included with NetWare 4.

- Macintosh networks are supported through NetWare for Macintosh, also included with NetWare 4.

We'll look at the MPR in Chapter 11, NetWare for Macintosh in Chapter 16, and TCP/IP in Chapter 17.

# Networking Standards and Topologies

S
O FAR, WE'VE been talking about the services NetWare offers, assuming you already have a server and workstations wired together on a network. But how are networks wired? We'll now look at the physical aspects of networking—the types of wiring and the standards for communicating over these wires.

## Networking Basics

The field of network technologies has an entire language of its own, so let's start with the basics. Here are a few of the terms you'll need to understand about networking:

- *Topologies* are the different types of physical network layouts. These are usually referred to as shapes, such as star and ring.

- *Protocols* are the "languages" computers use in talking over the network. These define how data should be sent.

- *Standards* are set to ensure that network devices all operate in the same manner and can be connected. There are many standards in networking, including Ethernet, ARCnet, and Token Ring.

- *Network nodes* are the devices on the network—both clients and servers.

- *Bandwidth* is the maximum speed data can travel through the network. This is usually measured in Mbps, or megabits per second.

## Network Topologies

A network topology defines the shape of the network; in other words, it describes where the wires are connected. This is called a *physical topology;* there are also *logical topologies,* which define the order in which the network data travels through the various nodes. Today's networks use several common topologies, described in the following sections.

### The Bus Topology

In a bus topology all machines are connected to one cable, referred to as the *bus.* Data is sent along the bus and picked up along the way by the intended recipient. An example of such a bus is shown in Figure 1.3.

**FIGURE 1.3**

A network using a bus topology

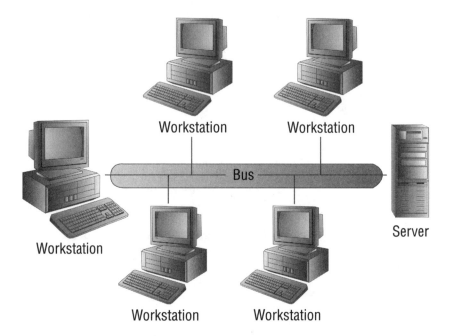

The major disadvantage of a bus topology is that it is vulnerable to wiring problems. Since the data must pass through the entire bus cable, a problem anywhere on the bus can cause several machines—or even the entire network—to go down. This is similar to old-fashioned Christmas lights, in which one dead bulb disables the entire string.

*A large network may use several separate buses; a problem on one bus usually doesn't affect the others.*

### The Star Topology

A star topology is an improvement over a bus. Rather than connecting the machines to each other, each is connected with its own wire to a central *hub*. This type of network is shown in Figure 1.4.

**FIGURE 1.4**

A network that uses a star topology

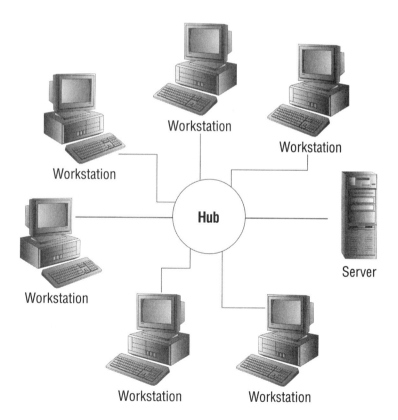

Because each node on the network has its own wire, a problem with one computer will usually be isolated to that computer. This makes star networks much easier to maintain and troubleshoot than bus networks; if a computer loses its connection to the network, you know exactly which wire to check.

The device at the center of the star is the hub. This is sometimes referred to as a *concentrator* or *repeater*. The hub is typically a small box with several network connections on it; the wires to the individual nodes of the network are connected to these ports.

Hubs are available in a more sophisticated model called an *intelligent hub*. This device includes indicators for each of the nodes and makes it much easier to diagnose problems. Many hubs include features to notify the administrator when there is a problem.

*Remember, the server is just another node on the network; it uses the same type of port the workstations do. The hub doesn't detect any difference between clients and servers.*

### The Ring Topology

In a ring topology, the nodes are connected to each other in a ring. Data passes through each node in turn until it reaches the node it was intended for. A network that uses this topology is shown in Figure 1.5.

The ring topology is used chiefly by the Token Ring standard, popularized by IBM. This system uses *token passing* to transmit data; packets called tokens are passed from machine to machine. If a node has data to transmit, it adds it to a token and sends it on its way.

## Networking Standards

Topologies are a good way of visualizing a network, but you can't wire a network using just a topology. You have to use a particular type of wiring, a particular topology, and devices such as network cards and hubs, and they all have to work together. Luckily, this is easy if you follow one of the common standards.

Chances are the network at your company uses one of the standards described in the following sections. Each uses different cabling, network cards, and other devices, and each has its advantages and disadvantages.

**FIGURE 1.5**

A network that uses a ring
topology

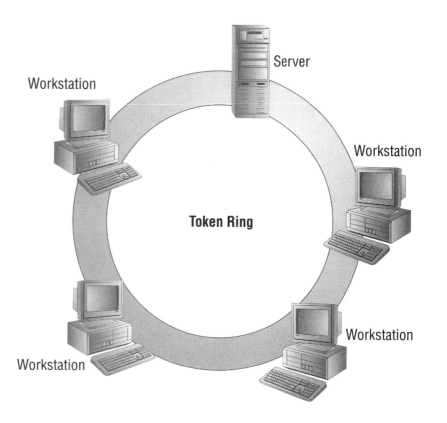

### Ethernet

Xerox, Intel, and Digital Equipment Corporation developed the Ethernet standard. The first version was produced in the 1960s, and the current standard, Ethernet 2.0, was developed in 1982. It is the most commonly used network topology. Estimates for Ethernet usage range from 60 to 90 percent of all networks in the world.

Most commonly, Ethernet uses one of two cable types:

- *10baseT Ethernet* uses UTP (unshielded twisted-pair) cables, similar to the cable used for telephone systems. These cables are wired in a star topology (although it still forms a logical bus) using a 10baseT hub.

■ *10base2 Ethernet* uses coaxial cable (called RG-58). It is wired in a bus topology. One cable connects all the nodes on a network segment, and special "T" connectors attach this cable to each network card. At each end of the bus, a device called *terminator* is attached. This device completes the circuit and prevents data from being lost.

The maximum bandwidth for Ethernet is 10Mbps. In practice, it's usually slower because of network cards, PC processing power, header information, and delays as data is transmitted through the hub. Speeds of 2- to 5Mbps are common.

Because of its advantages in reliability and ease of wiring, 10baseT is the current favorite. The hubs required are relatively inexpensive and usually include convenient diagnostic features.

You'll still see 10base2 Ethernet in many networks. It does have its advantages, even in some new types of networks. For example, if you have a computer on each desk in a classroom, you can easily connect them all to the network using a single stretch of cable.

### ARCnet

Datapoint Corporation developed ARCnet (Attached Resources Computer Network) in the late 1970s. It was a very popular topology for some time but was never quite as popular as Ethernet. Although ARCnet has few advantages for new types of networks, it is still in use in many existing networks.

Like Ethernet, ARCnet can use a variety of cabling standards. It typically uses coaxial cable, but it uses twisted-pair if the equipment supports it. Because most of the existing ARCnet networks are old, coax cable is the most common type.

The nodes in an ARCnet network are wired in a star topology to a central hub. However, ARCnet requires a specific configuration for each node: you have to define a node number for each one, and these numbers must be unique. For this reason ARCnet can be difficult to troubleshoot.

ARCnet operates at a maximum speed of 2.5Mbps, and in practical terms 50 to 60 percent of that speed is typical. Thus, it pales by comparison to Ethernet. However, the speed is largely dependent on the number of nodes; for smaller networks, ARCnet can run quite quickly. Several standards for faster varieties of ARCnet have been developed over the years, but none has become very popular.

Much of the equipment that connects this type of network is proprietary and a bit expensive. ARCnet is not very practical for new networks because of its relatively high cost and lack of support. For at least the next few years, though, don't be surprised to find yourself supporting an ARCnet network.

### Token Ring

The IEEE developed the Token Ring standard, but it didn't become popular until IBM introduced a revised version of the standard. Token Ring works well for high-traffic networks and is widely used in systems that need to link NetWare networks with IBM mainframes. Although Token Ring is not as common as Ethernet, many companies do use it.

The *Ring* in the name refers to the logical topology; physically, Token Ring uses a star topology, so one node's problems can't affect any other nodes. In fact, Token Ring takes this one step further: each node checks on its neighbors and can quickly report a failure.

The original Token Ring specification allowed speeds of 1- to 4Mbps. IBM's version allows speeds up to 16Mbps. IBM standards define the cable types, which include shielded twisted-pair (STP), unshielded twisted-pair (UTP), and fiber-optic cable. Multistation Access Units (MAUs) are used as hubs to connect nodes to the Token Ring network.

There are some considerations specific to Token Ring. Configuration can be difficult, and much of the equipment is proprietary. It is reasonably easy to work with, though, and can achieve high speeds and extreme reliability.

### FDDI

The FDDI (Fiber-optic Distributed Data Interface) standard is designed around fiber-optic cable and high-speed connections. It has some amazing capabilities: the network can operate at speeds of up to 100Mbps, can accommodate up to 1000 nodes, and can work with connections as much as 62 miles (100 kilometers) apart.

These capabilities don't come without a price. FDDI network cards and hubs are expensive, and fiber-optic cable costs as much as ten times more than good-quality twisted-pair cable. Thus, FDDI is used only when it's required—in networks that require high speeds, a large number of nodes, or long distances between nodes.

Because of its high cost and the fact that FDDI is a relatively new standard, it is not a common network configuration. You will usually see it only in large

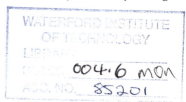

corporations and in high-tech areas such as CAD and data acquisition. In addition, FDDI is often used as a network *backbone,* connecting multiple networks and multiple buildings.

The topology of FDDI is most similar to Token Ring. It uses a logical ring topology and is physically wired as a star. The hubs used in FDDI are designed specifically for high-speed fiber-optic communication and are quite expensive.

FDDI is extremely reliable and can survive in situations where other networks would easily fail. However, you may find it hard to work with because the fiber-optic cable is expensive and requires special tools for installation. A new standard, called CDDI (copper distributed data interface) provides an alternative, supporting similar speeds using category 5 twisted-pair cable. The types of cables are covered in detail in Chapter 14.

### ISDN and ATM

ISDN (Integrated Systems Digital Network) is a new standard that can replace conventional analog phone lines with digital lines. In its basic form it can support speeds of up to 2Mbps—nothing amazing for a network, but revolutionary for a phone-system link.

Although ISDN is over ten years old, it arrived late in the United States. It is now available in many large cities but may be costly because the phone company must provide service. ISDN is becoming a popular way to connect to the Internet at faster speeds than modems use.

ATM (Asynchronous Transfer Mode) is a high-speed network architecture, based on a broadband ISDN, that allows multiple communications over the same wire. It is already in use in some corporate networks, but since it's new, it can be expensive and difficult to implement. It uses fiber-optic cabling, but a new standard will allow it to use UTP cable.

The current ATM standard offers an effective throughput of 155.52Mbps—over 15 times the speed of Ethernet. Future versions are expected to increase this to 622Mbps and even further. Speeds up to 2.4Gbps (Gigabits per second) have been tested and will undoubtedly become available in the next few years. The ATM working group, an organization of companies, is still developing the latest ATM standards.

In addition to the expense of fiber-optic or category 5 cabling, the devices needed to implement ATM on a network—switches and hubs—are currently quite expensive. For that reason it's probably not an economical choice except for networks that need a tremendous amount of speed.

### Fast Ethernet

The popular Ethernet standard, with a maximum transmission speed of 10Mbps, is showing its age. Some companies are already replacing it with 100BaseT, also known as Fast Ethernet. This is a standard that allows up to 100Mbps communication.

Although Fast Ethernet uses the same type of cabling as Ethernet 10baseT (unshielded twisted-pair, category 5), it requires six pairs of wires rather than the two pairs required by normal Ethernet. Thus, cabling may be just a bit more expensive. Hubs and NICs that support this standard currently cost roughly twice as much as their 10Mbps counterparts.

The IEEE has approved 100base-T as a standard for fast Ethernet, and it is becoming popular; about 650,000 adapters were shipped in 1995. Most of the cards and hubs that support these protocols also support conventional Ethernet, allowing you to upgrade the network a segment at a time. Although 100base-T equipment costs more than conventional Ethernet, it is becoming quite economical compared to ATM and FDDI. Because of this, many network managers are using it as an alternative to those standards—and even to replace them.

# *Summary*

THIS CHAPTER HAS discussed the basics of networking with Net-Ware 4, including the following:

- NetWare 4 uses a client-server network architecture and a dedicated server. A NetWare 4 network can include several components: servers, workstations, peripherals such as printers, network cards, and wiring. Because of the complexity of such a network, a network administrator often has a full-time job keeping it working.

- A NetWare server offers certain services to the network. These include, but are not limited to, file sharing, printer sharing, directory services, security, data integrity, messaging, and communications services. Separate servers may offer additional services.

- The actual wiring in a NetWare 4 network can use a bus, star, or ring topology. The most common standards used with NetWare are Ethernet, ARCnet, Token Ring, and FDDI. Two newer standards, ISDN and ATM, offer faster data transport at a price.

# DOS and Windows

CHAPTER

2

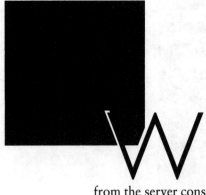

HAT'S A CHAPTER on DOS and Windows doing in a book about NetWare? Well, as we discussed in Chapter 1, you can't perform all your duties as a network administrator from the server console. You need to use a workstation for many tasks. A DOS workstation is required for many of the NetWare utilities, and without a basic knowledge of DOS, you'll have trouble maintaining files on the NetWare server.

You'll also need to understand DOS to get DOS clients working and to support them. The same goes for Windows. Additionally, the NWADMIN (NetWare Administrator) utility, the most important utility in NetWare 4, runs only under Windows.

This chapter doesn't cover the extreme basics, such as how to turn on your computer, what a disk drive is, or how to click with the mouse. We'll focus on the technical details that are important to the NetWare administrator: the commands you'll need to understand, the limitations you'll need to live with, and the files you'll need to modify to keep everything working.

## Understanding DOS

OS STANDS FOR Disk Operating System. This is a bit of a misnomer since it's not strictly a system for dealing with disks. DOS loads onto a PC when it is turned on and takes control at that point. DOS applications use the services of DOS to perform such tasks as displaying information on the screen, storing data in memory, and accessing disk drives.

There are several versions of DOS, but Microsoft's MS-DOS is by far the most common. DOS has been dominant for years in the PC industry and remains as the backbone of Microsoft's current environments, Windows and Windows 95.

# DOS Basics

In case you haven't worked extensively with DOS before, we'll take a quick tour of its basic features. This will include the various DOS versions, the process of installing DOS on a PC, the way files and directories are stored on a DOS disk, and the important files you'll need to use to configure a DOS machine.

### Versions of DOS

MS-DOS (Microsoft Disk Operating System) was the first operating system for IBM PCs. It was originally purchased by Microsoft from a small (and now unknown) software company. It was then licensed to IBM for inclusion with the first PCs, and the rest is history. Although IBM released it under their own name (PC-DOS), Microsoft retained the rights to it and soon licensed it to the many emerging PC clone manufacturers.

Speaking of history, the very first version of DOS was an attempt to copy a much older operating system, CP/M. If you've seen CP/M, you may find parts of DOS painfully familiar. You'll also notice some similarities to UNIX.

At the time of this writing, the current version of MS-DOS is 6.22. This is probably the last version of DOS that will be released separately, because Microsoft is focusing development on Windows 95 and other graphical systems that do not require DOS. (Although there's a version of DOS built into Windows 95, called DOS 7.0, it's not available separately.)

You can roughly judge the age of PCs in a network by the version of DOS that is installed on them. You will still see DOS 5.0 on many network workstations, and DOS 3.3 is not uncommon. There are even a few machines still running DOS 1.0. Most of these machines could benefit from a DOS upgrade. The latest versions are more versatile, include more commands, and can support higher levels of hardware. DOS versions below 4.0, for example, can't access more than 32MB per disk partition.

Because DOS has had many upgrades and at least three different manufacturers in the past five years, it's rare to find a network where all the DOS machines are running the same DOS version. Each manufacturer's version operates a little differently than the others, and not all software will run on all DOS versions. Here are the two other major versions you may run into:

- IBM has continued to develop the DOS it licensed from Microsoft. The latest version, PC-DOS 7.0, is newer than any version of MS-DOS and includes a variety of new features, including better memory management and a sophisticated text editor. However, with the dominance of Microsoft's products, it has little hope for success.

- Digital Research produced DR-DOS. It evolved through several major versions, all slightly improved from their competing MS-DOS versions. About the time MS-DOS 6 was released, Novell bought DR-DOS 6.0 from Digital, hoping to take some of the PC market from Microsoft. Novell later released an upgraded version as Novell DOS 7.0, but it flopped in the marketplace. Novell has since abandoned the product.

You may have noticed that all the competing versions of DOS have similar version numbers; this is not a coincidence, but a game PC software vendors like to play. They're afraid potential customers will judge products by comparing their version numbers, so they make sure they match the competition. One of the most blatant examples of this is Microsoft's word processor, Microsoft Word. When the long-awaited upgrade to Word 2.0 was released, it was called Word 6.0. This happened to coincide with the release of WordPerfect 6.0, Microsoft's major competitor.

*Since the non-Microsoft versions of DOS are fairly uncommon, we'll focus on MS-DOS throughout this chapter. However, you'll find that most of the information still applies to those versions.*

### Installing DOS

These days, most PC-compatible computers include a version of DOS already installed; however, you'll undoubtedly find the need to install DOS on machines that have been repaired or upgraded or just aren't working correctly.

The MS-DOS installation process is simple; you place the first disk in the drive and turn the computer off and on. The installation routine guides you through the process and handles all the details. You simply need to insert the appropriate disk when necessary.

Since most MS-DOS disks are intended for installation on a new PC, you may run into problems if you try to reinstall it. The installation routine will often fail to run after politely informing you that you already have DOS and must be making a mistake.

You can avoid this warning and complete the installation by removing the current version of DOS first. If the drive is empty, you can simply reformat it; otherwise, you'll need to delete the following files:

- Everything in the C:\DOS directory

- The COMMAND.COM and MSDOS.SYS files in the root directory

See the section "Using DOS Commands" later in this chapter for details on performing these tasks.

*The MS-DOS installation program may give you an option to format the hard drive; since this will erase all the information on the drive, be sure this is what you want to do before you agree to it.*

### Files and Directories

One of the most important tasks of DOS is to manage the storage of data on the computer's disk drives. In this section we'll look at the DOS *file system*, which manages this storage. As you'll see in Chapter 4, NetWare's file system is similar. Here are the units of storage DOS uses to divide a disk:

- A *file* is the basic unit of data storage. A word processor document, a data file, and an executable program are all considered files.

- DOS uses a *directory* to organize files into groups and subgroups.

- A *disk partition* is part of a disk that has been set aside for use by DOS, NetWare, or another operating system. In a DOS-only machine, a single partition is typically used for the entire disk.

**FILE NAMES AND PATHS** When you store a file in DOS, you give it a file name. DOS file names have followed the same format since version 1.0, and you may find it a little archaic if you're used to UNIX or the Macintosh. In fact, at times you may find it downright frustrating.

A DOS file name actually consists of two parts:

- A *file name*, which can be up to eight characters

- An *extension*, which can be up to three characters

A period divides the file name from the extension; for example, FILENAME.TXT, CONFIG.SYS, and A.DAT are all valid DOS file names. The extension usually indicates a file's type. Although there is no official list of extensions, these are some common ones:

| EXTENSION | DESCRIPTION |
| --- | --- |
| .TXT | A text file |
| .SYS | DOS system files |
| .EXE, COM | Executable program files |
| .BAT | A batch file (list of DOS commands) |
| .DOC | A word processor document |
| .WK1, .WK3, .WKS, Lotus 1-2-3 | Spreadsheet files |
| .XLS | A Microsoft Excel spreadsheet |
| .DAT | A data file |

Many other extensions are used for various purposes; particularly with Windows applications, practically every application has its own type of files, each with its own extension.

*DOS doesn't require specific extensions for files, but Windows does. Windows uses extensions to associate files with their applications. This allows you to double-click a file and run its corresponding application.*

**FILE-NAMING RULES** Along with the eight-character limit on file names, DOS has some other file-naming rules you should be aware of:

- File names may not contain spaces.

- File names are not case sensitive; you can use lower- or uppercase, but DOS stores all file names in uppercase.

- File names may not contain periods, except to separate the file name and extension.

- The following characters are not allowed:

  ```
  *  ?  [  ]  < >  ,  "  ;  :  /  \  +  =
  ```

- DOS reserves several file names for its own use:

  ```
  AUX
  CLOCK$
  COM1
  COM2
  COM3
  COM4
  CON
  LPT1
  LPT2
  LPT3
  NUL
  PRN
  ```

**DIRECTORIES**  To group files logically, DOS uses a system of directories and subdirectories. The organization of a DOS disk begins with the *root directory*, and directories are created under it. Each of these may have a virtually unlimited number of subdirectories underneath it.

When you specify a file name including its directory (called the *path* to the file), you use a backslash (\) to separate the directories. The initial backslash refers to the root directory. If you specify a drive letter, follow it with a colon (:). If you leave out the drive or directory name, the current drive and directory are assumed.

As a final rule, which you might recognize from UNIX, DOS uses a single period (.) to indicate the current directory and a double period (..) to indicate a parent directory. Table 2.1 shows some examples using all these features.

| | PATH NAME | DESCRIPTION |
| --- | --- | --- |
| **TABLE 2.1**<br>DOS Directory Naming | C:\ | Root directory of drive C |
| | C:\DOS | DOS directory under root of C |

| | PATH NAME | DESCRIPTION |
|---|---|---|
| **TABLE 2.1**<br>DOS Directory Naming<br>(continued) | \DATA | DATA directory under root of current drive |
| | \ | Root directory of current drive |
| | HOME | HOME directory under current directory |
| | ..\FRED | FRED directory under current directory's parent |
| | . | The current directory itself |
| | .. | The current directory's parent directory |
| | C:\DOS\TEMP | TEMP directory under DOS under C root |

**FILE ATTRIBUTES** You can give DOS files (and directories) a number of attributes. These are flags that DOS sets for the file, indicating that it is a certain type of file. DOS and various applications may set these automatically, or you can set them manually using the ATTRIB command (explained in the section "Using DOS Commands" later in this chapter).

DOS supports the following file attributes:

- **H (Hidden):** Hidden files are not usually displayed in a directory listing, but you can still use them by specifying their exact names.

- **R (Read Only):** You cannot write to, rename, or delete the file.

- **S (System):** DOS uses system files. This attribute also implies the Read Only and Hidden attributes.

- **A (Archive):** DOS automatically sets this flag to indicate that a file has changed. Backup programs use this information.

The NetWare file system is similar to the DOS file system and also includes file attributes; however, the list for NetWare is much longer. We'll discuss NetWare's file system in Chapter 4.

**WILDCARDS** When you specify a file name in a DOS command, you can often use *wildcard* characters. These characters allow you to specify a pattern that matches one or more files. These are the wildcards DOS uses:

| | |
|---|---|
| * | Represents any number of characters |
| ? | Represents a single character (or no character) |

You can use these wildcards in both the file name and the extension. If a wildcard matches more than one file, DOS usually performs the action on all the files that match. This can be useful, for example, for deleting all the files in a directory. Table 2.2 lists a few examples and what they mean.

| **TABLE 2.2** | PATTERN | MATCHES |
|---|---|---|
| Wildcard Characters in DOS | *.* | All files |
| | *.DAT | All files with the .DAT extension |
| | FILE1.* | All files with the name FILE1 and any extension |
| | *.D* | All files with extensions beginning with D |
| | F*.* | All files with names beginning with F |
| | F*.DAT | All DAT files with names beginning with F |
| | FILE?.DAT | FILE1.DAT but not FILE17.DAT |
| | ??.DAT | All DAT files with two-character names |

# Configuring DOS

In this section we'll look at the basics of configuring DOS and keeping it working on a PC. We'll start with a review of PC memory management and then examine the CONFIG.SYS and AUTOEXEC.BAT files, which you'll need to modify to change the configuration of a PC.

### DOS Memory Management

You'll come across several types of memory when managing DOS machines. The Intel line of processors started with the 8088, which was limited to 640K of RAM (Random Access Memory). Although the newer processors have overcome this limit, DOS and PC applications must still respect the 640K limit for some purposes. Figure 2.1 shows the layout of memory DOS uses. Here are the divisions of memory in DOS:

- **Conventional memory:** The original 640K of memory. Many programs, particularly some device drivers (software required to use hardware devices), are still limited to this area.

- **Upper memory:** The memory just above the 640K area, which includes a total of 384K. Your video card, NIC, and other hardware components use a sizable amount of this space. Conventional 640K and the upper 384K add up to the first 1024K—the first megabyte of RAM.

- **Expanded memory (XMS):** This memory uses a 64K block of conventional memory called the *page frame* to access the higher areas of memory, swapping memory in and out of the block. This system is rarely used in today's PCs, but it remains as a standard.

- **Extended memory:** The memory above 1MB. A computer with 16MB of RAM has 15MB of extended memory. Today's PCs can access this memory without swapping, but use of extended memory still requires a different method of access than conventional memory.

- **High memory:** A 64K area that begins at the 1MB boundary. It is addressed by HIMEM.SYS, a device driver that allows the use of high memory. This driver is shipped with recent versions of DOS and Windows. The most common use of high memory is for part of the COMMAND.COM file in DOS 5 and 6.*x* products from Microsoft. This allocation scheme allows DOS to take a much smaller portion of the precious 640K area.

**FIGURE 2.1**

DOS uses several areas of memory.

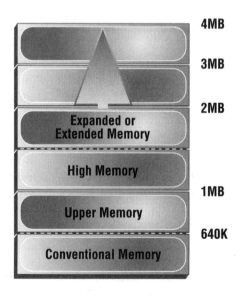

### DOS Startup Files

When a DOS machine boots, it reads two special files to manage its configuration:

■ CONFIG.SYS is read first. It includes special commands unique to this file and is used to set parameters and load device drivers.

■ AUTOEXEC.BAT is read second. It's a simple list of DOS commands, which are executed in order.

You may need to edit these files to manage a PC's configuration or to resolve a conflict between types of software. You can use the DOS EDIT utility, described in the section "Using DOS Commands" later in this chapter, to do this. The following sections describe each file, and the commands typically included, in detail.

**CONFIG.SYS**  The CONFIG.SYS file configures various parameters that DOS uses and loads device drivers and memory management utilities. The commands used in this file are unique and unrelated to DOS commands.

Here are the contents of a typical CONFIG.SYS file:

```
DEVICE=C:\DOS\HIMEM.SYS
DEVICE=C:\DOS\EMM386.EXE NOEMS
DOS=HIGH,UMB
LASTDRIVE=Z
FILES=40
BUFFERS=25
```

Let's take a closer look at each command.

| COMMAND | DESCRIPTION |
|---|---|
| HIMEM.SYS | A driver that allows use of the high-memory area |
| EMM386.EXE | The expanded memory manager. This example uses the NOEMS option. This means that no expanded memory will be allocated, but the upper-memory area is made available to programs |

| COMMAND | DESCRIPTION |
|---|---|
| DOS=HIGH,UMB | Specifies that DOS will be loaded into high memory. This is a feature of MS-DOS 5.0 and higher. The UMB keyword provides upper-memory blocks for application use |
| LASTDRIVE=Z | Specifies the last drive letter used for DOS drives. This command also controls network drives and can affect which drives you can use to access network information |
| FILES=40 | Specifies the number of DOS file handles that are available. This controls how many files DOS can have open at one time. A setting of 40 or 50 works for most applications, but some, such as database applications, may require a higher number. When these applications are connected to the network, 70 or 80 is a more practical minimum |
| BUFFERS=25 | Specifies the number of buffers available for file reads and writes. These buffers hold information going to or from the disk. A higher number of buffers allows faster disk access because more data can be handled in a single operation |

**AUTOEXEC.BAT**   The AUTOEXEC.BAT file is much easier to understand because all the commands in this file are simply DOS commands. This file is called a *batch file*. You can create other batch files to run specific sets of commands.

Since the commands in AUTOEXEC.BAT are executed each time the computer is started, it is typically used to load TSR (terminate-and-stay-resident) programs, such as network drivers, and to start programs, such as a NetWare login or a menu program. Here's a typical AUTOEXEC.BAT file:

```
C:\DOS\SMARTDRV.EXE
PROMPT $P$G
PATH C:\DOS;C:\WINDOWS;C:\
CD\NWCLIENT
LSL
```

```
3C5X9
IPXODI
VLM
F:
LOGIN MAIN\BOB
```

This file loads a TSR called SMARTDRV.EXE (a disk cache program), sets the DOS prompt and path, switches to the NWCLIENT directory, loads the network drivers (LSL, 3C5X9, IPXODI, and VLM), switches to drive F, and executes the LOGIN command to log in to the network. You'll find an explanation of each of these DOS commands in the next section.

## Using DOS Commands

When you boot a DOS machine, you find yourself at the command interpreter, which is managed by the COMMAND.COM program. It's what you use to give commands to DOS. The prompt for a DOS command typically looks like this:

```
C:\>
```

This prompt shows the current directory (currently, the root of drive C). Because this is often the current directory, many users refer to the DOS prompt as the C prompt.

If you're unfamiliar with DOS commands, you might find them a bit daunting. If you're used to the Macintosh, you'll find them cryptic and confusing; on the other hand, if you come from a UNIX background, you'll be used to a command line, but you'll find that the DOS command line isn't nearly as powerful or versatile as most UNIX shells.

Two DOS features should help you maintain your sanity while working with DOS:

- Typing **HELP** at the prompt gives you a menu-based help system, with descriptions of most commands.

- Typing any command followed by the /? switch gives a brief description of that command's options.

DOS commands typically include the command name, a file name or two, and one or more *switches,* which specify different options. Switches are indicated with a forward slash (/), not to be confused with the backslash (\) that indicates directory paths.

*We've used all capitals for the DOS command examples here. However, DOS commands are not case sensitive, and neither are file names, so you can use either upper- or lower-case. Commands enclosed in parentheses are alternate versions of the command; you can use either version.*

### CD (CHDIR): Change Current Directory

DOS keeps track of a current directory during your command-line session. This is the directory that is used by default when you refer to a file and is usually displayed in the DOS prompt. The CD command allows you to change your current directory. For example, this command makes the root directory current:

```
CD \
```

and this command makes the TEMP directory under the DOS directory current:

```
CD \DOS\TEMP
```

You can use a relative path name to specify the directory. For example, if you are in the DOS directory, this command takes you to the TEMP directory under the DOS directory:

```
CD TEMP
```

### CHKDSK: Check a Disk for Errors

The CHKDSK command checks the drive you specify (or the current drive) for errors and displays statistics about it, including the total amount of space and the amount of free space. Here's an example of CHKDSK output:

```
D:\>chkdsk
Volume Serial Number is 195D-08FA

    21,583,872 bytes total disk space
         2,048 bytes in 1 hidden files
         6,144 bytes in 2 directories
     3,637,248 bytes in 93 user files
    17,938,432 bytes available on disk
```

```
    2,048 bytes in each allocation unit
   10,539 total allocation units on disk
    8,759 available allocation units on disk

  655,360 total bytes memory
  602,336 bytes free
```

CHKDSK may also report one or more errors. You may be able to use a special switch, /F, to correct the errors. CHKDSK has only minimal error-correction abilities. You may want to try SCANDISK, a more sophisticated program provided with DOS 6.0 and above. However, CHKDSK still works, and you may prefer it in many cases—it gets simple jobs done more quickly.

## CLS: Clear the Screen

The CLS command simply clears the screen and gives you a new DOS prompt. This isn't particularly useful at the prompt unless you need to hide evidence of what you're doing, such as playing a game during work hours. However, it can be useful in batch files. If you're displaying a message to the user, you may want to clear the screen first to make it easy to read.

## COPY: Copy Files

The COPY command copies files from one location to another. The command line specifies the source path and file, followed by the destination path and file. If you omit the full path in either case, the current directory is assumed. Here are some examples:

| COMMAND | DESCRIPTION |
| --- | --- |
| COPY C:\DOS\FORMAT.EXE A:\FORMAT.EXE | Copies the FORMAT.EXE file from the C:\DOS directory to the root directory of the A drive |
| COPY C:\CONFIG.SYS | Copies the CONFIG.SYS file in the drive C root directory to the current directory |
| COPY *.DAT *.BAK | Copies all the DAT files in the current directory to the same directory and gives the copies the .BAK extension |

If you don't specify a file name for the destination, DOS uses the file name of the source. This can be very useful with wildcards. For example, this command copies all files from the C:\DOS directory to the C:\BACKUP directory:

```
COPY C:\DOS\*.* C:\BACKUP
```

*COPY has a limited set of capabilities. If you need to copy files in multiple directories, look at the XCOPY command.*

### DEL (ERASE): Delete Files

This is one of the essential DOS commands; it can also be one of the most dangerous if you're not careful. You specify the name of the file on the command line, and it is deleted, or removed from the disk. (See the UNDELETE command if you want to reverse the action.) For example, this command deletes the README.TXT file in the current directory:

```
DEL README.TXT
```

You can use DEL with wildcards, which can make it much more dangerous. For example, this command deletes all the files in the current directory:

```
DEL *.*
```

Since this is a drastic action, DOS prompts you to type **Y** before deleting the files. Be sure you really want the files erased before doing so. If you use this technique, subdirectories under the directory are not deleted, nor are the files inside them. The DELTREE command provides a solution for this situation.

### DELTREE: Delete an Entire Directory

Before DOS 6, deleting an entire directory, including subdirectories, was a difficult task. You couldn't use the RMDIR (remove directory) command unless a directory was empty, so you had to delete the files in each subdirectory, remove each subdirectory, and then delete the files in the main directory and remove it. If there were several nested subdirectories, this could take quite a while.

DOS 6 introduced a solution: the DELTREE command. This command accepts the name of a directory and deletes the directory, including the files and subdirectories underneath it. For example, this command deletes everything under the DATA directory:

```
DELTREE DATA
```

*Be very careful with the DELTREE command. It usually prompts you to type **Y** before deleting, but you will receive no further warning. In addition, files deleted with this command cannot be undeleted.*

### DIR: Display a Directory Listing

The DIR command simply displays a directory listing. It's probably the command you'll use most often. It displays each file name, along with the size of the file. You can also use switches to make things easier to read:

| COMMAND | DESCRIPTION |
| --- | --- |
| DIR /P | Pauses after each screenful of file names |
| DIR /W | Uses a wide format, which displays names only in multiple columns |
| DIR /A | Includes all files, even hidden and system files |
| DIR /S | Includes files in subdirectories under the current directory (DOS 6 only) |

You can use DIR with wildcards to search for a file. For example, this command displays all files with the .DAT extension:

```
DIR *.DAT
```

You can combine this feature with the /S switch, available in DOS 6 and above, to search an entire drive. The following command lists all the files with an .EXE extension. (Be sure you are in the root directory when you type this command.)

```
DIR *.EXE /S
```

### DISKCOPY: Copy a Disk

Use the DISKCOPY command to copy the contents of a floppy disk to another blank disk. You can specify the source and destination drives on the command line. The following command copies the contents of drive A to drive B:

```
DISKCOPY A: B:
```

More often, the following command is used:

```
DISKCOPY A: A:
```

This command uses a single drive. It reads the source disk in drive A and prompts you to insert the destination disk.

*DISKCOPY copies all the information on the disk, byte by byte, rather than by file. Because of this, only disks with identical formats can be used. This is why you will usually use the same drive for source and destination.*

### ECHO: Display a Message

The ECHO command simply echoes (displays) the text you type after the command. For example, the following command displays the word *Hello:*

```
ECHO Hello
```

This command may seem useless, but it's very handy for batch files. For example, to give instructions to the user, use this command:

```
ECHO Enter your network password below.
```

A variation of this command allows you to control the display of DOS commands. Use ECHO ON to turn them on and ECHO OFF to turn them off. These commands control whether the commands are displayed and affect only batch files.

### EDIT: Edit a File

The EDIT command starts the DOS editor, which is included with DOS 5.0 and above. Using this command is a convenient way to edit a file, such as the AUTOEXEC.BAT or CONFIG.SYS file. The DOS editor is shown in Figure 2.2.

This editor allows you to do any basic editing you need and includes features to insert and delete blocks, copy data between files, and search and replace. It's self-explanatory, with a friendly menu, but you may want to use the help system (press the F1 key) to learn the details of its operation.

*IBM's PC-DOS doesn't include EDIT. It does include a full-screen editing program, called simply E. E is a bit less friendly than EDIT but can actually be more powerful. E is also included with OS/2.*

FIGURE 2.2

The DOS editor allows
you to edit a file.

```
 File  Edit  Search  Options                                    Help
                           CONFIG.SYS
DEVICE=C:\DOS\HIMEM.SYS /testmem:off
DEVICEHIGH=C:\DOS\EMM386.EXE NOEMS X=D000-DFFF
REM The above line changed by CardSoft(TM) 3.1 Installation Utility
REM DEVICE=C:\DOS\EMM386.EXE NOEMS x=d800-dbff
rem DEVICE=C:\DOS\EMM386.EXE RAM x=d800-dbff
BUFFERS=40
REM The following line was removed for TurboTax:
REM FILES=40
REM The following line was added for TurboTax:
FILES = 100
DOS=HIGH,UMB
LASTDRIVE=Z
FCBS=4,0
rem ^^DEVICEHIGH=C:\SERVICES\ECD.EXE
STACKS=9,256
REM CardSoft(TM) 3.1 PCMCIA DRIVERS
rem ^^DEVICEHIGH=C:\CARDSOFT\SSCIRRUS.EXE
rem ^^DEVICEHIGH=C:\CARDSOFT\CS.EXE
rem ^^DEVICEHIGH=C:\CARDSOFT\CSALLOC.EXE
rem DEVICEHIGH=C:\CARDSOFT\ATADRV.EXE
rem DEVICEHIGH=C:\CARDSOFT\MTSRAM.EXE
MS-DOS Editor   <F1=Help> Press ALT to activate menus          00001:001
```

### FORMAT: Format a Disk

The FORMAT command prepares a disk for its first use. Hard drives are almost always already formatted, but you may need to reformat a hard drive to correct a major error, to erase the data, or when you install or partition the drive. You will also frequently use this command on floppy disks.

To use the FORMAT command, you specify the drive to format on the command line. This command formats the disk in drive A:

```
FORMAT A:
```

As a safeguard, you need to type **Y** after pressing ↵ to continue the format. In addition, DOS versions 5 and above attempt to save the data on the disk so you can use the UNFORMAT command to bring it back. If you wish to erase the data for good, use the /U switch.

*Even UNFORMAT doesn't work all the time. Be careful not to format any disk, especially a hard disk, unless you're prepared to lose the existing data on the disk—or you have a recent backup.*

### MD (MKDIR): Create a New Directory

MD is the command you use to create a new directory. The directory is created under the current directory unless you specify an entire path to the new directory. The following command creates a directory called TEMP under the current directory:

```
MD TEMP
```

### MEM: Display Available Memory

The MEM command displays a summary of the available memory, including conventional, extended/expanded, and high memory. This command is available in DOS 5.0 and above. Here is an example of its output:

```
Memory Type          Total       Used        Free
---------------    --------    --------    --------
Conventional           640K         52K        588K
Upper                  187K        187K          0K
Reserved               384K        384K          0K
Extended (XMS)      19,269K     18,245K      1,024K
---------------    --------    --------    --------
Total memory        20,480K     18,868K      1,612K

Total under 1 MB       827K        239K        588K

Largest executable program size       588K (602,016 bytes)
Largest free upper memory block         0K  (0 bytes)
MS-DOS is resident in the high memory area.
```

You can also add the /C switch to the MEM command. This displays much more information, including an exact list of the TSR programs that are currently in memory and which areas they are using.

### MORE: Display a File One Page at a Time

The MORE command displays a text file, pausing after each screen of text. This command is meant to be used as a *pipe*; this means that another program's output, or a file, can be displayed with the utility. You may be familiar with the use of pipes from UNIX.

To simply display a file, you can use the following command. The < symbol means to use the file as input to MORE.

```
MORE <filename
```

To display the output of a command, you use the pipe (|) symbol:

```
MEM /C | MORE
```

This is very useful for commands such as MEM, which do not pause during their display.

### MOVE: Move a File

The MOVE command, found only in DOS 6.0 and above, is similar to COPY, but it erases the old version of the file. For example, the following command moves all files in the DOS directory to the DOSBACK directory:

```
MOVE C:\DOS\*.* C:\DOSBACK
```

### PATH: Display or Modify the Search Path

DOS maintains a *search path,* or a list of directories that will be searched for executable files when you type a command. You separate the directories in the path with semicolons. The PATH command sets the path and is usually used in AUTOEXEC.BAT. Here's a typical PATH command:

```
PATH C:\;C:\DOS;C:\WINDOWS
```

Sometimes it's useful to add a directory to the current path; you can do this with an environmental variable, like this:

```
PATH %PATH%;C:\NEWDIR
```

We'll look at environmental variables in the discussion of the SET command.

### PAUSE: Wait for a Keystroke

This is an extremely simple command. It displays the message "Press any key to continue..." and waits for a keystroke. This is another command that's useless at the DOS prompt but very handy in batch files. For example, the following commands display a message to the user and wait for a keystroke to indicate that the user understands:

```
ECHO This computer is for use by official personnel only.

PAUSE
```

As a more useful example, if you include a command such as MEM or DIR in a batch file, you can use PAUSE to pause after the command's output, which gives you a chance to read it.

### PRINT: Print a Text File

The PRINT command sends a text file to a printer. Since NetWare printers act like local printers, this command works with either type of printer. However, NetWare provides a command, NPRINT, that offers many more printing options. NPRINT will be explained in Chapter 8.

### RD (RMDIR): Remove an Empty Directory

The RD command simply removes a directory. You can use this command only if the directory is empty. For example, the following command removes an empty TEMP directory under the current directory:

```
RD TEMP
```

*To remove a non-empty directory, including its contents, use the DELTREE command in DOS versions 6.0 and above.*

### REN: Rename a File

The REN command changes the name of a file. For example, to change the name of the FILE.TXT file in the current directory to FILE.DAT, use this command:

```
REN FILE.TXT FILE.DAT
```

You cannot rename a directory with the REN command. However, NetWare provides a command, RENDIR, you can use for this purpose. In addition, you can use the DOS 6 MOVE command to rename a directory.

### SCANDISK: Scan a Disk for Errors

The SCANDISK command, included in DOS versions 6.0 and above, provides an enhanced, full-screen alternative to the CHKDSK command. It checks the directory for errors, displays information about the disk, and scans its surface for bad sectors. The SCANDISK screen is shown in Figure 2.3.

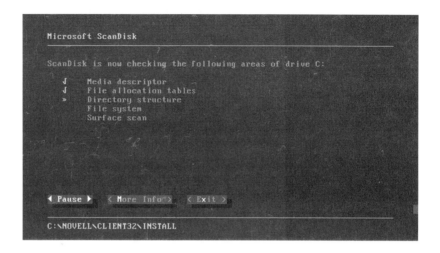

## SET: Set an Environmental Variable

The SET command sets an *environmental variable*. These are special values maintained by DOS, each with its own name. The path is stored in one such variable. Typing **SET** by itself lists all the currently defined variables.

Each variable has a name associated with it. The following command sets a variable called DOSDIR to C:\DOS:

```
SET DOSDIR=C:\DOS
```

Both DOS and various applications use environmental variables. For example, many DOS applications use the path defined in the TEMP variable for temporary files. NetWare applications use a special variable, NWLAN-GUAGE, to indicate the language they will display messages in.

We'll look at uses for environmental variables when we discuss NetWare login scripts in Chapter 9. Another use for them is in a batch file. You can include a variable's contents by using percent signs around its name; for example, you can use the following command to add to the path:

```
SET PATH=%PATH%;C:\NEWDIR
```

The %PATH% is expanded into the contents of the PATH variable. The following example displays information to the user:

```
ECHO Your current path is: %PATH%
```

### TYPE: Display a File

The TYPE command displays the contents of a file. For example, this command displays the CONFIG.SYS file:

```
TYPE C:\CONFIG.SYS
```

TYPE doesn't pause at each screen of text, so you might find the MORE command more useful (no pun intended).

### UNDELETE: Recover a Deleted File

The UNDELETE command *tries* to recover a file that has been deleted. You must include the name of the file (wildcards are allowed) on the command line after the UNDELETE command.

If you use it immediately after deleting the file, UNDELETE is usually successful. If not, there is a good chance the file has been written over and cannot be recovered. For this reason, never count on the UNDELETE command.

### XCOPY: Copy Files with Options

XCOPY is similar to the COPY command but includes a few more options and some extra capabilities. Most important is the /S switch, which allows you to copy all the files in a directory, including subdirectories. The following command copies all files under the C drive to the D drive:

```
XCOPY C:\*.* D:\ /S
```

This command includes many more options. For a complete list of XCOPY's options, type **XCOPY /?**.

# Using Microsoft Windows

ONSUMERS AND APPLICATION vendors widely consider DOS to be obsolete, and the reason is Windows. When Microsoft introduced Windows 3.0 in 1990, it took the computing world by storm. Users could manage their computers by means of a friendly, graphical interface, and without the irksome DOS prompt.

Windows 3.1 was released in 1992 to correct some rather nasty bugs. Not everyone was enthralled with Windows. Many power users still preferred DOS; it was faster, more reliable, and could run on more machines. Macintosh users, who have had a graphical interface since 1984, were not impressed. Microsoft's attempt wasn't nearly as reliable or as friendly as Apple's, but Microsoft had the budget to market it, and Windows installations now outnumber Macintoshes by about 20 to 1.

If you're used to a Macintosh, or the X-Windows system on UNIX workstations, you may find Windows a bit confusing, or perhaps a bit silly. Microsoft added many of the capabilities found in these systems to the latest version of Windows, Windows 95. However, we'll be talking about Windows 3.1 in this section since it's still the most common desktop operating environment.

# Windows Basics

In this section we'll take a quick look at the basics of Windows, for the uninitiated. We'll discuss the various versions of Windows and the features you'll use most often. If you need more detailed information, consult the Windows manual or one of the hundreds of books on the subject.

### Versions of Windows

Windows has evolved through several versions in its lifetime. It was actually released in 1985 as Windows 1.0; however, it was neither sophisticated nor popular at the time. Version 2.0, released in 1987, was not particularly popular either. All the excitement started with version 3.0. Since then there have been several updated versions:

- Windows 3.1 was the upgrade that made Windows what it is today. It fixed most of the bugs in version 3.0 and added new features.

- Windows for Workgroups was released later in 1992 as an enhanced version of Windows 3.1. It includes peer-to-peer networking and several other improvements.

- Windows 3.11 (1993) is a minor update that fixes some bugs, mostly associated with incompatibilities on certain computer systems. Most users don't need to upgrade to this version.

- Windows 95, released in late 1995, is the latest version at this writing. Since it's a major update and is quite different from Windows 3.*x*, we'll cover it in the section "Using Windows 95" later in this chapter.

### Installing Windows

Since Windows 3.*x* runs on top of DOS, you'll need to have DOS version 5.0 or above installed first. The installation routine for Microsoft Windows is simple. You insert the first Windows disk in the floppy drive and start the SETUP program. The installation program prompts you for each of the disks (usually five or six). The start of the installation process is shown in Figure 2.4.

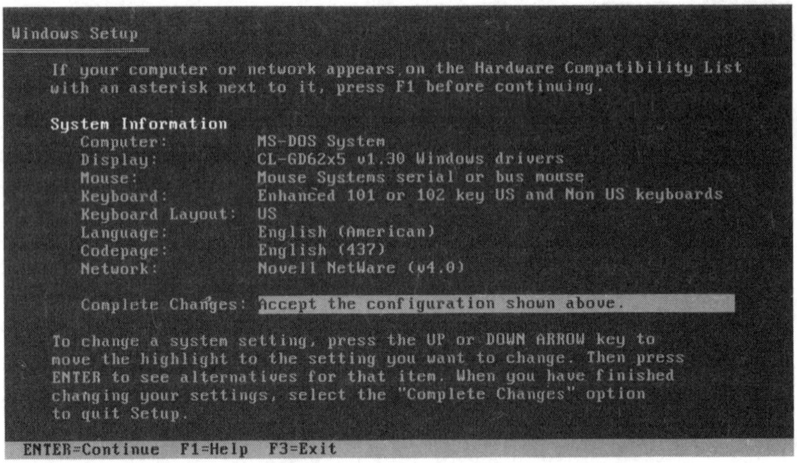

**FIGURE 2.4**

Windows installation program

```
Windows Setup

     If your computer or network appears on the Hardware Compatibility List
     with an asterisk next to it, press F1 before continuing.

  System Information
     Computer:          MS-DOS System
     Display:           CL-GD62x5 v1.30 Windows drivers
     Mouse:             Mouse Systems serial or bus mouse
     Keyboard:          Enhanced 101 or 102 key US and Non US keyboards
     Keyboard Layout:   US
     Language:          English (American)
     Codepage:          English (437)
     Network:           Novell NetWare (v4.0)

     Complete Changes:  Accept the configuration shown above.

  To change a system setting, press the UP or DOWN ARROW key to
  move the highlight to the setting you want to change. Then press
  ENTER to see alternatives for that item. When you have finished
  changing your settings, select the "Complete Changes" option
  to quit Setup.

ENTER=Continue   F1=Help   F3=Exit
```

Windows offers the choice of a simple or custom installation; the custom installation includes some extra options, including installing only portions of the package. A full Windows 3.1 installation takes between 5 and 10MB on a hard drive.

Windows uses a system of *virtual memory* to compensate for the varying amounts of memory between computers. When it runs out of physical memory, it swaps some of the contents of memory that is not currently being used to a file on the disk. This allows even a 4MB machine to run Windows; however, the constant swapping will slow you down considerably.

When you install Windows, it creates a *swap file* to be used as the virtual memory. Be warned that the default size shown is often more than you need. You should enter a more appropriate number; a number two to three times the number of megabytes of memory in your computer is a good choice if your memory is under 16MB. If you have 16MB or more, you can use a small swap file—4MB or 8MB should be sufficient.

If you have plenty of memory, you may be tempted to use no swap file at all, and if you're a Macintosh user, the mere mention of virtual memory probably makes you cringe at the slow speed. However, because of the way Windows handles physical and virtual memory, it runs better with a swap file, regardless of the memory size. 4MB is a good minimum size for systems with large amounts of memory.

### Program Manager

The first screen you see when you start Windows is Program Manager, shown in Figure 2.5. This is a simple shell program that allows you to run programs by clicking icons. The icons are placed into program groups, which are represented by smaller windows, to categorize them. The organization is that simple; you can't have an icon outside a program group, and you can't have a group inside another group.

**FIGURE 2.5**

Windows 3.1 Program Manager

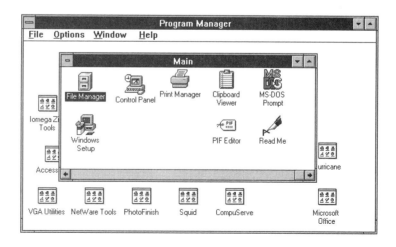

Applications in Windows can be Windows applications, which use icons, windows, buttons, and so on, and DOS applications. Most DOS applications will run under Windows, but not all of them. In addition, a DOS application may run more slowly than normal and may not multitask properly.

### File Manager

Another important Windows utility is File Manager. It allows you to copy, rename, move, and delete files and offers a friendly alternative to the DOS command line. File Manager is shown in Figure 2.6.

**FIGURE 2.6**

Windows 3.1 File Manager

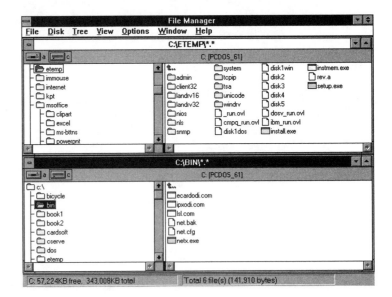

File Manager shows the contents of a directory in the right-hand window. You can highlight a file in the window by clicking it and then perform an action on that file. You can also select multiple files using the following techniques.

- Hold down the Ctrl key and click multiple files, including nonconsecutive files, to select them all at once.

- Select a file and hold Shift while selecting another. All the files between the two in the list are selected.

*Program Manager and File Manager are not remarkably sophisticated. However, Windows does allow you to use third-party programs in their place, and many such alternatives are available. Norton Desktop for Windows, from Symantec, is one such product.*

## Configuring Windows

Although Windows is friendlier than DOS, it isn't always perfect, and sometimes you need to modify its settings to get it working properly. Windows includes a Control Panel application to set many of these settings, but you must set some by manually editing a configuration file.

### The Control Panel

The Control Panel is found in the Main program group in Program Manager. It's actually an application called CONTROL.EXE. The main Control Panel screen is shown in Figure 2.7.

**FIGURE 2.7**

The Windows Control Panel lets you change some settings.

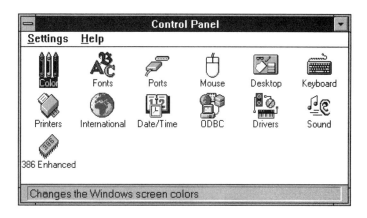

The Control Panel is actually a menu that allows you to run some small applications, called *applets*. Each applet is a control panel for a different aspect of the system. Depending on the configuration of the computer you're working on, there may be a different set of applets than the one we've shown. Table 2.3 lists some of the common applets and their descriptions.

| TABLE 2.3 Common Applets | APPLET | DESCRIPTION |
|---|---|---|
| | Color | Allows you to set the colors of windows and text |
| | Fonts | Allows you to install and remove TrueType fonts |
| | Ports | Allows you to control baud rate and other settings for the computer's serial ports |
| | Mouse | Controls settings for the mouse |
| | Desktop | Allows you to configure background colors and patterns, screensavers, and other desktop parameters |
| | Keyboard | Allows you to change settings for the keyboard |
| | Printers | Allows you to install and remove printers and change their settings |
| | International | Controls country-specific parameters, such as date and numeric formats |
| | Date/Time | Allows you to set the current date and time |
| | Drivers | Allows you to add and remove drivers, usually for sound cards and other multimedia devices |
| | Sound | Allows you to choose sounds for certain events, such as opening and closing windows |
| | 386 Enhanced | Allows you to change settings for virtual memory and other 386-specific parameters |

### Windows Configuration Files

Windows uses two main files to maintain configuration information. These files include drivers to be loaded, parameters, and information specific to the user. They are stored in the WINDOWS directory, with these names:

- **WIN.INI:** Stores user information and defaults for Windows and some applications

- **SYSTEM.INI:** Stores more technical information, such as communication parameters, printer ports, and device drivers

Both of these files are divided into sections for specific categories. For example, the 386 processor multitasking parameters are stored in a section of SYSTEM.INI labeled [386 Enhanced].

You can modify both of these files with a text editor, such as the DOS EDIT command discussed earlier in this chapter. However, be careful—if you make an incorrect change, you can prevent Windows from starting. Be sure to make a backup copy of both files before modifying them.

*Most of the settings you can control with the Control Panel actually make changes to the SYSTEM.INI and WIN.INI files. You can make changes manually or using the Control Panel. However, many of the settings in these files are not available in the Control Panel.*

In addition to the files named above, many Windows applications use their own file of initialization parameters. These files have an .INI extension and are stored in the WINDOWS directory. For example, the initialization file for Microsoft Excel might be EXCEL4.INI.

# Using Windows 95

MICROSOFT STARTED MARKETING the fabled "new Windows" sometime in 1993. It was hot news for quite a time, although little was known about it. At the time, it was called by Microsoft's code name, Chicago. Finally, in 1994, Microsoft announced that the new version would be called Windows 95. The actual product hit the shelves in August 1995, just in time to justify its name.

Windows 95 claims many advantages over Windows. Instead of running on top of DOS, it is integrated as one operating system. It also includes much better multitasking capabilities and is a bit more stable than Windows 3.1. It can run DOS applications, Windows 3.1 applications, and the new 32-bit Windows 95 applications.

Technically, a version of DOS, which identifies itself as DOS 7.0, is still inside Windows 95. However, this version of DOS is not currently available by itself. It's not well documented—but it performs almost exactly the same as DOS 6.22.

*We'll give you a brief tour of Windows 95 and a start at configuring it for your users here. For further details consult one of the many books about Windows 95, such as Mastering Windows 95 by Robert Cowart (Sybex 1995, 0-7821-1413-X).*

## What's New in Windows 95

Windows 95 includes many new features and a whole new look. (It may not look entirely new if you've seen a Macintosh). A typical Windows 95 desktop is shown in Figure 2.8.

**FIGURE 2.8**

A typical Windows 95 desktop

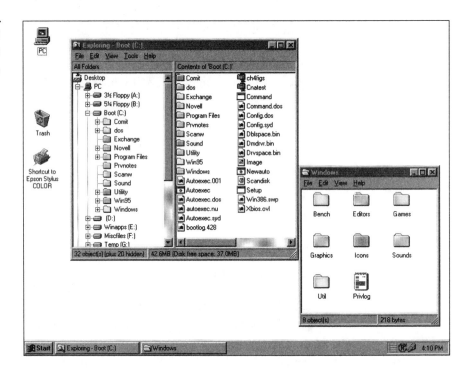

Program Manager has been replaced with the Start menu. To access it you click the Start button, in the lower-left corner of the screen. Unlike Program

Manager, this menu allows you to create subgroups within groups. You can also create icons on the desktop itself to run programs or create folders with multiple icons inside them.

To the right of the Start button, the task bar stretches across the screen. The task bar includes icons and text for each program that is currently running. You can switch between them by clicking the buttons. The "tray" at the right end of the task bar displays special-purpose icons (such as a resource meter) and, if desired, a clock.

## Configuring Windows 95

If you've dealt with Windows 3.1, configuring Windows 95 should not be difficult. Many of the same configuration files and applications are included. However, there are some differences, as you'll learn in the following sections.

### The Control Panel

Like Windows 3.1, Windows 95 includes a Control Panel. In fact, they are very similar. You start the Control Panel from the Settings menu under the Start button. The Windows 95 Control Panel has a new look. (Actually, it looks just like any other window in Windows 95.) It's shown in Figure 2.9.

**FIGURE 2.9**

The Windows 95 Control Panel has a new look but functions much the same as the one in Windows 3.1.

As you can see, the Windows 95 Control Panel includes many of the same applets as the old one. It also includes some new options, including a System option for technical details and a Passwords option that allows you to configure users' access to the system.

### Configuration Files

The SYSTEM.INI and WIN.INI files are still found in Windows 95, but many of their settings are no longer used. However, you will still need to modify these files at times. Also, many applications use an INI file, just as the old Windows versions did.

### The Registry

Many of the settings in WIN.INI and SYSTEM.INI, and in various applications' INI files, have been moved to a database Windows 95 calls the *registry*. Like the files it replaces, the registry includes various parameters. Each parameter has a label, called a key, and a value. The labels are organized into a directory-like structure with categories and subcategories.

The registry is not a text file, so you can't edit it with any ordinary editor. Windows 95 includes a special editor for the purpose, called the Registry Editor, or REGEDIT for short. This editor is shown in Figure 2.10.

**FIGURE 2.10**

The Windows 95 Registry Editor

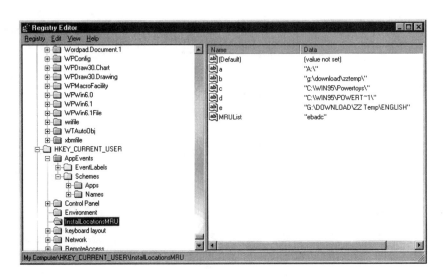

*The cautions about INI files go double for the registry; you can make changes that will crash your PC and prevent it from rebooting. To avoid this situation, be sure to make a backup of the registry. You can do this by using the Export option from REGEDIT. Also, the registry is actually stored as two hidden files in the Windows directory, SYSTEM.DAT and USER.DAT. You can copy these files to make a backup, but you must exit to a DOS prompt first.*

# Summary

N THIS CHAPTER we've looked at the most popular PC operating systems: DOS, Windows, and Windows 95. You should now have a basic familiarity with these systems, and an idea of how to configure them for your users.

- DOS was the first operating system for PC compatibles. It uses a command-line interface and allows you to run DOS applications. MS-DOS, from Microsoft, is the most common, but alternate versions have been developed by IBM and Novell.

- Windows 3.*x* gives you a friendlier, graphical alternative but still runs under DOS. It runs both DOS and Windows applications. It can multi-task to a point, running multiple applications at once.

- Windows 95 is the latest system from Microsoft. It still includes DOS but is much more tightly integrated. Multitasking has been greatly improved. It can run DOS and Windows applications, along with new 32-bit Windows 95 applications.

In the next chapter we'll continue to work with DOS and Windows. This time, the emphasis will be on the client software, which you can use to attach these systems to the network. We will also look at the client for OS/2.

# Configuring Workstations

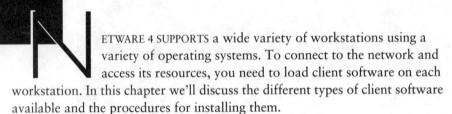

ETWARE 4 SUPPORTS a wide variety of workstations using a variety of operating systems. To connect to the network and access its resources, you need to load client software on each workstation. In this chapter we'll discuss the different types of client software available and the procedures for installing them.

We will cover the following client software in this chapter:

- Client 32 for DOS and Windows, the latest client for DOS and Windows 3.1*x*

- Client 32 for Windows 95, for Windows 95 workstations

- The NetWare DOS Requester, which supports DOS and Windows 3.1*x* and can be used with Windows 95

- The NetWare OS/2 Requester, supporting IBM's OS/2 operating system

Client software is also available for Macintosh computers. Because of the complex issues involved in connecting NetWare and Macintosh networks, and the features available, we have devoted Chapter 16 to Macintosh connectivity. Refer to that chapter for information about the Macintosh client.

# Client 32 for DOS and Windows

ITH THE RELEASE of Windows 95, Novell began to develop a new client software to replace the earlier clients. This software, called Client 32, is a fully 32-bit client with additional capabilities. In April of 1996 Novell released a beta version of Client 32 for DOS and Windows 3.1, which provides these benefits to older operating systems. This software has become the standard in the latest version of NetWare 4.

## Benefits of the 32-Bit Client

Client 32 includes several new features that make it more sophisticated than any previous NetWare client. Some of its benefits are listed here:

- The installation process is streamlined and simplified.

- Client 32 can be configured more conveniently from a friendly, Windows-based interface than by editing the NET.CFG file. Much of the configuration is automatic and changes itself when needed.

- NDS is fully supported, like the DOS Requester.

- Login scripts can be executed from Windows. Using the DOS Requester, you have to use a DOS login to execute a script.

- Installation includes NAL (NetWare Application Launcher), a new Windows-based menu system that can be configured through NDS.

- Administration is simpler. The client can intelligently upgrade itself using scripting tools.

## Installing the 32-Bit Client

At this writing, Client 32 for DOS and Windows 3.1 is available in two forms:

- You can use the *network installation* over the network.

- You can use the *disk installation* from disks.

The procedure for installing the 32-bit client is the same with either package, except that you'll need to change disks as requested by the disk version. Follow these steps to begin installation of the 32-bit client:

1. Change to the mapped drive and directory containing a network installation, or insert the first disk and switch to that drive.

2. Type **INSTALL** to start the installation program.

3. Press ↵ on the disclaimer. You are now presented with the installation options screen, shown in Figure 3.1.

**FIGURE 3.1**

Choose which 32-bit
client components
to install.

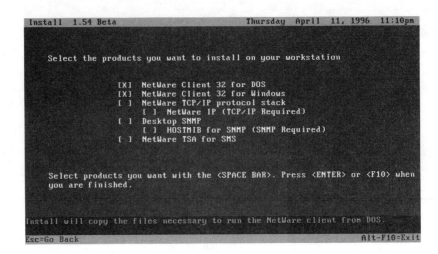

```
Install  1.54 Beta                        Thursday  April  11, 1996  11:10pm


    Select the products you want to install on your workstation


               [X]  NetWare Client 32 for DOS
               [X]  NetWare Client 32 for Windows
               [ ]  NetWare TCP/IP protocol stack
                  [ ]  NetWare IP (TCP/IP Required)
               [ ]  Desktop SNMP
                     [ ]  HOSTMIB for SNMP (SNMP Required)
               [ ]  NetWare TSA for SMS



    Select products you want with the <SPACE BAR>. Press <ENTER> or <F10> when
    you are finished.


Install will copy the files necessary to run the NetWare client from DOS.

Esc=Go Back                                                     Alt-F10=Exit
```

The installation options include the following:

- **NetWare Client 32 for DOS:** Installs the DOS 32-bit client

- **NetWare Client 32 for Windows:** Installs the Windows 3.1 components of the 32-bit client

- **NetWare TCP/IP protocol stack:** Use to install support for the TCP/IP protocol

- **Desktop SNMP:** Provides support for the Simple Network Management Protocol (SNMP)

- **NetWare TSA for SMS:** Installs the Transport Service Agent (TSA) for DOS, which allows an SMS backup application to back up the files on the workstation

For a typical Client 32 installation, you'll select the first two options; this is the default. After you have chosen the products to install, press ↵ to continue. You are now presented with two choices for the Windows client, as shown in Figure 3.2:

- **Do you plan to use more country codes than the one currently running on your machine?** Specify whether you intend to install support for a different language or country. This affects which NetWare client language files are installed.

■ **Do you want to set the shared Windows path?** This option allows you to indicate the path you are using for a shared version of Windows. If you are using a shared version of Windows, be sure to set this option.

**FIGURE 3.2**

The Client 32 installation program asks additional questions about Windows support.

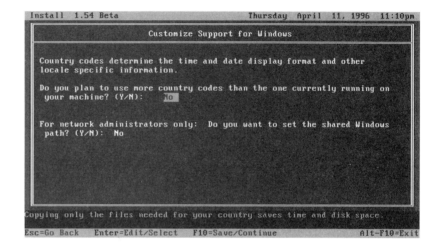

After you have answered these questions, press F10 to continue the installation. You now see a list of network drivers to choose from, as shown in Figure 3.3.

**FIGURE 3.3**

Choose a driver to match your network card.

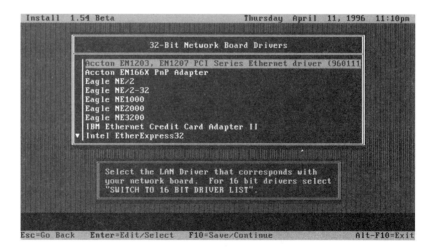

The list shows the 32-bit network drivers that are available. These are a new standard to match the 32-bit client software, and drivers may not be available for your particular card. Luckily, Client 32 also supports the older 16-bit drivers (MLIDs) the DOS Requester uses.

If there is a 32-bit driver to match your network card, you should select it since it will be more efficient. Otherwise, scroll to the end of the list and select the SWITCH TO 16-BIT DRIVER LIST option to see a list of available 16-bit drivers, as shown in Figure 3.4.

**FIGURE 3.4**

Client 32 also supports 16-bit network drivers.

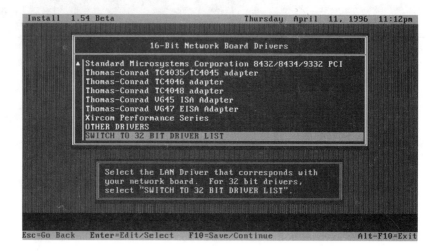

If your card is not represented in either list, you may be able to choose a compatible card; many cards are compatible with Novell's NE2000 specification. Otherwise, you will need a driver, usually provided on a disk that came with the network card. If you have such a disk, follow these steps:

1. Select the OTHER DRIVERS option at the end of the 16-bit or 32-bit list, depending on which type of driver you have available.

2. Enter the drive letter or path to the new driver.

After you have selected the appropriate network card, press ↵. You are now presented with a list of parameters that can be configured for your network card. Figure 3.5 shows a typical list of parameters. Some of the parameters you may encounter are explained here:

- **Base I/O Port:** Specifies the memory address used to communicate with the NIC. Set this to match the setting of your network card.

- **Hardware Interrupt:** This is the interrupt, or IRQ, setting used to communicate with your NIC. Set this to match the setting of your network card.

- **Media Frame Types:** These are communication methods you can use. You should choose the same frame type as the server is running. Usually, the Ethernet_802.2 frame type is used in a NetWare 4 server. You can support more than one frame type if you need to connect to servers using different types. This slightly affects the speed and memory use of the client.

- **Memory I/O Address:** This is an area of higher memory used to communicate with some high-speed network cards. Most cards do not require this setting.

- **Optional Node Address:** This sets the network card address, if available. Most network cards do not enable this setting. ARCnet cards usually require a unique number for this setting, and it should match the setting of the card itself.

**FIGURE 3.5**

Select the parameters to match the network driver to your network card.

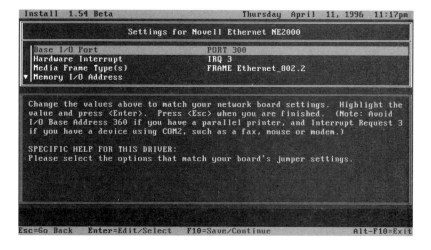

After you have entered the appropriate settings for your network card, press F10 to continue the installation. You now see the Installation Configuration Summary screen, shown in Figure 3.6.

**FIGURE 3.6**

Select the final options to install the 32-bit client.

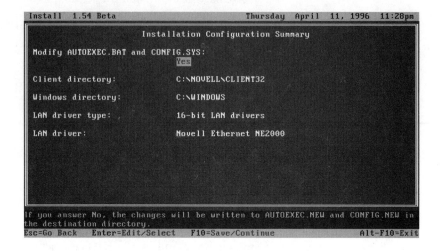

You can enter choices for the following options:

- **Modify AUTOEXEC.BAT and CONFIG.SYS:** Determines whether these files will be modified to automatically load the 32-bit client. The default is Yes.

- **Client directory:** Choose a directory on the workstation to install the new client software. The default is C:\NOVELL\CLIENT32.

- **Windows directory:** Select the directory where Windows 3.1 is installed, typically C:\WINDOWS.

- **LAN driver type:** This should already indicate the type of LAN driver you chose earlier. If not, select either 16-bit or 32-bit to indicate the driver type.

- **LAN driver:** This confirms the LAN driver you have chosen. You can change the setting here before you continue.

If you are satisfied with the options displayed, press F10 to complete the installation. All the required files will now be copied. An installation status screen, shown in Figure 3.7, displays the current progress of the installation.

**FIGURE 3.7**

Client 32 installation is now in progress.

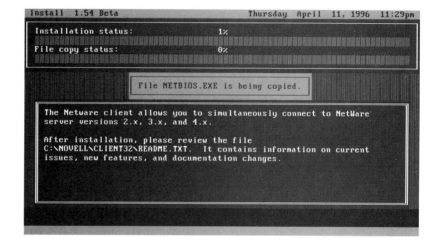

After all files are copied, you should see the final screen of the installation, shown in Figure 3.8. This screen indicates that the installation was successful and gives you additional instructions if needed. It also names the files that were changed.

**FIGURE 3.8**

Client 32 installation is now complete.

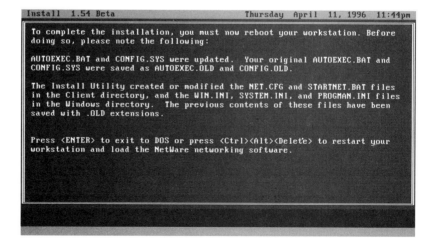

You must now reboot your workstation. If you allowed the installation program to modify the AUTOEXEC.BAT and CONFIG.SYS files, the 32-bit client will automatically load, and you should attach to the server.

## How Client 32 for DOS and Windows Works

During the Client 32 installation, the files needed for Client 32 to run are installed in the directory you have chosen, typically C:\NOVELL\CLIENT32. Your AUTOEXEC.BAT file is modified to run a file called STARTNET.BAT in the CLIENT32 directory. This batch file is similar to the STARTNET.BAT file the DOS Requester uses, but the Client 32 version uses a few more files. A typical STARTNET.BAT file is shown here:

```
SET NWLANGUAGE=ENGLISH

C:\NOVELL\CLIENT32\NIOS.EXE

LOAD C:\NOVELL\CLIENT32\LSLC32.NLM

LOAD C:\NOVELL\CLIENT32\CMSM.NLM

LOAD C:\NOVELL\CLIENT32\ETHERTSM.NLM

LOAD CNE2000.LAN PORT=300 FRAME=Ethernet_802.2 INT=3

LOAD C:\NOVELL\CLIENT32\IPX.NLM

LOAD C:\NOVELL\CLIENT32\CLIENT32.NLM
```

The most important component of the 32-bit client is NIOS.EXE, the NetWare Input/Output Services. This file provides the basic services the rest of the client software programs use. In addition, it provides support for the NLM architecture.

The rest of the client software files have the extension .NLM, which you should recognize—it stands for NetWare Loadable Module, the standard used for programs that run on the file server. The Client 32 NLM files follow the same architecture but are intended for client-side use. The LOAD command, provided with the 32-bit client, loads these files into memory.

*Although most of the client NLMs are different from the NLMs used on the server, LAN drivers are one exception. If servers and workstations use the same LAN cards, they can use the same drivers.*

# Client 32 for Windows 95

INDOWS 95 HAS some significant differences from Windows 3.1*x,* including a 32-bit architecture and better multitasking abilities.

Since Windows 95 is still built upon the foundation of DOS, you can use the DOS Requester with Windows 95. However, it will not provide all the features of a true 32-bit client and may not even be entirely stable. Luckily, Novell has released a solution: Client 32 for Windows 95.

## Benefits of Client 32 for Windows 95

Along with the benefits of Client 32 for DOS, which we explained earlier in this chapter, Client 32 for Windows includes the following features:

- The installation process is integrated into Windows 95, using the standard installation routines where possible.

- Login scripts can be executed within Windows 95.

- Windows 95 is fully supported by the Windows 95 version of Client 32, allowing you to use the standard Login and Network controls.

## Installing Client 32 for Windows 95

Like the DOS and Windows 32-bit client, Client 32 for Windows 95 is available either as individual disks or as a full package you can install across the network. Depending on which method you are using, perform one of these steps to begin the installation:

- If you are using a network installation, run SETUP.EXE from the ENGLISH directory under the installation directory.

- If you are using disks, run the SETUP.EXE program on the first disk.

In either case you should already be running Windows 95. Use the Run command under the Start menu to run the appropriate SETUP program. After you start SETUP, you are presented with a disclaimer. Click Yes to accept the license agreement and continue the installation.

You now see an introductory dialog box, as shown in Figure 3.9. You can view the README file from here to view additional documentation. When you are ready to begin, click the Start button in the dialog box.

**FIGURE 3.9**

Beginning the Client 32 for Windows 95 installation program

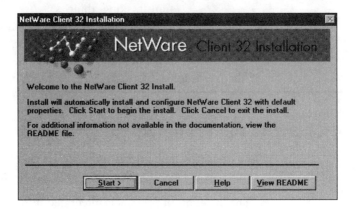

Once you start the Client 32 installation, your existing NetWare client software—the DOS Requester or the Microsoft Client that comes with Windows 95—is removed. You are not asked to confirm this.

As the installation starts, you have to wait several minutes while a driver database is built. After this is complete, you are presented with a dialog box asking whether you wish to set default properties, as shown in Figure 3.10. You can do this at any time, but it's a good idea to do it immediately. Answer Yes to this dialog box.

Now you see the Client 32 Properties dialog box, as shown in Figure 3.11. This dialog box allows you to define parameters for the client to use and is similar in function to the NET.CFG file in the DOS Requester. The first tab in the dialog asks for four options:

- **Preferred Server:** Specifies the default server to attach to when the client software loads.

- **Preferred Tree:** Specifies a Directory tree to log in to. You can specify a server or tree, but not both.

**FIGURE 3.10**

The Recommended
NetWare Client 32
Properties dialog box
allows you to set
parameters to connect to
a NetWare 4 server.

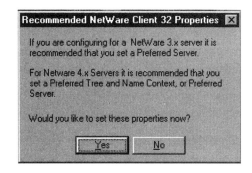

- **Name Context:** The default context to be used. This is the NDS container where your user ID is found.

- **First Network Drive:** The first drive to be used for network mappings.

**FIGURE 3.11**

Use the Client 32
Properties dialog box to
select parameters for
attaching to the network.

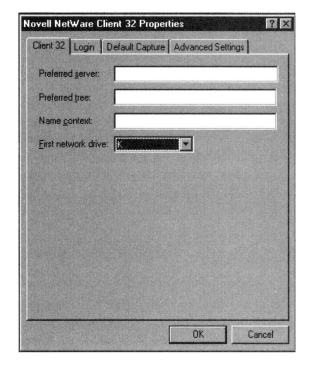

You may also need to set options in the other three tabs of the Client 32 Properties dialog box. These tabs include various types of settings:

- **Login:** Select whether to log in to a tree or a server and whether to use a login script.

- **Default Capture:** Allows you to select a network printer as the default workstation printer and to specify parameters for printing.

- **Advanced Settings:** Provides a list of named settings, similar to the names in the NET.CFG file in the DOS Requester. You can provide a setting for each name. This dialog box is shown in Figure 3.12.

**FIGURE 3.12**

The Advanced Settings tab provides a variety of named settings.

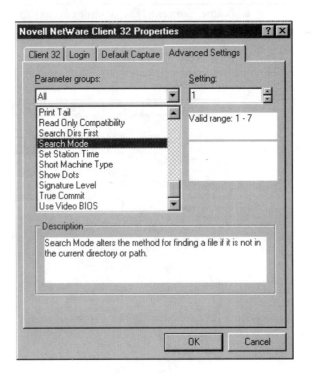

After defining the properties you want, click the OK button. The files needed for the 32-bit client are now installed. (If you are installing from disks, insert the appropriate disks when prompted.)

After the installation concludes, you must restart the computer. After Windows 95 restarts, Client 32 becomes available, and you can connect to the network.

# The NetWare DOS Requester for DOS and Windows

N THE EARLY days of NetWare (versions 3.11 and earlier), client software for DOS could be a nightmare. One of the components, IPX.COM, had to be generated for each workstation configuration, making it difficult to administer. In addition, this software, called the NetWare Shell, was not fully integrated with DOS.

The ODI specification was later introduced to simplify things. It allowed a more modular approach and did not require the IPX.COM file. This specification was used with NETX, the same NetWare shell.

With NetWare 3.12, Novell introduced an alternative to NETX—the NetWare DOS Requester. This is a modular system that you can easily change to match each workstation's configuration. It also integrates better with DOS and provides support for Windows. With NetWare 4.1, the DOS Requester became the standard for client software.

Although Client 32 has replaced the DOS Requester in the latest version of NetWare 4 and is emerging as a new alternative, the DOS Requester is still used in the majority of installations. We'll look at the details of installing, configuring, and using the DOS Requester in the sections that follow.

## Installing the DOS Requester

Novell provides a simple, automated installation program for DOS clients using the DOS Requester. This program installs the DOS Requester and other network components and provides a default configuration. You can also use it to install drivers for Microsoft Windows.

The installation routine is called INSTALL and runs from any DOS workstation. You can install the NetWare client software from disks, from the CD-ROM that NetWare 4 comes on, or from a directory on the network:

- **Installing from disks:** Place the first disk in the drive. Switch to that drive by typing **A:** or **B:**. Type **INSTALL** to start the installation.

- **Installing from CD-ROM:** Switch to the CD-ROM drive. Change directories to \CLIENT\DOSWIN. Type **INSTALL**.

- **Installing from the network:** Map a drive to the SYS: volume of a NetWare 4 server and then change to the \PUBLIC\CLIENT\DOSWIN directory. Type **INSTALL** to begin.

Which method you choose depends on the configuration of the machine. If a machine has a CD-ROM drive, the CD-ROM method will be faster. The network method is fastest of all but requires that you already have a connection to the network. This method is usually practical only when you are upgrading from earlier client software.

After starting the INSTALL program, you see the screen shown in Figure 3.13. You can now enter your choice for six installation options:

1. **Destination directory:** Enter the directory for the client software. This is usually C:\NWCLIENT.

2. **Modify AUTOEXEC.BAT and CONFIG.SYS:** Select Yes if you want the INSTALL program to modify your workstation's AUTOEXEC.BAT and CONFIG.SYS files.

3. **MS Windows support:** Select Yes if you want to install files for Microsoft Windows support. Be sure the correct Windows directory is selected. You can press ↵ to customize settings. The customization options allow you to enable international support and to select a network installation of Windows.

4. **Configure workstation for backup:** Select Yes if you wish to enable backup support for your workstation. This option installs the DOS TSA (Target Service Agent) to allow SBACKUP (or other SMS backup software) to back up the files on your local drives.

5. **Network board driver:** Press ↵ to see a list of network drivers. Select the one for your network card. If your card is not listed, select Other Drivers and select a disk or another path for the driver provided by the network card manufacturer.

6. **Start installation:** Press ↵ to begin the installation process. The next screen displays the progress of the installation.

**FIGURE 3.13**

Installation options for the DOS client INSTALL program

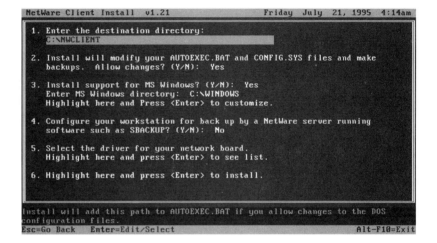

After completing the installation process, reboot the workstation to load the network drivers. The installation process makes the following changes to your workstation:

- Copies the network client software, including LSL, IPXODI, VLM, and the network driver, to a directory on your workstation, usually C:\NWCLIENT.

- Creates a batch file called STARTNET.BAT in the NWCLIENT directory. This file loads the network software in the correct order.

- Modifies the AUTOEXEC.BAT file to run the STARTNET.BAT file, thus loading the network software.

- Modifies the CONFIG.SYS file to include the LASTDRIVE=Z parameter. This parameter is required for the DOS Requester.

- Copies several files to the Windows directories if you selected to install files for Windows support. These files include the NetWare User Tools program and several DLLs (Dynamic Link Libraries) for network access.

- If desired, installs the TSA for your workstation (TSA_DOS.EXE) and adds it to the AUTOEXEC.BAT file if you chose to enable backup support.

- Creates a NET.CFG file in the workstation's NWCLIENT directory. This file stores settings for the client software.

# How the DOS Requester Works

The DOS Requester isn't the simplest piece of software. It actually consists of several components that interact, each providing a specific function. Before we discuss the components of the DOS Requester, let's take a look at the underlying architecture.

Your workstation communicates with the NetWare server through the use of one or more *protocols*. The principal communications protocol for Net-Ware workstation connections is IPX. Your network may support additional protocols, such as TCP/IP and AppleTalk.

## The IPX Protocol

The IPX (Internetwork Packet Exchange) protocol is the standard protocol for NetWare networks. IPX divides data into *packets*. These packets contain the data that is to be transmitted, along with the addressing information that determines the workstation or server the packet should be sent to. NetWare networks use three main addresses:

- The *IPX external network number* is set for all servers that share a common network wire, or *segment*. Multiple servers in the same net-work segment use the same number. NetWare uses this number to transmit data across multiple networks.

- The *IPX internal network number* is set at each server. NetWare uses this number to locate the server on the network, and it must be unique.

- Each workstation has a *network address*. NetWare uses this address to locate a specific workstation on the network. Usually, network addresses are set in hardware in the network card and cannot be changed. Each network card in a server also has a unique network address.

### The ODI Specification

ODI (Open Data-Link Interface) is a specification used with the IPX protocol for DOS workstations on the network. ODI allows workstations or servers to use multiple protocols on the same network. Each workstation can use a combination of protocols on the same network card. This allows your workstation to communicate with the NetWare 4 network and other systems, such as mainframe computers, concurrently.

In addition, the ODI specification provides a modular way of installing network drivers. When a network adapter is replaced, only one file—the network driver—needs to be replaced.

### Components of the DOS Requester

The NetWare DOS Requester consists of four separate programs and associated files. These client software programs are TSR programs, which stay in memory and operate in the background while the workstation performs other tasks. When you load the client software, you must do so in a certain order:

```
LSL.COM

LAN driver (MLID)

IPXODI.COM

VLM.EXE
```

Although they are loaded in this sequence, the data flows through these components in a different order: the LAN driver, LSL, IPXODI, and finally the DOS Requester itself (VLM.EXE). Figure 3.14 illustrates the flow of data through these components. The following sections describe each component in detail.

**FIGURE 3.14**

Data passes through several components between the workstation and the server.

**NETWORK CARD DRIVER [MLID]** The LAN driver is the software that communicates with the network card. After the data is sent across the network and received by the network card, this program converts it into a standard format that the NetWare client software understands. The type of LAN driver used for NetWare 4 is called an MLID, or Multiple Link Interface Driver. This is a term for any driver that supports the ODI specification.

The LAN driver is the only part of the client software that is not guaranteed to come with NetWare 4. Although NetWare provides drivers for common network cards, you should use the most current driver provided by the manufacturer of the network card. That driver should be included on a disk that came with the card. You may be able to obtain the latest version from a BBS or Internet service provided by the card manufacturer.

**LSL (LINK SUPPORT LAYER)** The LSL handles the ODI specification. This program communicates with the protocols, such as IPX, and makes the connection between these protocols and the network card. The TSR program used for LSL is LSL.COM.

**IPXODI (IPX PROTOCOL FOR ODI)** The IPXODI.COM program handles the IPX protocol. Packets are created and passed on to the LSL for processing by the network card. If you use other protocols, such as TCP/IP or AppleTalk, you load them along with (or instead of) IPXODI.

**THE NETWARE DOS REQUESTER** The NetWare DOS Requester provides the final layer of communication. The DOS Requester is responsible for communications with DOS and the application software on the workstation. The DOS Requester allows DOS applications to use network resources, such as files and printers, as though they were local to the workstation.

The DOS Requester program is called VLM.EXE. This program is actually a shell that loads subprograms called Virtual Loadable Modules (VLMs). Each of the VLMs provides a specific service. VLMs are modular, so they can be loaded and unloaded as needed. You can conserve memory by loading only the components you need.

## Using the DOS Requester

To use the DOS Requester you simply load the client software programs in the correct order after loading DOS. You can do this by switching to the

C:\NWCLIENT directory (or the client directory you specified) and executing the commands in this order:

```
LSL

LAN Driver

IPXODI

VLM
```

Since this is probably something you want to use each time a network workstation is turned on, you can automate the process with a batch file. The INSTALL program creates a batch file called STARTNET.BAT, which we'll look at in the next section.

Should you need to unload the drivers—for example, to change the configuration—you can do so by adding the /U switch to each program. The programs must be unloaded in reverse order. Here are the commands for unloading the drivers, assuming you are using the NE2000 LAN driver:

```
VLM /U

IPXODI /U

NE2000 /U

LSL /U
```

You cannot always unload the DOS Requester components. If certain applications or drivers are run after the client software, it will be unable to unload itself. In these cases you need to reboot the computer.

## Customizing the DOS Requester

Settings for the DOS client are provided through the use of a *configuration file* called NET.CFG. The following sections explain the changes you can make to workstation NET.CFG files and to the STARTNET.BAT batch file. By modifying these files, you can customize your users' connections to the network.

### Modifying the NET.CFG File

The NET.CFG file contains the settings for the DOS client software. This file is usually located in the C:\NWCLIENT directory on the workstation. Each workstation has its own NET.CFG file. Here are the contents of a typical file:

```
Link Driver NE2000

      Frame Ethernet_802.2

      PORT 300

      INT 5

NetWare DOS Requester

      FIRST NETWORK DRIVE = F

      SHOW DOTS = ON

      NAME CONTEXT = "OU=MKTG.O=IVR_INC"

      PREFERRED TREE = IVR_TREE
```

The NET.CFG file is divided into sections. Two typical sections are shown in the preceding file. The Link Driver section contains settings for the network card. If you are using multiple cards, there can be more than one Link Driver section. These settings must match the hardware settings of your network card. The NetWare DOS Requester section contains settings for the DOS Requester.

You can place several important commands in the NetWare DOS Requester section:

| COMMAND | DESCRIPTION |
| --- | --- |
| FIRST NETWORK DRIVE | Determines the first drive letter to be used for mapping network drives. Usually, the first drive is F |
| PREFERRED TREE | Specifies the NDS tree to attach to, if more than one tree is available |
| PREFERRED SERVER | Can be used instead of PREFERRED TREE to specify a server to attach to. You can specify a tree or server but not both |

| COMMAND | DESCRIPTION |
| --- | --- |
| NAME CONTEXT | Determines the workstation's *default context*. When a user logs in without specifying an NDS container, NetWare looks for the user login name in the default context |
| SHOW DOTS | If ON, indicates that the "." and ".." entries (current and parent directories) should be included in directory listings, as DOS does. This provides compatibility with some DOS applications |

You can place many other commands in the DOS Requester and other sections of NET.CFG files. Appendix E includes a complete list of these options.

You can edit the NET.CFG file using any text editor, such as the EDIT program built into MS-DOS (versions 5.0 and above). If you make changes to these settings, you'll need to reboot the workstation to reload the network software with the new settings.

## Using the **INSTALL.CFG** File to Modify **NET.CFG** Files

In a typical network you'll find yourself needing to make the same changes to each user's NET.CFG file after installing the client software. Rather than requiring you to make these changes manually, NetWare provides an easier way. By using the INSTALL.CFG file in the installation directory, you can change all the files at one time. The INSTALL.CFG file provides settings to the INSTALL program for all aspects of installation.

The [REQUESTER] section of the INSTALL.CFG file contains settings that will be copied into the DOS Requester section of each workstation's NET.CFG file. You can load this file into a text editor and customize these items to suit your network.

*Always make a backup copy of the INSTALL.CFG file before modifying it. This file controls the installation process, and making changes to some parts of the file could cause the installation process to fail.*

### Customizing the **STARTNET.BAT** File

Another file, called STARTNET.BAT, is also created in the NWCLIENT directory. This is a DOS batch file. The commands in the STARTNET.BAT file load the network software for the workstation. A typical file looks like this:

```
SET NWLANGUAGE=ENGLISH

C:\NWCLIENT\LSL.COM

C:\NWCLIENT\NE2000.COM

C:\NWCLIENT\IPXODI.COM

C:\NWCLIENT\VLM.EXE
```

You can modify this file with any text editor. You may need to do this to load a different network driver, to change the workstation's language setting, or to provide other parameters to the network software. For example, you can add the /MC option to the VLM.EXE line to force the VLMs to be loaded in conventional memory instead of expanded memory. This memory allocation scheme may resolve some conflicts with other software.

## Installing and Using Windows 3.1 Client Software

The DOS client INSTALL program can also install the Microsoft Windows client software. The Windows client software works with the DOS Requester to provide access to all network resources. It also provides an easy way to manage network resources from the Windows environment.

NetWare Windows client software includes the following:

- Drivers for more efficient handling of mapped network drives.

- Drivers to allow printing to network printers.

- A control panel, called NetWare Settings, to customize the Windows client software.

- Pop-up message support. You can display messages sent from other workstations or the server (such as disk error and printer status messages) in a pop-up window over the currently running Windows application.

- NetWare User Tools. This Windows utility allows you to change drive mappings, set printer CAPTURE settings, and specify other options.

*The client software discussed here is meant for use with Windows 3.1, 3.11, or Windows for Workgroups. You can use it with Windows 95, but it lacks some of the features of the 32-bit client.*

## Using the Network Control Panel

After the Windows client software is installed, a new Network icon is created on the Control Panel. Double-click this icon to see a dialog box for changing settings for the Windows client. This dialog box, shown in Figure 3.15, allows you to modify NetWare client settings:

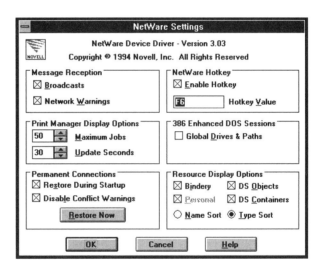

- **Message Reception:** Allows you to specify whether to display messages sent from other users and warnings from the server in a pop-up window over your current application. You can enable or disable broadcasts (messages from users) and warnings (messages from the network server) separately.

- **Print Manager Display Options:** Controls the number of network printing jobs that will be displayed in the Windows Print Manager.

- **Permanent Connections:** Enables permanent connections to printers, servers, and drive mappings that will automatically be restored each time you start Windows. You can up set these connections using the NetWare User Tools program, described in the next section.

- **NetWare Hotkey:** Allows you to use a function key to access the NetWare User Tools program.

- **Global Drives and Paths:** Makes DOS sessions under Windows share the same drive mappings.

- **Resource Display Options:** Controls the types of resources displayed in NetWare User Tools and how these resources are sorted.

### Using NetWare User Tools

You can run the NetWare User Tools program from an icon in the NetWare program group or by pressing a hotkey (if you enabled this key in the NetWare Settings dialog box). This program allows you to perform the following functions, using a simple drag-and-drop interface:

- Change CAPTURE settings for printers

- Change drive mappings

- Attach to and detach from servers and Directory trees

- Display a list of users on the system and send messages to other users

The Help button in the NetWare User Tools window provides access to a friendly help system, which explains the specifics of the available options. Figure 3.16 shows an example of a NetWare Drive Connections screen in NetWare User Tools.

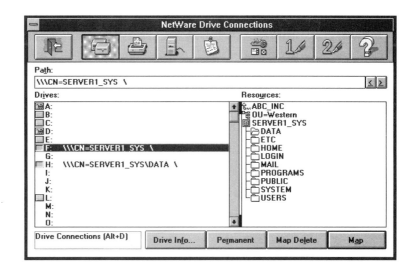

# Using the OS/2 Client Software

NETWARE ALSO PROVIDES support for the IBM OS/2 operating system. Users at OS/2 workstations can attach to the server or to the NDS tree and can access shared files and printers just like DOS and Windows clients. DOS and Windows programs running within OS/2 can also access the network.

Because OS/2 can work with the standard DOS file system, you can use OS/2 clients on your network without installing additional software on the file server. However, OS/2 includes the HPFS (High Performance File System). This system allows long file names (up to 255 characters with lowercase letters) and extended attributes (other information, such as file descriptions). To take advantage of these features, you need to install the OS/2 *name space* on the server.

*Since the OS/2 name space allows longer, more versatile file names, you can also use it to support the long file names of Windows 95. At this writing, a specific name space for Windows 95 has not yet been released.*

### Adding the OS/2 Name Space

The OS/2 name space allows HPFS files to be stored on your server. You can install the name space by using the following commands at the file server console:

| COMMAND | DESCRIPTION |
| --- | --- |
| LOAD OS2 | Loads the protocols used for the OS/2 name space. This is an NLM called OS2.NAM. After the name space is installed, this module loads automatically when you mount the volume |
| ADD NAME SPACE OS2 TO SYS | Adds the name space to the volume and allocates space to store HPFS file names. You can use any volume name in place of SYS. These changes are permanently written to the volume, so you execute this command only once |

After you have installed the name space, you can use the HPFS features on your server. Note the following considerations:

- Extended OS/2 naming information is accessible from OS/2 clients only. You can access the files from DOS clients, but long file names may be truncated. Since an OS/2 client can also access DOS file names, you can use an OS/2 client to copy or rename the files using DOS names; however, you lose the extended name information when you do this.

- The name space module (OS2.NAM) should load automatically when you mount the volume. If this module fails to load or is unloaded, files that use OS/2 naming will be inaccessible until the module is loaded.

### Installing the OS/2 Requester

The NetWare Client for OS/2 gives OS/2 workstations access to NetWare 4 and NDS. It includes the NetWare OS/2 Requester, which is the OS/2 equivalent of the DOS Requester and which provides the same functions.

To begin the installation, run the INSTALL program. There are two ways to do this:

- Place the NetWare 4 CD-ROM in a local or networked drive. Change to that drive and type **INSTALL** from the OS/2 command prompt.

- Run the MAKEDISK program from the CD-ROM or the SYS:PUBLIC\ CLIENT\OS2 directory on a server. This program allows you to create a set of installation disks for the OS/2 client. You can then run INSTALL from the first disk.

The INSTALL program includes several options, including an option to display built-in documentation. To install the client software, select Requester on Workstation from the Installation menu. You can choose from four types of installations:

- **Edit CONFIG.SYS and Copy All Files:** The default. It installs all the client software, including the LAN driver, and modifies the OS/2 CONFIG.SYS file to load the network client software.

- **Only Edit CONFIG.SYS:** Makes changes to CONFIG.SYS only. This is useful if you have already installed the client software.

- **Only Copy Requester Files:** Copies the OS/2 client files to your workstation but does not modify CONFIG.SYS.

- **Only Copy ODI LAN Driver Files:** Allows you to copy optional LAN driver files from the installation directory. Drivers are provided for several common network cards. You can choose from this list or insert a disk provided by the network card manufacturer.

Choose one of the options above (usually the first one) and click the OK button to begin the installation process. Choose a LAN driver; all files are copied or modified in accordance with your selection.

After the client software has been installed, reboot the workstation. You can now use the OS/2 version of the LOGIN program to log in to the network. After logging in, you can access network drives from the OS/2 desktop.

The installation program also installs a program called NetWare Tools for OS/2. This program is very similar to the Windows NetWare User Tools program described in the section "Using NetWare User Tools" earlier in this chapter. It allows you to map network drives, set up printer capturing, and log in and out of servers and Directory trees.

# Logging in to the Network

**A**FTER YOU HAVE installed the appropriate client software for your operating system, you need to log in to the network before you can begin using its resources. This is the process of entering your user ID and password to authorize your use of the network. A login script may be executed, performing default actions.

*You need a valid username and password to log in. Consult Chapter 5 for the steps to create a new user.*

## Logging in under DOS and Windows 3.1

Using either the DOS Requester or the new Client 32, you use the DOS LOGIN.EXE program to begin your network session. Follow these steps:

1. Load the client software. If you have added the commands to AUTOEXEC.BAT, this software should load automatically when you turn on the workstation.

2. From the DOS prompt, switch to the first network drive. This drive depends on the setting in NET.CFG but is typically F.

3. Type **LOGIN** to access the LOGIN program.

4. Enter your username and password at the prompts.

This completes the login process. If you have a login script, it executes immediately after you log in. You can use a login script to set up default drive mappings, printers, and other settings. Chapter 9 discusses login scripts.

You can also log in from Windows 3.1 by using NetWare User Tools, described earlier in this chapter. However, this will not run a login script and may not always work with DOS applications running under Windows.

## Logging in with Windows 95

After you have installed Client 32 for Windows 95, restart the computer. Each time you start Windows 95, you immediately see a dialog box to log in to the network. Enter your username and password to log in. If you have a login script, it will be executed.

The settings used to log in, such as whether to log in to a server or an NDS Directory tree, were configured when you installed the 32-bit client. You can change these settings by selecting Network from the Windows 95 Control Panel, highlighting the NetWare 32-bit client entry, and clicking the Properties button.

## Logging in with OS/2

Although OS/2 can run DOS applications, you should use the OS/2 version of the LOGIN utility to log in to the network. This provides access to the network for all the programs you run, including DOS, Windows, and OS/2 applications.

You can log in from an OS/2 prompt using the following steps:

1. Switch to the NETWARE directory, typically on drive C.

2. Type **LOGIN**.

3. Enter your username and password.

You can also log in using the OS/2 User Tools program. You can change the settings in this program to automatically display a login dialog when you start OS/2, similar to the capabilities of Windows 95.

OS/2 can execute a login script, but it is a special OS/2 login script. You need a separate script for OS/2 if you wish to use this feature. The normal login scripts defined through NDS are DOS login scripts and will not be executed.

# *Summary*

N THIS CHAPTER we've discussed the various types of software PC clients can use to access the network:

- Client 32 for DOS and Windows is the latest client for these operating systems. It is included with the latest version of NetWare 4 and is emerging as a new standard.

- The NetWare DOS Requester supports DOS and Windows 3.1. This was the previous standard for these systems and is still the most common client software in use. Both the DOS Requester and Client 32 support NDS; older software, such as the NetWare Shell, did not. The DOS Requester includes support for pop-up windows, graphical login, and other Windows features.

- Client 32 for Windows 95 supports Windows 95 workstations.

- The NetWare OS/2 Requester supports IBM's OS/2 operating system and gives it the same capabilities as the DOS Requester, including NDS support. The OS/2 Requester allows graphical login and logout and provides friendly tools for managing drives, printers, and other parameters.

Each type of client software requires specific tasks to install and configure it. Once you have installed and run the client software, you need to log in to the network. Logging in verifies that you are a valid user, connects you to the network resources, and optionally runs a login script.

After you've logged in, one of the most important resources you can use is the file system. In the next chapter we'll look at the NetWare 4 file system, which you use to store and organize data on the server.

# The NetWare 4
# File System

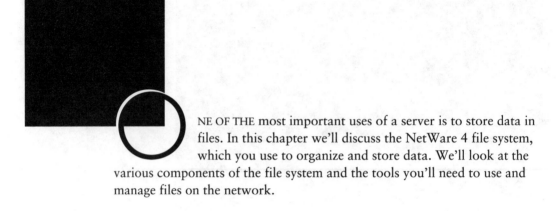

NE OF THE most important uses of a server is to store data in files. In this chapter we'll discuss the NetWare 4 file system, which you use to organize and store data. We'll look at the various components of the file system and the tools you'll need to use and manage files on the network.

# Components of the File System

IRST, LET'S TAKE a look at what makes up the NetWare 4 file system. (For the most part, this information also applies to earlier NetWare versions.) We'll start with the largest unit, the disk drive itself, and work our way down to the individual files stored there. Figure 4.1 shows how these components fit together. The following sections describe each component separately.

The NetWare file system evolved from CP/M and UNIX, as the DOS file system did, so you'll notice many similarities. Nevertheless, the NetWare file system is unique, and using it requires particular tools and techniques.

It's important to note that although the NetWare file system is organized in very nearly the same way as DOS, it does not actually use DOS and is not compatible with it. Once you've formatted a drive for use with NetWare, you can access the files on it only through the NetWare server. You can't boot DOS on the server machine, for example, and read the files. Chapter 13 explains the process of installing and formatting drives for use with NetWare.

**FIGURE 4.1**

Components of the
NetWare file system

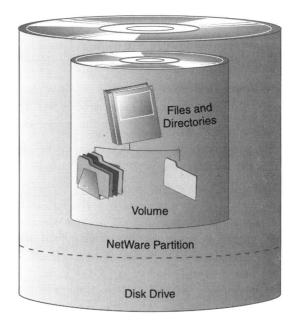

Files and Directories

Volume

NetWare Partition

Disk Drive

## Disk Drives

The files in the NetWare file system are stored on a disk drive in the Net-Ware 4 server. Since a server is just a PC-compatible machine that runs NetWare, the drives it uses are at least similar to the drives a typical PC uses, and often the same. However, you must install them in a specific manner.

To access and use the drive, NetWare requires a driver for the specific drive type. You can use the following types of drives with NetWare 4:

- SCSI (Small Computer Systems Interface, usually pronounced "scuzzy") drives have long been the standard for servers. They are fast and reliable, and they are available in many configurations. The driver you use depends on the SCSI controller.

- IDE (Integrated Drive Electronics) drives are currently the most inexpensive option for PCs. They are not as fast as SCSI, but they are suitable for most small servers. NetWare includes a driver, IDE.DSK, that works with most IDE drives.

- EIDE (Extended IDE) is a revised version of the IDE standard that has become popular in recent years. Although based on IDE, it is faster and more versatile and includes most of the advantages of SCSI. EIDE drivers are available to work with NetWare.

- MFM, ESDI, and other old drives have been used in servers, but they are not recommended for new servers. These may use a custom driver provided with the drive or the generic ISADISK driver.

## Disk Partitions

NetWare does not actually work with entire disk drives; to NetWare, the largest division within a disk drive is a disk partition. A partition is simply an area of the disk drive that has been set aside for NetWare's use.

You may have partitioned disks in DOS before, using the FDISK program. This program allows a large disk to be treated as several smaller disks; for example, a 680MB hard drive might be divided into a 400MB partition and a 280MB partition. After you have set up the partitions, DOS recognizes the disk as two separate drives.

*In both DOS and NetWare, changing the partitioning of a disk drive erases all data on the drive. Be sure you have a backup before changing partitioning.*

NetWare uses the same type of partitioning as DOS to set aside space. However, in a DOS setup, all the partitions are DOS partitions; a NetWare server's drive typically has a DOS partition and a NetWare partition. If you boot DOS on the server, only the DOS partition is accessible.

Since you use DOS to load NetWare on the server, you usually need a DOS partition. A typical NetWare server with one drive has a small DOS partition; the minimum size is 5- to10MB, but 20MB is more practical. This partition stores DOS itself, the server program (SERVER.EXE), and any drivers you need. After the disk driver is loaded, the NetWare partition becomes accessible.

*You cannot use FDISK to create a NetWare partition. You must use the NetWare INSTALL program, described in Chapter 13, for this purpose.*

# Volumes

Although partitioning sets aside a portion of the disk for NetWare's use, NetWare does not store files directly in the NetWare partition. Instead, it uses *volumes*. A volume is the most important disk storage unit in NetWare.

Volumes are similar to separate disk drives, or partitions, in DOS; each has its own name and contains its own directory of files. However, a volume does not necessarily correspond to a single disk drive or partition. A NetWare partition can contain several volumes, and a volume can span several partitions, even on different drives. Regardless, NetWare treats a volume as a single, unified storage space.

Volume names in NetWare can be up to eight characters long and are followed by a colon. The first volume is created when you install a server and is always named SYS:. This volume stores the NetWare operating system and utilities and is essential to the server's operation.

NetWare sets aside a portion of each volume to store the *directory entry table,* or *DET*. This table is similar to the FAT (file allocation table) on a DOS disk. The DET stores an entry for each file, including its name, its attributes, and where it can be found on the disk.

# Files and Directories

Like DOS, NetWare stores data on a volume in files, using a system of directories to organize these files into logical groups. In this section we'll look at the conventions and systems NetWare 4 uses to organize files.

### File-Naming Rules

When you install NetWare, you can choose between two formats for file names: DOS format and NetWare format. The NetWare format allows both upper- and lowercase letters and foreign characters. The NetWare format can cause incompatibilities with DOS programs, and Novell recommends against its use; however, it can be useful in some applications. Each file on the volume has a name you use to identify it. If you selected DOS file names when you installed the server, the rules for file names on the NetWare volume are the same as for DOS. This similarity with DOS was built into NetWare to allow it to work well with DOS. For example, you can copy files from a DOS disk to a NetWare volume and back without worrying about the names of the files.

The rules you should follow for DOS-compatible names were given in Chapter 2. If you have chosen the NetWare format, you are allowed to use additional characters in the names. There are also alternate name spaces for OS/2, UNIX, and Macintosh, which we'll look at later in this chapter.

### Directories

Like DOS, NetWare 4 organizes files into directories and subdirectories. Each directory can have any number of directories under it, so the volume organization is something of a tree structure. Figure 4.2 shows a simple directory structure.

**FIGURE 4.2**

Files and directories are organized in a tree structure.

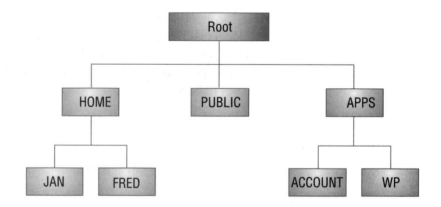

The first directory on a volume is the root directory, as it is in DOS. You can store files directly in this directory, but this method would lead to poor organization. Instead, you should create directories to organize the files.

When you set up a server, several directories are created automatically under the root directory of the SYS: volume. NetWare uses them for various purposes:

- SYSTEM contains NetWare server utilities, configuration files, and NLMs. Most tasks performed on the file server use the SYSTEM directory.

- PUBLIC contains utilities that run from a workstation. By default, all users on the network have access to PUBLIC.

- MAIL stores configuration files for each user. This directory is used mainly for access by bindery-based clients. Third-party e-mail systems may also use it.

- ETC contains sample files for the TCP/IP protocol. TCP/IP is an optional protocol you can use to integrate NetWare with UNIX systems and the Internet. We'll discuss TCP/IP further in Chapter 14. The ETC directory is also used by some third-party applications.

## File Attributes

Like DOS, files on a NetWare volume can be given attributes. These are flags you can set to give the file a certain behavior; the system may also set them to indicate something about the file—for example, that it has changed or is compressed. You can set file attributes using the FLAG command, NWADMIN, or FILER, all of which we'll discuss later in this chapter.

NetWare 4's list of attributes is much longer than that of DOS. Table 4.1 lists the possible attributes. Many of these attributes concern NetWare 4 features, such as file compression and disk suballocation, which we'll discuss in Chapter 12.

| **TABLE 4.1** Attributes Available in NetWare 4 | **ATTRIBUTE NAME** | **DESCRIPTION** |
| --- | --- | --- |
| | A (Archive Needed) | NetWare sets this attribute automatically when a file is changed. Backup programs use this flag to indicate which files need to be backed up |
| | Ci (Copy Inhibit) | Stops users from copying the file (Macintosh files only) |
| | Cc (Can't Compress) | NetWare sets this attribute to indicate that no significant amount of space would be saved by compression |
| | Dc (Don't Compress) | Prevents a file or directory contents from being compressed |

| | ATTRIBUTE NAME | DESCRIPTION |
|---|---|---|
| **TABLE 4.1**<br><br>Attributes Available in<br>NetWare 4<br>(continued) | Di (Delete Inhibit) | Prevents a file or directory from being deleted; this applies only to Macintosh file systems |
| | Dm (Don't Migrate) | Prevents file or directory contents from being migrated to an optical jukebox, tape, or other high-capacity storage |
| | Ds (Don't Suballocate) | Causes the file to be written in whole blocks, regardless of whether block suballocation is enabled |
| | Ic (Immediate Compress) | Causes the file, or all files in the directory, to be compressed immediately when written |
| | M (Migrated) | Indicates files that have been migrated to high-capacity storage |
| | H (Hidden) | Prevents a file or directory from being shown in the directory listing. This attribute affects DOS programs only; the NDIR utility shows hidden files if the user has the File Scan right |
| | I (Indexed) | Activates the turbo FAT indexing feature on the file |
| | N (Normal) | Normal is not an actual file attribute; the FLAG command uses it to assign a default set of attributes (Shareable, Read/Write) |
| | P (Purge) | Causes the file to be purged (erased) immediately when deleted. The file cannot be recovered using the Salvage option |
| | Ri (Rename Inhibit) | Prevents the user from renaming the file or directory; this applies only to Macintosh file systems |
| | Ro (Read Only) | Prevents users from writing to, renaming, or erasing the file. Ro automatically sets the Ri (Rename Inhibit) and Di (Delete Inhibit) attributes |
| | Rw (Read/Write) | Allows both reading and writing to the file. This attribute is set when the Ro (Read Only) attribute is cleared |
| | S (Shareable) | Allows multiple users to access the file at the same time |

| TABLE 4.1 | ATTRIBUTE NAME | DESCRIPTION |
|---|---|---|
| Attributes Available in NetWare 4 (continued) | Sy (System) | Indicates files the system uses. A combination of the Read Only and Hidden attributes |
| | T (Transactional) | Indicates that the file is a TTS file and is protected by the Transaction Tracking System. You can use this feature only with applications that support TTS |
| | X (Execute Only) | Prevents the file from being modified, renamed, or copied. Once set, this attribute cannot be removed except by deleting the file. Use this attribute for executable files only |

### Alternate Name Spaces

OS/2, UNIX, Macintosh, Windows NT, and Windows 95 offer two advantages over DOS file names: they can be longer (up to 256 characters), and they can include lowercase letters, some punctuation, and spaces. Thus you can give your files names such as "Revised Financial Report for October 1997" instead of FNOCT97R.DOC.

If you use OS/2, Macintosh, or another operating system, you may be dreading the thought of using DOS file names for all your files on the server. Luckily, you don't have to. NetWare supports a variety of name spaces that allow you to store files on the server using non-DOS names.

The alternate name spaces provided with NetWare 4 are the following:

- The *Macintosh name space* allows Macintosh-compatible names.

- The *Long Filenames name space* allows long file names in Windows 95, OS/2, and Windows NT.

- The *NFS name space* is used for UNIX-compatible names.

To support one or more of these schemes, you need to add the name space to a volume and load a special disk driver. Chapter 13 will discuss this process. After you have added a name space, you can still use DOS file names if you wish.

# Managing Files and Directories

I
N THIS SECTION we'll take a look at the tools you can use to manage the files and directories stored on your NetWare server. Some tools are provided with NetWare, and others may come with DOS or Windows or from a third-party provider.

Since NetWare uses a DOS-compatible file system, you can use any DOS or Windows file management utility; however, the ones we'll describe here have special features that make them ideally suited to files on the NetWare server.

*Although you can use third-party utilities to rename, copy, or delete files, utilities that attempt to modify the FAT directly—such as disk editors and directory sorters—will not work on NetWare files.*

## Managing Files with **NWADMIN**

NWADMIN, the NetWare Administrator utility, is possibly the most important utility in NetWare 4. You use it to manage NDS objects, which we'll discuss in the next chapter. In addition, you can use it to manage files.

### Getting Started with **NWADMIN**

You'll use the NWADMIN utility frequently throughout this book. This utility can run on a Windows or Windows 95 workstation. Follow these steps to start NWADMIN:

1. Log in to the network.

2. Start Windows (or Windows 95).

3. Select Run from the File menu, or from the Start menu in Windows 95.

4. Type **NWADMIN** as the name of the file to run. (The path should not be necessary.)

You should now see the main NWADMIN screen, shown in Figure 4.3.

**FIGURE 4.3**

You can use NWADMIN
to manage files, along
with other aspects of
NetWare.

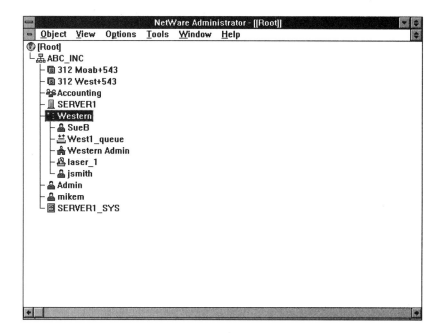

**FIGURE 4.3**

You can use NWADMIN
to manage files, along
with other aspects of
NetWare.

## Browsing a Volume

NWADMIN calls the process of navigating through a directory tree *browsing*.
You can browse the files and directories in a volume in two ways:

- Double-click the name of a volume to expand the listing to the names of
  files and directories under the root directory of the volume, as shown in
  Figure 4.4.

- Click the volume name once to highlight it. Select Tools from the menu
  bar, and then select Browse to open a new window that shows only the
  volume, as you can see in Figure 4.5.

After you open the volume for display, you can navigate through the directories. Double-clicking a directory opens that directory. If you select a file or
directory, the Object menu includes options that allow you to perform file
operations, such as copy, move, rename, and delete. In addition, the Details
option on the Object menu allows you to view the attributes of the file, along
with the trustees, which you'll learn about in Chapter 7. The Details dialog is
shown in Figure 4.6.

**FIGURE 4.4**

Double-click a volume name to view the contents of the volume in the main NDS window.

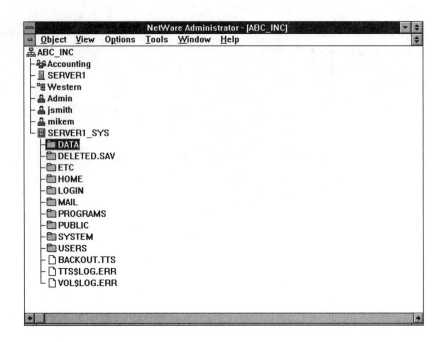

**FIGURE 4.5**

The Browse option on the Tools menu allows you to open a new window for viewing the directory.

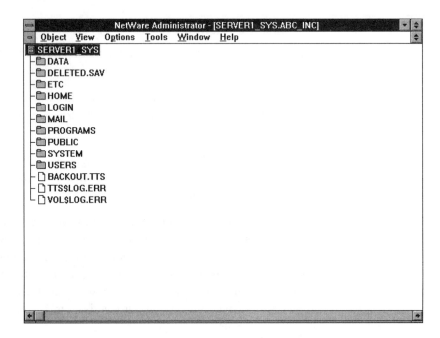

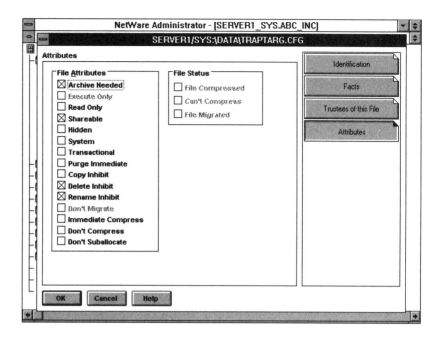

NWADMIN also allows you to manage files using Windows' *drag-and-drop* feature. If you drag a file into a directory with the mouse pointer, you can move or copy the file. This feature is similar to dragging and dropping in the Windows File Manager or Windows 95 Explorer.

## Managing Files with FILER

NetWare provides a DOS alternative for managing files: the FILER utility. Although not quite as friendly as NWADMIN, FILER provides all the options for the file system that NWADMIN does. Unlike NWADMIN, FILER is strictly for the file system—it cannot manage NDS objects.

### The FILER Main Menu

You start the FILER utility by typing **FILER** at the DOS prompt. You then see the main FILER menu, shown in Figure 4.7. Here's a quick overview of the options you'll find; we'll cover the most important ones in detail in the following sections.

- **Manage Files and Directories:** This is the option you'll use most often. It allows you to browse through the directory of a volume and perform actions such as copying, renaming, and deleting files.

- **Manage According to Search Pattern:** This is an alternative to the previous option. It provides the same function but first allows you to enter a template to choose which files to manage, using wildcard characters. This option lets you quickly find the type of files you're looking for.

- **Select Current Directory:** This option allows you to choose a new current directory, which will be used for the options listed above. By default, the directory you are in when you type **FILER** is used.

- **View Volume Information:** With this option you can view information about the various disk volumes on the network—free space, total space, and so forth.

- **Salvage Deleted Files:** Use this option to view a list of files that have been deleted and, if desired, restore them.

- **Purge Deleted Files:** Allows you to remove any deleted files that are being saved on a volume and free the associated space.

- **Set Default Filer Options:** Allows you to set several settings for the FILER utility, such as the order in which files and directories are sorted in the display.

**FIGURE 4.7**

The FILER utility provides a DOS alternative for managing files.

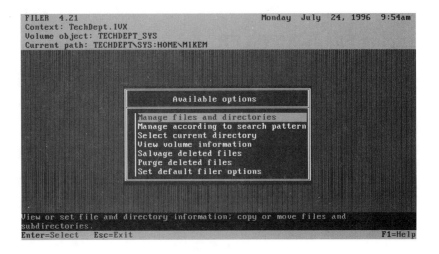

### Managing and Browsing Files and Directories

When you select the Manage Files and Directories option in FILER, you see a listing of the current directory, as shown in Figure 4.8. You can move the highlight to different files using the arrow keys, or use F5 to mark multiple files. Once you've chosen a file or directory, you can perform the following functions:

- Press F10 to manage a selected file. You can delete, rename, or copy the file or change its attributes and security information.

- Press F10 to manage a selected directory. You can rename it or delete it (including its contents) and change attributes and security information.

- Press ↵ to switch to a selected directory. You'll see a list of files in the directory.

**FIGURE 4.8**

FILER shows a list of files and directories.

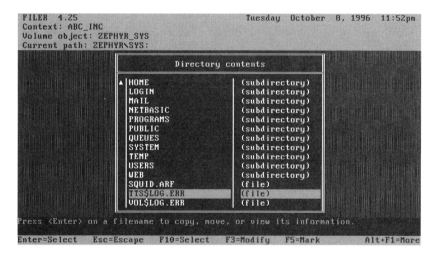

FILER gives you an easy way to manage file attributes. Press F10 to manage the file or directory. Select File Attributes to see the file attributes display, as shown in Figure 4.9. To add an attribute, press Ins and select the new attribute; to remove an existing attribute, press Del.

**FIGURE 4.9**

FILER shows a list of current attributes for a file.

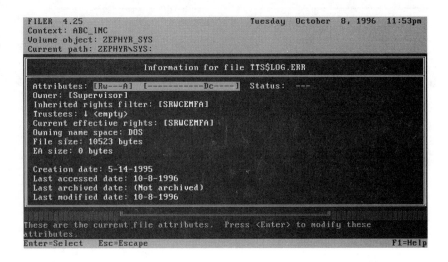

```
FILER  4.25                               Tuesday  October  8, 1996  11:53pm
Context: ABC_INC
Volume object: ZEPHYR_SYS
Current path: ZEPHYR\SYS:
┌────────────────────────────────────────────────────────────────────────┐
│                    Information for file TTS$LOG.ERR                       │
│  Attributes: [Rw---A]  [----------Dc----]  Status:  ---                   │
│  Owner: [Supervisor]                                                      │
│  Inherited rights filter: [SRWCEMFA]                                      │
│  Trustees: ↓ <empty>                                                      │
│  Current effective rights: [SRWCEMFA]                                     │
│  Owning name space: DOS                                                   │
│  File size: 10523 bytes                                                   │
│  EA size: 0 bytes                                                         │
│                                                                           │
│  Creation date: 5-14-1995                                                 │
│  Last accessed date: 10-8-1996                                            │
│  Last archived date: (Not archived)                                       │
│  Last modified date: 10-8-1996                                            │
│                                                                           │
└────────────────────────────────────────────────────────────────────────┘
These are the current file attributes.  Press <Enter> to modify these
attributes.
Enter=Select    Esc=Escape                                        F1=Help
```

## Managing Deleted Files

When you delete a file on a NetWare volume, it is not actually removed from the disk. Instead, it is marked as deleted but remains on the disk. Deleted files are retained until the disk space is low or until you purge them yourself.

Previous versions of NetWare provided a SALVAGE utility to manage deleted files. FILER allows you to do this in NetWare 4. To access this option, use the Salvage Deleted Files option from the main FILER menu, as shown in Figure 4.10.

*NWADMIN also includes a Salvage option from the Tools menu, which serves the same purpose.*

You see a list of deleted files in the current directory. Files in deleted directories are stored in a special directory on each volume called DELETED.SAV. Since a file can be created and deleted repeatedly, you might find several versions of a file; the deletion date should help you determine which one you need.

Once you've located the file you need, you can press ↵ to salvage (restore) it. You can also press F10 to access additional options, such as purging the file so that it can never be recovered.

If you're concerned about disk space or security, you can purge all the deleted files on a volume using the Purge Deleted Files option from the FILER main menu.

**FIGURE 4.10**

FILER allows you to list and salvage deleted files.

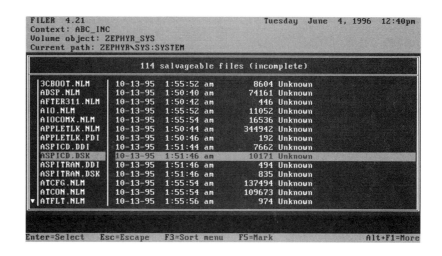

```
FILER 4.21                                Tuesday  June  4, 1996  12:40pm
Context: ABC_INC
Volume object: ZEPHYR_SYS
Current path: ZEPHYR\SYS:SYSTEM

                        114 salvageable files (incomplete)

    3CBOOT.NLM      10-13-95   1:55:52 am        8604 Unknown
    ADSP.NLM        10-13-95   1:50:40 am       74161 Unknown
    AFTER311.NLM    10-13-95   1:50:42 am         446 Unknown
    AIO.NLM         10-13-95   1:55:52 am       11052 Unknown
    AIOCOMX.NLM     10-13-95   1:55:54 am       16536 Unknown
    APPLETLK.NLM    10-13-95   1:50:44 am      344942 Unknown
    APPLETLK.PDI    10-13-95   1:50:46 am         192 Unknown
    ASPICD.DDI      10-13-95   1:51:44 am        7662 Unknown
    ASPICD.DSK      10-13-95   1:51:46 am       10171 Unknown
    ASPITRAN.DDI    10-13-95   1:51:46 am         494 Unknown
    ASPITRAN.DSK    10-13-95   1:51:46 am         835 Unknown
    ATCFG.NLM       10-13-95   1:55:54 am      137494 Unknown
    ATCON.NLM       10-13-95   1:55:54 am      109673 Unknown
  ▼ ATFLT.NLM       10-13-95   1:55:56 am         974 Unknown

Enter=Select    Esc=Escape    F3=Sort menu    F5=Mark            Alt+F1=More
```

*Unlike the UNDELETE command in DOS, a deleted file in NetWare can always be recovered—unless it has been purged.*

## Managing Files with Command-Line Utilities

Along with the DOS command-line utilities discussed in Chapter 2, NetWare provides a few utilities of its own. Like the DOS commands, you can use these commands at the DOS prompt, assuming you're logged in to the network. Typically, after the command name, you specify the file to act on and other options.

*As with most DOS commands, you can display a detailed list of options for each of the following commands by using the /? switch after the command.*

### FLAG

The FLAG command provides a simple method of managing file attributes from the command line. It is similar to the ATTRIB command in DOS but deals strictly with NetWare file attributes. You can use FLAG with both files and directories on NetWare volumes, but not on local DOS files.

The FLAG /D command allows you to view the attributes for a file. You can change a file's attributes by specifying the name of the attribute, along with a plus or minus sign to specify whether to add or remove the attribute. For example, this command adds the Sh (Shareable) attribute to the PEOPLE.DAT file:

    FLAG PEOPLE.DAT +Sh

*The plus sign is optional when adding an attribute since adding the attribute is the default action.*

You can also use wildcards to specify more than one file. The following command sets all the files in the current directory to Read/Write:

    FLAG *.* Rw

Along with the normal list of attributes given earlier in this chapter, FLAG allows you to specify two special keywords for combinations of attributes:

| KEYWORD | DESCRIPTION |
| --- | --- |
| ALL | Specifies a combination of the A, Ci, Di, H, Ic, P, Ri, Ro, Sh, Sy, and T attributes |
| N (Normal) | Specifies the Rw attribute and removes all others |

*FLAG also includes options to change the ownership of a file and control search modes. Appendix A provides details about these options.*

## NCOPY

The NCOPY command is similar in function to the XCOPY command in DOS, but it may be more efficient. When you copy a file from one network directory to another, the command takes place entirely on the file server, without copying any files into the DOS workstation's memory. NCOPY is typically used to copy entire subdirectories of files quickly and easily.

*NCOPY copies a file with its attributes but does not copy trustee assignments (rights) or file ownership to the new file. You will need to modify these areas yourself after copying the file.*

NCOPY has many options, but you will use the following ones most often. Appendix A provides a more detailed list.

| OPTION | DESCRIPTION |
|--------|-------------|
| /S | Indicates that subdirectories of the source directory will also be copied |
| /E | Indicates that empty subdirectories will also be copied. These are normally skipped with the /S option |
| /V | Indicates that all data written to the destination file or directory will be read back (verified). This option slows down the copy process but guarantees that the copy will be reliable |

Here are some examples to illustrate the use of NCOPY:
The command

```
NCOPY C:\DOS\*.* F:\BACKUP\DOS /S/E/V
```

copies all the files in the DOS directory on drive C, including subdirectories and empty subdirectories, to the BACKUP\DOS directory on drive F, with verification.
The command

```
NCOPY F:\DIR1 F:\DIR2
```

copies all the files in DIR1 to DIR2. Subdirectories are not copied.
The command

```
NCOPY F:\SYSTEM\*.TXT G:\SYSTEM
```

copies all the text files in the SYSTEM directory on drive F to the SYSTEM directory on drive G.

*You may have noticed that you can use local directories as the source or destination of NCOPY. However, if you use NCOPY, one of the directories must be on a network volume.*

## NDIR

NDIR is a NetWare-specific alternative to the DIR command in DOS. Along with the typical list of files, NDIR includes the information only NetWare knows—file ownership and attributes.

More than for just listing files, NDIR is useful for searching for a particular file, even if you don't know its whole name. For example, if the user SUE is searching for a file and all she knows is that she created it in the past week, you can type

```
NDIR F:\ /SUB /OW EQ SUE /CR AFT 3-14-97
```

Obviously, NDIR can be complicated. Luckily, the /? switch gives you a list of options anytime you need it. We list all the options in Appendix A. Here are a few more NDIR commands, to illustrate the flexibility of this command.

The command

```
NDIR
```

lists all files in the current directory, using the default format.

The command

```
NDIR * /R
```

displays a list of rights for each file in the current directory.

The command

```
NDIR F:\*.TMP /SUB
```

lists all files with a .TMP extension on drive F, including those in subdirectories.

The command

```
NDIR F:\* /SUB /OW EQ SUE.ACCT.STECH
```

lists all files owned by the user SUE on the network drive F. If the user is in the current context, the full distinguished name is not necessary.

The command

```
NDIR F:\PUBLIC\* /CR BEF 03-22-97
```

lists all files in the PUBLIC directory created before March 22, 1997.

## NPRINT

NPRINT allows you to quickly send a text file to a network print queue. For example, the following command sends all files with the .TXT extension in the current directory to the LASER1 print queue:

```
NPRINT *.TXT Q=LASER1
```

You'll learn more about the NPRINT command, and about NetWare printing, in Chapter 8.

### RENDIR

The RENDIR command renames a directory. On the command line, you simply specify the old name followed by the new name. For example, the following command renames the BACKUP directory on the SYS: volume, giving it the new name TEMP:

```
RENDIR SYS:BACKUP TEMP
```

You can use RENDIR on local drives, as well as on NetWare volumes. This is very convenient since some DOS versions are conspicuously missing a command to rename directories. (The MOVE command in DOS 6.0 and above can do this.)

## Alternatives for File Management

There is no rule that you have to use NetWare utilities to manage files on the NetWare server. Since NetWare uses a DOS-compatible file structure, you can use practically any DOS or Windows file-management utility. Here are some you may be familiar with:

- The DOS commands described in Chapter 2 can be used on NetWare files.

- The DOSSHELL program, in DOS versions 5.0 and earlier, provides a friendly file-management interface.

- The Windows 3.1*x* and Windows NT File Manager allow you to manage files in a manner similar to NWADMIN.

- The Explorer in Windows 95 provides most of the same functions.

All of these utilities can perform basic file maintenance—renaming, copying, moving, and deleting files—but since they're not NetWare utilities, they are unable to manage NetWare's special features—ownership of files, rights to files, and file attributes. They also cannot manage deleted files.

Another disadvantage of using non-NetWare utilities is that they may not retain file attributes, rights, and ownership information if you copy files or move them to a new location. If you need the same rights, ownership, and attributes to apply, use a NetWare utility—NWADMIN or FILER.

# Mapping Network Drives

I N THIS SECTION we'll discuss NetWare 4's system of *drive mappings*. These allow you to map drive letters to NetWare volumes, or portions of them. Drive mappings are essential for accessing a NetWare volume from clients.

While DOS uses drive letters, such as C and D, to indicate the various disks (or partitions) in a computer, NetWare uses named volumes, such as SYS:, for the purpose. Drive mappings provide a bridge between these two systems—allowing, for example, a DOS client to access the SYS: volume by referring to drive F.

## Network Drives and Search Drives

There are actually two distinct types of drive mappings in NetWare. Understanding the difference between these types is essential to managing the network. Here is a summary of the two types of mappings:

*Network drives* map a DOS drive letter you choose to a directory on a NetWare volume. This type of mapping simply allows the DOS client to treat the NetWare volume, or part of it, as a local drive.

*Search drives* provide the same function as network drives—making a DOS drive letter represent a NetWare volume—but serve another important purpose. When you type a command at the DOS prompt, all the defined search drives are searched for the command. Thus, you can use search drives to indicate directories that applications are using.

Search drives are numbered 1 through 16 and are searched in that order. They are also assigned DOS drive letters, but you cannot control which letters. Search drives are automatically assigned available drive letters, starting with Z and going back through the alphabet.

*Search drives are similar to the PATH command in DOS. In fact, NetWare changes the PATH to match the search drive settings. For this reason, you should not alter the PATH while logged in to the network. Unlike the PATH command, search drives are used for locating data files—not just commands.*

## The MAP Command

To set up drive mappings of both network drives and search drives, you use the MAP command. This command provides a variety of options for mapping drives. We'll explain the two main variations of the MAP command in the following sections. You can use the MAP command by itself to display a list of current drive mappings of both types.

### Mapping Network Drives

You use the simplest syntax of the MAP command to map a network drive. You specify the drive letter to use and the volume and directory to correspond to it on the command line. For example, this command maps drive F to the SYS: volume:

```
MAP F: = SYS:
```

More commonly, you'll specify a particular directory to set the drive mapping to. This sets the current directory for that drive; when the user switches to that drive, the directory will be set. The user can, however, change the current directory. Here is an example that maps the G drive to the SYS:PUBLIC directory:

```
MAP G: = SYS:PUBLIC
```

There is a final option for mapping network drives: the MAP ROOT command. This command allows you to specify a directory, and the user and applications treat that directory as the root. For example, this command:

```
MAP ROOT J:=SYS:ETC
```

maps drive J to the ETC directory under SYS:. However, as far as the user or an application can tell, ETC acts like the root directory. The user cannot change to any directory above this "fake root." This technique is often used to avoid confusing users, and to fool some older applications that expect to be run from the root directory.

*MAP ROOT isn't completely secure. Although users can't change to directories above a fake root, they can change to directories below it. Users can also tell which directory is acting as root by entering the MAP command. The mapping can also be changed by some applications.*

A final option of MAP allows you to map the next available drive (in alphabetical order) to a directory, without specifying the drive. The MAP NEXT command assigns the next drive letter to the SYS:SYSTEM directory:

```
MAP NEXT SYS:SYSTEM
```

### Mapping Search Drives

You use a variation of the MAP command to map search drives. Instead of a drive letter, you type the letter **S**, followed by the search drive number, on the command line. For example, this command maps the first search drive to the SYS:PUBLIC directory:

```
MAP S1:=SYS:PUBLIC
```

If this is the first search drive you have mapped, the drive would be assigned a drive letter of Z, but you don't need to use this drive letter in the command.

Since the order of search drives is important, you can use some special forms of the MAP command to change the order:

| COMMAND | DESCRIPTION |
|---------|-------------|
| MAP INS | Inserts the directory into the list at the numeric location you specify. The remaining drives are renumbered |
| MAP DEL | Deletes the specified search drive from the list |

*There is no MAP NEXT for search drives; however, using MAP S16: forces NetWare to choose the next available number (not necessarily 16), so it performs the same function.*

A search drive functions like a network drive; you can switch to that drive, and the directory specified in the MAP command will be current. However, if you use the CD command on the drive, you aren't just changing the current directory, you're also changing the directory for that search drive. For this reason you should avoid using the CD command on mapped drives unless you intend to change the search path.

## Mapping Drives with **NETUSER**

NetWare 4 provides a utility called NETUSER that provides a convenient way to change drive mappings, printer redirection, and other settings. The main screen of NETUSER is shown in Figure 4.11.

**FIGURE 4.11**

NETUSER allows you to change your current settings.

```
FILER  4.25                              Tuesday  October  8, 1996  11:53pm
Context: ABC_INC
Volume object: ZEPHYR_SYS
Current path: ZEPHYR\SYS:




                          Available options

                          Salvage menu

                          View/recover deleted files.
                          Salvage from deleted directories.
                          Set salvage options.




View and/or recover deleted files.
Enter=Select    Esc=Escape                                        F1=Help
```

The changes you make with NETUSER last only until you log out of the network. Here are the steps to map a drive using NETUSER:

**1.** Start the NETUSER utility by typing **NETUSER** at the DOS prompt.

**2.** From the main menu, select Drives.

**3.** Choose the drive to map and the directory, and press ↵ to map the drive.

# Using Applications on the Network

NE OF THE important jobs of a network administrator is to install applications on the network and get them running. Depending on the application, this can be a very easy process—or a very hard one. We'll give an overview of how to organize and plan your directory structure and then present some of the techniques you may need to use to get an application working.

## Organizing Files and Directories

One of the things that separates a well-running network from a cobbled-together one is the use of a good directory structure. If you're lucky enough to be setting up a network from scratch, plan the files and directories carefully so that things will be easy. If you're not, your network probably works as is—but moving toward a more organized structure will make it more efficient for both you and the users.

Let's start with an example of a badly planned directory structure, like the one shown in Figure 4.12. This directory just grew as the network and users needed it and was never actually planned. It has several glaring problems:

- Applications are not stored in a consistent place. Many are stored directly under the root directory.

- Data is stored in several different places; a user might have trouble finding the appropriate place.

- There is no attempt to separate data according to users or departments.

**FIGURE 4.12**

A poorly planned file system

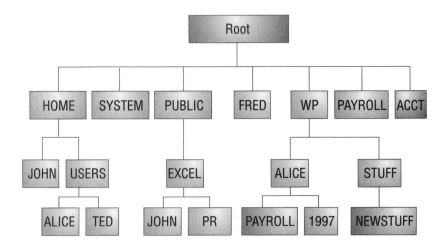

A corrected directory is shown in Figure 4.13. Here are some tips to follow in planning your directory structure:

■ Use a central APPS directory to store applications, each in its own subdirectory. This makes it easy to assign rights to users to run the applications, without allowing them to delete or modify the executable files.

■ A central DATA directory makes it easy to set rights, once again. In addition, you can easily choose this directory when making a backup.

■ When you create users, you are asked to create a home directory for each user. It's best to place these under a central directory, such as HOME or USERS. Users are given full rights to their home directories and can store data files there.

■ If there are many data files, split them in some logical fashion, such as by department, by workgroup, or by user.

■ One good strategy is to give each user a DATA directory under that user's home directory. Users should use this directory (or subdirectories underneath it) for their personal documents and the global DATA directory for documents that concern a whole department or the whole company.

**FIGURE 4.13**

A well-planned file system

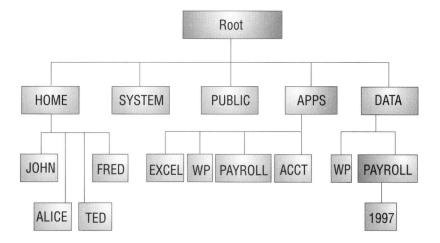

## Making Applications Work

The vast majority of major applications available today are *network-aware*. This means they can be installed onto the NetWare network and will usually manage all the details of their configuration for you, which can be very convenient. Often, these applications also allow multiple users to access the same files.

Unfortunately, many applications are not network-aware or not built for multiple users at all. The biggest offenders in this area are proprietary systems, such as an industry-specific accounting package or one developed in-house. Luckily, you can usually convince even these applications to run.

To install such an application, you specify the network directory—such as F:\APPS\ACCT—to install to. Once you've done that, follow these guidelines:

- Give all users (or the appropriate users) read rights to the directory.

- Since some applications write temporary files in the application directory, you may have to give users the write right to the directory also. In this case you should give the executable files the Ro (Read Only) attribute to prevent users from modifying them.

- If possible, specify a different directory for data files and temporary files. Consult the program's documentation.

- In a single-user program, users will usually be able to access the program at the same time but will not be able to use the same data file. You may be tempted to let them do so by adding the Sh (Shared) attribute to the data files; however, this rarely works with single-user applications and may corrupt the files.

If all else fails, call the technical support number for the application. Even though their product might not officially support NetWare networks, they are the most common type of network in the world; chances are good that they've dealt with your problem before.

# *Summary*

N THIS CHAPTER we looked at the NetWare 4 file system, which you use to store data on disks in the server. Components of the file system include disks and partitions, volumes, directories, and files. We covered these topics:

- The syntax required for file names and paths, and the limitations on them. In most cases these limitations are very similar to those of the DOS file system.

- The utilities you can use to manage files on the NetWare server. The most important of these are NWADMIN and FILER. In addition, you can use DOS and Windows commands and utilities, and several NetWare-specific commands.

- The MAP command, including the types of drives you can mapped, the techniques of storing applications and data efficiently on the network, and how to get applications to work properly using the network.

Although the file system is an important part of NetWare 4, you'll also need to understand NDS, which you use to organize users and network resources. In the next chapter we'll begin a detailed look at NDS and its features.

# Managing Objects with NDS

CHAPTER

5

I N EARLIER CHAPTERS we mentioned NetWare Directory Services, or NDS, several times. Since NetWare 4 is built around NDS, it's hard to explain much about NetWare 4 without reference to NDS. In this chapter we'll delve into the details of NDS itself. We'll start with a discussion of how NDS organizes the network resources and then give detailed instructions to allow you to manage the most important resource—the users.

# How NDS Organizes the Network

I N A NETWARE 4 network, there are many things to keep track of—users, printers, volumes, servers, and so forth. NetWare uses a database to keep track of all of these. In NetWare 3.1x, this database is the *bindery*—a simple database with information about each component. Each server maintains a separate bindery; this arrangement is called a *server-centric* organization. If a user needs access to multiple bindery servers, you have to log in to each one separately to give it access. A diagram of this type of organization is shown in Figure 5.1.

This method works fine for small networks—those with one location and only a few servers—but in a large, multiserver network, maintaining many binderies can be confusing.

*You may have heard of a product called NNS, or NetWare Naming Services. This was a precursor to NDS, available as an add-on to NetWare 3.1x servers.*

In NetWare 4 the bindery has been replaced by the NDS Directory. Unlike the bindery, the Directory can be organized in a tree-like structure. More

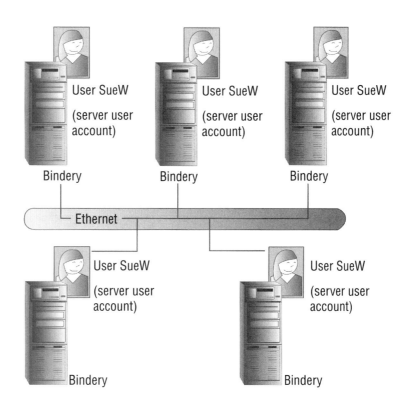

**FIGURE 5.1**

In the server-centric organization of older versions of NetWare, each server keeps a separate database of users, printers, and other objects.

important, NDS is *network-centric*—one NDS Directory can store information about all the components of the network. Figure 5.2 shows a network-centric structure.

*To avoid confusion between the Directory in NDS and disk directories, we will use a capital D when referring to the NDS Directory throughout this book.*

## Benefits of NDS

Before we explain the technical details of NDS, let's discuss its advantages over a conventional network organization, such as the bindery of NetWare 3.1x. We've already mentioned that NDS allows for better organization and a single database for the entire network. We'll look at these and other advantages in detail in the next sections, as well as the NDS features that provide them.

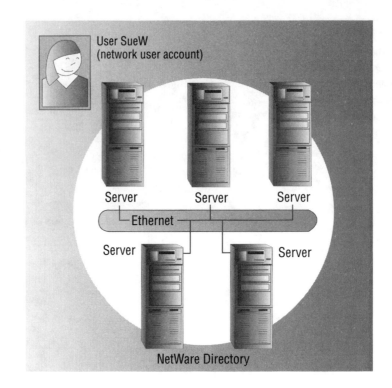

**FIGURE 5.2**

NetWare 4 uses a
network-centric
organization in which the
NDS Directory stores
information about all the
components on
the network.

### Better Organization

NDS organizes all the components of the network in a tree-like structure called the Directory. The Directory is usually represented by an upside-down tree, as shown in Figure 5.3. This organization is similar to a disk directory. It starts with a single object called the [Root] object. The Directory tree is then divided into smaller groupings, often related to departments of the company.

*Following Novell's convention, we'll use square brackets when referring to the [Root] object to avoid confusion with a disk's root directory. We'll represent the [Root] object with a small picture of the Earth.*

The objects that divide the Directory tree are called container objects. You can subdivide these objects as needed. Each user, printer, server, volume, or other network component is represented by what is called a leaf object in the

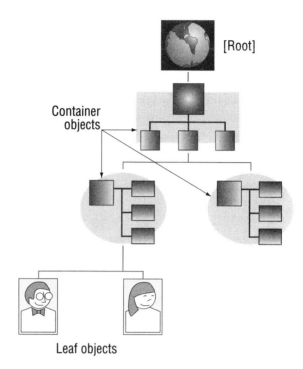

[Root]

Container
objects

Leaf objects

Directory tree, stored under a particular container object. We'll look more at the types of objects later in this chapter.

### Easy Administration

Using NetWare 2.$x$ and 3.1$x$, you can allow a user to access more than one server. However, this can be a complicated process; you have to log in as an administrator for each server and create an account for the user on each one.

Because NDS is network-centric, it makes a large network much easier to maintain. When you create a User object to represent a user on the network, the user can access any part of the network, including files stored on any server. You can easily give them access to all the servers from a single utility.

The NDS Directory can be split into sections, called partitions, and replicas of these partitions can be stored on multiple servers. This allows you to access the Directory quickly from anywhere on the network.

### Better Security

Although you don't have to give access to each server individually, NDS offers a wide variety of security options. You can restrict a user to one server, one volume, or a particular section of the NDS tree. You can give a user managing rights—the right to create or delete users and other NDS objects. You can assign these rights for the entire Directory or, more often, for a portion of the NDS tree.

Since a single Directory tree can manage a very large network, it may be too much work for a single administrator. Luckily, you can create multiple administrators in NDS, giving each the ability to control a portion of the Directory.

NDS security is a complicated subject, and probably the most complicated part of NDS. Chapter 7 goes into the details of NetWare 4 security.

### Expandability

Another advantage of NDS is that it is *scaleable.* This means it should work as easily with a small network as with a very large one. In practice, it's obviously easier to work with a tiny network than a huge one. However, NDS allows you to easily expand the network from one size to another. You can add a server, a volume, or even an entire location to the existing NDS tree.

NDS trees can also be *merged,* or combined into a single tree. This makes it easy to create a large-scale network organization gradually. You can start with several trees, one for each department, and later connect and integrate them into a single, global Directory.

NetWare 4 and NDS also provide an ability called internetworking to integrate with other networks. You can easily connect your NetWare 4 network with other NetWare 4 networks, with earlier versions of NetWare, other networking systems, or larger networks, such as the Internet. You can even manage earlier versions of NetWare from within NDS.

The NetWare Directory is also compatible with other Directory Services, particularly the X.500 standard, an international specification for network directories. NDS is based on the X.500 specification and includes most of its features, although it is limited in some areas and is not a hundred percent compatible.

### Reliability

An important feature of NDS is its reliability, or *fault tolerance.* Two NDS organization techniques provide high reliability:

- *Partitioning* allows you to divide the NDS tree into sections, or partitions. You can store each partition on a different server.

- *Replication* allows you to store copies, or *replicas,* of a partition on multiple servers.

If you use these features correctly, no one server is needed in order to keep the NDS database intact. If a server containing a partition goes down or is damaged, replicas of the partitions on other servers can take over. Figure 5.4 shows a typical setup of partitions.

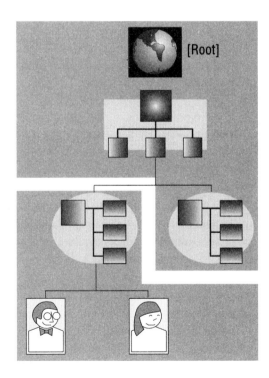

The best thing about the fault-tolerant features of NDS is that they are automatic. As you add servers to the network, NDS stores replicas of the NDS database on them by default. Because it is stored on multiple servers, NDS is called a *distributed database*.

This default provides a measure of reliability with a minimum of maintenance. However, when your network contains four or more servers, you'll need to make decisions and configure the partitioning and replication. We'll cover the ins and outs of planning NDS organization in Chapter 6.

### Directory Services

Although the main purpose of the NDS Directory is to manage the users and other objects in the NetWare 4 network, it can also be extended and used for other purposes. For example, many e-mail systems store their addressing information in the NDS database, and third-party applications can add data to the Directory for their own use.

*NAL (NetWare Application Launcher), the new menu system provided with the latest version of NetWare 4, provides a new use for NDS: storing information about applications. This will be explained in Chapter 9.*

## Structure of the Directory

As we've mentioned, every network resource is represented by an object in the NDS Directory. There are about 30 types of objects that can be placed in the Directory, but they all fall into two categories:

- You use *container objects* to organize other objects; they do not represent actual resources themselves. These objects are similar to subdirectories in a disk's directory.

- *Leaf objects* represent actual network resources and reside within one or more container objects.

Figure 5.5 is a diagram of a Directory tree including many of these objects. In the following sections we'll discuss these types of objects and describe some of the objects of each type. We'll begin with the [Root] object, a special type of container object.

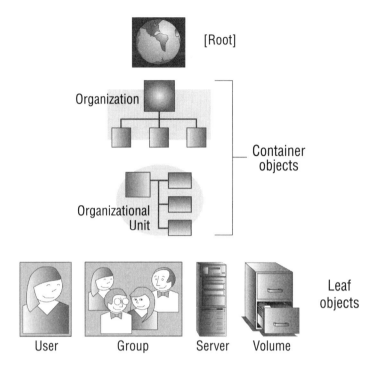

FIGURE 5.5

The NDS Directory tree consists of container and leaf objects.

[Root]

Organization

Container objects

Organizational Unit

User   Group   Server   Volume

Leaf objects

## The [Root] Object

At the top, or root, of the upside-down tree that represents the NDS Directory is the [Root] object, as shown in Figure 5.6.

The [Root] object performs the same function as the root directory on a disk. It is the ultimate container object; every object in the Directory tree is under the [Root]. This is more than an arbitrary distinction; because all objects in the tree lie under the [Root] object, you can use it when you need to make changes or assign rights that should affect every object in the tree.

Although the [Root] object is a container object, it acts like no other container object. It is created automatically when NDS is initially installed. It always has the name [Root]. You cannot delete or rename it, and you can change only a few of its parameters.

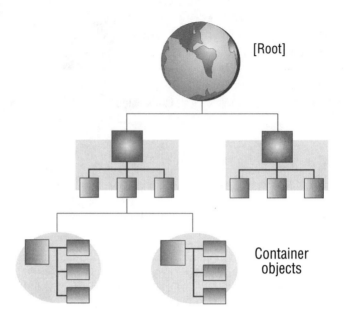

[Root]

Container
objects

## Container Objects

As mentioned earlier in this chapter, you use container objects to organize the Directory tree. The container objects form the structure of the NDS Directory and are vital to its organization. Container objects can contain leaf objects—representations of actual network resources—or they can contain other container objects. This allows you to finely subdivide the organization of the Directory.

The available container objects in NetWare 4 are Country, Organization, and Organizational Unit. Each has its own uses and can contain certain types of objects.

**COUNTRY** The Country object is the highest-level container object. You can place it directly under the [Root] object and use it to divide a multinational corporation into sections, a separate one for each country. However, it is very rarely used, and Novell recommends against its use, even for networks that do span multiple countries.

So if you shouldn't use it, what is the Country object doing in NetWare 4? The answer lies in the X.500 standard, upon which NDS is based. The

Country object is part of that standard, so NetWare 4 includes it for compatibility. Thus, if your NetWare 4 network interconnects with another type of network and relies on the X.500 standard to share a Directory between them, you may need to use the Country object.

*If you're intimately familiar with the X.500 standard, you may wonder what became of the Locality object; the standard uses it to form a subdivision under the Country object. NetWare 4 does not support the Locality object; however, you'll find a few references to it in Novell's documentation. A future version of NetWare may support it.*

The Country object is the only object with a restriction on the names you can use. If you use Country objects, you must name them using a standard two-character abbreviation for each country. The X.500 standard also defines these two-character abbreviations. For example, US is the United States, UK is the United Kingdom, and FR is France. Some are not so easy to remember, such as CH (Switzerland) and DE (Germany); this is because each abbreviation is based on the native language of its country or is a common abbreviation of the country name.

If you're a frequent Internet user, you may have noticed the two-letter country designations that end almost every non-US address. These are the same two-letter codes used by NetWare 4 and the X.500 standard. You can find a complete list of these codes in the Novell manuals.

**ORGANIZATION** Since few networks use the Country object, the Organization object is typically the first level under the [Root] object. The Directory tree must have at least one Organization object. You use this object to indicate a major division, such as a company, university, or department.

Most smaller companies use a single Organization object, typically named after the company itself. Only large corporations, universities, and governments need to use more than one Organization object; when they do, these objects are named after the major divisions of the network. You must place Organization objects directly under [Root], or under a Country object if you're using one. The top level of a Directory tree for a large university is shown in Figure 5.7.

**ORGANIZATIONAL UNIT** The final container object is the one you'll use most often. You use the Organizational Unit object to subdivide the Organization object. Thus, this is the object that lets you really organize the objects in the Directory.

**FIGURE 5.7**

Use the Organization
object to indicate major
divisions of the network.

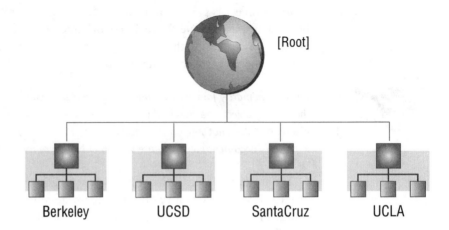

**FIGURE 5.7**

Use the Organization
object to indicate major
divisions of the network.

You cannot create an Organizational Unit object directly under [Root]. You must place it under an Organization object or another Organizational Unit. You can nest Organizational Units many levels deep, allowing for a complex organizational structure.

Typically, the first level of Organizational Units divides an Organization into a small number of important divisions. These might represent the locations of a company, such as Burbank and Boise, or the departments, such as Inventory and Sales. The top levels of a Directory tree organized by location are shown in Figure 5.8.

There is no hard and fast rule as to which categories you should use to divide the network, but they should be similar to the divisions of the organization or company itself. For example, if a single Accounts Payable department handles the bills for an entire company, there is little point in having a separate Accounts Payable Organizational Unit for each location. On the other hand, Accounts Payable might be one of the top levels of the tree. We'll look at the details of NDS planning, and the various methods of organization, in Chapter 6.

## Leaf Objects

Container objects are strictly for organization—they don't represent actual network resources. Leaf objects do the real work. These objects are the "leaves" of the Directory tree and represent the actual users, servers, and other resources of the network.

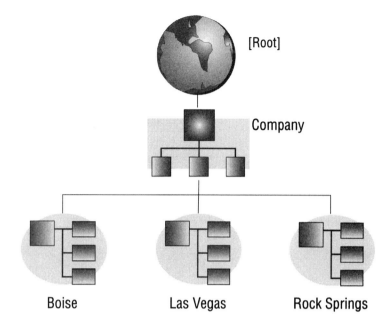

When you perform most of the configuration tasks of an administrator—such as creating a user, changing a password, or assigning rights—you are actually manipulating leaf objects in NDS. We'll describe the actual steps in performing some of these tasks later in the chapter.

There are many types of leaf objects—about 26 in all. Let's take a look at a few of the most important ones here; you'll run into the others elsewhere in this book. A sample Directory tree showing the most common leaf objects is shown in Figure 5.9.

**USER OBJECTS** Probably the first NDS object you'll work with as a NetWare 4 administrator is the User object. This object represents a user of the network. Before a user can access the network, you must create a User object for that user. This object includes information about the user, such as name, address, and password.

Any changes you need to make in the way users access the network—giving them rights to files, changing their passwords, or assigning them as administrators over other users—are made through changes to the User object corresponding to that user. You can also make changes to multiple users with a Group object.

**FIGURE 5.9**

Some of the most
common leaf objects
and their icons

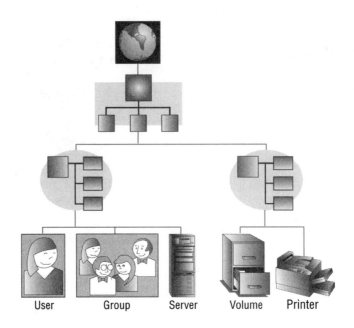

| User | Group | Server | Volume | Printer |

**GROUP AND ORGANIZATIONAL ROLE OBJECTS** Group objects allow you to create a logical grouping of users. For example, you could assign all users who need to access a spreadsheet program as members of a Spreadsheet group. This allows you to assign the rights they will need as a group rather than by modifying individual user objects.

This may sound similar to the use of a container object, such as the Organizational Unit, but Group objects are different. A Group object is a leaf object and simply contains a list of members. Each of the members receives the rights of the Group object. Members of a group can be from the same container, or even from different containers across the Directory tree.

An Organizational Role is a similar object. It allows you to define a role that a user (or more than one user) can fill. For example, suppose your company has a computer operator who is assigned to come in the wee hours of the night and insert tapes for a backup. This user would need the rights to read the files to be backed up and to run the backup software.

However, suppose the position of computer operator is a thankless job and is filled by a new person every few days. As an administrator, you would have to create a new User object for each new employee and give each of them the required rights. Using an Organizational Role simplifies this task: just create the new user and assign that user to the Organizational Role.

Of course, your company probably doesn't have a turnaround this high, and backups can usually be automated. However, the Organizational Role object can be very useful for any responsibility that rotates among different employees. An important use for this object is in creating administrators for portions of the network. We'll discuss this in Chapter 7.

**SERVER OBJECTS** The Server object represents a server on the network, running NetWare 4. It includes information such as the location of the server and its address on the network. NetWare uses this object to locate a server when a user attempts to log in to it or map a drive to one of its volumes.

Unfortunately, you can't install an additional NetWare 4 server just by creating a Server object. As a matter of fact, you normally shouldn't create this type of object; it is created automatically when you install a new server on the Directory tree. We'll cover the details of installing a NetWare 4 server in Chapter 13.

*You can actually delete and re-create a Server object if you are careful to use the same parameters, such as Network Address. This may be useful if you are temporarily removing the server from the network.*

**VOLUME OBJECTS** A Volume object represents a disk volume on a NetWare server. This object stores information about the volume, including the server it resides on. The actual data on the volume—files and directories—is separate from NDS and is not part of this object. The object is simply a pointer to the physical volume.

As with the Server object, you will not normally need to create a Volume object. It is created and named automatically when a new volume is installed on a server in the Directory tree. The NDS Volume object is named after the server name and the name you give the volume; for example, the Volume object for the SYS: volume on the STT1 server would be named STT1_SYS.

**PRINTER, PRINT QUEUE, AND PRINT SERVER OBJECTS** The parameters needed to set up printing on the network are also stored in NDS. There are three objects involved:

- The Printer object represents an actual printer.

- The Print Queue object represents a print queue, which keeps track of documents to be printed.

- The Print Server object represents a print server, which controls the printing process.

These objects, and other configuration needed for printing, are discussed in detail in Chapter 8.

# NDS Properties and Values

Each NDS object has a list of *properties,* or categories of information that can be specified about the object. For example, a User object's properties include First Name, Last Name, Location, and Telephone Number. The contents of the property are called the *value.* For example, the value of a User's Last Name property might be Smith, and the value of the Location property might be Kansas City.

Not all properties apply to all objects; for example, a user doesn't have a network address, and a printer doesn't have a telephone number. For this reason each type of object has its own list of properties. All User objects share the same list of properties, all Printer objects share a different list, and so forth. Each individual object has its own values for the properties.

### Required and Optional Properties

Some properties are required, and others are optional. For example, the required properties for a User object are Login Name and Last Name. You must specify values for these properties when you create the object. You can specify a value for optional properties, such as Telephone Number, but you don't need to.

Which of the optional properties you use are up to you. When you plan the network, you should decide which values to use and which to ignore. For example, a small company might have little use for the Telephone Number property since all the users have the same telephone number. For a large corporation, on the other hand, a list of telephone numbers for various users can be essential. This is one of the considerations of NDS planning, which we'll discuss in Chapter 6.

Most of the optional properties are not used by NetWare itself but are included strictly for your own use. To make these optional properties useful, you should choose a consistent method of assigning values to them. For example, if some telephone numbers are entered with area codes and some without, it will be difficult to search for a particular telephone number.

### Single and Multiple Values

Most properties are *single-value* properties; they can have only one value. For example, a user can have only one last name. Other properties, though, are *multivalue* properties, which can contain more than one value. One example is the Telephone Number property, which can store several alternate phone numbers for a user.

You also use a multivalue property when you set up a Group. The Group object has a Members property, which can contain multiple values. Each value is the name of a User object to be assigned as a member of the Group.

### The NDS Schema

Internally, NetWare stores all the objects and property values in the Directory according to a set of rules called the *NDS Schema*. The schema is installed when NDS is installed and specifies the following types of information:

- Which types of objects can exist

- Which properties each object has

- Which values a property can have

You won't normally have to worry about the schema, or even know it's there. Third-party programs can alter the schema, allowing them to store their own information in the Directory as a property of objects. For example, an e-mail application might add properties such as Email Address to User objects.

One thing to be aware of is that when the schema is changed, it changes the way NDS information is stored. If you ever have to reinstall NetWare 4, replace a server, or restore from a backup, you will need to reinstall the application so it can modify the schema; otherwise, the NDS data could become corrupt.

# Naming Objects in NDS

As the file system does, NDS has a set of rules for naming objects. You can access any object in the Directory if you know its name and its location in the Directory tree. The following sections describe the different types of syntax you can use to refer to NDS objects and how to determine the name for each object.

### Object Names

Each object in a Directory tree has an *object name*. NetWare 4 has standards for naming each type of object. The object name is usually the most obvious name for the object; a user's object name is the login name, and a server's object name is the server name. The object name is also referred to as the object's *common name*. For example, the common name for user JSMITH would be the same as the login name, JSMITH.

An object's common name isn't enough to identify the object uniquely. NDS allows you to create users or other objects with identical object names, as long as they are in different container objects. To completely identify the object, you also need to know where it is in the tree.

### Understanding Context

In a file system, you can have hundreds of files with the same name—as long as you store them in different directories. NDS is no different. For example, the Directory tree in Figure 5.10 has two users named JAMES. NetWare can tell them apart because they reside in different containers. The container an object resides in is called its *parent object*.

An object's *context* is a description of the object's location in the tree. The context includes the name of the object's parent object and its parent objects. You describe a context using a list of container objects, beginning with the object that is the most distant from [Root]. Use a period to separate the names. For example, if the Organizational Unit IDAHO is under the Organization WESTERN in the Country US, the context for any leaf object under IDAHO is

```
.IDAHO.WESTERN.US
```

When you are logged in to the network, NetWare keeps track of your *current context,* or default context. This is usually the context that contains your User object. When you access a resource without specifying its full location, NetWare looks for it in the current context. The current context is similar to the current directory in the DOS and UNIX file systems.

### Distinguished Names

By combining an object's common name with its context, you can determine its *distinguished name.* Since this name includes the name and location of the

**FIGURE 5.10**

Users in different container objects can have the same name.

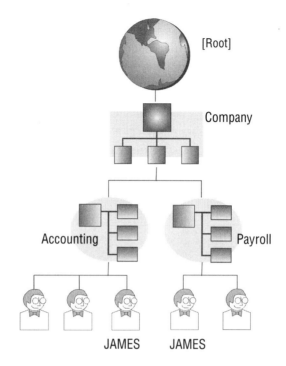

object, it is a unique name for the object. Although two objects can have the same common name, each will have a unique distinguished name.

Distinguished names begin with a period and also use a period between object names. For example, if the User object JOHN is in the Organizational Unit MARKETING, which is in the Organization ABC, John's full distinguished name is

```
.JOHN.MARKETING.ABC
```

## Relative Distinguished Names

To avoid having to specify all the container objects higher in the Directory than a particular object, you can use a *relative distinguished name,* or *RDN.* The RDN relies on your current context and starts there instead of at [Root] to look for the object.

Remember the period that begins a full distinguished name? If you leave it out, the name is considered to be an RDN. The simplest example of using an

RDN is to access an object that is in your current context. For example, if your current context is .ACCT.PHILCO (the ACCT Organizational Unit under the PHILCO Organization) and you want to access a printer called PRINTER1 in the same context, you can simply specify its name as

```
PRINTER1
```

When an object is outside your current context, you can still use an RDN. Enter a period at the end of the RDN to move up a level in the Directory tree. For example, if you are in the .ACCT.PHILCO context and you wish to access a printer called PRINTER2 in the MKTG.PHILCO context, the RDN is

```
PRINTER2.MKTG.PHILCO.
```

You can use multiple periods to move up more than one level in the Directory tree. However, this is rarely needed except in the most complicated networks; it's usually easier to simply use the full distinguished name in these cases. Figure 5.11 shows the different RDNs you could use to refer to PRINTER2 from different contexts.

**FIGURE 5.11**

The relative distinguished name to refer to an object differs depending on your current context.

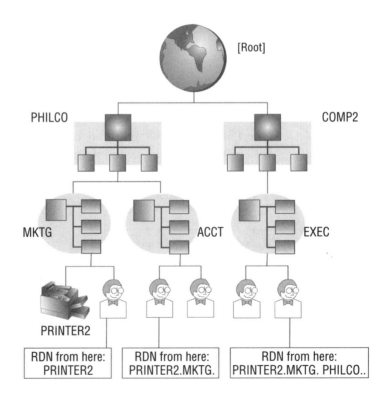

### Typeless Names and Typeful Names

So far, we've been using *typeless* names. They include the names of objects but not the types of objects. For instance, in the distinguished name .SUE.PR.ACCT.WNC, we know that SUE is a common name, but we don't indicate whether PR, ACCT, and WNC are Organizations or Organizational Units. We can make an educated guess, and NetWare can too. You can use type-less names in almost any situation where NetWare asks for an object's name.

Nevertheless, a more formal method of naming is possible: *typeful* naming. As the name implies, this kind of name includes the type for each object. These are the available object types:

C       Country

O       Organization

OU      Organizational Unit

CN      Common Name

To make the typeful name, add the object type and an equal sign to each object. The typeful name for the user SUE mentioned above would be

.       `.CN=SUE.OU=PR.OU=ACCT.O=WNC`

You must understand typeful names because you'll need to use them occasionally. For the vast majority of NDS tasks, however, the typeless name works fine, and it is much easier to type.

# Using the NWADMIN Windows Utility

NOW THAT YOU understand the basics of NDS, we'll look at the steps required to manage NDS, particularly for creating and managing users. The most important utility for the purpose is NWADMIN, or NetWare Administrator. This is a Microsoft Windows utility included with NetWare 4, and it allows you to create and manage all types of NDS objects.

*If you wish to manage NDS objects from DOS, you can use the NETADMIN utility, described later in this chapter.*

## Running NWADMIN

The NWADMIN program is stored in the PUBLIC directory of the SYS: volume, so it should be available to you if you are logged in to the network. You can follow these steps to quickly run NWADMIN:

**1.** Log in to the network.

**2.** Start Windows (or Windows 95).

**3.** Select Run from the File menu, or from the Start menu in Windows 95. Type **NWADMIN** as the name of the file to run. (The path is not necessary.)

You now see the main NWADMIN screen, shown in Figure 5.12.

**FIGURE 5.12**

NWADMIN is the most important utility for managing NDS objects.

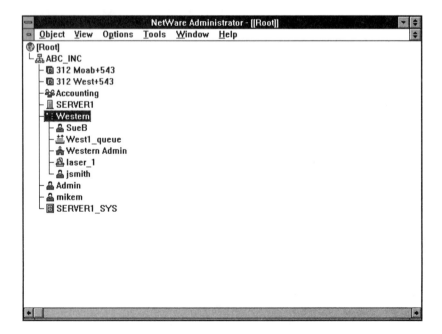

Since you'll be running NWADMIN frequently as a network administrator, it's a good idea to create an icon for it on your desktop, to allow you to run it conveniently, at any time. In Windows and Windows 95, you can simply specify this command line when you create an icon:

```
F:\PUBLIC\NWADMIN.EXE
```

You may have to specify a different network drive if F is not mapped to your SYS: volume.

*To run NWADMIN, you must be running network client software that supports NDS, such as the 32-bit client or the NetWare DOS Requester. See Chapter 3 for specific information about client software.*

## An Overview of **NWADMIN**

Since NWADMIN is the most important utility you need to understand to manage a NetWare 4 network, we'll begin with a quick tour of its various menus and features. NWADMIN includes features to manage NDS objects and their properties, to manage partitioning and replication, and even to manage the file system.

Let's take a look at the menus:

- **Object menu:** Allows you to create, rename, or delete an object; modify properties; and control object rights. Before you select an option from this menu, highlight the object you want to affect. You can also right-click a highlighted object to view its Object menu.

- **View menu:** Provides several options that allow you to control the way NDS objects are displayed. These options include setting the current context, choosing objects to include, sorting objects, and expanding or collapsing the display.

- **Options menu:** Allows you to set several options related to the behavior of the program. Selecting each of the options toggles the option's status. A check mark is displayed to the left of each activated option.

- **Tools menu:** Provides options to open new NWADMIN windows and start other programs. The options include Partition Manager, which you use to manage partitions and replicas; an option to salvage deleted files; and the Remote Console, which allows you to access a server's console from your workstation.

You should now have a basic idea of the features and uses of NWADMIN. Now let's examine the steps you take to create User objects and manage their properties.

## Creating a New User

Probably one of the first tasks you'll be asked to do as a network administrator is to create a new User object. You must create a new User object each time an additional user needs to access the network (usually, whenever an employee is hired). Follow these steps to create a new user:

1. Highlight the container object under which you wish to create the new User object.

2. From the NWADMIN Object menu, choose Create to see a list of object types you can create.

3. Select User Object to see the Create User dialog box, as shown in Figure 5.13.

4. Specify the Login Name and Last Name properties. These are the required properties for a User object.

5. Click the Create button to complete creating the User object.

The Create User dialog box also contains four check boxes, which you can use to set additional options:

- **Use User Template:** Copies the default settings for a new User object from a user template. (User templates are discussed in the next section.)

- **Define Additional Properties:** Brings up the Details dialog box to allow you to set values for the other properties of the object.

- **Create Another User:** Returns you to the Create User dialog box after you have created a user so you can create another user immediately.

- **Create Home Directory:** Sets up a home Directory for the user in the file system and allows you to specify its location (the server, volume, and Directory).

**FIGURE 5.13**

You must define certain properties when creating a User object.

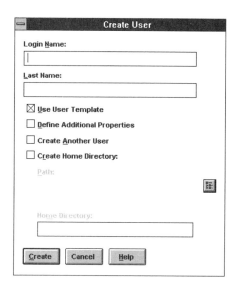

After creating the user, you'll want to define any optional properties that you have chosen to use. You can do this using the Details option, which we'll describe in a moment.

## Creating a User Template

Most of the users in your network will have certain things in common. For example, they probably all work for the same company and will need access to the same basic list of applications. Rather than having to create hundreds of users and enter the information for each one's properties, you can use Net-Ware 4's *user template* to create users quickly.

The user template isn't a separate kind of NDS object; as a matter of fact, it's nothing more than a User object named USER_TEMPLATE. However, you can check Use User Template in the Create User dialog box to easily define a user with default values in the properties of your choice.

Each container object (context) can have a separate user template, which controls the defaults for users created in that container. The first time you select the User Template option, a User object is created in the highlighted container. Next, you see the Details dialog box for the template, as shown in Figure 5.14. The property values you assign to this User object can be copied when a new user is created in the container.

**FIGURE 5.14**

Enter the default values
for new users in the user
template.

```
┌──────────────────────── User : USER_TEMPLATE ────────────────────────┐
│ Identification                                                         │
│                                                    ┌─────────────────┐ │
│   Login Name:   USER_TEMPLATE.Western.ABC_INC      │  Identification │ │
│                                                    └─────────────────┘ │
│   Given Name:   user template                      ┌─────────────────┐ │
│                                                    │   Environment   │ │
│   Last Name:    template                           └─────────────────┘ │
│                                                    ┌─────────────────┐ │
│   Full Name:                                       │ Login Restrictions│ │
│                                                    └─────────────────┘ │
│   Generational                                     ┌─────────────────┐ │
│   Qualifier:            Middle Initial:            │Password Restrictions│ │
│                                                    └─────────────────┘ │
│   Other Name:                                      ┌─────────────────┐ │
│                                                    │Login Time Restrictions│ │
│   Title:                                           └─────────────────┘ │
│                                                    ┌─────────────────┐ │
│   Description:                                     │Network Address Restriction│ │
│                                                    └─────────────────┘ │
│                                                    ┌─────────────────┐ │
│   Location:                                        │     Mailbox     │ │
│                                                    └─────────────────┘ │
│   Department:                                      ┌─────────────────┐ │
│                                                    │Foreign EMail Address│ │
│   Telephone:                                       └─────────────────┘ │
│                                                    ┌─────────────────┐ │
│   Fax Number:                                      │Print Job Configuration│ │
│                                                    └─────────────────┘ │
│                                                    ┌─────────────────┐ │
│                                                    │   Login Script  │ │
│  ┌──────┐  ┌────────┐  ┌──────┐                    └─────────────────┘ │
│  │  OK  │  │ Cancel │  │ Help │                                        │
│  └──────┘  └────────┘  └──────┘                                        │
└────────────────────────────────────────────────────────────────────────┘
```

*The user template affects only users created after you create or modify the template. It does not affect any existing users.*

## Managing Properties and Values

The Details option on the Object menu allows you to view all the properties of an object and specify or change their values. For example, when you highlight a User object and select Details, you see the dialog box shown in Figure 5.15.

Properties are divided into categories. The categories and properties displayed depend on the type of object you are modifying. Use the buttons along the right side of the dialog box to select a category. You can then fill in the values of properties to change existing values.

After you've made changes to the property values, be sure to click the OK button to save the changes to the Directory. If you click the Cancel button instead, the changes will be ignored.

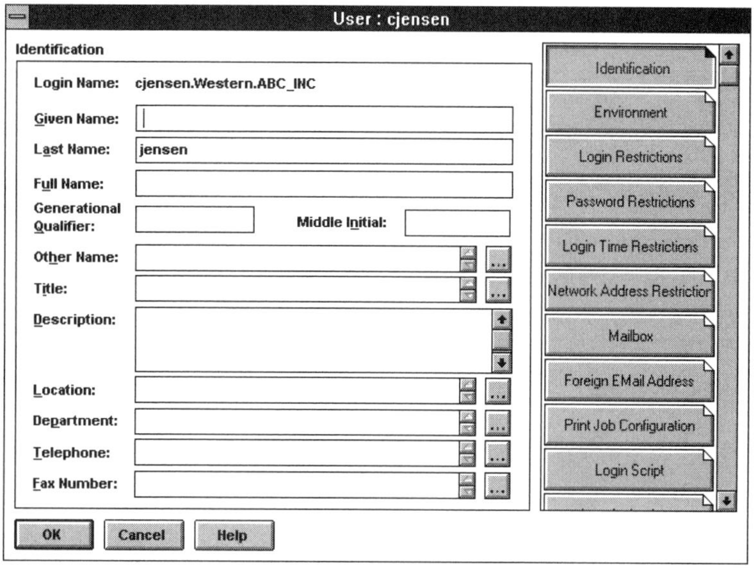

**FIGURE 5.15**

The Details option on the
Object menu allows you
to view and change an
object's properties.

**FIGURE 5.15**

The Details option on the
Object menu allows you
to view and change an
object's properties.

# Deleting and Maintaining Objects

The Object menu of NWADMIN also allows you to delete, rename, and move
User objects and other NDS objects. You can also search for objects that have
certain names or characteristics.

### Deleting an Object

The Delete option of the Object menu allows you to delete an object. You can
use this option to remove any leaf object or empty container object. (You
cannot delete a container object unless you first delete all the objects within
the container.) After selecting Delete, you are prompted to confirm that you
wish to delete the object.

Deleting a User object immediately prevents that user from logging in and
accessing the network. You'll need to do this whenever a user leaves the company. If the user has simply moved to a different department, you can use the
Move option, described later in this section.

### Renaming an Object

The Rename option of the Object menu allows you to change an object's common name. After selecting Rename, type the new name for the object. The Rename dialog box also contains two options that you can control with check boxes:

- **Save Old Name:** Adds the object's old name to the object's Other Names property. This allows you to track an object after renaming it.

- **Create Alias in Place of Renamed Container:** For container objects, check this box to create an Alias object with the old name of the container. An *alias* is a special NDS object that points to another object. In this case, the Alias object points to the new location; this allows users to continue using the old name to refer to the object. Alias objects are described in detail in Chapter 6.

### Moving a Leaf Object

The Move option on the Object menu allows you to move a leaf object from one container to another. Select the leaf object you wish to move and then select the Move option. You see the Move dialog box, shown in Figure 5.16. Browse the Directory to find the destination container object and then select OK. This can be useful when reorganizing the Directory tree or if a user changes departments within the organization.

**FIGURE 5.16**

To move a leaf object, use the Move option on the Object menu, and select the container object into which you want to move the leaf object.

*You cannot move a container object using the Move option. Instead, you must use Partition Manager, described in the next chapter.*

### Searching for an Object

The Search command on the Object menu allows you to search the Directory tree for objects with certain property values. The options in the Search dialog box, shown in Figure 5.17, allow you to set specific parameters for the search.

**FIGURE 5.17**

The Search command allows you to find objects with certain property values.

```
┌─────────────────────────────────────────────────┐
│ ─                    Search                       │
├─────────────────────────────────────────────────┤
│ Start From:                                       │
│ ┌─────────────────────────────────────┐  ┌───┐  │
│ │ Western.ABC_INC                     │  │ ▣ │  │
│ └─────────────────────────────────────┘  └───┘  │
│   ☐ Search Entire Subtree                         │
│ Search For:                                       │
│ ┌────────────────────────────┐ ┌──┐              │
│ │ User                       │ │ ▲│              │
│ └────────────────────────────┘ └──┘              │
│ ─────────────────────────────────────────────    │
│ Property:                                         │
│ ┌────────────────────────────┐ ┌──┐              │
│ │ Department                 │ │ ▲│              │
│ └────────────────────────────┘ └──┘              │
│ ┌──────────────┐ ┌──┐ ┌───────────────────┐      │
│ │ Equal To     │ │ ▲│ │ Accounting        │      │
│ └──────────────┘ └──┘ └───────────────────┘      │
│                                                   │
│ ┌──────┐ ┌────────┐ ┌──────┐ ┌──────┐ ┌──────┐   │
│ │  OK  │ │ Cancel │ │ Save.│ │ Open.│ │ Help │   │
│ └──────┘ └────────┘ └──────┘ └──────┘ └──────┘   │
└─────────────────────────────────────────────────┘
```

These options work as follows:

- **Start From:** Allows you to specify a container object where the search will begin. If you check the Search Entire Subtree box, NWADMIN searches all the objects in child containers of the container; otherwise, the search is confined to a single container. The Browse button to the right of the Start From value allows you to select a container from a graphical display of your Directory tree.

- **Search For:** Allows you to specify the type of object that will be searched for, such as User, Printer, or Server.

- **Property:** Specifies the property you want to find. The list of properties here depends on the type of object you have selected.

Beneath the Property option are two boxes that allow you to specify a condition for the search. In the box on the left, you can choose whether to find properties that are equal to or not equal to a value you indicate or that are present or not present.

The Save button allows you to save the search parameters to a file. You can use the Open button in the Search dialog box to load these saved search parameters later. In this way you can keep a library of frequently used search criteria and perform specific searches quickly. For example, you could set up a search to quickly list all the Printer objects in the Directory tree.

After the search is completed, you see a list of objects that meet the criteria you selected. On those objects, you can then perform any of the operations described in this chapter.

## Assigning Rights

After creating a user, you usually need to give that user rights to certain files and directories, or perhaps to certain NDS objects, such as printers. You can use the following NWADMIN options from the Object menu to assign rights:

- **Rights to Files and Directories:** Allows you to define file system rights for the user

- **Rights to Other Objects:** Allows you to give the user rights to other NDS objects

- **Trustees of This Object:** Allows you to give other users (or other NDS objects) rights to manage this user

Since NetWare 4 security is complicated, we've devoted a chapter to it. See Chapter 7 for the details of using these options to assign rights.

# Using the NETADMIN DOS Utility

ESPITE THE RECENT rise of Windows and Windows 95, your network probably includes several machines that still spend most of their time in DOS. You may even prefer to work in a DOS environment. You can perform most of the tasks for managing NDS using the NETADMIN utility, which runs under DOS. This utility includes most of the features of NWADMIN.

*One thing lacking from NETADMIN is the management of the file system—files, directories, and deleted files. You can use FILER, described in Chapter 4, to manage these parts of the network from DOS. Partition Manager in NWADMIN is also not included in NETADMIN; you can use PARTMGR, described in Chapter 6, for this purpose.*

Like NWADMIN, NETADMIN is stored in the SYS:PUBLIC directory on a file server. You run NETADMIN by typing **NETADMIN** at the DOS prompt. NETADMIN's main screen is shown in Figure 5.18.

**FIGURE 5.18**

NETADMIN is a DOS-based utility for managing NDS objects.

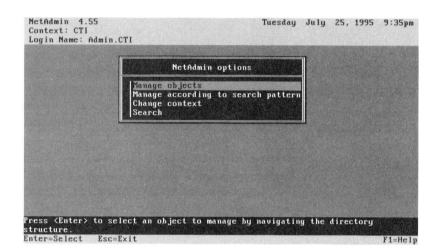

The main NETADMIN menu offers the following options:

- **Manage Objects:** Lists objects in the Directory tree and allows you to modify, delete, rename, and move them

- **Manage According to Search Pattern:** Allows you to enter a pattern to search for and then lists only objects that match the pattern

- **Change Context:** Changes your current context

- **Search:** Allows you to search for a specific type of object or for objects with certain property values

Most commonly, you'll use the Manage Objects option. This takes you to a Directory tree display, as shown in Figure 5.19. From this screen you can browse the tree. Press ↵ after selecting a container object to see the objects in the container. When you find the object you want to manage, select it. You can now perform any of the actions described in the following sections.

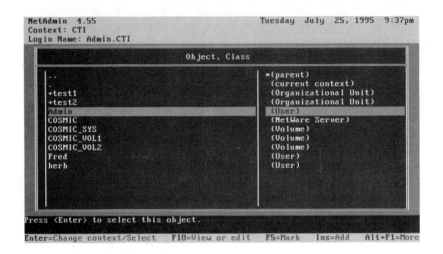

**FIGURE 5.19**

The Manage Objects option in NETADMIN displays a list of objects in the NDS Directory.

*You can switch between NETADMIN and NWADMIN anytime you wish. Changes made in one will always affect the other. Changes may not take effect until you exit the utility.*

## Creating a New User

Creating a user in NETADMIN is similar to NWADMIN. Follow these steps:

1. From the main NETADMIN menu, select Manage Objects.

2. Highlight the container object in which you wish to create a new user.

3. Press Ins (Ins is used in most NetWare DOS utilities as a Create option) to see a list of object types you can create.

4. Select User object and press ↵ to see the next screen.

5. Enter the required properties for the new User object: the Login Name and Last Name properties, as shown in Figure 5.20.

6. Press F10 to create the new User object.

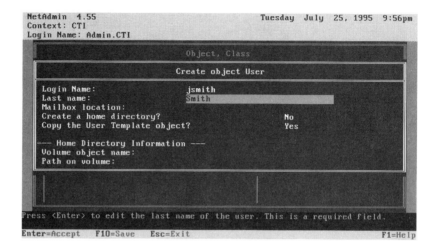

**FIGURE 5.20**

NETADMIN prompts you for the required properties of a User object.

*NETADMIN doesn't include a feature to create a User Template automatically. However, you can do so simply by creating a User object in the appropriate context, using USER_TEMPLATE as the login name. Then give that User object the properties you wish to give new users by default.*

## Managing Properties and Values

To manage an object's property values, highlight the object and press F10. Select Actions ➢ View or Edit Properties of This Object. The next menu lists the property categories for the type of object you selected. The property categories for a User object are shown in Figure 5.21.

Select the category of properties you wish to modify and press ↵. NETADMIN displays a list of properties in the category and their current values. You can change any of these values by typing a new value and pressing ↵. After you've made your changes, press F10 and then Esc to save the changes and exit.

**FIGURE 5.21**

NETADMIN displays a
list of property categories
for a User object.

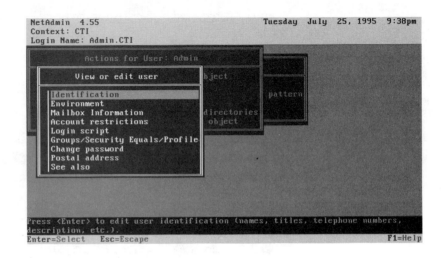

## Deleting and Maintaining Objects

To delete, rename, or otherwise modify an object using NETADMIN, you
can highlight it and press F10. This brings up the Actions menu, shown in
Figure 5.22. This menu is similar to the Object menu in NWADMIN; it
describes the various actions you can perform on the object.

**FIGURE 5.22**

The Actions menu allows
you to manage an object
or its properties.

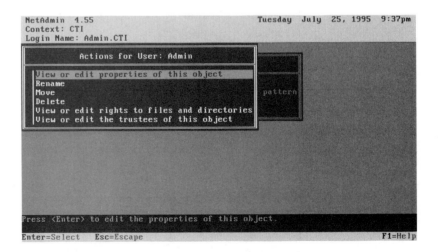

Once you've selected the function from the Actions menu, you are prompted
for additional information. You can then press F10 to complete the action.

# Summary

N DS, OR NETWARE Directory Services, is a fundamental part of Net-Ware 4. You use it to organize all of the network's components and resources—users, printers, groups, servers, volumes, and so on. NDS is a global, distributed database that allows for a network-centric organization.

Here are the main topics we presented:

- Each resource is represented by an object in NDS. Each object has a set of properties, or categories of information. The data entered in each property is called its value. Properties can have single or multiple values. Some properties are required, while others are optional.

- Each NDS object has an object name, or common name, and a location in the Directory tree, or context. The context and common name together make up the distinguished name. You can use a relative distinguished name to address an object relative to the current context. Names can be either typeless or typeful.

- The main utilities for managing NDS are NWADMIN (Windows) and NETADMIN (DOS). Using one of these utilities, you can create new objects, rename, move, or delete existing objects, and modify property values.

In the next chapter we'll look at some of the more complicated aspects of NDS, including partitioning and replicating, and the process of planning and organizing a Directory tree for your network.

# Designing and Organizing NDS

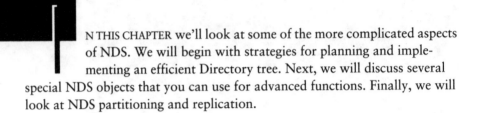

I N THIS CHAPTER we'll look at some of the more complicated aspects of NDS. We will begin with strategies for planning and implementing an efficient Directory tree. Next, we will discuss several special NDS objects that you can use for advanced functions. Finally, we will look at NDS partitioning and replication.

# Planning the Directory Tree

N ETWARE 4.1 CAN organize your network and its resources much better than any previous version of NetWare could. However, NetWare can't do this by itself. To establish an efficient NDS organization, you'll need to do a bit of planning—preferably before you set up the network.

In the following sections we'll look at the benefits of a well-organized Directory tree and the steps you take to set one up. We will also take a look at the default organization NDS provides and explain why it is inadequate.

## Advantages of an Efficient NDS Organization

Why do you need an efficient NDS organization? Here are some of the advantages a well-organized Directory tree provides:

- **Simplified administration:** You can make administration easier by organizing users and resources into containers and groups.

- **Ease of access:** Users can quickly find the network resources they need to access.

- **Improved security:** Whether your network is managed by one administrator or several, you can keep security tight with the features of NetWare 4 and NDS.

- **Fault tolerance:** By placing replicas and partitions strategically, as you'll see later in this chapter, you can eliminate the risk of data loss in the event of a server crash.

- **Optimized network traffic:** By using partitions and replicas and managing time synchronization, you can minimize the traffic over wide area network (WAN) links.

- **Transparent upgrade:** You can upgrade your server to NDS easily. In a multiserver network, you can upgrade specific portions of the network at a time to minimize the impact of the transition.

- **Flexibility:** You can change a well-planned Directory as the network evolves, with minimal impact on users.

## Default NDS Organization

Before we look at a well-organized Directory tree, let's examine a poorly organized one. Figure 6.1 shows a Directory tree with a single Organization object under the [Root] object. All the network's resources are in this container. This arrangement happens to be the default organization. In other words, if you make no effort to organize NDS yourself, this is how your Directory tree will appear.

Since the default organization places all the objects in a single container, it provides few of the advantages we listed above. It can be as confusing as a messy, cluttered desk. Luckily, it's never too late to start organizing the Directory—but as with the desk, the longer you wait, the harder the task will be.

*Although the default organization gives you few of the powerful advantages of NDS, most small networks have little need for those advantages anyway. If you have a small network with one server and 20 or fewer users, the default organization will usually work fine. However, it might cause problems as the network grows larger and more complicated.*

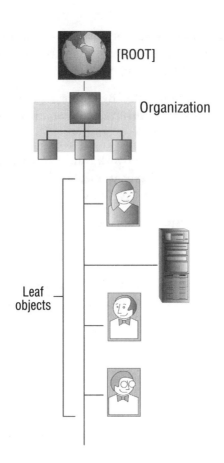

**FIGURE 6.1**

The default NDS organization places all objects in the Directory under a single Organization object.

[ROOT]

Organization

Leaf objects

## Designing the Upper Levels

The most important task in designing an effective Directory tree is the design of the upper levels. These are the most important divisions within the Directory. In addition, they will be the most difficult to change later, so you should take care in planning them.

The highest level in the Directory, of course, is the [Root] object. Under the [Root] is an Organization object that represents the company or other organization. Some larger companies and universities use multiple Organization objects.

The next level or two are the major divisions of the company; they are constructed with Organizational Units. You can base these on locations, divisions of the company, workgroups, or a combination of these strategies. We will look at each of these strategies in the following sections.

### Organizing by Location

Companies with multiple locations often use the *locational* strategy. In this approach you create Organizational Unit objects for each of the physical locations of the company, as shown in Figure 6.2.

**FIGURE 6.2**

A locational organization uses an Organizational Unit object for each physical location.

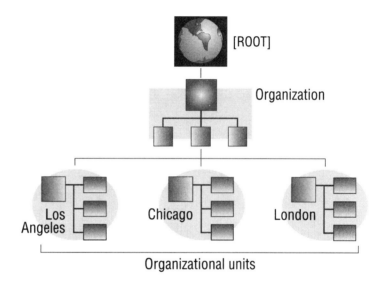

This strategy provides a simple organization and makes it easy to create partitions. A large company might choose to have a different LAN administrator at each of the locations. This type of network management is easy to implement using the locational strategy.

You can also organize locations using the Country object, which you place directly under the [Root], above the Organization objects. Country objects should be used only in large, multinational corporations or for compatibility with other networking systems. If you use a Country object, its name must be a valid two-character country abbreviation (determined by the X.500 standard), as explained in Chapter 5.

The locational structure works well when the locations of a company are managed separately. However, if employees in various locations work closely together on projects, a divisional, workgroup, or hybrid organization, described in the following sections, may be more practical.

*Be sure to consider partitioning and replication, discussed later in this chapter, as you decide whether to use a locational organization. One of the most important benefits of this organization is to minimize traffic in a wide area network.*

### Organizing by Division

A common Directory tree organization uses the *divisional* approach. This strategy divides the tree into Organizational Unit objects based on divisions or departments of the company, such as Sales, Accounting, Research, Production, and so on. The structure of NDS will resemble the company's organization chart. In Figure 6.2, the Organizational Unit objects represent cities. Here they would represent divisions of the company instead.

This is a good strategy to use when there are clear divisions within the company, as with most medium-size and large companies. Since users within a division often require access to the same data and applications, administration is simplified.

### Organizing by Workgroup

The organization of modern companies often includes *workgroups,* which are groups of users who perform similar tasks, usually on the same project. You could organize your Directory tree according to these workgroups. Your Organizational Units might have names like "Project A," "Government Research," and so forth.

Since workgroups can be flexible, and a user may belong to more than one group, you may find it useful to use Group objects instead of a container object to arrange some workgroups. Usually, the workgroup organization is combined with other strategies, as described in the next section.

### Using a Hybrid Organization

For many companies, particularly large ones, you'll find that none of the above strategies is ideal. A *hybrid,* or combination, approach, based on the organization of the company, may be the solution. The hybrid approach combines the strengths of two or more types of NDS organization.

Figure 6.3 shows one example of a hybrid organization. In this example the company's Directory tree is organized at the top level by location, with locations in Los Angeles, Chicago, and London. Each location is then organized by department. Each location has its own Sales department to handle local sales. The Research department for the corporation is located in Los Angeles, and the Accounting department is based in London.

**FIGURE 6.3**

Example of a hybrid
organization. This tree is
divided by location and
then by department.

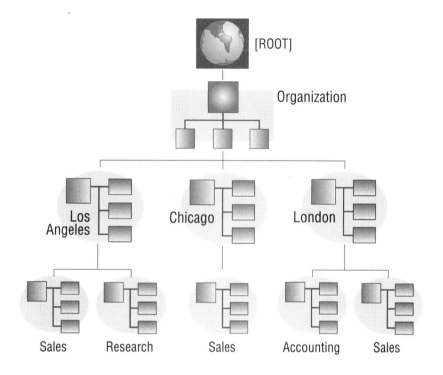

The example in Figure 6.4 takes another combination approach. This company is administered from a central location. The tree is organized by divisions of Accounting, Marketing, and Sales. The Marketing department works strictly from the Denver office. The other departments have an office in each location.

Figure 6.5 illustrates a more elaborate hybrid organization. The first level is divided by departments: Marketing, Technical, and Accounting. The Accounting department has an office in each of two locations. The Technical department is further subdivided into Research, Service, and Support. Finally, the Research department is organized into workgroups.

## Designing the Lower Levels

Although the planning is not as critical as for the upper levels, you should give some consideration to the structure of the lower levels of the Directory tree. Depending on how you've organized the upper levels, the lower-level design may be left to separate administrators.

**FIGURE 6.4**

Another example of hybrid organization. This tree is organized by department and then by location.

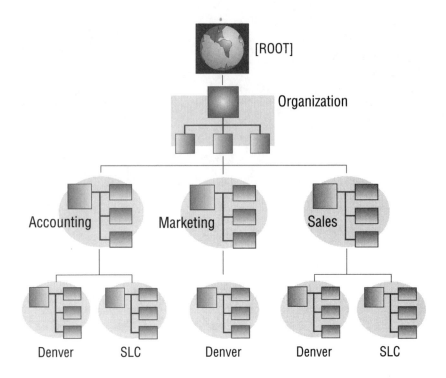

At the lower levels, divisions are usually based on subdepartments of the organization, or workgroups. These divisions are subject to change more frequently than larger divisions, but you can modify them easily.

You may want to group together User Objects and other objects in an Organizational Unit if they use the same applications or resources or if they will need the same security access. The Group and Organizational Unit objects provide an alternative to container objects for this purpose.

*Avoid dividing the Directory tree unnecessarily at the lower levels. Too many divisions can complicate administration and decrease the stability of the NDS database.*

## Establishing Network Standards

Along with planning the structure of the Directory tree, you should establish standards for object names, properties, and values. This makes the network easier to manage in the long run. We'll look at the types of standards you should be concerned with and how to document them properly in the following sections.

**FIGURE 6.5**

Example of a more
complex hybrid
Directory tree
organization. This tree is
organized by depart-
ments, locations, and
workgroups.

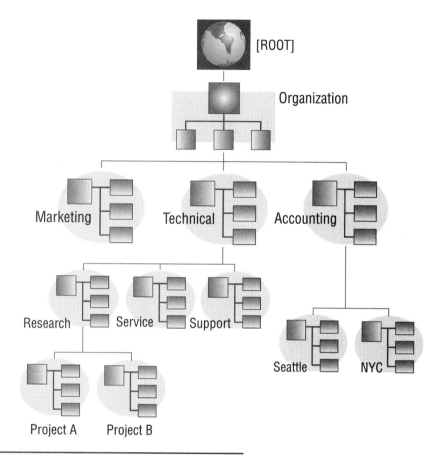

### Choosing an Object-Naming Standard

By using consistent naming procedures, you make network administration more efficient. For example, it will be easy to locate users, printers, servers, and other network objects that you need to maintain. Users will also benefit from consistent object names. For example, when sending e-mail, a user will have no trouble determining another user's name.

The following sections offer some guidelines for naming objects on your network.

**USER LOGIN NAMES** Typical standards for user login names include some combination of names and initials:

- First name, last initial, as in JOHNS: For small companies, this user-naming standard might be the best solution since employees probably know each other by their first names. However, this combination can result in duplicate names and may cause confusion when employees are also known by nicknames.

- **First initial, last name, as in JSMITH:** This is another common method. There is slightly less chance of duplicate names, which makes it easier to determine the user the name refers to.

- **First initial, middle initial, last name, as in JDSMITH:** More complicated schemes such as this one are often needed in larger companies. There is very little chance of duplication.

It is also important to determine what you will do if two users have names that would produce the same username. For example, you might decide to add a middle initial or, as a last resort, a number. If you find you have to do this often, you may be better off with a different naming scheme.

*Traditionally, many administrators limit user login names to 8 characters. Although NDS allows 64-character names, some e-mail systems require 8-character names. In addition, 8-character names will work better if you also use an earlier version of NetWare on the network. These systems are less and less common, though, so you may not need to worry about this on your network.*

**GROUPS, ORGANIZATIONS, AND ORGANIZATIONAL UNITS** Because Organizations and Organizational Units usually identify divisions, locations, or workgroups in the company, you should name them after the entity they represent. Use concise names; you might need to type them when referring to users by distinguished name. For example, you might use MGMT for Management, ACCT for Accounting, AP for Accounts Payable, and NYC for New York City.

Give Group objects names that represent their function, such as DATAENTRY for the data entry group or PROJECT1 for users working on a particular project. If the group was created to give users access to an application directory, it might be named for that application, such as WORDPROCESSING or BACKUP.

**OTHER OBJECTS** You should also have a standard procedure for naming other types of objects in the Directory tree. Names should be concise and meaningful to users. Here are some examples:

- Servers are often named based on their location, such as EAST1, NYC, or BLDG3. Keeping server names short helps users who need to type the name of a server to log in. Server names must be unique, even if they are in different containers.

- Volumes are given NDS names automatically when you create them. The name combines the server name and volume name, such as EAST1_SYS.

- Printers are typically named according to the printer type and location, such as LJ4_BLDG3 or DMP_WEST.

- Name print queues according to their purpose or to refer to the department that uses them or the type of form they will be printed on, as in ACCTG or CHECKS.

## Choosing Standard Properties

You should also determine which properties to use for each object and how to format the property values. Look carefully at the lists of properties for all the objects—users, printers, servers, and so on—and decide which properties will be useful. Then establish a consistent format for each property value.

For example, if you decide to use the Location property to specify the building number on a college campus, you should choose how to format the location: Building #17 or B17 or BLDG17. Following a consistent format makes it easy to perform searches, such as finding users in a certain building.

## Documenting Your Standards

In addition to planning the naming standards you'll use on your network, it is important to create a *standards document*. This document should describe your company's standards for naming objects and formatting property values. If the network has multiple administrators, they should all receive a copy of the standards document.

Here is what the users portion of the standards document might look like for a typical small company:

**User Names:** First initial plus last name (for example, JSMITH). Up to eight characters. If a name is a duplicate, add a middle initial.

**Properties to be defined:**

Given Name (first name)

Last Name (full last name)

Telephone (include area code)

Title (full title)

Location (building number in this format: BLDG XX)

## Implementing NDS

After you've planned an NDS structure, the next step is to implement it. If you're creating a brand-new network, this step is easy. Just create the basic Directory structure, and fill in the details as the company grows.

For existing networks, the process can be more complicated. Luckily, there is no rule that you must implement NDS on all servers at once. A common strategy is to create separate Directory trees for different departments and later merge them into a larger tree. We'll look at the process of merging trees, as well as adding and removing servers from the network, in Chapter 12.

# Using Special NDS Objects

C HAPTER 5 INTRODUCED you to the NDS objects you will use most often: Users, Groups, container objects, and so on. In this section we'll describe some of the less common objects. While not essential to your network, these objects can make some tasks easier.

## Alias Objects

As described in Chapter 5, an alias is simply another name for an object. You use the Alias object to store an alternate name for an object; its properties include a pointer to the location of the original object. You can create Alias objects using NWADMIN; in some cases they are also created automatically.

The main reason to create an Alias object is to make a resource, such as a printer, in one container available to users in another container. For example, users in the ACCT Organizational Unit might need to access a printer in the MKTG Organizational Unit. You can create an alias for the printer in the ACCT container; as far as users will know, this makes the printer local to their container. They can access it without specifying a different container.

In addition, NWADMIN automatically creates an Alias object to help users find an object that has been moved or renamed. When you move or rename an object, you can check the Create Alias in Place check box in the Move or Rename dialog box. This creates a pointer to the new object from the old object.

## Directory Map Objects

The Directory Map object is a special object that points to a directory in the file system. This object allows you to simplify MAP commands and makes it easier to maintain the system when an application or data directory is moved.

To create a Directory Map object, you set the Directory Path property to the path the Directory Map object will point to. First, though, you need to find the Volume object in the NDS tree.

As an example, suppose you created a Directory Map called WP to point to the directory you use for word processing files, SYS:APPS\WP. Users who wish to map a drive to that directory could simply type a MAP command such as this:

```
MAP F:=WP
```

This might make the MAP command easier to type than one that includes the entire directory name—but Directory Map objects have a more important benefit. Because they point to a directory, they allow you to move the directory easily and update the pointer.

As an example, suppose you moved word processing files to a different volume to make more space available on the SYS: volume. The new location is VOL2:APPS\WP. Rather than changing all users' login scripts to point to the new directory and telling everyone about the change, you simply have to point the Directory Map to the new location. Once you've done so, users can use the MAP command listed above to reach the new directory.

## Application Objects

Application objects were added in version 4.11 of NetWare. These objects are something like a Directory Map object, but they represent all the information needed to run a particular application. They are used by NAL, the menu system described in Chapter 9.

The Application object's properties include the location of the application and the directories users will need to access to use it.

## Organizational Role Objects

We looked at Group objects in the previous chapter. Groups allow you to combine users, whether in a single container or different containers, and give them similar rights or properties.

An Organizational Role provides a similar function but is typically used for only one user. The user is called the *occupant* of the Organizational Role and is set in the Organizational Role object's Occupant property.

While Group objects are often used for access to the file system, Organizational Roles are typically used for security. You can give a set of rights to an Organizational Role and then make one or more users occupants of that Organizational Role. These users all receive the same rights.

An Organizational Role is often used for tasks that a user needs rights to perform. For example, a user might be assigned to do backups and assigned as an occupant of a "backup" Organizational Role. In addition, Organizational Roles are useful for assigning administrators to control portions of the file system or the Directory tree.

*Since the main use for Organizational Roles is in dealing with NetWare 4 security, we'll look at the Organizational Role object in detail in Chapter 7.*

## Profile Objects

Each user in NDS has a login script—a series of commands that are executed each time the user logs in. Along with user login scripts, there are other types: container login scripts, default login scripts, and profile login scripts.

The Profile object has its own login script. You can assign users to a Profile object as an easy method of giving them all the same login script. This script is executed after the container login script and before the user login script.

You can create a Profile object in any container for this purpose and then assign users to this profile. The User object has a Profile property for this purpose; each user can be assigned to only one profile. Users in a Profile don't need to be in the same container.

Group objects also provide a way to group users, regardless of their container; however, Group objects have no login script, so the Profile object provides a way to do this.

*We'll take a closer look at the types of login scripts and their uses, along with more information about the Profile object, in Chapter 9.*

# Partitioning and Replication

N DS PROVIDES INCREASED reliability through partitioning and replication. *Partitioning* divides the Directory tree into sections, and *replication* stores copies of partitions on separate servers. We'll look at the details of this process in the following sections; in addition, we'll discuss the strategies you should use when planning the partitions and replicas in your network.

## The Basics: NDS Partitions

By default, all the objects in the Directory tree are part of a single partition, called the [Root] partition. You can assign any container object, and the objects underneath it, as separate partitions. You can refer to a partition by using the name of its container object. For example, Figure 6.6 shows a Directory tree with three partitions: the [Root] partition, the MGMT partition, and the ACCOUNTS partition.

Like NDS objects themselves, partitions are organized in a hierarchy beginning with the [Root] partition. Partitions can be referred to as parent and child partitions, based on the partition they lie under. You create a new partition by splitting an existing partition into a parent and child partition.

## Types of Replicas

Each copy of a partition is called a *replica*. The term can be a bit confusing; even if there is only one copy of a partition, it is still referred to as a replica. There are four types of NDS replicas. You use each for a particular purpose, as described in the following sections.

**FIGURE 6.6**

A Directory tree divided
into three partitions

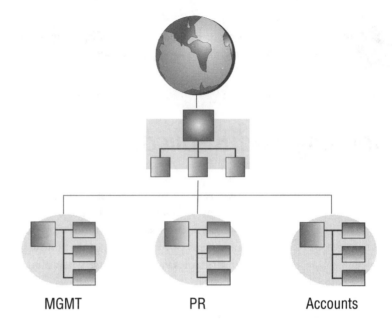

MGMT　　　　　PR　　　　Accounts

**MASTER REPLICAS** NetWare 4 creates a *master replica* when you define a partition. This replica controls all partition operations, including creating, merging, and moving partitions. The master replica also controls replica creation, deletion, and repair.

There can be only one master replica for each partition. When objects are changed in a master replica, the same change automatically occurs on all replicas of that partition. The server that stores the master replica of a partition must be accessible before you can *split* the partition (create a new partition) or merge it with another partition.

**READ/WRITE REPLICAS** Read/write replicas contain the same information as the master replica, but each partition may have multiple read/write replicas. Changes made to these replicas are also reproduced automatically on all other replicas of the same partition. However, you cannot use read/write replicas when splitting or merging a partition.

If your network loses a master replica, you can change one of the read/write replicas to master replica status. Read/write replicas support the login process by providing authentication.

**READ-ONLY REPLICAS** Use read-only replicas on servers where reads of the partition are necessary but writes are to be prevented. Because read-only

replicas do not support the authentication process, they have limited usefulness. These replicas contain the same information as the master and read/write
replicas but do not allow for alteration of objects. You can use them for
searching and viewing objects. They can also be useful as backup replicas.

**SUBORDINATE REFERENCE REPLICAS** You do not create subordinate reference replicas. NDS creates these replicas automatically. Subordinate references do not contain object data; instead, they point to a replica that does.
They do not support user authentication, object management, or even object
viewing.

NDS creates subordinate references on a server when a replica of a partition appears on that server without a replica of that partition's child. A subordinate reference is simply a pointer describing the location of the child
partition or its replica.

Subordinate references ensure that there is efficient access to relevant portions of the NDS database on each server. NDS automatically removes the
subordinate reference if the child partition's replica is added to the server.

Although you don't have to create subordinate reference replicas, you will
have to worry about their effects on network traffic. We'll look at these issues
in Chapter 12.

## Planning Partitions and Replicas

When the first server is installed, NDS creates and stores a single partition on
that server's SYS: volume. The next server installed into the existing NDS tree
simply expands the partition. The third and fourth servers receive a read/write
replica of the partition. All servers installed after that do not receive any replicas by default.

This default replication scheme will work for small to medium-size networks (up to about 5 servers and 100 users). Beyond that, consider partitioning based on location within the WAN. If you used a locational strategy to
organize the Directory tree, the partitions will be simple.

## Using the NWADMIN Partition Manager

You can set up partitions and replicas using the Partition Manager utility,
which you can access from NWADMIN's Tools menu. The initial Partition
Manager screen is shown in Figure 6.7.

**FIGURE 6.7**

Partition Manager allows you to manage partitions and replicas.

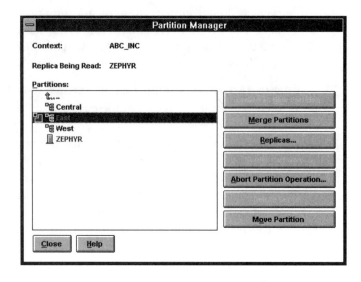

We'll look at each of the tasks you can perform with this utility in the following sections. You can also use the DOS-based PARTMGR utility, described later in this chapter, for most of these functions.

*In NetWare version 4.11, the Partition Manager utility has been replaced with a new utility, NDS Manager. Along with the functions described here, NDS Manager includes several useful functions for troubleshooting. These features are described in Chapter 12.*

### Splitting (Creating) a Partition

The process of creating a new partition is called splitting the partition since you are actually taking some objects away from one partition and placing them in another. Follow these steps to split a partition:

1. Select the container object that will be at the root of the new partition.

2. Click the Create As New Partition button.

3. Select Yes to split the partition.

This process, and most of the other partitioning changes you can make, may take several minutes (or longer) since they must be copied to all the servers in the network.

### Deleting a Partition

The opposite of splitting a partition is merging partitions. In this process a child partition is deleted and the objects in it are moved to the parent partition. Follow these steps to merge a partition with its parent:

1. Select the container object at the root of the partition to be deleted.

2. Click the Merge Partitions button.

3. Select Yes to confirm the merge.

### Moving a Container Object

You may have noticed in Chapter 5 that you couldn't move a container object and the objects underneath it using NWADMIN. You can do this using Partition Manager; it is a powerful tool for reorganizing the Directory tree.

For Partition Manager to work, the container to be moved must be at the root of its own partition. Follow these steps:

1. Select the container at the root of the partition.

2. Click the Move Partition button.

3. Select the destination context (container) for the partition.

4. Click the OK button to begin the move process. The process may take several minutes.

### Creating and Managing Replicas

To manage replicas of a partition, highlight the partition's root object and click the Replicas button. The list of replicas for the partition is shown in a separate window, as you can see in Figure 6.8. You can use the buttons in this dialog box to perform the following functions:

- **Add Replica:** Create a new replica

- **Delete Replica:** Remove an existing replica

- **Change Type:** Change a replica's type

- **Send Updates:** Force the replicas to synchronize

- **Receive Updates:** Update the replica list with any changes that have been made

**FIGURE 6.8**

Partition Manager shows the list of replicas for a partition.

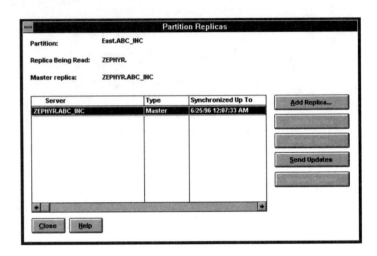

## Using the PARTMGR Utility

You can use the PARTMGR utility from DOS to perform many of the same functions as Partition Manager. You run this program by typing **PARTMGR** at the DOS prompt. The initial PARTMGR screen is shown in Figure 6.9. To use this utility, follow the same steps as for Partition Manager, which we described earlier in this chapter.

Select the Manage Partitions option from the main PARTMGR screen, and you see a list of container objects and partitions, as shown in Figure 6.10. The word *(Partition)* after an entry indicates that this container object is at the root of a partition. From here, you can work with partitions:

- Press ↵ to expand container objects. Select the "." or ".." entry to move up the Directory tree.

- Press F10 on a container object to create a new partition starting with that container.

■ Press F10 on a partition's root object to manage the partition. You can merge the partition with its parents, view its list of replicas, or abort a partition operation you have already started.

■ Server objects are also shown on the list. Press F10 on a server to see the list of replicas stored on that server.

**FIGURE 6.9**

The PARTMGR utility provides a DOS alternative for managing partitions and replicas.

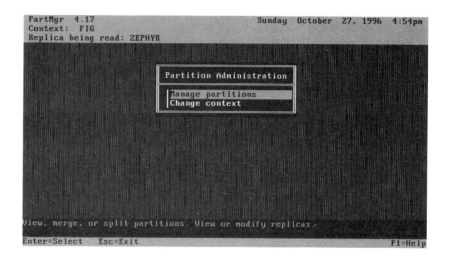

**FIGURE 6.10**

PARTMGR shows a list of container objects and partitions.

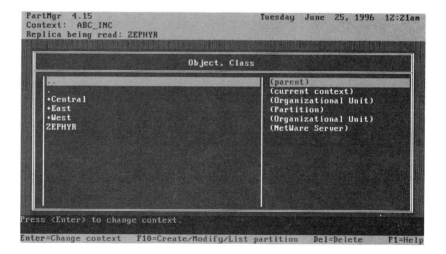

# Summary

N THIS CHAPTER we've discussed the advanced features of NDS, which is the central structure of a NetWare 4 network. These are the main points we covered:

- Although NDS provides many advantages, it is most effective with a well-planned Directory tree.

- Common organizational methods are by location, by division, and by workgroup.

- Special NDS objects that serve a variety of purposes include the Alias object, the Directory Map object, the Organizational Role object, and the Profile object. Using these objects can simplify access to network resources and make the network easier to manage.

- NDS partitioning and replication allow you to keep multiple copies of the NDS database on separate servers. A well-planned system of partitions and replicas prevents data loss and allows easy access to resources.

In the next chapter we'll move on to one of the most complicated—and most powerful—features of NetWare 4: security. We'll look at the features that allow you to secure both the file system and NDS.

# Securing the NetWare 4 Network

7

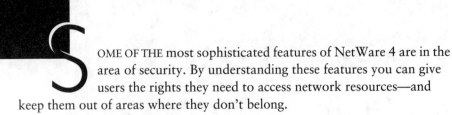

SOME OF THE most sophisticated features of NetWare 4 are in the area of security. By understanding these features you can give users the rights they need to access network resources—and keep them out of areas where they don't belong.

We'll begin the discussion of NetWare 4 security with a look at trustees—the basic building blocks of security. We will then discuss the two major types of security in NetWare 4: file system security and NDS security.

# Understanding Trustee Rights

YOU MANAGE NETWARE 4 security by assigning rights to *trustees*. A trustee is any user or other object that has rights to a file, directory, or NDS object. User objects are the most common trustees, but you can use any object as a trustee. Here are the most common types of objects used as trustees in the file system or in NDS:

- **[Root] object:** You can assign trustee rights to the [Root] object, but this practice can be dangerous because all users in the Directory tree are given these rights. For small networks, assigning rights to the [Root] object can be an easy way to assign rights to publicly available files, such as those in the PUBLIC subdirectory.

- **Container objects (Organization objects and Organizational Unit objects):** Since an Organization object is usually a major division of the Directory tree, the same warning given about the [Root] object applies here. You should assign rights to an Organization object only for files that need to be made available to the entire organization.

Organizational Units provide a much better approach. Since these containers are usually specific to a particular department or class of users, you can give rights assigned here to logical groups of users. The advantages of a well-designed Directory tree become obvious when you are assigning rights to these containers.

■ **Organizational Role and Group objects:** You can use Organizational Role objects or Group objects when files are not needed by all members of a container object. These types of objects allow you to keep tight control over who can access these files. This strategy may be useful for applications that you want to restrict to a specific set of users.

■ **User objects:** Assigning rights to a User object can be useful when only a certain user should have access to a file or directory. It's generally considered bad practice to assign the same rights to multiple users, but you may find it to be the most convenient way to assign those rights. If you find yourself assigning the same rights to several users, consider using a Group or container object instead.

■ **The [Public] trustee:** The [Public] trustee is a special object that does not represent an actual object in the Directory tree. Instead, it provides a method of assigning rights to all users attached to the network—*even those who are not logged in*. Obviously, it would be very dangerous to assign rights to this trustee. Use this method only for special cases. NetWare 4 assigns a minimal set of rights to this trustee to enable users to log in.

# Understanding File System Security

B Y CONTROLLING ACCESS to the file system, you can protect data from users who should not access it. In addition, you can give users access to the directories and files they need while keeping those files safe.

# File System Rights

A trustee can have several types of rights to a file or directory. These rights specify which actions the trustee can perform in that file or directory. If a user is assigned rights in a directory, these rights are called *explicit rights* or *trustee rights*. Users can also receive *group rights* from a group they belong to. Table 7.1 lists the available file system rights.

| **TABLE 7.1**<br>Available File System<br>Rights | RIGHT | DESCRIPTION |
|---|---|---|
| | Read [R] | Reads data from an existing file |
| | Write [W] | Writes data to an existing file |
| | Create [C] | Creates a new file or subdirectory |
| | Erase [E] | Deletes existing files or directories |
| | Modify [M] | Renames and changes attributes of files |
| | File Scan [F] | Lists the contents of a directory |
| | Access Control [A] | Controls the rights of other users to access files or directories |
| | Supervisor [S] | Grants all other rights |

### Inherited Rights

If a user is a trustee of a directory, the rights are *inherited* into subdirectories of that directory. The *Inherited Rights Filter* (IRF) controls which rights can be inherited. You cannot use the IRF to grant rights; it can only block or allow rights that were given in a parent directory.

The IRF is simply a list of the rights a user or other trustee can inherit for that directory or file. If a right is included in the IRF, it can be inherited. If you leave a right out of the IRF, no user can inherit that right for that directory or file.

### Effective Rights

Users' rights in a directory begin with the rights granted explicitly to them or any group they belong to and any rights they have inherited from a parent directory. The IRF then filters the inherited rights, and the end result is called the user's *effective rights* in the directory. Effective rights are what NetWare actually looks at when controlling user access.

For example, in Figure 7.1, user RALPH has been given the rights RWMF in the DATA directory. He inherits the same rights in the AP directory because the IRF allows all rights [RWCEMF]. In the AR directory, however, the IRF limits his rights to R and F. Although the C right is included in the IRF, user RALPH does not receive this right because he did not have it in the DATA directory.

**FIGURE 7.1**

Effective rights are the actions a trustee can perform in a file or directory.

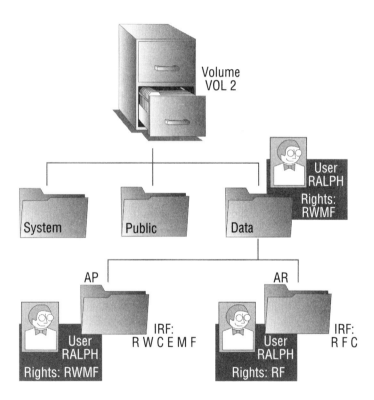

## Managing File System Security

Since you can manage files using NWADMIN, as described in Chapter 4, you might have guessed that you can also manage file system security this way. In addition, FILER gives you the same capabilities. We'll look at the methods you can use in NWADMIN in the following sections.

*Remember, although NETADMIN is a DOS alternative to NWADMIN, it cannot manage files or file system security. If you need to manage security from DOS, use the FILER utility.*

### Assigning Trustee Rights

You can assign trustees to a file or directory, or you can assign files to a user or other trustee. We'll look at both of these processes, using the NWADMIN utility, in the following sections. You can also use FILER, which we discussed in Chapter 4.

*To assign rights using FILER, press F10 after selecting the file or directory you wish to manage and select the Trustees option.*

**ASSIGNING TRUSTEES TO A FILE OR DIRECTORY** In NWADMIN you can assign trustees to a file or directory by following these steps:

1. Browse the NDS tree to locate the Volume object, and double-click to browse its directory structure.

2. Select a file or directory, and select Object ➤ Details. The Details screen for the file appears.

3. Click the Trustees of this Directory button, located along the right side of the Details screen, to display the trustees information for a directory, as shown in Figure 7.2.

4. Select a trustee (if trustees are already assigned to the directory) to see the rights for that user in the directory.

5. Add or remove rights by clicking the check boxes to the left of their names.

6. Add a new trustee by clicking the Add Trustee button. This presents the Select Object dialog box, which allows you to select a user, a group, or another object, as shown in Figure 7.3.

7. Assign rights to the new trustee by clicking the check boxes. The Read and File Scan rights are granted by default.

**FIGURE 7.2**

Click the Trustees of This Directory button to display the current trustees of the directory.

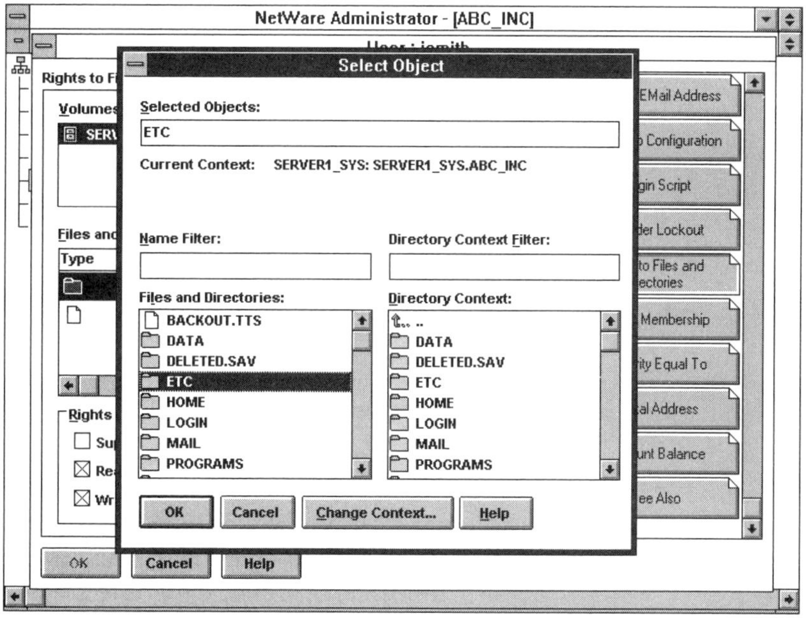

**FIGURE 7.3**

After clicking the Add Trustee button, use the Select Object dialog box to find the user or other object to be added.

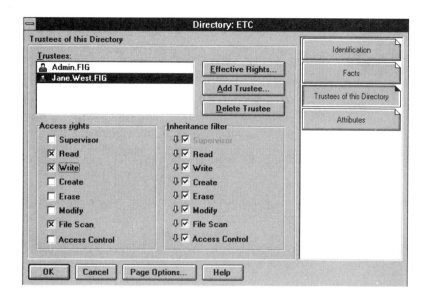

*NWADMIN provides a shortcut for accessing the Details option. After selecting the file or directory, click the right mouse button to display a pop-up menu. The Details option is listed first. Other options you can access from this menu depend on the type of object selected.*

**ASSIGNING FILE RIGHTS TO A USER** An alternate method of assigning file system rights is to start with the user. This method also works with other objects, such as groups and containers. Follow these steps:

1. Navigate through the NDS tree and highlight the user (or other object) whom you want to add as a trustee.

2. Select Object ➤ Details. The Details screen for the user (or other object) appears.

3. Select the Rights to Files and Directories button.

4. Select which volumes are to be displayed. The simplest way is to use the Find button, which allows you to quickly find all volumes in the current Directory tree. All directories and files the user has rights to are displayed, as shown in Figure 7.4.

5. Click the Add button to add the user as a trustee to another directory or file. You'll see the Select Object dialog box (refer to Figure 7.3), which allows you to select files.

6. Highlight a file or directory after it has been added to the list, as in Figure 7.4. NWADMIN displays the rights the trustee has. By default, these are Read and File Scan.

7. Click the check boxes to add or remove rights.

### Modifying the Inherited Rights Filter (IRF)

You can view and modify an IRF for a directory by using the Details screen, which is the same screen that displays the trustees for that directory. To display this screen, select the directory, choose the Details option (from the Object menu or the pop-up menu that appears when you press the right mouse button), and then click the Trustees button.

In the Inheritance Filter list, you can change the inheritance status for each right by clicking its check box. An arrow icon to the left of the check box

**FIGURE 7.4**

The current trustee rights given to a user are displayed when you click the Rights to Files and Directories button.

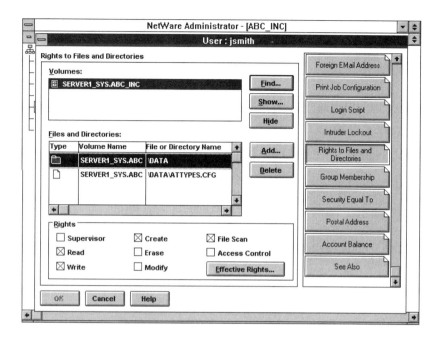

shows you whether the right is allowed or blocked. (A filled arrow means the right can be inherited.)

### Displaying Effective Rights

An Effective Rights button appears in both the trustee's Rights to Files and Directories screen and the directory's Trustees screen. Click this button to view the current effective rights for the trustee in that directory. Rights the user has been granted are displayed in black. Those that the user does not have are grayed. Figure 7.5 shows the Effective Rights dialog box.

The effective rights in this dialog box are updated whenever you view them; the user doesn't have to log in or out to display the current effective rights. However, when you make a change to a user's rights, you must save the changes with the OK button before the Effective Rights dialog box can reflect those changes.

**FIGURE 7.5**

Effective rights of a user
can be displayed for the
file or directory.

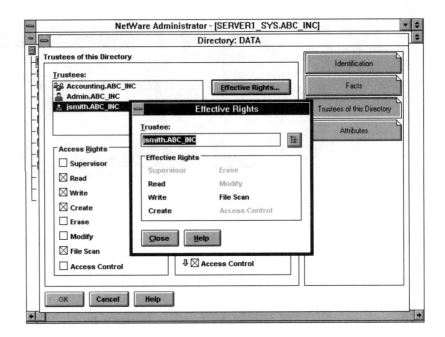

**FIGURE 7.5**

Effective rights of a user can be displayed for the file or directory.

# Understanding NDS Security

WHILE FILE SYSTEM security allows you to control access to volumes, files, and directories on a server, NDS security controls access to objects in the NDS Directory: users, groups, printers, and entire organizations. You can control users' ability to modify and add objects and to view or modify their properties. With an understanding of NDS security, you can assign users the rights they need in the Directory while maintaining a secure network.

## Login Security

NDS provides *login security* for the network. A user who needs to access the network must log in and enter a password. This password is encrypted and then compared with the encrypted version of the User object's Password property. Since encrypted passwords are used, there is little risk of passwords being "snatched" across the network.

Of course, no amount of login security will be effective if your users use simple passwords or no password at all. Be sure to require passwords on the network and advise users not to use common words or names.

# Trustee Rights

Like the file system, NDS security assigns rights through the use of trustees. An object trustee is any user (or other object) that has been given rights to the object. The list of trustees for an object is called the *Access Control List,* or *ACL.* Each object has a property containing the ACL.

While the file system has a set list of rights a trustee can receive, NDS security provides two categories of rights: object rights and property rights. We'll look at each of these in the following sections.

### Object Rights

Object rights are the tasks a trustee can perform on an object. The five types of object rights are listed in Table 7.2.

**TABLE 7.2**

Object Rights

| RIGHT | DESCRIPTION |
| --- | --- |
| Supervisor | The trustee is granted all the rights listed below. Unlike the Supervisor right in the file system, the NDS Supervisor right can be blocked by the Inherited Rights Filter (IRF) |
| Browse | The trustee can see the object in the Directory tree. If the Browse right is not granted, the object is not shown in the list |
| Create | The trustee can create child objects under the object. This right is available only for container objects |
| Delete | The trustee can delete the object from the Directory. To delete an object, you must also have the Write right for All Properties of the object |
| Rename | The trustee can change the name of the object |

## Property Rights

Property rights are the tasks a trustee can perform on an object's properties. These rights allow the trustee to read or modify the object's property values. There are five types of property rights, as listed in Table 7.3. Note that they are not the same as the types of object rights.

**TABLE 7.3**

Property Rights

| RIGHT | DESCRIPTION |
| --- | --- |
| Supervisor | The trustee is given all the property rights listed below. Once again, the IRF can block this right. Trustees with the Supervisor object right are automatically given supervisory rights to all properties of the object |
| Compare | The trustee is allowed to compare the property's values to a given value. This allows the trustee to search for a certain value but not to look at the value itself |
| Read | The trustee can read the values of the property. The Compare right is automatically granted |
| Write | The trustee can modify, add, or remove values of the property |
| Add Self | The trustee is allowed to add or remove itself as a value of the property. For example, users who are granted the Add Self right for a group can add themselves to the group. The Write right automatically grants the Add Self property |

Property rights can be granted in two ways: All Properties or Selected Properties. You can choose one of these methods from NWADMIN's Rights to Other Objects dialog. If you select All Properties, the same list of rights is granted to each of the properties of the object.

*Avoid assigning rights to All Properties of an object. Since the ACL is one of the object's properties, assigning rights to All Properties gives the trustee the right to add or remove trustees from the list. Because this is a security risk, use Selected Properties for all users except administrators.*

When granting rights to Selected Properties, you are allowed to activate or deactivate each of the property rights for each property of the object. This option allows you to fine-tune the security and allow access only to what is needed.

An object trustee can have both All Properties rights and Selected Properties rights for the same object. Selected Properties rights override the All Properties rights for that property. For example, you could grant the Supervisor right to All Properties for an object trustee and then use Selected Properties to limit rights to certain properties. Rights without a Selected Properties assignment follow the All Properties assignment.

## Inherited Rights in NDS

Like the file system, NDS uses a system of inherited rights. When an object trustee is given rights to a container object, the trustee also receives the same rights for all children of the object. Inheritance affects both object rights and property rights.

### Object Rights Inheritance

Object rights are inherited in the same fashion as file system rights. When a trustee is given object rights for an object, the rights are inherited by child objects. The trustee receives rights for these objects also, unless the rights are blocked.

### Property Rights Inheritance

Property rights can be inherited in the same manner as object rights, with one exception: only rights given with the All Properties option can be inherited. If a trustee is given rights to Selected Properties of an object, child objects cannot inherit those rights. The reason is that each of the different types of objects, such as users and Organizational Units, has a different list of properties.

### Blocking Inherited Rights

When a trustee is given rights to a container object, the rights flow down the Directory tree until they are blocked. You can block inherited rights in two ways: with a new trustee assignment or with the IRF.

**EXPLICIT ASSIGNMENTS** You can block the rights a trustee can inherit for a particular object by giving the trustee a new explicit assignment to the object. For example, in Figure 7.6, user RON is given full rights [SBCDR] to the entire NHA_CO Organization. However, RON has been given a new explicit assignment of Browse and Rename only [BR] for the Orlando Organizational Unit. While RON receives full rights in the Tampa Organizational Unit, his rights in Orlando are limited to [BR] by the new trustee assignment.

**FIGURE 7.6**

You can block inherited rights with a new explicit assignment.

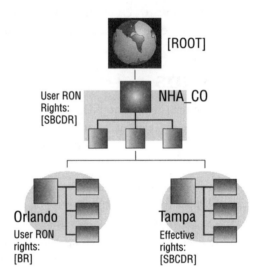

You can use a new trustee assignment to block rights, as in the example, or to add additional rights. The new trustee assignment replaces the rights that would have been inherited. (The trustee assignment is also called an explicit assignment.) Because an explicit assignment blocks inherited rights, you do not need to consider inherited rights if an explicit assignment has been granted.

### The Inherited Rights Filter (IRF)

Each NDS object has an IRF for object rights. The IRF is a list of the rights a user can inherit for the object. For example, in Figure 7.7, user JANS has been given the [BCDR] rights to the Accounting Organizational Unit. She inherits these same rights in the AP Organizational Unit, which has the default IRF. The IRF for the PR Organizational Unit has been set to [SBR], so JANS's rights in PR are limited to [BR].

Each object also has an IRF for property rights. Like the rights themselves, the IRF can be set for All Properties or Selected Properties. You can also set an IRF for All Properties and set different IRFs for certain Selected Properties. Remember, the rights are inherited only if they were assigned to All Properties for the parent object.

**F I G U R E 7.7**

You can use the Inherited
Rights Filter to block
inherited rights.

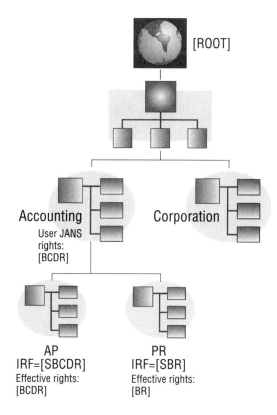

[ROOT]

Accounting
User JANS
rights:
[BCDR]

Corporation

AP
IRF=[SBCDR]
Effective rights:
[BCDR]

PR
IRF=[SBR]
Effective rights:
[BR]

## Security Equivalence

In several situations in NDS, a trustee automatically receives all the rights
given to another trustee. This is referred to as *security equivalence*. By understanding these equivalences, you can easily grant rights to users and make sure
unnecessary rights are not granted. There are two types of security equivalence: implied and explicit.

### Implied Security Equivalence

When you give rights to a container object, all objects within the container
receive the same rights through security equivalence. If one of these objects
is a container object, the objects underneath it also receive the rights. This is
referred to as *implied security equivalence* or *container security equivalence*.

For example, as you can see in Figure 7.8, giving a trustee assignment to the Accounting Organizational Unit would give the same rights to the Payables and Billing Organizational Units and all leaf objects under them. Giving a trustee assignment to the [Root] object would give the same rights to all objects in the entire tree.

**FIGURE 7.8**

In implied security equivalence, rights given to a container are passed on to objects within the container.

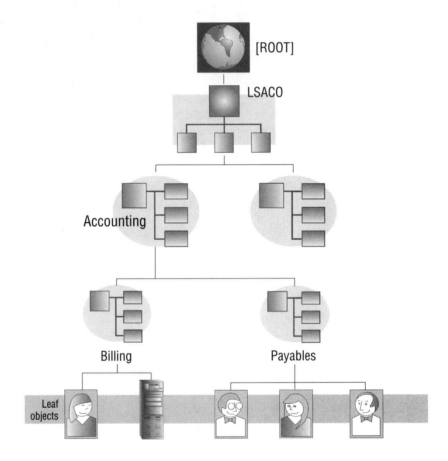

Because rights flow from container objects to their children, you may be tempted to describe this process as inheritance. However, it is not inheritance, according to the NetWare definition. Inheritance means that rights given to a trustee for a container object are given to the same trustee for the object's children.

It is important to understand the difference between inheritance and implied security equivalence because the IRF does *not* affect security equivalences. This distinction can be one of the most difficult concepts to master in NDS security. You can avoid confusion by remembering these rules:

- An object *inherits* the trustees assigned to its parent objects. The IRF can block these rights.

- A trustee is *security equivalent to* its parent objects. The IRF cannot block these rights.

These concepts are further illustrated in Figure 7.9. Look carefully at the Directory tree shown there and consider the following statements about the objects in the Directory.

- The CORP Organizational Unit has been given full rights to the ACCTG Organizational Unit. (CORP is a trustee of ACCTG.)

- The ADMIN and PAYROLL Organizational Units both have an IRF of [BR] (Browse and Rename only).

- JANE receives full rights [SBCDR] to objects in the ACCTG Organizational Unit. This is because JANE has an implied security equivalence to the CORP container object. The IRF given to the ADMIN Organizational Unit does not affect JANE's rights.

- JANE inherits full rights to all objects in the PAYABLES organizational unit, including the User objects FRED and SUE.

- JANE's rights to the User object TOM are limited to [BR] by the IRF of the PAYROLL Organizational Unit.

### Explicit Security Equivalence

A second, much simpler type of security equivalence is also available: *explicit security equivalence.* This is a security equivalence that is specifically given to a user. You can assign explicit security equivalences in three ways:

- Each user has a Security Equal To property. You can add users or other objects to this list, and the user receives the rights given to those objects.

- If a user is assigned to the membership list of a Group object, the user becomes security equivalent to the Group object.

- If a user is an occupant of an Organizational Role object, the user becomes security equivalent to the Organizational Role object.

**FIGURE 7.9**

This Directory tree shows examples of both inherited rights and implied security equivalence.

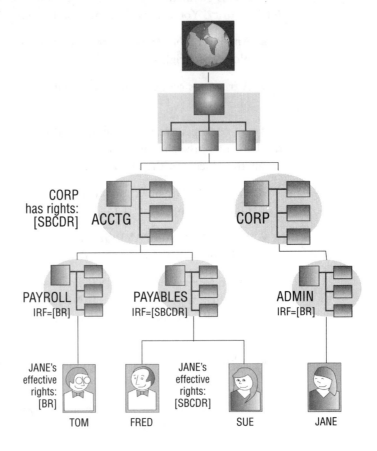

All explicit security equivalences are listed in the user's Security Equal To property. Security equivalences the user receives through an Organizational Role or Group membership are automatically added to this list.

*Security equivalences cannot be combined or "nested." For example, if user JOHN is made security equivalent to another user, WENDY, and WENDY is made security equivalent to the ADMIN user, JOHN does not become security equivalent to ADMIN and does not receive administrative rights. He receives only those rights given to (or inherited by) WENDY's User object.*

# Managing NDS Security with **NWADMIN**

You can use NWADMIN to manage NDS security. You can start with the trustee or with the object and add trustees, delete them, modify their rights, or view the current rights. We'll look at some common tasks using NWADMIN in the following sections.

## Viewing Trustee Rights

Like so many other things in NetWare, there is more than one way to view trustee rights in NWADMIN. You access both of these options from the Object menu or from the right-click pop-up menu when you have highlighted an object:

- **Trustees of This Object:** This option allows you to view a list of trustees for the object you have selected, as shown in Figure 7.10. You can then select a trustee to view detailed information.

- **Rights to Other Objects:** This option allows you to view a list of objects of which the selected object is a trustee. First, enter a context to search in. You can then select an object from the list to view the trustee's rights to the object, as shown in Figure 7.11.

**FIGURE 7.10**

The Trustees of This Object option allows you to view an object's trustee list.

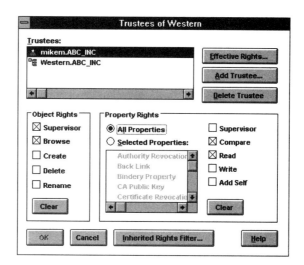

**FIGURE 7.11**

The Rights to Other
Objects option allows you
to list a trustee's rights.

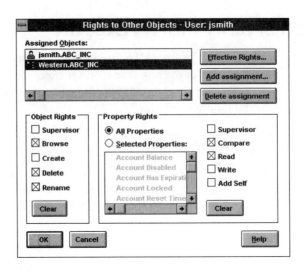

Each of these screens includes all the possible rights for the object. A check box to the left of each option displays whether the right is granted and allows you to grant or revoke the right.

### Adding a Trustee

Similarly, you can add a trustee in two ways. The first is to add trustees to an object:

1. With an object highlighted in the Directory tree, select Object ➤ Trustees of This Object.

2. Click the Add Trustee button to access the Select Object dialog box, shown in Figure 7.12.

3. Find the object that will become a trustee in the Select Object dialog box and save the changes.

The trustee is added to the list. You can change the trustee's rights, as described in the next section.

A second way to add a trustee is to add objects to a trustee:

1. Highlight an object in the Directory tree and Select Objects ➤ Rights to Other Objects.

FIGURE 7.12

To add a trustee, select
the object from the
Directory tree.

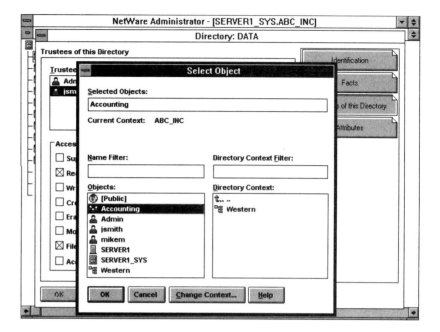

**FIGURE 7.12**

To add a trustee, select
the object from the
Directory tree.

**2.** Click the Add Assignment button to access the Select Object dialog box.

**3.** Select the object the trustee will have rights to and save the changes.

The object is added to the list of objects the trustee has rights to. You can change these rights, as described in the next section.

### Changing Object and Property Rights

While either the Rights to Other Objects or Trustees of This Object dialog box is displayed, you can change the object rights given to the trustee. Simply select the trustee or object and click the check box to the left of each type of right to grant or revoke that right.

You can also change property rights from either of these dialog boxes. You can assign rights for all properties by selecting All Properties and then checking or unchecking the box to the left of each property right.

To assign rights to selected properties, click the Selected Properties button. You are presented with a list of properties that depends on the type of object.

Select the property you want to change rights for and check or uncheck the boxes as appropriate.

*A check mark is displayed to the left of each property you have changed the rights for. Unchecked properties have not been changed in Selected Properties and will default to the setting for All Properties.*

### Modifying the IRF

You can change the IRF from the Trustees of This Object dialog box. Follow these steps:

1. Highlight an object in the Directory tree and select Object ➤ Trustees of This Object.

2. Click the Inherited Rights Filter button to display the dialog box shown in Figure 7.13.

3. To change the IRF for object rights, use the check boxes on the left. A checked box means the right is allowed for inheritance, and an unchecked box means the right is blocked. An arrow or blocked arrow to the left of the check box indicates your selection.

4. To change the IRF for All Properties, click the All Properties button and then check or uncheck the box to the left of each possible property right.

5. To change the IRF for Selected Properties, click the Selected Properties button and then select the property to be changed. Check or uncheck the appropriate boxes. A check mark to the left of the property name indicates that the All Properties IRF is overridden for this property.

### Displaying Effective Rights

An Effective Rights button appears in both the Trustees of This Object and the Rights to Other Objects dialog boxes. Click this button to view the current effective rights of the user for the object. Rights the user has been granted are displayed in black. Those the user does not have are grayed. Figure 7.14 shows an example of the Effective Rights display. If you have made changes to a trustee's rights, you must click OK to save the changes before the Effective Rights display can reflect those changes.

**FIGURE 7.13**

You can change a user's inherited rights by clicking the check box for each type of right.

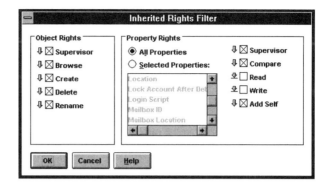

**FIGURE 7.14**

You can display a trustee's effective rights for an object.

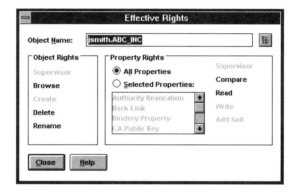

*By viewing the Effective Rights display, you can easily check to determine whether you have assigned rights correctly. It is a good idea to check the effective rights whenever you have made changes because of the interaction between explicit, inherited, and group rights.*

# *Summary*

N THIS CHAPTER we've looked at the various aspects of security in Net-Ware 4 and examined the following issues:

- NDS security begins with a trustee—a User object (or other object) that has been given rights to another object. Just about any NDS object can be a trustee.

- File system security allows you to assign rights to a file or directory to a trustee, and NDS security allows you to grant rights to an NDS object.

- You can manage both types of security using the NWADMIN utility. You can also use FILER to manage security within the file system.

Security is a complicated issue, so the next chapter will be a welcome change of pace. We'll discuss NetWare 4 printing, including all aspects of setup, NDS objects for printing, and troubleshooting.

# NetWare 4
# Printing

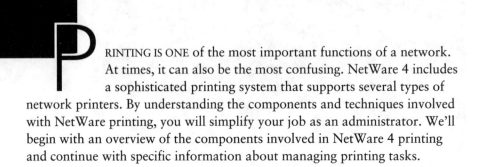

**P**RINTING IS ONE of the most important functions of a network. At times, it can also be the most confusing. NetWare 4 includes a sophisticated printing system that supports several types of network printers. By understanding the components and techniques involved with NetWare printing, you will simplify your job as an administrator. We'll begin with an overview of the components involved in NetWare 4 printing and continue with specific information about managing printing tasks.

# Components of NetWare 4 Printing

**I**N NETWARE 4, several components are involved in printing: print servers, print queues, and printers. Each of these is a physical object and is represented by an object in NDS. You can create these objects under NDS and maintain them from within the NWADMIN utility. Additional components include the CAPTURE utility, which redirects print jobs from DOS, and the port driver (NPRINTER), which completes the interface between the user and the printer. The components of NetWare 4 printing are shown in Figure 8.1 and described in the following sections.

**FIGURE 8.1**

Several components interact to provide network printing services.

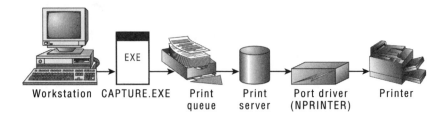

Workstation   CAPTURE.EXE   Print queue   Print server   Port driver (NPRINTER)   Printer

# Print Queues

When you send a document to a network printer, it first goes to a *print queue*. The print queue stores each set of data, or *print job*, it receives. The jobs are sent, one at a time, to the print server. Print queues serve two purposes:

- Allow users to continue working while the printer prints. Once the workstation sends the job to the print queue, NetWare performs the printing, without using the workstation.

- Allow multiuser printing. Many users can add jobs to the queue at once, and they will be printed in the order received. Each print job is completed before the next one begins.

The properties of the Print Queue NDS object store information about the print queue. This includes information about the print queue itself and information about each of the print jobs. The actual print jobs are stored on a file server volume. You choose this volume when you create the Print Queue object, as described in the section "Creating Print Queue Objects" later in this chapter.

# Print Servers

The *print server* controls the printing process: it accepts print jobs from print queues and sends them to the appropriate printers. In NetWare 3.1*x*, print servers were limited to 16 printers; in NetWare 4 this limit has been increased to 255. This allows you to easily use a single print server for the entire network, although in practice this may slow down the server. The properties of the Print Server NDS object provide identification information and define the list of printers the server can send jobs to. You can create this object using NWADMIN or PCONSOLE, as described in the section "Creating Print Queue Objects."

Along with the NDS object, you must run the print server software (PSERVER.NLM) on a server. This is the program that actually controls the printing process. In some cases, a hardware device—such as a printer interface or the printer itself—acts as a print server.

# Printers

You must create a Printer object to represent each printer on the network. The properties of the Printer object identify the printer and list the print queues the printer can accept jobs from. Other properties define the printer type and how it is connected. Printers can be attached to a server, to a workstation, or directly to the network. Printer types are described in the following sections.

### Server Printers

You can connect printers to a printer port on a server. This is the simplest connection method; it is easy to configure and use. Before you configure a printer this way, you should be aware of these issues:

- You must have an available port (serial or parallel) on the server for each printer. A typical PC-compatible machine has one to three parallel ports and two serial ports.

- The printer usually needs to be located near the server. The limit for a parallel printer cable is about 15 feet, although you can extend it with third-party devices. Serial printers have a longer range (about 300 feet).

- You do not need to load the print server (PSERVER.NLM) on the same server the printer is attached to. However, you must run NPRINTER on that server. NPRINTER is described in the following sections.

### Remote (Workstation) Printers

You can also attach a printer to a workstation. These printers are called workstation printers or *remote printers*. The print server sends each job to the workstation, and the workstation sends it to the printer.

To use a remote printer, you run the NPRINTER.EXE program on the workstation. This TSR program sends data to the printer. You can run up to seven copies of NPRINTER on your workstation to drive multiple printers. A single workstation can have a maximum of three parallel and four serial printers.

Since NPRINTER is a TSR program, you can continue to use the workstation while data is being sent to the printer. Of course, you must leave the workstation turned on to keep the printer available to network users.

Remote printing does have a few disadvantages:

- The workstation can be slowed down if a printer is used heavily or if multiple printers are supported. This is doubly true if Windows is running on the workstation.

- If the workstation crashes or is turned off by a well-meaning user, the printer is unavailable to network users.

- Each remote printer uses a small amount of memory (about 10K) on the workstation. This can add up, especially if users need to run large DOS applications.

*You can run Windows on a workstation that supports remote printers. To do this, you must run NPRINTER for each printer before starting Windows. NPRINTER is reasonably reliable under Windows, but some Windows applications can cause instability.*

To use NPRINTER, specify the printer name on the command line. For example, the following command might be used to remotely attach the Check_Printer Printer object:

```
NPRINTER .Check_Printer.ABC_INC
```

*If you use a workstation printer as a network printer, be sure to use the CAPTURE command on the workstation to send jobs to the queue. If the user prints to the printer locally, network print jobs may be interrupted, and the workstation may crash.*

### Network-Connected Printers

A network-connected printer is attached directly to the network. This capability is built into many high-end printers, and you can attach many others to the network with an add-on card. Hardware devices are also available to interface the network to one or more printers.

Directly connected printers can be configured in one of two modes:

- **Remote mode:** The printer acts as a remote (workstation) printer. Instead of NPRINTER.EXE running on a workstation, the hardware device handles these functions. This configuration is better than a workstation printer because no workstation is slowed by printing.

- **Queue server mode:** The printer acts as a separate print server. Jobs are sent directly from the print queue to the printer. This can be the best arrangement because the load on the server is insignificant.

Many printers and interfaces are not yet NDS-aware; however, you can use network printers developed for NetWare 3.1*x* on NetWare 4 networks with no problems. You need to enable Bindery Services (discussed in Chapter 11) to use printers or hardware print servers without NDS support.

To determine which mode to use, consult the documentation for your printer or network interface. Most network printers also include an installation program that can create the needed bindery or NDS objects and configure the printer.

### Printer Redirection with CAPTURE

Some applications (such as WordPerfect and most Windows applications) support NetWare printing directly. You can select a print queue to print to rather than a printer port. For applications that do not provide this support, you can use the CAPTURE utility to send data to the print queue.

CAPTURE is a TSR program that *redirects* printing to a print queue. You specify a local printer port (usually LPT1, LPT2, or LPT3) with the CAPTURE command. After the CAPTURE command is executed, any data the workstation sends to that port will be redirected to the network queue you specified.

The simplest CAPTURE command specifies the local port to redirect and the network queue to redirect to. For example, this command redirects the workstation's LPT1 port to a print queue called WEST41_Q:

```
CAPTURE /L=1 /Q=WEST41_Q
```

NetWare 4 also allows you to specify a printer name rather than a queue name. This command captures the LPT2 port to a printer called PRINTER5:

```
CAPTURE /L=2 /P=PRINTER5
```

*Even if you specify a printer to capture to, a print queue is used. NetWare finds the first available print queue serviced by the printer you specify. Since NetWare must search for a queue, you can improve performance by specifying the queue name rather than the printer name.*

The CAPTURE utility has a wide variety of options to control the printing process. Use forward slashes (/) or spaces to separate the parameters. CAPTURE options are summarized here:

- **AU (Autoendcap) or NA (No Autoendcap):** Allows jobs to be sent as soon as the application is finished sending the job to the printer. Not all applications support this option. Autoendcap is enabled by default. You can use the NA option to deactivate it.

- **B=*text* (Banner) or NB (No Banner):** Specifies whether a banner is printed before the job. The *banner* is a page that describes the job and the user who sent it; you can use it to send printouts to the appropriate people. If you specify the B option, follow it with text to be included at the bottom of the banner, such as **B=ACCOUNTING**. A generic banner is printed by default.

- **C=*number* (Copies):** Specifies the number of copies to be printed. By default, one copy is printed.

- **CR=*filename* (Create File):** Allows you to redirect printing to a file instead of a printer. You can later send the file to a printer.

- **D (Details):** Displays details about a captured port. Use the L option (described below) to specify the port.

- **EC (End Capture):** Ends capturing to the port. This option replaces the ENDCAP command in NetWare 3.1*x*. Any job that is currently being sent is completed. There are three options for EC:

| | |
|---|---|
| EC L=port | Ends capturing for the specified port. If no port is specified, LPT1 is assumed |
| EC ALL | Ends capturing for all ports |
| ECCA | Ends capturing and cancels the current job. Nothing is sent to the print queue |

- **F=*number or name* (Form):** Allows you to specify a form to be used with print jobs. Forms are defined with the PRINTDEF utility or in NWADMIN and are described in the section "Creating Print Job Configurations and Forms" later in this chapter. No form is used by default.

- **FF (Form Feed) or NFF (No Form Feed):** Specifies whether a *form feed* character is sent to the printer after the print job is completed. This option ensures that printing for the next job starts at the top of a page. Most applications send a form feed by default. In these cases using the FF option results in unnecessary blank pages being printed between jobs. The default action is FF (Form Feed).

- **/? or /H (Help):** Displays a list of options for the CAPTURE command.

- **HOLD (Hold Job):** Specifies that print jobs are to be held in the print queue and not printed. You can later release the jobs using PCONSOLE or NWADMIN.

- **J=*name* (Specify Job):** Selects a print job configuration to be used. A *print job configuration* contains options similar to CAPTURE options, and you can use its name with no other options. You can create print job configurations using the NWADMIN or PRINTCON utility.

- **K (Keep):** Tells CAPTURE to keep your print job even if the capture has not ended correctly. A capture may not end correctly if your workstation is disconnected or turned off while a job is being printed. Without the Keep option, the job is discarded when this happens. With the option, the job is kept in the queue. Jobs are discarded by default.

- **L=*number* or LPT*n* (Local Port):** Specifies the logical port number to redirect to the queue. You can use numbers from 1 to 9, as described at the end of this section. The options L=2 and LPT2 both select the LPT2 port for redirection. If you don't specify a port, LPT1 is assumed.

- **NAM=*name* (Banner Name):** Specifies a name to be included at the top of the banner. The default is your login name. This option also activates the Banner option.

- **NOTI (Notify) or NNOTI (No Notify):** Specifies whether you are notified when the print job has finished printing. If Notify is enabled, you receive a message on your screen or in a pop-up window (under Windows) when the job has completed. Notify is enabled by default.

- **P=*name* (Printer) or Q=*name* (Queue):** Use these options to specify a printer or queue for the port to be redirected to. You can use only one or the other of these options.

- **S=*name* (Server):** Specifies a file server name for the queue. This option is used for bindery-based queues only.

- **SH (Show):** Use this option by itself to display the current CAPTURE parameters for each port.

- **T=*number* (Tab Spacing) or NT (No Tab Conversion):** Specifies the number of spaces to use in place of tab characters in the document. Use the default NT option if you wish to have the tab characters sent to the printer without conversion.

- **TI=*number* (Timeout):** Specifies a timeout in seconds to be used to end a print job. If the specified number of seconds elapses with no data having been sent to the printer, the job is considered finished and sent to the print queue.

When you use CAPTURE, data is sent to a print job in the specified queue. The following three events can end the job and send it to the printer:

- You can end capture with the EC option. This sends the job to the printer and discontinues CAPTURE.

- You can set a timeout with the TI option. If the specified number of seconds elapses with no printing having occurred, NetWare assumes the job is finished and sends it. The port remains captured for future jobs.

- You can set the AU (Autoendcap) option. This allows applications to tell NetWare when they are finished with the printer. If the application supports it, this option is the fastest method. If the application doesn't support it, you can make it do so by setting both this option and a timeout.

If you are using the NetWare DOS Requester or Client32, redirection is not limited to the standard printer ports (LPT1, LPT2, and LPT3). You can use port numbers up to 9. To do this, you must add a line to the workstation's NET.CFG file in the NetWare DOS Requester section to specify the number of allowed ports:

```
NETWORK PRINTERS = 9
```

*The port numbers used in the CAPTURE command are logical ports. These have no relation to physical ports, the actual ports used to connect printers. A workstation does not need to have a physical port available in order to capture a logical port.*

If your workstation does have a physical port with the specified number, the CAPTURE command overrides the printer and sends data to a print queue instead. To print to a local printer (a printer hooked to a physical port on your workstation), you must either use the EC option to end capturing to that port or not capture the port. You can also define your workstation's printer as a network printer, as described earlier in this chapter.

### The Port Driver (NPRINTER)

Before data is sent to the printer, it is sent to the port driver. The *port driver* is run by the NPRINTER program, at either a workstation or a server. NPRINTER receives data from the print server and transmits it to the printer. You can run NPRINTER in one of three ways:

- For a printer connected to a server, load NPRINTER.NLM on the server. If the printer is attached to the same server the print server (PSERVER.NLM) is running on, NPRINTER is loaded automatically when you load PSERVER. You can also attach the printer to a different server and load NPRINTER.NLM manually on that server.

- For remote (workstation) printers, run the NPRINTER.EXE program, described in the section "Remote (Workstation) Printers" earlier in this chapter.

- You do not need to run NPRINTER for directly connected network printers. Software equivalent to NPRINTER is built into the printer or interface.

# *Managing Printing with NWADMIN*

BECAUSE PRINTING SERVICES have been integrated into NDS, you can use NWADMIN to manage all aspects of printing. The tasks include creating the objects required for printing, configuring them, and managing print jobs in print queues.

# Creating Objects for Printing

You can use NWADMIN to create the objects required for printing. The properties of these objects control how they interact and define the devices used for printing. To enable printing with NDS, you must create a Print Server object and at least one Printer and one Print Queue object.

You can create these objects anywhere in the Directory tree. However, to provide easy access, it is best to create all of them in the same context as the users who use them, or as close to it as possible. You can create the objects in any order.

## Creating the Print Server Object

You must create a Print Server object for each server that runs PSERVER and for directly connected network printers that use queue server mode. Since each print server can provide access to up to 256 printers, you typically need only one Print Server object for the entire network.

To create the Print Server object, follow these steps:

1. Highlight the context to create the Print Server object in.

2. Select Object ➤ Create.

3. Select Print Server as the type of object.

4. Enter the Print Server name in the Create Print Server dialog box, which is shown in Figure 8.2.

The Print Server object is created. You can change its properties by selecting Object ➤ Details.

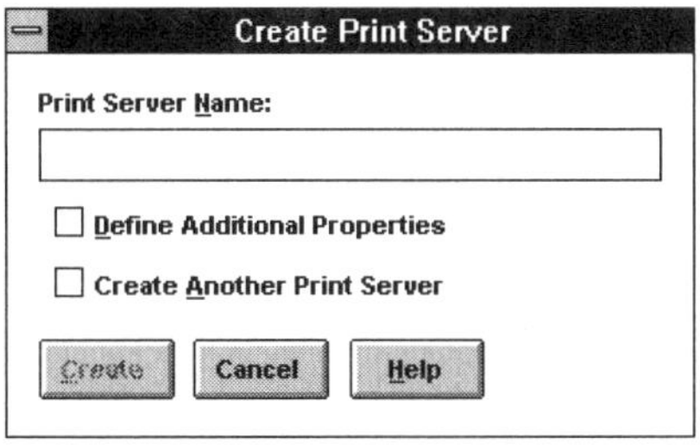

**FIGURE 8.2**

Enter the print server name to create a new print server.

| Create Print Server |
| --- |
| Print Server **N**ame: |
| ☐ **D**efine Additional Properties |
| ☐ Create **A**nother Print Server |
| Create   Cancel   **H**elp |

You use the properties of the Print Server object to identify the print server and to specify parameters. Several pages (categories) of properties are available. These are described in the following sections.

**IDENTIFICATION** The Identification page specifies information about the Print Server object. Identification information includes the name, network address, status, and other information. You enter this information on the Identification properties page, which is shown in Figure 8.3. Most of these properties are optional. You can use the Change Password button to choose a password for the print server; this password will be required when PSERVER.NLM is loaded at the server. The status of the print server is also shown on the Identification properties page. If the print server is running, you can disable it with the Unload button.

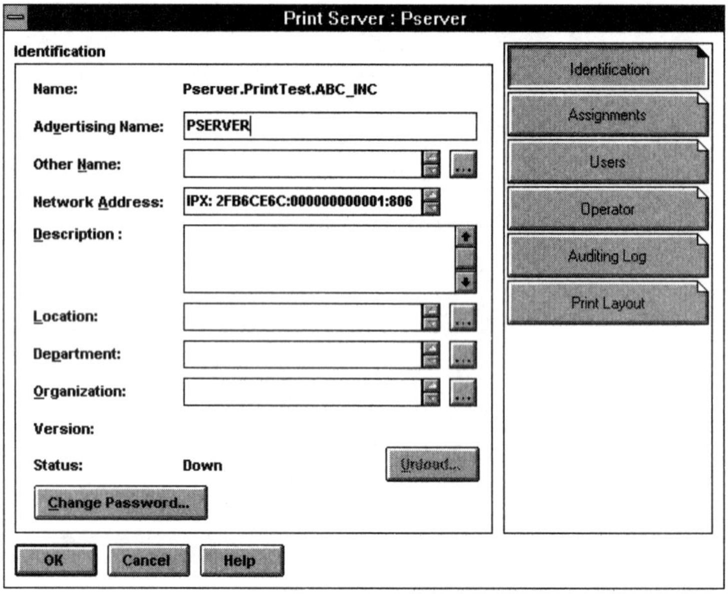

**FIGURE 8.3**

The Identification properties page specifies information about the Print Server object.

**ASSIGNMENTS** The Assignments page lists the printers that have been assigned to the server. After you create the Printer object, you can use the Add button to add the printer to the list. Only printers in this list can receive jobs from the print server. The Assignments properties page is shown in Figure 8.4.

**FIGURE** 8.4

The Assignments
properties page lists the
printers that have been
assigned to the print
server.

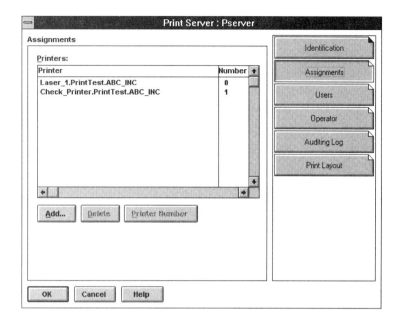

**USERS** You can use the Users page to specify which users can send jobs to printers in the print server. You can add specific users to this list or use groups or container objects to provide access to multiple users.

**OPERATOR** You can use the Operator page to specify one or more users who have Operator privileges on the print server. These users can unload the print server and perform other control functions. This list can include individual users; you can also use an Organizational Role object here to assign a print server operator.

**AUDITING LOG** The Auditing Log page, shown in Figure 8.5, provides a powerful *auditing* feature for printing. If this is enabled, a log of the print server's activities is maintained. Each print job is added to the log, and the information in the log specifies whether printing was successful, which printer the print job went to, and how long it took to print the job. To activate the auditing feature, use the Enable Auditing button. The text on this button then changes to read Disable Auditing, and you can use the button to stop the auditing process.

**FIGURE 8.5**

The Auditing Log page
allows you to audit
printing.

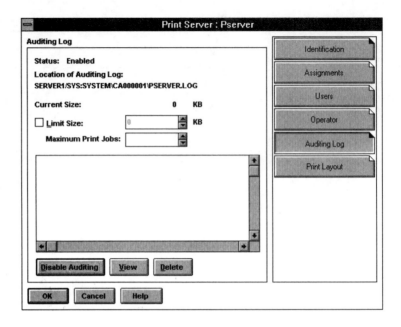

**FIGURE 8.5**

The Auditing Log page allows you to audit printing.

**PRINT LAYOUT** The Print Layout page allows you to view the configuration of the print server graphically. This powerful feature allows you to determine how printing has been configured and to troubleshoot printing problems. The Print Layout properties page is shown in Figure 8.6.

The print server, print queues, and printers are shown with lines between them to define their relationship. You can watch for two indicators of printer problems:

- An icon with a red exclamation mark is displayed to the left of an object that is not functioning. This icon means the print server is not running, the printer is not connected, or the print queue is not accepting jobs.

- A dashed line is displayed instead of a solid line if the connection is a temporary one and will not be reestablished the next time the print server is loaded.

### Creating Print Queue Objects

You must create at least one print queue for each printer on the network. A print queue can also be serviced by multiple printers, and multiple queues can

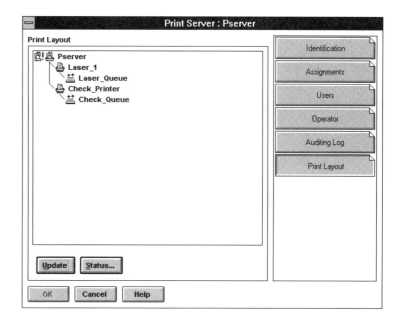

**FIGURE 8.6**

The Print Layout properties page provides an illustration of how the print components interact.

be routed to a single printer. In addition to NetWare 4 print queues, you can define a Print Queue object that sends print jobs to a queue on a bindery-based server. This makes it easy to integrate bindery and NDS printing.

To create the Print Queue object, follow these steps:

1. Highlight the context to create the print queue in. For easiest access, you should place it in the same context as users who use this queue.

2. Select Object ➤ Create.

3. Select Print Queue as the type of object to create. You see the Create Print Queue dialog box, shown in Figure 8.7.

4. Select whether this print queue is an NDS queue or will reference a bindery queue.

5. Select a name for the print queue. For bindery queues, enter the name as it appears on the bindery server.

6. Select a volume to store print queue entries on. For NDS queues, this can be any volume; for bindery queues, it should be the SYS: volume on the bindery server.

7. Click the Create button to create the Print Queue object.

**FIGURE 8.7**

Enter the required information to create a new Print Queue object.

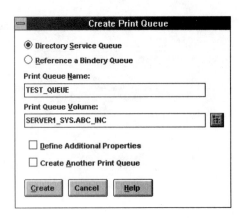

After the Print Queue object is created, highlight it, and select Object ➤ Details to define its properties, which are discussed in the following sections.

**IDENTIFYING THE PRINT QUEUE**  The Identification properties page, shown in Figure 8.8, allows you to view and change identifying information for the print queue. In addition, three check boxes in the Operator Flags section of the page allow you to control the print queue's behavior:

- **Allow Users To Submit Print Jobs:** Controls whether users can add jobs to the print queue. If this option is turned off, users receive an error message when they attempt to print to a port that has been redirected to the queue.

- **Allow Service By Current Print Servers:** Controls whether entries in the queue are printed by the print servers. If you turn off this option, entries are added to the queue but are not printed until it is turned back on.

- **Allow New Print Servers To Attach:** Controls whether new print servers can be attached to the print queue. If you turn this option off, all current print servers continue to print, but new ones are not able to attach.

**VIEWING QUEUE ASSIGNMENTS**  The Assignments properties page allows you to view the objects that have been assigned to this print queue. These include print servers that are authorized to obtain entries from the queue and printers that are set up to print jobs from the queue.

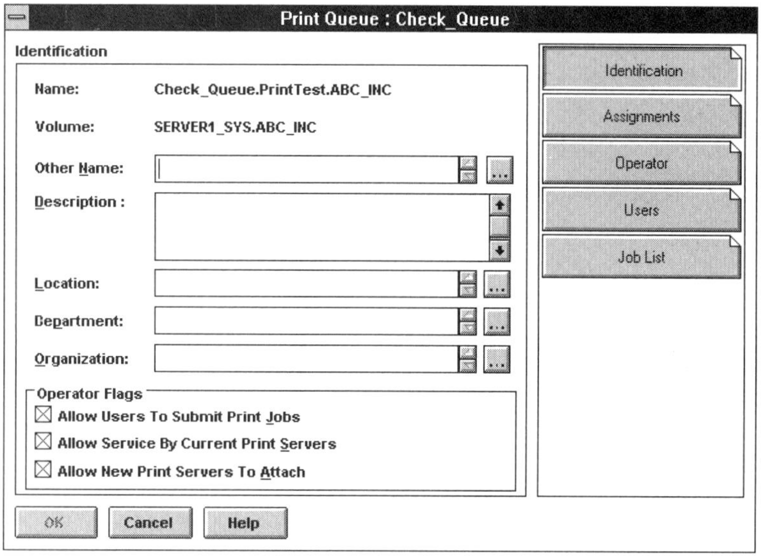

**FIGURE 8.8**

The Identification properties page shows information about the print queue and allows you to control it.

```
Print Queue : Check_Queue
Identification
  Name:           Check_Queue.PrintTest.ABC_INC
  Volume:         SERVER1_SYS.ABC_INC
  Other Name:     [                    ]
  Description :   [                    ]

  Location:       [                    ]
  Department:     [                    ]
  Organization:   [                    ]
  ┌ Operator Flags ──────────────────────
  │ ☒ Allow Users To Submit Print Jobs
  │ ☒ Allow Service By Current Print Servers
  │ ☒ Allow New Print Servers To Attach

  [ OK ]  [ Cancel ]  [ Help ]
```

Buttons on right: Identification, Assignments, Operator, Users, Job List

*The properties on the Print Queue object's Assignments page are for your information only and cannot be changed. Changes to queue assignments are made on the Assignments properties page of the Print Server and Printer Object dialog boxes.*

**QUEUE USERS AND OPERATORS** The Users properties page allows you to specify a list of users who can submit jobs to the print queue. Use the Add button to add to this list. You can add individual users, but it is more common to add multiple users by using Group objects or container objects.

The Operator properties page allows you to specify users who can control print jobs in the queue, as described in the next section. You can include individual users in the list or use an Organizational Role object to assign a print queue operator.

**MANAGING PRINT JOBS** The final page of properties for the Print Queue object is the Job List properties page. This lists each of the print jobs that have been submitted to the queue and describes their status. This screen is shown in Figure 8.9.

**FIGURE 8.9**

The Job List properties
page lists print jobs
waiting in the print queue.

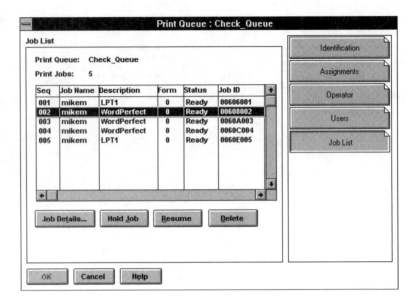

**FIGURE 8.9**

The Job List properties page lists print jobs waiting in the print queue.

You can use the Job List properties page to view the jobs that have been sent to the printer. In addition, you can manage the jobs with the following functions:

- **Job Details:** Displays complete information about the highlighted job. This screen is shown in Figure 8.10. You can modify certain information, such as the job description, and place the job on hold if desired.

- **Hold Job:** Allows you to place a job on hold; the job is not printed until it is released.

- **Resume:** Allows a held job to be printed.

- **Delete:** Removes an entry from the queue.

## Creating Printer Objects

The Printer object is the final object required for network printing. You must create a Printer object to represent each printer on the network. You can create a Printer object by following these steps:

I. Highlight the context to place the Printer object in.

2. Select Object ➤ Create.

3. Select Printer as the type of object to create.

4. Enter a name for the printer, and click the Create button to create the object.

**FIGURE 8.10**

You can view details for an individual print job in the Print Job Detail screen.

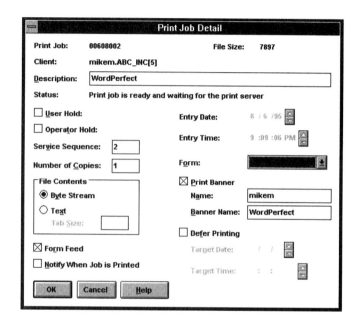

After the Printer object is created, you can modify its properties using the Details option from the Object menu. The properties of the Printer object allow you to identify the printer, specify how it is connected to the network, and specify print queues to print from. These properties are described in the following sections.

**SELECTING PRINTER ASSIGNMENTS** The Assignments properties page, shown in Figure 8.11, allows you to assign Print Queue objects to be serviced by the printer. You can use the Add button to add additional queues. The Priority field allows you to change a queue's priority, and the Delete button allows you to remove a print queue from the list.

**FIGURE 8.11**

The Printer object's
Assignments properties
page lists queues serviced
by the printer.

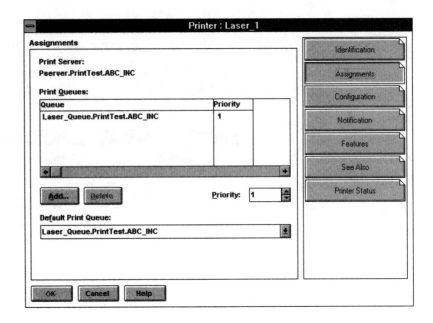

**FIGURE 8.11**

The Printer object's
Assignments properties
page lists queues serviced
by the printer.

The Default Print Queue option allows you to specify a print queue to be used when a user uses the P option in the CAPTURE command to specify the printer's name rather than a print queue.

**CONFIGURING PRINTERS** The Configuration properties page, shown in Figure 8.12, allows you to configure the printer. This page controls the type of port the printer is connected to, the communication parameters, and other settings. Available options on this screen include

- **Printer Type:** Allows you to specify the type of port, parallel or serial, the printer is attached to. You can also specify UNIX or AppleTalk printers.

- **Communication:** This button allows you to view parameters specific to the type of port used. The Parallel Communication screen for a parallel printer is shown in Figure 8.13. A different screen is shown for serial printers. You use these screens to specify the physical port the printer is attached to, speed of communication, and other settings.

- **Banner Type:** Specifies whether the banner used for the printer is in text (ASCII) or PostScript format. The PostScript format can be used on compatible printers only.

- **Service Interval:** Controls how often the printer checks for new jobs in the print queue. The default is 5 seconds.

- **Buffer Size in KB:** Controls the size of the buffer used to store data before it is sent to the printer. This can range from 3- to 20K. The buffer is stored in the RAM of the server or workstation that runs NPRINTER.

- **Starting Form:** Selects the default type of form for the printer.

- **Network Address Restriction:** Allows you to select a list of network addresses the printer can use.

- **Service Mode for Forms:** Specifies how form changes are managed.

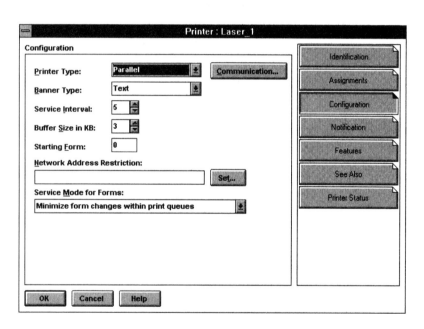

**FIGURE 8.12**

The Printer object's Configuration properties define the type of printer and its connection.

**OTHER PRINTER PROPERTIES** The remaining pages of printer properties allow you to identify the printer, provide notification for printer errors, and display printer status:

- **Identification:** Allows you to define a name and other information for the printer. Most of this information is optional.

- **Notification:** Allows you to list users who are notified when an error occurs at the printer.

- **See Also:** Allows you to reference other objects that are related to the Printer object. This is for your information only and is not used by NetWare.

- **Printer Status:** Displays the current printer status and information about the job that is currently printing.

**FIGURE 8.13**

The Parallel Communication screen allows you to define specific communication parameters for the printer.

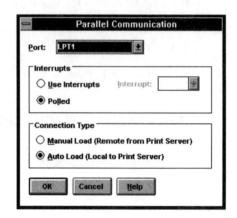

# Managing Printing with PCONSOLE

YOU MAY BE familiar with the PCONSOLE menu utility, which manages most aspects of printing in NetWare 3.1*x*. This DOS-based utility has been improved in NetWare 4.

If you prefer PCONSOLE to NWADMIN, you can use it to perform most of the same printing management tasks described so far in this chapter. In addition, PCONSOLE offers a Quick Setup feature that allows you to create all the objects needed for printing in one step. The main PCONSOLE menu is shown in Figure 8.14.

The following sections describe how to use PCONSOLE to set up and manage network printing. See the descriptions in the section "Managing Printing with NWADMIN" earlier in this chapter for details on the properties of the print objects.

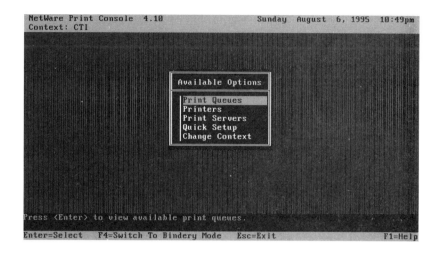

**FIGURE 8.14**

PCONSOLE is a DOS menu utility that allows you to control network printing.

## Using the Quick Setup Option

The Quick Setup option on PCONSOLE's main menu provides an easy way to set up network printing, without requiring you to know about the interaction between the print objects. Quick Setup creates each of the required print objects and assigns the correct properties for them to work together. You can use this option to create a working setup quickly and then examine and modify the objects if necessary.

After you select Quick Setup, you see the screen shown in Figure 8.15. You can specify a print server name, printer name, and queue name. Default names are provided. If the print server you specify does not exist, it is created automatically.

## Managing Printing Objects

PCONSOLE allows you to control the three types of objects required for printing: Print Queues, Printers, and Print Servers. You can create new objects and specify all their properties from within this utility. Most of the options are similar to the PCONSOLE utility in NetWare 3.1x.

**FIGURE 8.15**

The Quick Setup option creates all the objects required for network printing.

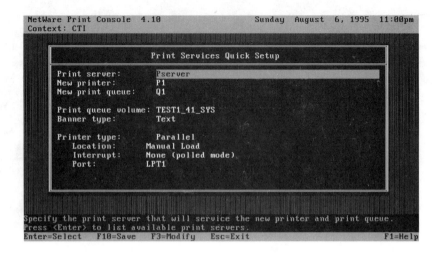

```
NetWare Print Console  4.10                    Sunday  August  6, 1995  11:00pm
Context: CTI

                         Print Services Quick Setup

        Print server:       Pserver
        New printer:        P1
        New print queue:    Q1

        Print queue volume: TEST1_41_SYS
        Banner type:        Text

        Printer type:       Parallel
            Location:       Manual Load
            Interrupt:      None (polled mode)
            Port:           LPT1


    Specify the print server that will service the new printer and print queue.
    Press <Enter> to list available print servers.
    Enter=Select   F10=Save   F3=Modify   Esc=Exit                      F1=Help
```

*You can perform many tasks in more than one way from PCONSOLE. For example, you can create Printer objects from the Print Server option rather than the Printers option. This makes it easy to find the option you need.*

### Print Queues

PCONSOLE's Print Queues option allows you to create and modify Print Queue objects and their settings. When you select this option, you see a list of currently defined print queues. Press Ins to create a new print queue, or press ↵ to view information for a print queue. From the Print Queue Information menu, shown in Figure 8.16, you can control the properties of the print queue and manage print jobs.

### Printers

PCONSOLE's Printers option displays a list of currently defined printers. You can create a new Printer object by pressing the Ins key from this screen. Press ↵ with a printer's name selected to display the Printer Configuration screen, shown in Figure 8.17. This screen allows you to set options for the printer type, communication options, and other properties of the Printer object.

**FIGURE 8.16**

The Print Queue Information menu allows you to monitor and control the print queue.

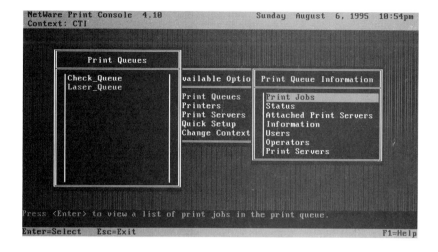

**FIGURE 8.17**

The Printer Configuration screen allows you to control the Printer object's properties.

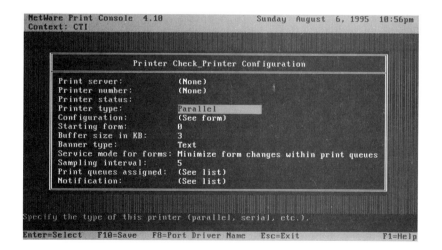

## Print Servers

Press ↵ with PCONSOLE's Print Servers option selected to view a list of currently defined print servers. You can press Ins to create a new Print Server object and press Del to delete a server. Press ↵ with the print server name selected to view the Print Server Information menu, shown in Figure 8.18. This menu allows you to define the properties of the print server.

**FIGURE 8.18**

The Print Server Information menu allows you to define the print server's properties.

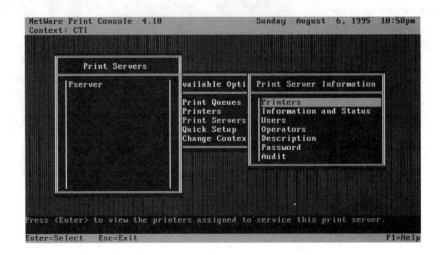

# Creating Print Job Configurations and Forms

N THIS SECTION we'll look at two features NetWare 4 provides to allow you more control over your printouts:

- You can use *printer forms* to specify commands to be sent to the printer at the beginning of a print job. You can also use different form types for different types of paper loaded into the printer. NetWare does not allow a job intended for one form to be printed until the form is mounted. You can create forms with the PRINTDEF utility or with NWADMIN.

- Custom *print job configurations* allow you to specify a list of options to be used in a CAPTURE command; you can then access the options with a single CAPTURE option. You can create print job configurations using NWADMIN or the PRINTCON utility.

In the following sections we explore how to create printer forms and print job configurations using the PRINTCON and PRINTDEF utilities from DOS and with NWADMIN in Windows.

# Using PRINTDEF and PRINTCON

The PRINTDEF and PRINTCON utilities, also available with NetWare 3.1*x*, have been improved in NetWare 4. You can use these utilities, or the NWADMIN utility, to create custom print configurations and to print forms. These forms and configurations are stored as properties of User and container objects in NDS.

### PRINTDEF: Defining Forms

The PRINTDEF utility, shown in Figure 8.19, allows you to create printer forms. Forms specify commands to be sent to the printer at the beginning of the job, based on the configuration of the particular printer. Forms are useful for printing in a specific font or size or on a certain type of paper. If you specify a form when printing, NetWare waits for that form to be mounted before printing the job.

The PRINTDEF main menu includes these options:

- **Print Devices:** Allows you to define devices (printers) to be used for forms. Several device definitions for common printers are included with NetWare 4.

- **Printer Forms:** Allows you to define forms for a selected type of printer.

- **Change Current Context:** Changes the current context, where the items you create will be stored.

By defining forms, you can control the printer's formatting functions for applications that do not directly support the printer. However, most modern applications, and all Microsoft Windows applications, provide printer support that makes printer forms unnecessary.

### PRINTCON: Creating Print Job Configurations

The PRINTCON utility, shown in Figure 8.20, allows you to create custom print job configurations. The configurations consist of a list of options, similar to the options for the CAPTURE command.

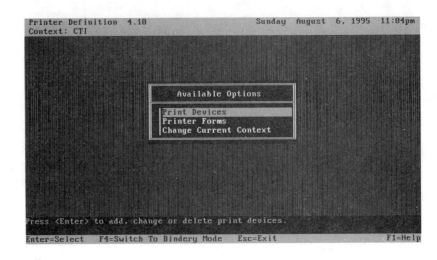

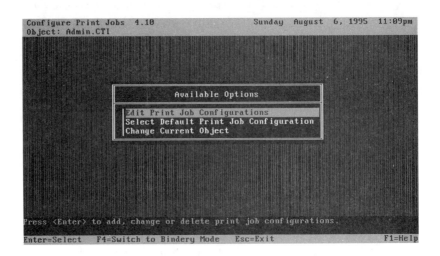

If you specify a print job configuration, you can omit all other CAPTURE options. For example, the following CAPTURE command will capture using a print job configuration called TEST:

```
CAPTURE /j=TEST
```

## Managing Forms and Print Jobs with NWADMIN

You can also control form definitions and print job configuration using the NWADMIN utility. The printer form information is stored as an attribute of each container object, and that information affects leaf objects in that container.

You can create print job configurations using the NWADMIN utility as follows:

- Give each user a Print Job Configurations property that can define configurations specific to the user.

- Give each Organization or Organizational Unit object a Print Job Configurations property. This allows you to define job configurations that any user in the container can use.

# *Summary*

N THIS CHAPTER we've looked at NetWare printing, one of the fundamental services of NetWare 4. Printing is handled by several components:

- Data to be printed first goes to a print queue. The print queue stores each set of data, or print job, it receives. The jobs are then sent, one at a time, to the print server.

- The print server accepts print jobs from print queues and sends them to the appropriate printer.

- You must create a Printer object to represent each network printer. The properties of the Printer object identify the printer and list the print queues the printer can accept jobs from.

- CAPTURE is a TSR program that allows you to redirect printing to a network printer. After the CAPTURE command is executed, any print jobs a workstation sends to this port are redirected to the specified network queue.

- Before data is sent to the printer, it is sent to the port driver. The port driver receives data from the print server and transmits it to the printer. The port driver is also called NPRINTER and is run by NPRINTER .EXE or NPRINTER.NLM.

To manage printing, you can use NWADMIN or the DOS PCONSOLE utility. You can create the needed objects, maintain them, and check their performance using these utilities.

In the next chapter we'll look at ways of making the network easier and more convenient for users: login scripts, which allow you to run commands each time a user logs in, and menus, which give the user a simple list of options for running programs.

# Using Login
# Scripts and
# Menus

S A NETWORK administrator, you'll quickly learn that the fewer steps a user has to perform for a particular task, the better. In this chapter we look at three areas of NetWare 4 that can make things easier for the users—and for the administrator. These include the following:

- Login scripts, which allow commands to be executed when the user logs in

- The NetWare menu system, which allows you to create friendly DOS-based menus

- NetWare Application Launcher (NAL), which provides a similar feature for users of Windows or Windows 95

# How Login Scripts Work

A *LOGIN SCRIPT* IS simply a list of commands to be executed when a user logs in. Login scripts use their own set of commands. Commands are available to set up the environment—for example, mapping drives and setting variables—and to execute programs.

## Types of Login Scripts

When a user logs in, one or more login scripts are executed. There are four types of login scripts, each with its own purpose. These are listed here in the order in which they are executed:

1. A *Container login script* can be defined for each container object in NDS. Only one container login script is executed, for the user's parent container.

2. A *Profile login script* is attached to a Profile object in NDS, a special object that defines a set of users who share a common login script.

3. A *User login script* can be defined for each individual user.

4. The *default login script* is executed for users who have no user login script defined.

### Container Login Scripts

You can create a container login script for any Organization or Organizational Unit object. This is the first script executed for users in the container. You can use this login script for drive mappings, printer settings, and other options that all users in the container need.

NetWare executes only one container login script—for the user's parent container. For example, in Figure 9.1, user JOHNM has the distinguished name JOHNM.AP.ACCT.AQP_CO. Although JOHNM is in the containers AP, ACCT, and AQP_CO, only the login script for AP is executed because AP is JOHNM's parent container. If the AP Organizational Unit has no login script, no container login script is executed.

### Profile Login Scripts

The Profile object is a special NDS object you can use to assign the same login script to several users. You can use a profile login script to execute a certain set of drive mappings or other commands for certain users in the directory, even if they are in different containers. We discuss the Profile object in the section "Creating Profile Login Scripts" later in this chapter.

### User Login Scripts

The final login script to execute is the user login script. You can use a user login script to execute specific commands for a particular user. One important use for the user login script is to override certain commands in the container login script.

*Create a user login script only if commands are specific to one user. If several users need the same script, a Profile login script is a better choice.*

**FIGURE 9.1**

Only one container
login script is executed
for each user.

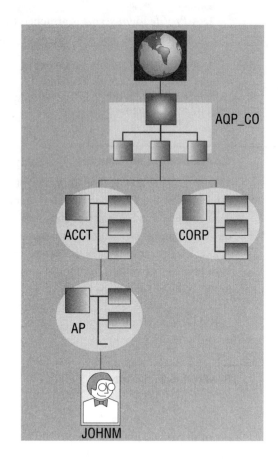

### The Default Login Script

The default login script is built in to the LOGIN utility. You cannot edit it. The default script is executed when a user has no user login script. The default login script provides a basic set of search and drive mappings—for example, a search mapping for the PUBLIC directory.

The default login script allows users to log in to a new system without having to create a login script. If you are using container or profile login scripts, the default login script may cause conflicts. You can prevent conflicts with a special login script command: NO_DEFAULT. If you include this command in the container or profile login script, it prevents the execution of the default login script, even if the user has no user login script.

The following are the commands the default login script executes. Login script commands are described in the next section.

```
MAP DISPLAY OFF
MAP ERRORS OFF
MAP *1=SYS:
MAP *1=SYS:%LOGIN_NAME
IF "%1"="ADMIN" THEN MAP *1:=SYS:SYSTEM
MAP INS S1:=SYS:PUBLIC
MAP INS S2:=SYS:PUBLIC\%MACHINE\%OS\%OS_VERSION
```

## Using Login Script Commands

A variety of commands are available for use in login scripts. These *login script commands* are unique to login scripts; you cannot use them at the command prompt, although some are similar to command-line utilities.

Some of the most useful login script commands are listed in the following sections. See the NetWare documentation for a complete listing.

### MAP

MAP is probably the most commonly used login script command. You can use this command to assign drive letters as network drives and search drives, just like the MAP command-line utility, with one exception: you cannot use the MAP NEXT command, which maps the next available drive letter to a directory, in login scripts.

In addition to the usual MAP commands, you can use two other commands in login scripts: MAP DISPLAY and MAP ERRORS. Both of these have a single parameter, ON or OFF.

| COMMAND | DESCRIPTION |
| --- | --- |
| MAP DISPLAY | Controls whether NetWare displays a list of drive mappings when the user logs in |
| MAP ERRORS | Controls whether NetWare displays map error messages as it executes the login script. These errors are usually caused by an invalid path or by a MAP command for a path the user does not have rights to |

### IF, THEN, and ELSE

You can use the IF command to execute a command or set of commands conditionally. The IF command is followed by a condition, then by the keyword THEN, and then a command or list of commands to be executed. Here is a simple IF command:

```
IF MEMBER OF "PAYABLES" THEN MAP F:=SYS:DATA\AP
```

In this example, the MAP command for drive F will be executed only if the user is a member of the PAYABLES group.

You can use two keywords for more sophisticated conditions:

- The ELSE keyword specifies commands to be executed when the condition is not met.

- The END keyword ends a complex IF statement. It must be used if the IF statement uses more than one line.

Here is a more complicated example of an IF command:

```
IF %LOGIN_NAME = "ADMIN" THEN
   MAP F:=SYS:SYSTEM
   MAP J:=VOL1:TOOLS\ADMIN
ELSE
   MAP F:=SYS:HOME\%LOGIN_NAME
   MAP J:=VOL1:TOOLS\PUBLIC
END
```

In this example, drives F and J are mapped to certain directories for the ADMIN user and to different directories for all other users.

The condition in the IF statement uses login script variables. NetWare sets these variables when running the login script. You can use them to test individual information for the user or workstation. You can also use these variables with the WRITE command, described below.

You can use another keyword, IF MEMBER OF, to perform actions based on group membership. The first example above uses this method. You can use IF NOT MEMBER OF to perform actions if the user is not a member of the specified group.

## INCLUDE

The INCLUDE command allows you to include another login script within the current script. The other script can be the script belonging to another container or profile or a DOS text file containing login script commands. Here are some examples:

- **INCLUDE .OU=VIP:** Runs the login script for the VIP Organizational Unit

- **INCLUDE SYS:PUBLIC\LOGIN1.TXT:** Executes commands from a text file

NetWare executes the commands in the other login script or file as though they were included in the current login script. If the login script or file ends with the EXIT command, the current login script ends; otherwise, the current script continues with the commands after the INCLUDE command.

## CONTEXT

You can use the CONTEXT command to set the current Directory context for the user. For example, the following command sets the context to the AP Organizational Unit under the main ZYX_CO Organization:

```
CONTEXT .AP.ZYX_CO
```

## WRITE

You can use the WRITE command to display a message to the user. You can use login script variables to display specific information for the user. For example, the following WRITE command is typically used to greet users:

```
WRITE "Good %GREETING_TIME, %FULL_NAME."
```

This displays a message such as, "Good Morning, Bob Smith." Another example displays the current time:

```
WRITE "The time is %HOUR:%MINUTE:%SECOND %AM_PM."
```

This displays a message such as, "The time is 11:30:23 AM." By taking advantage of the WRITE command, you can advise users of conditions that may affect their use of the network.

### DISPLAY and FDISPLAY

You can use the DISPLAY and FDISPLAY commands to display the contents of a text file when the user logs in. FDISPLAY uses a *filtered* format to display the file, removing printer codes and unprintable characters; DISPLAY writes the file to the screen in raw format. Here is an example of the FDISPLAY command:

```
FDISPLAY SYS:PUBLIC\NEWS.TXT
```

This command simply displays the NEWS.TXT file to the user during the login process.

You can use the display commands to display information, such as system news or warnings about system problems. You can also combine them with the IF command to display detailed error messages. For example, you might use the following FDISPLAY command to explain a printer error to the user:

```
#CAPTURE L=1 Q=LASER1_QUEUE
IF ERROR_LEVEL > 0 THEN FDISPLAY SYS:PUBLIC\PRTERROR.TXT
```

In this example, if the CAPTURE command fails, the PRTERROR.TXT file is displayed. This file could give instructions on correcting the problem or let users know who to call.

### REM or REMARK

The REM and REMARK commands allow you to insert a comment in the login script. You can also use a semicolon (;) or asterisks (***) to indicate a comment. The following are all comments:

```
REM The following commands set up drive mappings
***Be sure to include the user's mappings here***
;Don't try this at home
Remarkably enough, this line won't execute
```

### COMSPEC

You can use the COMSPEC command to specify the location of the COMMAND.COM file. DOS uses this file to run the command interpreter. Some DOS programs unload COMMAND.COM and reload it when they finish. If the location is not specified correctly, the work-station reports the error message "Unable to load COMSPEC" and requires rebooting.

You must use COMSPEC if your users are using a network version of DOS. If they run DOS only from their individual workstations, this command is not needed.

## PAUSE

The PAUSE command simply stops the login script until you press a key. This command can be useful in debugging login scripts; by including PAUSE in strategic places you can view messages that would normally have scrolled off the screen.

## Using DOS Commands in Login Scripts

You can also use any DOS command or program in your login scripts. Pre-cede each DOS command with the pound sign (#). DOS commands are most commonly used with the CAPTURE command to control network printing. You can use any DOS command, with the following restrictions:

- You should execute only DOS commands that return immediately, such as CAPTURE. If you wish to execute a menu or other program and end the login script, use the EXIT command.

- Don't use the pound sign with the MAP command. There is a login script version of MAP.

- You can't use the SET command to set DOS variables in a login script. You should use the DOS SET login script command instead.

- You can't execute a DOS batch file directly; instead, execute COM-MAND.COM with the /C parameter and the name of the batch file:

    ```
    COMMAND /C LOGIN.BAT
    ```

- Login scripts will also execute in Windows 95 and Windows 3.11. DOS commands may not produce the desired result under these operating systems.

### Ending Login Scripts

You can use the EXIT command to end the current login script. You can also include a command that executes at the DOS prompt after the user logs in. One use for EXIT is to run a menu, as described in the previous section.

Because the EXIT command ends the login script, it should be the last command in the script. In addition, the EXIT command prevents any further scripts from executing. Thus, if the EXIT command is included in the container login script, it prevents the profile and user login scripts from executing. If you include EXIT in the profile login script, it prevents the user login script from executing.

You can use the EXIT command by itself or follow it with a command in quotation marks, such as in this example, which would automatically execute a menu at the end of the login script:

```
EXIT "NMENU ACCT"
```

DOS executes the command after the login script has finished. NetWare actually places the command in the keyboard buffer, so DOS believes the user typed it. The size of the keyboard buffer limits the command to 14 characters. This trick works only under DOS; you can't use EXIT to execute a command in other operating systems.

If you are executing a DOS program that will stay running, such as NMENU, you should run it with the EXIT command. Although you can execute DOS commands anywhere in the script with the # prefix, the LOGIN.EXE program remains in memory while they execute. By passing commands to DOS using the keyboard buffer, EXIT executes the command after the LOGIN program has finished.

By default, users have the rights to edit their own user login scripts. You can add the EXIT command at the end of the container or profile login script if you wish to prevent user login scripts from executing.

## Variables for Login Scripts

One of the strengths of NetWare 4 login scripts is their ability to act on specific information, such as the current user's name or group memberships. For example, you could map a drive for all members of a certain group for access to an application. You can accomplish this through the use of login script variables.

*Login script variables* let you include changing information in a login script. You can use login script variables anywhere in the login script; NetWare substitutes the current value of that item. Use the percent (%) character at the beginning of each variable name to indicate that it is a variable. Variables may be uppercase or lowercase, but since some commands require them to be uppercase, it's best to use uppercase all the time.

Here are a few of the most common login script variables. For a complete listing, see the NetWare documentation.

- **MACHINE:** Specifies the type of computer being used; typically IBM_PC

- **OS:** Specifies the type of DOS, usually MS_DOS

- **OS_VERSION:** Specifies the DOS version, such as 6.22

- **STATION:** Represents the connection number (network address) of the workstation

- **LOGIN_NAME:** Gives the login name of the user

- **GREETING_TIME:** Specifies a time of day—MORNING, AFTERNOON, or EVENING

# Creating and Managing Login Scripts

YOU CAN CREATE and manage login scripts using NWADMIN or NETADMIN. The script is a property of its corresponding object—Container, Profile, or User. We examine how to create each kind of login script in the sections that follow.

*You can't modify the default login script; the only way to avoid its actions is to define a user login script or use the NO DEFAULT directive in the container or profile script.*

## Container and User Login Scripts

Container login scripts are a property of their corresponding container object. View the Login Script property category to modify the login script. User login scripts are a property of the User object, which also has a Login Script property category. Figure 9.2 shows a User login script being edited in NWADMIN.

**FIGURE 9.2**

Use NWADMIN to create and edit login scripts.

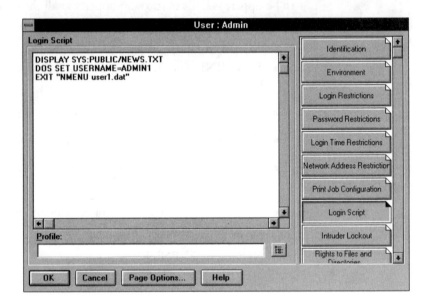

## Creating Profile Login Scripts

Profile login scripts are a property of a Profile object, which can be applied to one or more users. Follow the steps below to set up a profile login script. You can do this from NWADMIN or NETADMIN.

1. Create a Profile object. You can place this object in any container, but the logical place for it is in the same container as the users who need it.

2. Edit the Profile object's Login Script property and insert the desired commands.

3. For each user who will execute the profile login script, make that user's User object a trustee of the Profile object. As a minimum, the User object must have the Read [R] right for the Profile object's Login Script property.

**4.** Each User object has a Profile property. Edit each User object's Profile property, and select the Profile object you have created. You can select only one Profile object per user.

# The NetWare 4 Menu System

LOGIN SCRIPTS ALLOW you to configure the user's environment; however, once the login process is complete, the user is in control. NetWare 4 provides a way to give the user convenient access to applications with the NetWare *menu system*. Menus can be defined for any user or group of users and can run any DOS program.

*This is strictly a DOS menu system. NAL (NetWare Application Launcher) provides a similar capability for Windows. NAL is described in the section "Using NetWare Application Launcher" later in this chapter.*

## Menu Commands and Syntax

You can create a menu by placing menu commands in a menu *source file*. This file usually has the extension .SRC and can be created with any text editor. Here is an example of a simple menu source file. Figure 9.3 shows the menu that would result from this source file.

```
MENU 01, Tom's Menu
   ITEM DOS Prompt
      EXEC DOS
   ITEM File Management
      EXEC FILER
   ITEM Word Processing
      EXEC F:\APPS\WP\WP.EXE
   ITEM Exit this Menu
      EXEC EXIT
   ITEM Log out of the Network
      EXEC LOGOUT
```

**FIGURE 9.3**

The menu listing in the example would generate a menu screen like this.

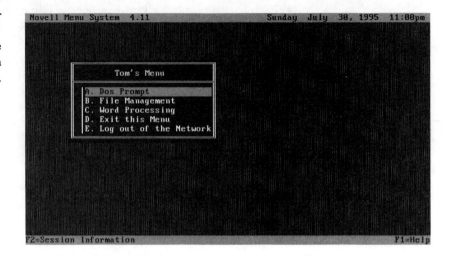

As you can see, the menu source file is composed of *menu commands*. These commands are specific to the menu system. For example, the MENU command begins the menu and specifies the title, and the ITEM command lists each option in the menu. There are actually quite a few menu commands, each with its own purpose. The following sections explain each of these in detail.

## MENU

You begin each menu file with the MENU command. Each submenu within the file also has a MENU command. Here is an example:

```
MENU 01, Applications Menu
```

After the MENU command, specify a number for the menu. This number identifies the menu. It can range from 1 to 255. The numbers don't have to be in order; you can use any unique number. You must use a different number for each MENU command within the file.

Place a comma after the menu number, and then include a name for the menu. Names can be up to 40 characters long, and you can use them to identify the type of functions included in the menu.

## ITEM

The MENU command is followed by ITEM commands. Each ITEM command defines an item to be included in the menu. You should indent the

ITEM commands by a few spaces to set them off from the MENU command. Here is a typical ITEM command:

```
ITEM File Management
```

A description of the menu item follows the ITEM command. It can also include several options. To use one of these options, place the option name in braces after the item description. The available options are

- {BATCH}: The menu program is unloaded from memory before executing the item. This can be useful for programs that require large amounts of memory. If this option is not used, a portion of the menu program is kept in memory, using about 32K.

- {CHDIR}: The current directory is saved, and after the item executes, this becomes the current directory again. You can use this option to avoid incompatibilities with applications that change to their own directories. Using the BATCH option automatically sets the CHDIR option.

- {PAUSE}: After the item is executed, the menu program displays a "Press any key" message and waits for you to respond before returning to the menu. You can use this option to make sure the output of the item is visible. For example, if you place the NDIR command in a menu item, you should include the {PAUSE} option so you can see the directory listing before returning to the menu.

- {SHOW}: Displays the name of the command being executed in the upper-left corner of the screen. This is useful for DOS commands or for NetWare command utilities that don't display their own titles.

The menu lists each item with a letter next to it. You can type the letter to execute the item. NetWare usually assigns these letters; however, you can use a final ITEM option to specify the letter for a menu option. You do this by using the caret (^) character and the desired letter as the first two characters of the item description. The following ITEM command specifies the letter *L*:

```
ITEM ^LLog out of the network
```

If you assign a letter to any item, you should assign letters to other items in the menu. If you don't, NetWare may choose the same letter for another option.

### EXEC

EXEC is the command that actually does the work in a menu. You can use it to run a program or command. Follow the EXEC command with the name of a DOS or NetWare command or utility or another executable program. If the program is not in a path referenced by a search drive or PATH entry, you need to specify the full path. Here is an example of the EXEC command:

```
EXEC FILER
```

In addition to specifying the name of a program, you can use special keywords with EXEC to perform specific functions. These include the following:

| COMMAND | DESCRIPTION |
|---|---|
| EXEC EXIT | Allows the user to exit the menu system and return to the DOS prompt |
| EXEC LOGOUT | Exits the menu and logs the user out of the network. The user is returned to the DOS prompt but needs to log in again before using any network resources |
| EXEC CALL | Executes a DOS batch file. After the batch file is completed, the user is returned to the menu |
| EXEC DOS | Allows the user to run a DOS shell from within the menu. The DOS prompt is displayed. After executing DOS commands, the user can type **EXIT** at the DOS prompt to return to the menu |

### SHOW

You can use the SHOW command in a menu item to execute a submenu. The number assigned in the MENU command for the submenu is used in the SHOW command to refer to it. For example, the following menu source file includes a submenu accessed with the SHOW command:

```
MENU 01, Main Menu
   ITEM NetWare Utilities
      SHOW 05
   ITEM Word Processing
      EXEC WP
```

```
ITEM Log out
    EXEC LOGOUT

MENU 05, NetWare Utilities Menu
   ITEM File Management
      EXEC FILER
   ITEM NDS Management
      EXEC NETADMIN
   ITEM Remote Console
EXEC RCONSOLE
```

The SHOW 05 command in the first ITEM command executes the sub-menu numbered 05. You must include this submenu in the same menu source file. The first menu in a file is the main menu and is executed when the menu starts. Other menus in the file are submenus and must be called by number with SHOW commands to execute. Submenus can also use the SHOW command to execute another menu. Submenus are opened in a window on top of the main menu, as shown in Figure 9.4.

**FIGURE 9.4**

Submenus allow you to organize categories of options.

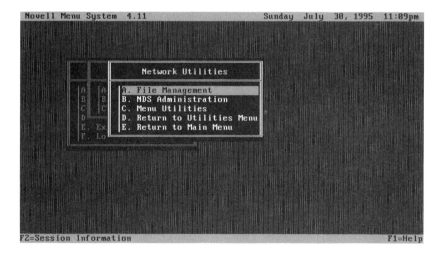

## LOAD

The LOAD command is similar to the SHOW command in that it also executes a different menu. However, the LOAD command allows you to do this with a menu in a different file. Here is an example of a menu item that uses LOAD:

```
ITEM Accounting Menu
     LOAD ACCT
```

The file the LOAD command refers to must be in the current directory or in a path assigned to a search drive. This is not a menu source file but a menu data file, as discussed in the section "Compiling the Menu" later in this chapter.

### GET

You can use the GET commands to get input from the user before the EXEC command executes the program. This input can be used to pass information to an application program or to provide a friendly interface to DOS or NetWare command-line utilities. Three GET commands are available:

| COMMAND | DESCRIPTION |
|---|---|
| GETO | Gets *optional* input from the user. The user can press Enter and leave the input blank |
| GETR | Specifies *required* input. The user cannot execute the program without entering a value |
| GETP | Assigns the input value to a variable (%1, %2, and so on), which allows you to specify commands to the program using these variables. You can also use the values of the variables for later commands |

The GET commands require a specific format, which is the same for all three commands. Here is an example:

```
GETR Enter User Name: { } 10,GUEST,{ }
```

The following components make up a GET command:

- The GET command itself: GETO, GETR, or GETP.

- The values in braces are the *prepend* and *append* values. These are placed at the beginning and end of the value on the command line. These values can be left blank, but the braces must be included.

- Following the prepend value is a number (10, in this example). This number is the maximum number of characters the user is allowed to enter.

- Following the length is the default value. This value is placed between commas. It is displayed as the default when the user is prompted, and if the user presses Enter, this value is used. If you do not wish to use a default value, your GET command must still include two commas, with nothing between them.

The main purpose of GET commands is to make command-line utilities friendlier. For example, the following menu item provides an interface to the NCOPY command-line utility:

```
ITEM Copy Files {PAUSE}
   GETR Source File: { } 15,,{ }
   GETR Destination: { } 15,,{ }
   EXEC NCOPY
```

When the user selects the Copy Files option in the menu, the following actions are performed:

**1.** The user is prompted for the source file and allowed to enter up to 15 characters. This dialog is shown in Figure 9.5.

**2.** The user is prompted for the destination file and allowed to enter up to 15 characters. Both this item and the previous one are required.

**3.** The NCOPY command is executed with the two GETR values as parameters. This copies the source file to the destination file.

**4.** Because we used the {PAUSE} option, the system pauses after the NCOPY command finishes. After seeing whether the command is successful, the user can press any key to return to the menu.

## Creating and Configuring a Menu

The process of creating the menu source file will be simpler if you do a bit of planning first. Be sure you know the list of applications the user should have access to, with their full paths, and any special commands needed. You may wish to create a flowchart that represents the menu before beginning. An example of a menu flowchart is shown in Figure 9.6.

**FIGURE 9.5**

The GET menu
commands allow the user
to enter information.

**FIGURE 9.6**

Develop a complete plan
before creating the menu.

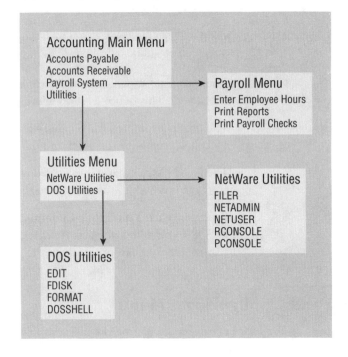

### Creating the Source File

You can create a menu source file using any text editor, such as EDIT under DOS or Notepad under Windows. Save the file as an ASCII file with the SRC extension. Use the menu commands, described earlier in this chapter.

### Compiling the Menu

After you have created the menu source file, you must *compile* it before it can be used. You compile a menu source file with the MENUMAKE utility. This utility reads the file and creates a *menu data file*. This file has the same name as your source file, with .DAT as the extension. The menu data file is the file you use to execute the menu.

To compile your menu, you should be in the directory that contains the menu source file. Simply type **MENUMAKE** followed by the name of the source file. You do not need to include the .SRC extension. Here's an example:

```
MENUMAKE MYMENU
```

This command would read the file MYMENU.SRC and compile it into a data file called MYMENU.DAT.

If MENUMAKE finds any errors in the source file, it stops without creating the menu data file. If this happens, read the error message carefully. You must then edit the source file to eliminate the error and use the MENUMAKE command to restart the compile process.

*Once MENUMAKE has compiled your menu, the menu data (DAT) file is used to execute the menu; the source file is no longer needed. However, since the DAT file cannot be changed, you should save the source file so you can make changes to the menu later.*

### Executing the Menu

Once you have successfully compiled your menu with the MENUMAKE utility, you can run the menu. You use the NMENU command (provided by a batch file called NMENU.BAT in the SYS:PUBLIC directory) to execute a menu. To run a menu, simply type **NMENU** *filename*, where *filename* is the DAT file created by the MENUMAKE utility. This file must be in your current directory or search path. You do not need to specify the .DAT extension.

### Automatic Execution with Login Scripts

Although you should run the menu from the DOS prompt to test it, you will probably want to run it automatically from the user's login script. You can do this by using the EXIT login script command. Here's a typical command to start a menu from a login script:

```
EXIT "NMENU TOM"
```

Because the EXIT command uses the workstation's keyboard buffer to pass information, the command in the quotation marks is limited to 14 characters. This should be sufficient for any NMENU command, but there is not enough room to specify a full path. Be sure the DAT file for the menu is located in the user's default directory (usually the user's home directory) or in the search path.

# Using NetWare Application Launcher

ALTHOUGH THE NETWARE menu system works well for DOS applications, it can't be used with Windows applications. *NetWare Application Launcher* (*NAL*), introduced with NetWare 4.11, allows you to configure applications for users under Windows—and it's much easier to learn than the menu commands.

When running NAL, a user is shown a window with a list of icons, each representing an application that can be run. This may sound familiar—Windows itself provides the same feature. However, NAL provides several unique features that make it ideal for network users:

- It can be centrally managed through NDS. You can quickly add an application and give users access to it. When an application is moved, you can change its information, and all users will have access to the new location.

- You can specify network drives and/or printers to be configured before the application executes and to be restored to normal after it finishes.

- You can configure scripts (similar to login scripts) that execute before and after the application.

- The user cannot add programs or modify them—only the administrator is allowed to modify the applications.

We examine the details of NAL in the following sections.

## Creating and Managing Application Objects

Although users use NAL to launch programs, the most important feature of this system exists behind the scenes. The NDS schema in NetWare 4.11 has been modified to include several new objects. These are called Application objects, and each can store information about a particular application on the network.

As you might expect, you can create Application objects using NWADMIN. You can create them in any context in the Directory tree, but ideally they should be located in the same context as the majority of the users who will use them. Alternatively, you may wish to store all the Application objects in a special Organizational Unit for convenient management.

### Creating the Object

To create an Application object, select Object ➤ Create from the main NWADMIN menu. You choose one of four different object types, depending on the application's operating system:

- Application (DOS)

- Application (Windows 3.*x*)

- Application (Windows 95)

- Application (Windows NT)

You are then asked to define the required properties for the Application object, as shown in Figure 9.7. Enter the following information about the application:

- **Application object name:** Enter a name for the Application object; this is usually the name of the application itself.

- **Path to executable file:** Enter the full path to the application's executable (EXE) file. You can also click the box to the right of this field to browse through the Directory tree and volumes to find the file.

- **Define additional properties:** Check this box if you wish to define additional properties (described below) for the application.

- **Create another application:** Check this box if you wish to create another Application object with similar attributes.

**FIGURE 9.7**

Enter the required
properties for the
Application object.

### Application Object Properties

You can define a wide variety of properties for each application object. If you check the Define additional properties option when you create a new Application object, the properties dialog is shown automatically; otherwise, you can modify the Application object's properties by highlighting it and choosing Object ➢ Details from the NWADMIN menu.

The initial properties dialog for an Application object is shown in Figure 9.8. As with other objects, there are several pages of property categories. The property categories for an Application object include the following:

- **Identification:** This includes the required name and executable file properties. In addition, you can specify an icon to represent this application in NAL.

- **Environment:** Allows you to specify a working directory and command-line parameters, typically necessary only for DOS applications. This property page is shown in Figure 9.9.

- **Drives/Ports:** Allows you to specify up to three drive mappings and three printer captures that will be in effect while the application executes. This

**FIGURE 9.8**

The initial Application object properties dialog allows you to identify the application.

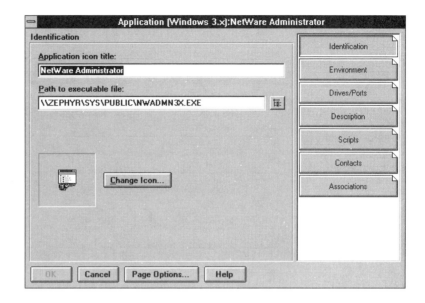

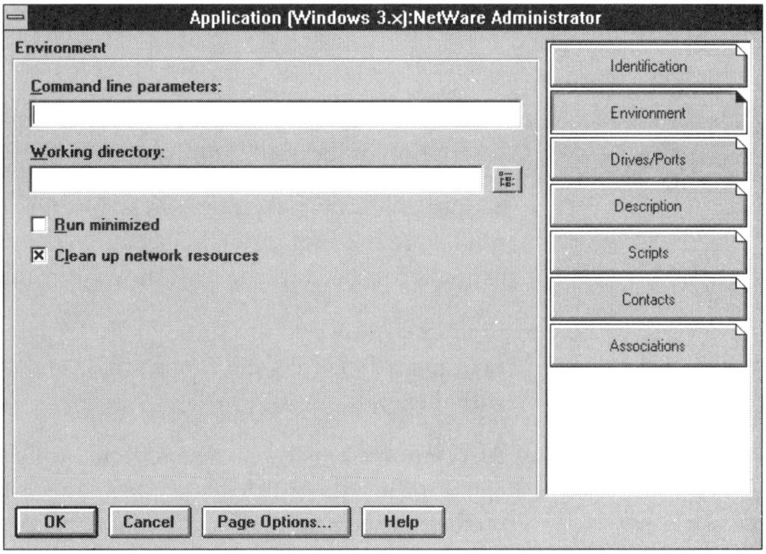

**FIGURE 9.9**

The Environment property category allows you to configure the application's environment.

makes it easy to keep a drive mapped for data files or force an application to use a certain printer. This property page is shown in Figure 9.10.

**FIGURE 9.10**

The Drives/Ports property category allows you to configure network drives and printer redirection.

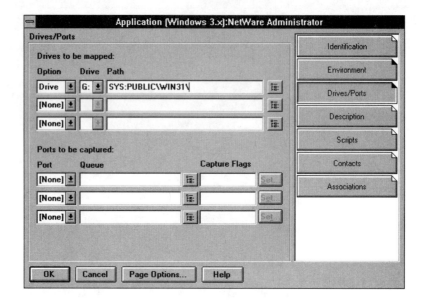

- **Description:** This is a simple text field that allows you to specify a description of the application.

- **Scripts:** Allows you to enter two scripts for the application—one to be run before the application launches, and another to run after the application is finished. This page is shown in Figure 9.11.

- **Contacts:** Allows you to specify a list of users who are responsible for the application; users can contact these individuals if they have problems with the application.

- **Associations:** This is where you decide which users have access to the application. Add or delete users from this list to include the application on their NAL menu. Users from the same container or different containers can be associated with the application.

**FIGURE 9.11**

The Scripts property category allows you to define application-specific scripts.

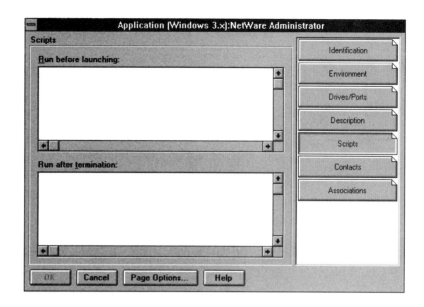

## Installing NAL on the Workstation

Depending on your users' needs, you may wish to give them access to NAL separately, or you may want it to run automatically. Choose one of these two methods:

- To allow the user to run NAL when needed, create an icon or shortcut for SYS:PUBLIC\NAL.EXE.

- To run NAL automatically, create an icon or shortcut as above, and add it to the Startup group.

NAL is available for both Windows 3.1 and Windows 95; if you run NAL.EXE, it will run the correct version depending on the operating system.

## Launching Applications with NAL

From the user's point of view, NAL works much like the Windows 3.1 Program Manager or the Windows 95 desktop. Each icon in the NAL window represents an application (defined by an Application object); double-clicking the icon launches the application. A typical NAL window with several icons is shown in Figure 9.12.

**FIGURE 9.12**

NAL allows the user to launch programs from icons.

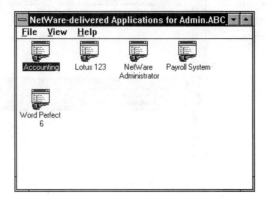

# *Summary*

|
|  N THIS CHAPTER you've learned several ways to make the network friendlier to users and easier to maintain for the administrator:

- Login scripts allow a list of commands to be executed when a user logs in. You can define separate scripts for containers, profiles, or individual users. A default login script is used if no user login script is defined.

- The NetWare menu system allows you to create DOS-based menus of applications for users. You can create a menu source file using menu commands and then compile it for use with the NMENU program.

- NetWare Application Launcher (NAL) allows you to manage users' access to applications through NDS. You can create applications as Application objects using NWADMIN and specify which users can access them.

You should now be better able to manage your users. In the next chapter we'll look at techniques for managing the server itself—bringing it up and down, using the server console, and configuring the server with various utilities and commands.

# Managing the Server

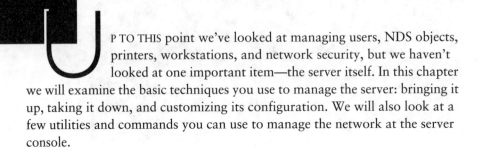

P TO THIS point we've looked at managing users, NDS objects, printers, workstations, and network security, but we haven't looked at one important item—the server itself. In this chapter we will examine the basic techniques you use to manage the server: bringing it up, taking it down, and customizing its configuration. We will also look at a few utilities and commands you can use to manage the network at the server console.

*This chapter covers the day-to-day tasks you perform at the server console. For tasks involved in installing and configuring servers, see Chapter 13.*

# Using the Server Console

HE NETWARE 4 server console refers to the keyboard and screen of the server itself. The server can't run any end-user applications, and it can't run the DOS and Windows utilities we examined in the earlier chapters. There *are* programs that can execute on the server, however. These include

- **Server commands:** Commands you type at the server's console prompt to perform various functions; these are built into NetWare.

- **NetWare Loadable Modules (NLMs):** Programs you can load and execute at the console using the LOAD command. Some, such as device drivers, stay in memory and provide functions, while others are utilities that display a screen and allow you to interact.

Let's begin with a look at the basics of working with the server console and then move on to specific descriptions of commands and utilities.

## Switching between Screens

The server console can make several screens available at any given time, depending on which NLMs are currently loaded. The one screen that is always present is the main console screen, or *colon prompt*. This screen prompts you with the name of the file server followed by a colon and waits for commands. The results of earlier commands are displayed. The console screen is shown in Figure 10.1.

**FIGURE 10.1**

The server console screen allows you to type commands.

```
    Hardware setting: I/O ports 300h to 31Fh, Interrupt Ah
    Node address: 080000292329
    Frame type: ETHERNET_II
    Board name: NE2000_1_EII
    LAN protocol: ARP
    LAN protocol: IP  address 128.0.0.1  mask FF.FF.0.0  interfaces 1

Tree Name: OAK_TREE
Bindery Context(s):
    ABC_INC

ZEPHYR:time
    Time zone string: "MST7MDT"
    DST status:  ON
    DST start:   Sunday, April 6, 1997   2:00:00 am MST
    DST end:     Sunday, October 27, 1996   2:00:00 am MDT
    Time synchronization is active.
    Time is synchronized to the network.
Wednesday, October 9, 1996   5:42:59 am UTC
Tuesday, October 8, 1996   11:42:59 pm MDT

10-08-96  11:43:21 pm:     RSPX-4.10-28
    Remote console connection granted for 2B2CCB96:0080C88129E2

ZEPHYR:
```

You can switch between the available screens on the file server with one of the following keystrokes:

- Pressing Alt+Esc switches to the next screen if more than one is open. You can use this keystroke repeatedly to rotate through the current screens.

- Pressing Ctrl+Esc displays a menu that allows you to choose a screen from the list.

## Using the Console Remotely

You might find it inconvenient to run to the server console each time you need to access it; things are even worse when your network has several servers in different locations. Luckily, NetWare 4 provides a solution. The RCONSOLE utility allows you to access the server's console from any DOS workstation.

*A version of RCONSOLE is also available for Macintosh workstations. This version is described in Chapter 16.*

In essence, RCONSOLE allows you to take over the screen and keyboard of the server. The server console itself follows along as you type commands. In fact, if two users access RCONSOLE at the same time, the server responds to both of them. This can be confusing if you don't know that another administrator is already using the server.

*Although you can run RCONSOLE from any workstation, it requires either its own password or the ADMIN password to access the server. Be sure your passwords are secure to avoid unauthorized tampering with the server.*

Before you can use RCONSOLE, you need to load two NLMs at the server. These NLMs handle the server's end of the communication. Type the following commands at the console prompt to load the needed NLMs:

```
LOAD REMOTE password

LOAD RSPX
```

The password specified in the command line will be required for users to access the server via RCONSOLE. If you do not specify a password, the ADMIN password is required.

To start the remote console, type **RCONSOLE** at the workstation's DOS prompt. Next, choose the connection type:

- Use SPX for a typical connection across the network.

- Select Asynchronous for a modem connection. (See the NetWare manuals for details of configuring a modem console connection.)

You will see a list of servers that are available—those that are running RSPX and REMOTE (see Figure 10.2). Select a server and press Enter. Type the remote console password. After you enter the correct password, you hear a beep and your screen displays the current server screen.

You can now perform any server functions. However, you can't use Alt+Esc or Ctrl+Esc to switch between screens while in RCONSOLE. Instead, use Alt+F3 and Alt+F4 to move back and forth through the different screens or Alt+F2 to display a menu of options.

To exit RCONSOLE, press Alt+F2 to display the menu and select the Exit Remote Console option. You are returned to the RCONSOLE menu. You can select another server or exit to DOS by pressing Esc.

**FIGURE 10.2**

RCONSOLE shows a list of available servers to connect to.

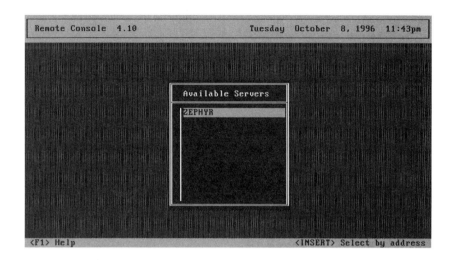

*RCONSOLE will work either full screen or in a window under Windows 3.1 or Windows 95, although in both cases it will display a warning indicating that some functions may not work correctly.*

## Bringing Up the Server

Most servers are kept running continuously. However, you may need to bring up the server if it has been shut down or turned off or has experienced a power outage.

Here's a quick summary of the steps needed to bring up a server. Depending on the setup of the server, these steps may happen automatically; we'll explain how to do that in the "AUTOEXEC.BAT and CONFIG.SYS" section later in this chapter. If things aren't automatic, follow these steps:

1. If your server has a bootable DOS partition, simply turn on the PC; if not, you will need to insert a DOS boot disk to start the server.

2. Once DOS has booted, you see the C prompt. Use the CD command to change to the directory where the server startup files were installed, usually C:\NWSERVER.

3. Type **SERVER** to start the file server.

The server console will now start. Commands in AUTOEXEC.NCF (discussed in the section "The AUTOEXEC.NFC File" later in this chapter) are executed. When all commands have been executed, you should see the console prompt.

It's that simple. If you have any trouble getting the server to start, see the section "The AUTOEXEC.NCF File." See Chapter 13 for detailed installation and configuration instructions.

*If problems occur during the server boot process, you may find the CONLOG utility useful; this will log all console messages to a file. See Appendix C for details about this utility.*

## Taking Down the Server

If the server is currently running, don't just turn it off to take it down. Doing so may cause corruption of files, not to mention that it may anger your users. Follow this procedure to bring the server down gracefully:

1. Use the MONITOR utility (described in the section "Using the MONITOR Utility" later in this chapter) to examine the list of current users. Ask them to log off; if they do not, they will be disconnected automatically when you take down the server and may lose work that was in progress.

2. After all users are logged out, switch to the console prompt.

3. Type **DOWN** to bring down the server. The process may take a minute or two.

4. Although most processes have been stopped, you are still at the console prompt. Type **EXIT** to return to DOS.

NDS relies on communication between servers. If you have more than one server in the network, you should avoid taking a server down for more than a few minutes. If you need to bring down a server for an extended period—or permanently—see Chapter 12 for instructions.

## Restarting the Server

Often you will want to bring down the server and immediately bring it back up. For example, this is necessary when you install new software or make changes to the server's configuration files. You could simply use the procedures described above to bring the server down and back up; however, NetWare 4 provides a simpler way. Follow these steps:

1. As above, check for logged-in users and log them out if necessary.

2. Type the **DOWN** command at the console prompt.

3. Rather than typing EXIT, type **RESTART SERVER**. This reloads the server immediately.

*If you are restarting the server due to a hardware problem or crash, this method may not work. In these cases it's best to turn the power off for a moment and then back on.*

# Server Configuration Files

IKE A WORKSTATION, the server uses several configuration files to determine how it operates. These include the following:

- **STARTUP.NCF:** This file loads device drivers needed to bring up the server.

- **AUTOEXEC.NCF:** Use this file to execute commands after the server starts.

- **AUTOEXEC.BAT and CONFIG.SYS:** Use these files to configure the DOS partition.

We'll take a closer look at each of these files in the following sections.

*You can also create your own command files—the server's equivalent of batch files. Place the commands in a file with the .NCF extension and type the name of the file (without the extension) at the console prompt to execute the commands.*

# The **STARTUP.NCF** File

The STARTUP.NCF file contains commands that the NetWare 4 server processes as soon as it comes up. Only certain types of commands can be placed in this file; it is usually used for disk drivers and memory allocation settings. If you need to execute other commands, you should use the AUTOEXEC.NCF file, described in the next section.

NetWare can't access the NetWare partition until a disk driver is loaded, so the STARTUP.NCF file is located on the DOS partition, in the same directory as the SERVER.EXE program. STARTUP.NCF usually contains just one command, which loads a disk driver. Here's an example command for loading the IDE disk driver:

```
LOAD IDE PORT=2f8 INT=A
```

After the disk driver is successfully loaded, NetWare can access the NetWare partition. The SYS volume is automatically mounted after the disk driver loads. The next file, AUTOEXEC.NCF, is located on this volume.

# The **AUTOEXEC.NCF** File

The AUTOEXEC.NCF file is read when the server starts and after the SYS volume has been mounted. This file is located in the SYS:SYSTEM directory. The commands in this file are executed after those in STARTUP.NCF. You can add just about any console command to this file.

The most important uses for this file are to specify the file server's name and internal network number and to load and bind the network drivers. You can also use it to specify the server's time zone and time synchronization information. Here's an example of a simple AUTOEXEC.NCF file:

```
SET TIME ZONE = MST7MDT

SET DAYLIGHT SAVINGS TIME OFFSET = 1:00:00

SET START OF DAYLIGHT SAVINGS TIME = (APRIL SUNDAY FIRST
   2:00 AM)

SET END OF DAYLIGHT SAVINGS TIME = (OCTOBER SUNDAY LAST
   2:00 AM)

SET DEFAULT TIME SERVER TYPE = SINGLE
```

```
SET BINDERY CONTEXT = .OU=GROUP1.O=WEST

FILE SERVER NAME WEST_23

IPX INTERNAL NET 44998

LOAD NE2000 PORT=300 INT=5 FRAME=ETHERNET_802.2

BIND IPX TO NE2000 NET=99
```

The file in this example was created automatically when the server was installed and includes the basics needed to run a server. You may need to add commands to this file when you install additional software on the server or if you wish to modify settings.

## AUTOEXEC.BAT and CONFIG.SYS

Although AUTOEXEC.BAT and CONFIG.SYS are DOS files rather than NetWare files, you may need to modify them in the process of configuring the server. The AUTOEXEC.BAT file is optional, but you can use it to start the server automatically when the machine is turned on. Here's an example:

```
CD \NWSERVER

SERVER
```

This is usually all you need. Because NetWare takes over after the SERVER command, you cannot use any DOS drivers or other software in this file. Anything you do load in DOS may cause conflicts with the server, so keep the file simple.

As for the CONFIG.SYS file, it is unnecessary for a NetWare server. DOS device drivers should not be loaded. When you first install DOS, the HIMEM .SYS and EMM386 drivers are installed; you must remove these to avoid conflicts with the server. The easiest way to ensure the proper configuration is to remove the CONFIG.SYS file entirely.

*The AUTOEXEC.BAT and CONFIG.SYS files are located in the root directory of the server's boot drive—usually drive C if you boot the server from a DOS partition, or drive A if you boot from a floppy. See Chapter 2 for more information about these files and their available commands.*

# *Using Console Utilities*

ETWARE 4 INCLUDES several utilities you can use at the server console to manage the server and the network. These include

- **INSTALL:** Allows you to install new server components or modify the server's configuration

- **MONITOR:** Allows you to track the performance of the server and manage users who are logged in

- **EDIT:** Allows you to edit configuration files

We explain each of these further in the following sections.

## Using the INSTALL Utility

You use the INSTALL utility in the process of installing NetWare 4. You can run it on an existing server to change installation parameters or to upgrade or install additional software. You can start this utility by typing **LOAD INSTALL** at the server console. The main INSTALL menu is shown in Figure 10.3.

**FIGURE 10.3**

The INSTALL utility allows you to install and configure the server and other products.

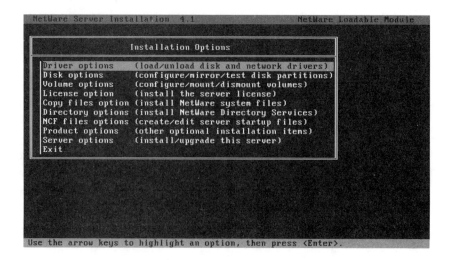

Following is a summary of the available options in the INSTALL utility. Because its main purpose is installation of the server, we'll examine it in more detail in Chapter 13.

■ **Driver options:** Allows you to load and unload LAN drivers and disk drivers.

■ **Disk options:** Allows you to create and modify partitions on a disk and use the disk-mirroring features.

■ **Volume options:** Allows you to create or remove volumes from a disk partition and to mount and dismount them.

■ **License option:** Adds or changes server licenses. These licenses determine the number of users who can simultaneously access the server.

■ **Copy files option:** Use this option on a new server to install NetWare utilities and other files into the SYSTEM and PUBLIC directories.

■ **Directory options:** Allows you to install or remove NDS.

■ **NCF files options:** Allows you to create or edit the AUTOEXEC.NCF and STARTUP.NCF files.

■ **Product options:** Allows you to add or remove optional products, such as online documentation.

■ **Server options:** Used to install a new server or upgrade an existing server.

## Using the MONITOR Utility

MONITOR is probably the utility you will use most often on the server. It is essentially your window into the server's operations. It displays information about users who are logged in, volumes that are available and in use, network traffic, and other parameters. The main MONITOR screen is shown in Figure 10.4.

The following sections explore some of the tasks you can perform with MONITOR. There are also many more complex uses, which Chapter 12 explains in detail.

**FIGURE 10.4**

The MONITOR utility
allows you to monitor
and manage the
network and server.

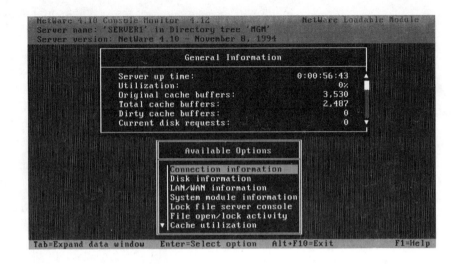

### Viewing Active Connections

To view a list of active connections—that is, users or other objects (such as print servers) that are currently attached to the network—select the Connection Information option from the main MONITOR screen. A list of users who are currently attached to the network is displayed, as shown in Figure 10.5.

**FIGURE 10.5**

MONITOR shows a
list of users currently
using connections on
the server.

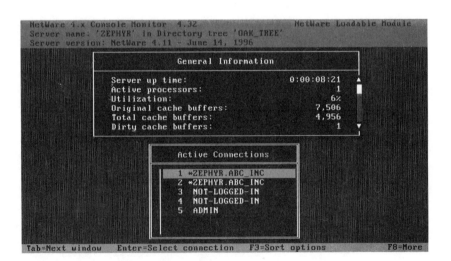

You can highlight one of the users in the list and press ↵ to display specific information about that user's session, including a list of files they currently have open. An example of this list is shown in Figure 10.6.

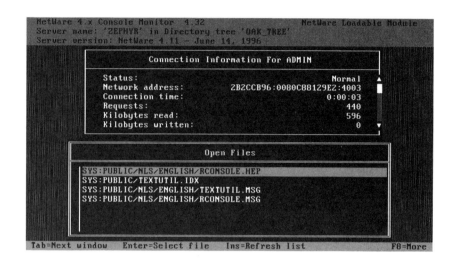

### Disconnecting a User

You can also terminate a user's access to the network from the Connection Information option of the MONITOR utility. Before you do this, check the list of files the user has open to make sure no data will be lost. To disconnect the user, press the Del key. You are prompted to type **Y** to disconnect the user.

From the user's point of view, all the resources of the network will disappear. The user will see a message indicating that he or she has been disconnected. You can also use the CLEAR STATION command, described later in this chapter, for this purpose.

# Using the EDIT Utility

The last utility we will look at in this chapter is also the easiest to understand. The EDIT utility provides a convenient way to edit a file on a server volume without using a workstation. Its functionality is similar to the DOS EDIT command, described in Chapter 2.

To edit a file, type **LOAD EDIT** followed by the name of the file. For example, this command loads the AUTOEXEC.NCF file:

```
LOAD EDIT SYS:SYSTEM/AUTOEXEC.NCF
```

In the case of AUTOEXEC.NCF and STARTUP.NCF, you can also start the EDIT utility from the INSTALL utility, as described earlier in this chapter. Loading the EDIT utility manually allows you to edit any file on the server. Figure 10.7 shows the EDIT utility in action.

**FIGURE 10.7**

The EDIT utility allows you to modify text files and configuration files.

```
NetWare Text Editor   4.14                      NetWare Loadable Module
              Current File "SYS:SYSTEM\AUTOEXEC.NCF"
set Time Zone = MST7MDT
set Daylight Savings Time Offset = 1:00:00
set Start Of Daylight Savings Time = (APRIL SUNDAY FIRST  2:00:00 AM)
set End Of Daylight Savings Time = (OCTOBER SUNDAY LAST  2:00:00 AM)
set Default Time Server Type = SINGLE
set Bindery Context = O=ABC_INC
file server name ZEPHYR
ipx internal net 307DFD75
load conlog  maximum=100
; Network driver LOADs and BINDs are initiated via
; INITSYS.NCF. The actual LOAD and BIND commands
; are contained in INITSYS.NCF and NETINFO.CFG.
; These files are in SYS:ETC.
sys:etc\initsys.ncf
#LOAD NE2000 INT=A PORT=300 FRAME=Ethernet_802.3  NAME=NE2000_1_E83
#BIND IPX NE2000_1_E83 NET=2B2CCB96
#LOAD NE2000 INT=A PORT=300 FRAME=Ethernet_802.2  NAME=NE2000_1_E82
#BIND IPX NE2000_1_E82 NET=6E371932
mount all
Alt+F10=Exit                                              F1=Help
```

# Using Console Commands

ALONG WITH THE utility NLMs, you can use a variety of commands at the console prompt. You already looked at the DOWN, EXIT, and RESTART commands, which you can use to bring the server up and down. The following sections describe some other common commands. For a complete list of console commands and utilities and their options, see Appendix C.

# BROADCAST

The BROADCAST command sends a message to users on the network. To use this command, specify a message to be sent and a user to send it to. You can send the message to all users who are currently attached to the network by leaving off the username. For example, the following command sends a message to all users:

```
BROADCAST "The system will be going down at 5:00"
```

You'll usually use this command to inform users about conditions that may affect their use of the network. You can use only one line for the message, so you can't carry on much of a conversation.

# CLEAR STATION

The CLEAR STATION command disconnects a user from the network and closes any files that user has open. Its function is similar to the disconnect option in the MONITOR utility, described earlier in this chapter. If the user has any files open, they may not be closed properly when you do this, so it's best to have the user log off normally; however, you may need to use this command if the workstation is not responding.

Use the connection number (listed in MONITOR) as the parameter in the CLEAR STATION command. You can also use the ALL keyword in place of the connection number to disconnect all users.

# CLS

The CLS command clears the screen of the file server. You can use it to erase information you have been displaying on the screen. Only the main console screen is affected. After this command executes, a new prompt is displayed at the top of the screen.

# CONFIG

The CONFIG command displays a summary of the server's configuration. This information includes the version of NetWare that is running, the number of licenses available, and the LAN drivers that are currently loaded. Figure 10.8 shows an example of the output of the CONFIG command.

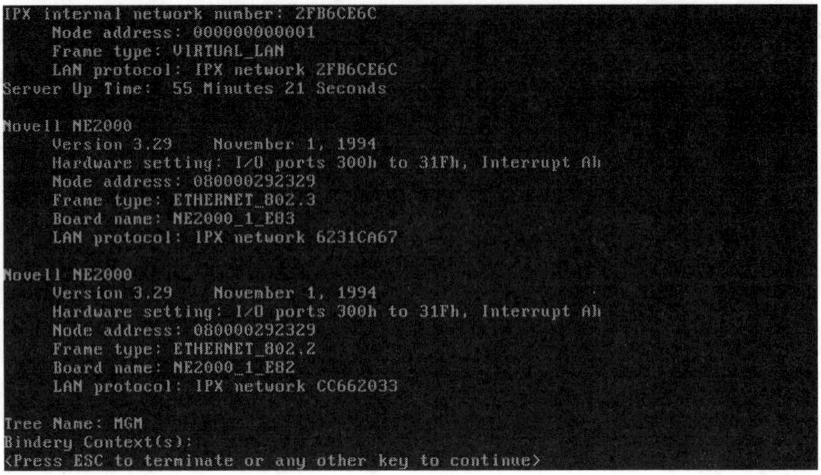

**FIGURE 10.8**

The CONFIG command displays a summary of the server's configuration.

```
IPX internal network number: 2FB6CE6C
    Node address: 000000000001
    Frame type: VIRTUAL_LAN
    LAN protocol: IPX network 2FB6CE6C
Server Up Time:  55 Minutes 21 Seconds

Novell NE2000
    Version 3.29    November 1, 1994
    Hardware setting: I/O ports 300h to 31Fh, Interrupt Ah
    Node address: 080000292329
    Frame type: ETHERNET_802.3
    Board name: NE2000_1_E83
    LAN protocol: IPX network 6231CA67

Novell NE2000
    Version 3.29    November 1, 1994
    Hardware setting: I/O ports 300h to 31Fh, Interrupt Ah
    Node address: 080000292329
    Frame type: ETHERNET_802.2
    Board name: NE2000_1_E82
    LAN protocol: IPX network CC662033

Tree Name: MGM
Bindery Context(s):
<Press ESC to terminate or any other key to continue>
```

## DISABLE LOGIN

The DISABLE LOGIN command prevents users from logging in to the server. It does not affect users who are already logged in. You can use this command to prevent additional users from logging in while you are attempting to bring down the server. Logins are enabled automatically if you restart the server; you can also use the ENABLE LOGIN command.

## DISMOUNT

The DISMOUNT command is the opposite of the MOUNT command; it dismounts a disk volume. Specify a volume name to be dismounted at the command line. For example, the following command dismounts the SYS volume:

```
DISMOUNT SYS
```

You will use this command when changing the server's configuration or troubleshooting; dismounting and remounting a volume is an easy way to check for disk errors. Use the MOUNT command to remount the volume and make it available to users.

## DISPLAY NETWORKS

The DISPLAY NETWORKS command can be useful for configuring communication between servers. This command displays a list of internal and

external network numbers that NetWare can detect on the server and other
servers it is communicating with.

## DISPLAY SERVERS

If you are on a multiserver network, DISPLAY SERVERS provides a way to
verify that the network connection is intact and servers are communicating
correctly. This command displays a list of servers that can be seen across the
network from the current server.

Because certain services, such as NDS and printing, use their own server
names, each server in your network may be listed several times in DISPLAY
SERVER's output. Figure 10.9 shows an example of the output of this command.

**FIGURE 10.9**

The DISPLAY SERVERS
command lists accessible
servers.

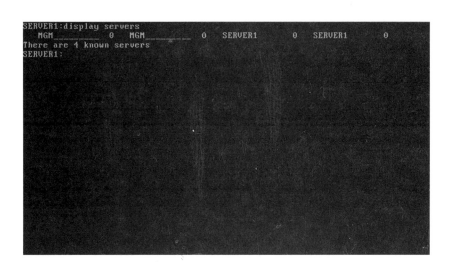

## HELP

The HELP command displays instructions for any server command.
For example, the following command displays a list of options for
the BROADCAST command:

```
HELP BROADCAST
```

The output of this HELP command is shown in Figure 10.10.

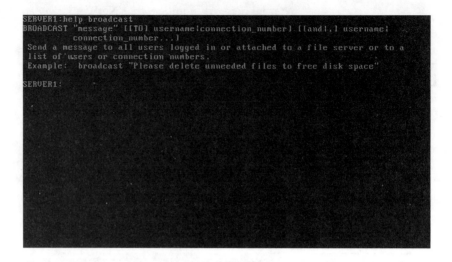

```
SERVER1:help broadcast
BROADCAST "message" [[TO] username|connection_number] [[and|,] username|
          connection_number...]
  Send a message to all users logged in or attached to a file server or to a
  list of users or connection numbers.
  Example:  broadcast "Please delete unneeded files to free disk space"

SERVER1:
```

# LOAD

The LOAD command loads an NLM into memory and executes it. After the NLM loads, you may see a screen provided by that utility. To remove the NLM from memory, use the UNLOAD command, described below.

# MOUNT

The MOUNT command mounts a disk volume, making it accessible to users on the network. As mentioned above, NetWare automatically mounts all available volumes when the disk drivers are loaded. You will need to use this command if you have installed a new volume or if you have used the DISMOUNT command to dismount it.

# MODULES

The MODULES command lists all the NLMs that are currently loaded. You may find this useful to determine which modules are running or whether a particular module, such as a LAN driver, was loaded correctly or is the correct version. The output of the MODULES commands lists the file name of each NLM, its version number, and a brief description. Figure 10.11 shows an example of the output of this command.

```
SERVER1:modules
IDE.DSK
   NetWare 4.01/4.02/4.10 IDE Device Driver
   Version 5.00     September 30, 1994
   Copyright 1994 Novell, Inc.  All rights reserved.
UNICODE.NLM
   NetWare Unicode Library NLM
   Version 4.10     November 8, 1994
   Copyright 1994 Novell, Inc.  All rights reserved.
DSLOADER.NLM
   NetWare 4.1 Directory Services Loader
   Version 1.25     October 22, 1994
   Copyright 1993-1994 Novell, Inc.  All rights reserved.
TIMESYNC.NLM
   NetWare Time Synchronization Services
   Version 4.13     October 14, 1994
   (C) Copyright 1991-94, Novell, Inc.  All rights reserved.
MSM.NLM
   Novell Generic Media Support Module
   Version 2.32     August 23, 1994
   Copyright 1994 Novell, Inc.  All rights reserved.
<Press ESC to terminate or any other key to continue>
```

## SET

The SET command allows you to modify parameters that affect the server's performance. For example, the following command disables file compression:

```
SET File Compression = OFF
```

There are literally hundreds of SET commands for different purposes. You can use the SERVMAN utility, introduced in Chapter 12, as an alternative to remembering the various commands. The most commonly used SET commands are listed in Appendix D.

## TIME

The TIME command gives you the time; in addition, it tells you the time synchronization status of the server. Time synchronization is explained in detail in Chapter 12. The output of the TIME command is shown in Figure 10.12.

## UNLOAD

The UNLOAD command removes an NLM from memory and terminates its execution. Although Novell requires all certified NLMs to be unloadable, this command can occasionally cause a server crash. If the NLM has a screen, you should use its exit option rather than this command if possible.

**FIGURE 10.12**

The TIME command displays the server's time and synchronization information.

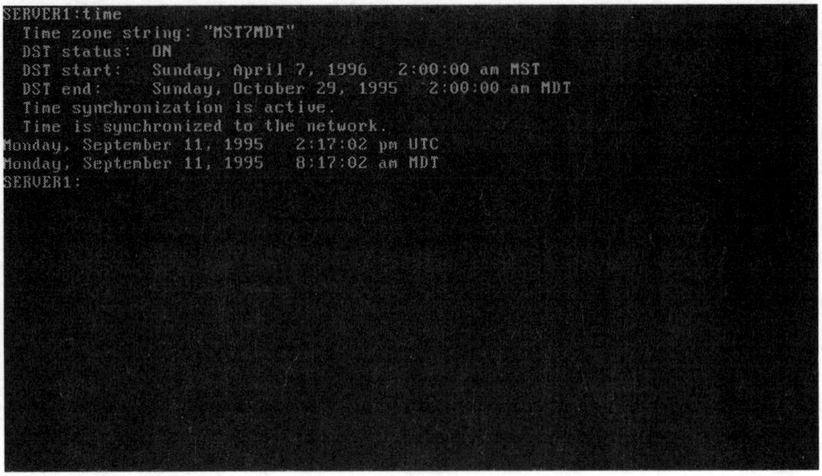

```
SERVER1:time
  Time zone string: "MST7MDT"
  DST status:  ON
  DST start:   Sunday, April 7, 1996   2:00:00 am MST
  DST end:     Sunday, October 29, 1995   2:00:00 am MDT
  Time synchronization is active.
  Time is synchronized to the network.
Monday, September 11, 1995   2:17:02 pm UTC
Monday, September 11, 1995   8:17:02 am MDT
SERVER1:
```

# Summary

N THIS CHAPTER we've examined the various tasks you can use to manage the network through the server console. We covered the following topics:

- Accessing the server console and switching between screens

- Using RCONSOLE to access the server remotely

- Bringing the server up, bringing it down, and restarting it quickly

- The files you can use to configure the server's behavior: AUTOEXEC
  .NCF, STARTUP.NCF, and the DOS files AUTOEXEC.BAT and
  CONFIG.SYS

- The INSTALL console utility, which allows you to change the server's configuration or install additional components

- The MONITOR utility, which allows you to view a list of users currently using the server, along with many other statistics about the network and server

- The EDIT utility, which allows you to edit server configuration files or any text file on a server volume

The next chapter covers the topic of managing an entire multiserver network. We'll explain how to network multiple NetWare 4 servers or NetWare 4 and NetWare 3 servers. We will also look at the options for keeping data safe by creating backups, and at the e-mail packages available for NetWare 4 networks.

# Managing the
# Network

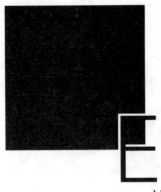

EVEN IN A single-server network, the process of managing the network is more than just managing the server and its wiring. You may have to deal with integration between different types of servers and keeping backups of data.

In this chapter we examine ways of integrating NetWare 3.1x servers into the network and of supporting NetWare 3.1x applications and client software directly with NetWare 4. We also look at backup strategies and the software you can use to keep the network backed up.

## Integrating NetWare 4 with NetWare 3.1x

AT THIS WRITING, NetWare 3.1x is still the most popular network operating system in the U.S. If your network has a few servers, there's a good chance that it includes at least one NetWare 3.1x server.

While upgrading all servers to NetWare 4 is the ideal solution, you may not be ready for this step—or you may not need to take it. NetWare 4 still supports the features of NetWare 3.1x and can even be used to help manage NetWare 3.1x servers. In the following sections we look at two features of NetWare 4 for working with NetWare 3.1x:

- Bindery Services, which allows NetWare 3.1x and older client software and applications to work with NetWare 4

- NetSync, which allows users and resources on NetWare 3.1x servers to be managed from within NDS utilities

*For basic information about NetWare 3.1x, including the ways in which it differs from NetWare 4 and how to administer it, see Chapter 15.*

# Managing Bindery Services

N DS, USED IN NetWare 4 to store information about network resources, is a radical departure from the bindery used in previous versions of NetWare. To remain compatible with older systems—both previous versions of NetWare and older client software—NetWare 4 includes *Bindery Services*.

Bindery Services uses one or more container objects to serve as a simulated bindery. All the leaf objects within these containers appear as a flat database to bindery-based clients. The container objects that act as a bindery are called the *bindery context*. The bindery context is set with a SET command or in the file server's AUTOEXEC.NCF file. You can set up to 16 different bindery contexts. All the contexts will appear as portions of the same bindery, as illustrated in Figure 11.1.

**FIGURE 11.1**

The contents of the bindery context container serve as a simulated bindery.

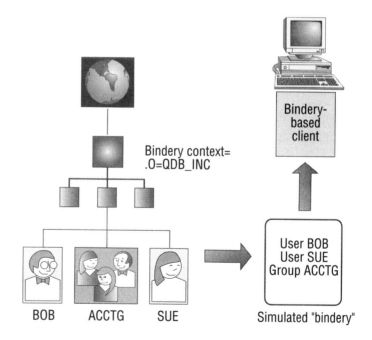

Bindery context=
.O=QDB_INC

Bindery-based client

User BOB
User SUE
Group ACCTG

BOB  ACCTG  SUE

Simulated "bindery"

When you upgrade your server from NetWare 3.1*x* to NetWare 4, NetWare 4 automatically creates a bindery context. All the users, groups, and print queues from the NetWare 3.1*x* bindery are created as objects under a single Organization object, which is defined as the bindery context. This may not be the most efficient arrangement, but it allows network users who are still using old NetWare clients and software to begin using NetWare 4 immediately after the upgrade.

When you install a new NetWare 4 server, NetWare 4 also creates a default bindery context. The context that contains the NetWare Server object is set up as the bindery context container. If you need a different bindery context or more than one, you must reset it manually.

## Planning Bindery Services

Although Bindery Services is set up automatically when you install NetWare 4, there are many things to be aware of when you are using Bindery Services on your server. In this section we examine the steps involved in planning and installing an efficient Bindery Services setup.

### Planning Considerations

It is important to plan the way Bindery Services will operate on your server. Because the bindery does not offer all the features of NDS, you must be careful to create NDS objects that will be compatible with bindery-based clients when necessary.

**OBJECT NAMING**  The common name of an object is used as its bindery name. Suppose a user has the following distinguished name:

    .CN=JIMS.OU=ACCT.O=ABCINC

To Bindery Services, this user is seen as simply JIMS. Since the bindery is flat, you cannot address objects in their containers. Because of this limitation, two problems can occur when using Bindery Services. These involve bindery-compatible naming and name conflicts.

**USING BINDERY-COMPATIBLE NAMES**  You need to use *bindery-compatible names* for objects in the bindery context container. For the common name of each object, follow the same rules that bindery-based objects follow in NetWare 3.1*x*:

- You cannot use spaces in the names. If you use spaces in an object's name, they are converted to underscores for Bindery Services.

- You cannot use the following special characters in bindery names:

  | $   | Dollar sign |
  |-----|-------------|
  | ?   | Question mark |
  | \   | Backslash |
  | /   | Forward slash |
  | "   | Quotation mark |
  | [ ] | Opening and closing square brackets |
  | :   | Colon |
  | \|  | Vertical bar |
  | < > | Opening and closing angle brackets |
  | +   | Plus sign |
  | =   | Equal sign |

- Names are limited to 47 characters. (NDS normally allows 64-character names.)

**NAME CONFLICTS** Because NDS objects with the same common name can exist in different contexts, object names can conflict with each other when you are using Bindery Services. If you have a single bindery context set on your server, this cannot happen. However, since you can assign up to 16 contexts as bindery contexts, you must be careful that no identical names exist in those contexts.

Figure 11.2 shows a Directory tree arrangement in which there could be name conflicts. If both .OU=SALES and .OU=SERVICE are set as bindery contexts, a conflict will occur because both contain a User object with the name FRED.

**CREATING NEEDED OBJECTS** If you are using Bindery Services to ensure compatibility with a bindery-based application, you may need to manually create several bindery objects that are not automatically created with Bindery Services.

When you install NetWare 3.1*x*, it creates the GUEST User object and the EVERYONE Group object. Bindery Services does not create these objects. If you have upgraded your server from NetWare 3.1*x*, these objects should have

**FIGURE 11.2**

When using multiple bindery contexts, you must be careful that name conflicts do not exist between any two contexts.

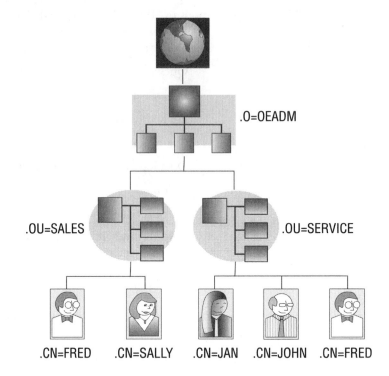

been created as objects in the bindery context. If your NetWare 4 server is a new installation, you need to create them manually.

For example, NetWare NFS (Network File System) requires that the group EVERYONE exist in the bindery. If you are installing Bindery Services and will be using NFS, you must create the group as a leaf object in the bindery context. You will also need to add all the bindery context User objects to this group. (The current version of NFS actually performs these steps automatically when it is installed.) If you have upgraded a NetWare 3.1x server, the EVERYONE group should have been transferred from the bindery.

Finally, NetWare creates the SUPERVISOR account when you install Bindery Services, but this is only a bindery object. Even when you upgrade a NetWare 3.1x server to NetWare 4, SUPERVISOR is not created in NDS and is not equivalent to the ADMIN object in NDS. The SUPERVISOR account retains Supervisor rights, but only for objects within the bindery context and for the server's file system.

### Limitations of the Bindery

Bindery-based clients will not be able to access all the information available through NDS. They will have access only to the information that a bindery would normally provide. Items not available to bindery clients include the following:

- E-mail name, phone number, and other extended addressing information

- Aliases and profiles

- Print job configurations

- NDS login scripts

Because bindery clients are logging in to a server-centric bindery environment located on one server, the login script they will access is the one in the MAIL directory on the server they log in to. This script must be maintained on that server, and it is not replicated to other servers. However, you can move the bindery-based login scripts to NDS using the UIMPORT utility provided with NetWare 4.

## Planning Bindery Contexts

For most networks, one bindery context is sufficient. In fact, early versions of NetWare 4 allowed only one bindery context. The ability to set up to 16 separate bindery contexts is new to NetWare 4. By taking advantage of this feature, you can have the benefits of Bindery Services without sacrificing the efficiency of a well-organized Directory tree.

In the Directory tree for the QDC Organization pictured in Figure 11.3, users in the ACCT and CORP Organizational Units both need access to Bindery Services. We can set the following as the bindery context:

```
.ACCT.QDC;.CORP.QDC
```

Leaf objects in both containers will act as objects in the simulated bindery. This is a powerful feature for combining NetWare 4 with earlier versions of NetWare.

To give users in both the ACCT and CORP Organizational Units access to Bindery Services, use multiple bindery contexts.

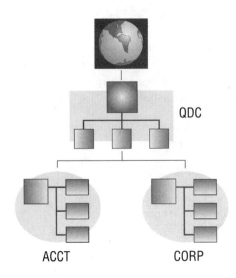

QDC

ACCT CORP

## Configuring Bindery Services

You must configure Bindery Services individually for each server that will allow bindery attachments. In addition, the server must have a master or read/write replica of the partition containing the bindery context.

### Setting the Bindery Context

You configure the bindery context for a server with the SET command. You can type this command at the server console, but it is usually more practical to add the command to the server's AUTOEXEC.NCF file. An easy way to do this is to use the SERVMAN utility, as follows:

1. At the server console, type **LOAD SERVMAN**.

2. Select Available Options ➤ Server Parameters.

3. Select Parameter Category ➤ Directory Services.

4. Select Directory Services Parameters ➤ Bindery Context.

5. Press ↵ to edit the bindery context. When you're finished, press Esc and select Yes to save your changes.

**6.** Press Esc twice to see the Update Options menu. Select the first option, Update AUTOEXEC.NCF and STARTUP.NCF Now. Press ↵ (or change the path to your AUTOEXEC.NCF file, if necessary).

**7.** Exit SERVMAN by pressing Esc twice and then selecting Yes.

If you need to set multiple bindery contexts, use a semicolon (;) to separate the contexts in the SET command. For example, the following command would set bindery contexts for the example in Figure 11.3:

```
SET BINDERY CONTEXT = .ACCT.QDC;.CORP.QDC
```

### Creating Needed Replicas

To use bindery emulation on a server, you must make sure the server contains a master or read/write replica of the partition containing each of the bindery context container objects. If the server does not contain such a replica, you must create it using either Partition Manager or the PARTMGR utility.

# Managing NetWare 3.1x with NETSYNC

I F YOU HAVE NetWare 3.1*x* servers on the network, you cannot normally manage them with NDS utilities. However, the NetSync utility, included with NetWare 4, allows this. NetSync lets you synchronize up to 12 NetWare 3.1*x* servers with a NetWare 4 server's bindery context. The NetWare 4 server and associated NetWare 3.1*x* servers are referred to as a *NetSync cluster*.

NetSync consists of two NLMs: one for the NetWare 4 server and one for the NetWare 3.1*x* servers. These NLMs continually synchronize the binderies of the NetWare 3.1*x* servers with the bindery context of the NetWare 4 server. When you install NetSync, all User and Group objects in the NetWare 3.1*x* servers are created as objects in the NetWare 4 Directory's bindery context, as shown in Figure 11.4.

After the NetSync installation, the NetSync NLMs act continuously to copy all objects in the NDS bindery context to each of the NetWare 3.1*x* servers. Each server's bindery is replaced with a "superbindery" containing all objects from all the bindery-based servers. Figure 11.5 shows how the binderies on two NetWare 3.1*x* servers might look before and after synchronization.

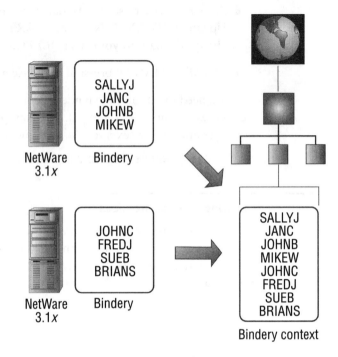

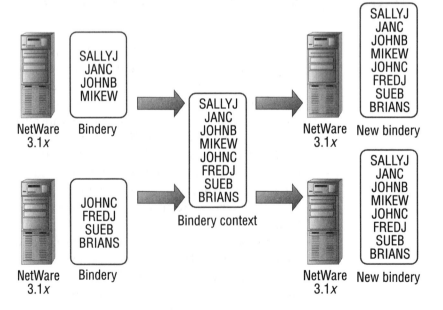

## Limitations of NetSync

Before you install NetSync, you should be aware of some limitations and special considerations.

After the bindery is synchronized with NDS, you should not manage objects with the SYSCON utility on the NetWare 3.1x server, because changes made in this way are not copied to the NDS bindery context. Instead, you need to perform all user management using NDS utilities. The same warning applies to maintaining printing services with the NetWare 3.1x version of the PCONSOLE utility. For those changes to be copied to the NDS bindery context, you need to use NDS utilities instead.

One exception to this rule is the accounting feature of NetWare 3.1x. Accounting information is not copied to the NDS objects, so you can still use SYSCON to maintain these features. Be sure not to change any other information while using SYSCON.

Another point to consider is that trustee rights to files and directories on the NetWare 3.1x server are not copied to NDS. You still need to maintain these from the NetWare 3.1x FILER utility. You can also use the SYSCON utility, but again, be sure not to make other changes in SYSCON. Similarly, you cannot use NWADMIN to maintain the NetWare 3.1x file system. You must use NetWare 3.1x utilities.

*The NetWare 4 server's bindery context must not be changed after NetSync is installed. If it is changed, users with bindery accounts will not be able to log in. This will also cause synchronization to be lost.*

User login scripts are moved to the Login Script property of the User object in Directory Services. However, the system login script from the NetWare 3.1x server is not copied. If you need to execute commands from the system login script, you must move them to the bindery context container object's login script.

## Installing NetSync

The following sections guide you through the installation of NetSync on a NetWare 4 server and on one or more NetWare 3.1x servers. To avoid any problems, follow all instructions carefully.

**Before You Begin**

You should perform the following tasks before installing NetSync:

1. Make sure the bindery context is valid and that this is where you want users from NetWare 3.1*x* servers to be copied.

If you have more than one bindery context set, NetSync copies users to the first one in the list. If this is not the one you want, you need to change the order of the contexts in the SET BINDERY CONTEXT command in the server's AUTOEXEC.NCF file.

2. Check for duplicate users and verify that no users are duplicated between the different bindery contexts of NDS and between these and any of the NetWare 3.1x servers.

The binderies of each of the NetWare 3.1*x* servers are combined with any objects already in the bindery context. If any users exist in more than one of these places, only one of them is copied. For example, if the User object FRED exists on two separate NetWare 3.1*x* servers, NDS creates only one FRED in the bindery context. It is best to resolve all conflicts by renaming or deleting users before beginning the synchronization process.

3. Be sure you have sufficient rights to perform the NetSync installation.

You must have full rights in the SYS:SYSTEM directory on the NetWare 4 server and on each of the NetWare 3.1*x* servers on which you wish to install NetSync. The installation program allows you to use different login names for the NetWare 3.1*x* servers.

**Installing NetSync on the NetWare 4 Server**

You must perform the NetWare 4 portion of the NetSync installation first. The NetWare 3.1*x* NetSync NLM will not install properly unless it is able to communicate with NetSync on the NetWare 4 server. Follow these steps:

1. Load the NetSync NLM on the NetWare 4 server. The NetWare 4 version of NetSync is called NETSYNC4.NLM. Use the following command at the server console:

```
LOAD NETSYNC4
```

You see a screen listing NetWare 3.1x servers that have been authorized for NetSync. (If this is your first installation, the list will be empty.) Press ↵ to continue.

**2.** Authorize the NetWare 3.1x server. You are presented with the NetSync Options menu. Select the first option, Edit Server List.

**3.** Press Ins to add a new entry to the list. You are asked to provide the following information:

- **3.1x File Server Name:** This is the name of the file server you wish to authorize for NetSync. If you are authorizing more than one server, enter the name of the first one.

- **NetSync Password:** Enter a password to be used by the NetSync program. This is not a user or administrator password, but a temporary password. You use it to establish communication between the NetSync modules on the NetWare 4 and NetWare 3.1x servers during installation. Remember this password. You are not required to use the same password for each NetWare 3.1x server, but it is easier to remember the passwords if you do.

- **Install NetSync Files on the 3.1x Server:** Answer Yes to copy the files needed for NetSync to the 3.1x server. Under most circumstances you will want to do this, although you would choose not to copy these files if the files were already installed or if you planned to install them manually.

- **Copy 3.1x Bindery to 4.x:** Answer Yes here to start the bindery synchronization process. Answer No only in special cases (for example, if you wish to install NetSync files but not use NetSync yet), because a negative response here will cause the servers to be out of synchronization.

**4.** Press Esc and then ↵. You are asked for a username and password for the NetWare 3.1x server. You need to use a username that has Read, Write, Modify, and Delete rights for the SYS:SYSTEM directory on the server. The safest way to ensure this is to use SUPERVISOR or a supervisor-equivalent user.

NetSync now begins copying files to the NetWare 3.1x server. When it is finished, you should get a message stating that copying was successful. If you do not, the most likely cause is insufficient disk space on the NetWare 3.1*x* server. If copying was not successful, you should resolve the problem (such as deleting files to make room on the server) and then reload NETSYNC3.

5. Press ⏎ to continue. The server you just installed should now appear in the Authorized 3.1x Servers list. You now have the option to modify the AUTOEXEC.NCF files on the NetWare 3.1*x* and NetWare 4 servers to automatically load NetSync.

6. If you wish to add other NetWare 3.1*x* servers to the NetSync cluster, repeat steps 2 through 5 for each server.

### Configuring the NetWare 3.1x Servers

You have now made the following changes to your NetWare 3.1*x* servers:

- You copied the NetSync programs to the SYS:SYSTEM\NETSYNC directory.

- You added to the AUTOEXEC.NCF file a command to load NETSYNC3.NLM.

- You installed updated versions of several system NLMs needed to run NetSync.

To finish the synchronization process, you must restart each of the NetWare 3.1*x* servers. Restarting them loads all the updated modules and the NETSYNC3 module. Follow these steps:

1. Make sure all users are logged out of the NetWare 3.1*x* server. Type the **DOWN** command at the server console. Type **EXIT** to return to the DOS prompt, and type **SERVER** to restart the server.

The server loads in the usual fashion and should automatically load the NETSYNC3 module. When NetSync starts for the first time, it presents you with the following prompt:

```
NetWare 4 Server Name:
```

2. Enter the name of the NetWare 4 server on which you installed NetSync. You are asked for the NetSync password. This is the password you assigned in step 3 of the previous section of this chapter.

After you enter the password, NetSync begins the synchronization process. This may take several minutes. NetWare first copies all the bindery information from the NetWare 3.1*x* server to the bindery context. Then it copies objects in the bindery context back to the NetWare 3.1*x* server.

You have now completed the NetSync installation. Try using NWADMIN to edit or create some users on the NetWare 3.1*x* servers to make sure these servers are correctly synchronized with NDS.

*Once NetSync is installed, you can no longer use SYSCON to manage users on the NetWare 3.1x server. You now must perform all administration with NDS utilities.*

## Using NetSync Options

The NetSync Options menu allows you to manage and fine-tune your synchronized servers. The menu becomes available in the NetWare 4 NETSYNC module after you have authorized at least one NetWare 3.1*x* server. A similar menu is available on the 3.1*x* server. This menu contains the following items:

- **View Active Log:** Allows you to view current events in the NetSync log file. NetSync maintains this file to keep track of operations involved in the synchronization process. This log is stored in a file called NETSYNC .LOG in the SYS:SYSTEM\NETSYNC directory. Each server maintains its own log file.

- **Log File Operations:** Allows you to maintain the log file. In the NetWare 4 server, you have the option to view the entire file. (In a NetWare 3.1*x* server, you must use a text editor to do this.) Other options allow you to control which events are shown on the log file screen, change the size of the log file, and delete the log file.

- **Edit Server List (NETSYNC4 only):** Allows you to add NetWare 3.1*x* servers to the NetSync cluster. You can also remove servers from the list. An additional option allows you to resynchronize a 3.1*x* server that is no longer synchronized, as explained in the next section.

- **Configuration Options:** Allows you to change some parameters that affect the synchronization process. For example, you can change the Watchdog Delay Interval, which is the amount of time a server waits before checking on the other servers in the cluster.

- **Move a Print Server (NETSYNC3 only):** Allows you to move the services of a NetWare 3.1*x* print server to a NetWare 4 print server.

- **Exit/Unload NetSync:** Terminates the NetSync NLM and returns to the server console. You should never unload the NETSYNC loadable modules in normal circumstances, but you may need to do this if you wish to discontinue using NetSync or to reconfigure the server. The server unloads NETSYNC automatically when you bring it down with the DOWN command.

## Resynchronizing a NetWare 3.1*x* Server

If you make any changes to a NetWare 3.1*x* server using bindery-based utilities such as SYSCON, you must resynchronize the server's bindery with NetSync. You do this through the NetSync Options menu's Edit Server List item.

When you select the server name, you are given an option to recopy the server's bindery. Choose this option only if you have lost synchronization. When you choose it, the information in the bindery overwrites any changes you have made using NetWare 4 utilities.

# Using Backup Software

A LTHOUGH NETWARE 4 can generally be trusted not to damage or erase the data you store on a server's volumes, there can still be problems. To keep your data safe, you should establish a backup strategy for the network.

NetWare 4 includes SMS (Storage Management Services), an architecture that allows data on the server, workstations, and even NDS data to be backed up. NetWare 4 also includes a basic backup application, SBACKUP. We look at these in this section, but we start with some suggestions for backup strategies.

# Backup Strategies

While installing a backup device and occasionally using it will help you avoid losing data, it's best to have a backup strategy—a detailed plan of when you will make backups, and what data will be included. There are several strategies you can use, each with its advantages and disadvantages.

## Full Backup

A full backup is the simplest type of backup, and the safest. It includes all the data on a volume or workstation. For servers with relatively small amounts of data storage, a regular full backup is the best solution. There are several advantages to this strategy:

- All files are available on each backup tape if you need to restore them.

- A minimum of configuration is required to run the backup.

There are disadvantages, however:

- The backup and restore process can be very slow with large amounts of data.

- If you have a large amount of data, a single backup tape may not be enough to hold a full backup.

## Incremental Backup

An incremental backup strategy begins with a full backup at regular intervals—perhaps once a week. Backups between the full backup store only the files that have changed since the previous backup.

For example, if you make a full backup on Monday, Tuesday's backup includes only the files changed since Monday's, Wednesday's backup includes only the files changed since Tuesday's, and so on. This system has a few advantages:

- Incremental backups are the quickest, as far as backup time is concerned.

- The latest changes are always available on the most recent tape.

However, there are some significant disadvantages to this strategy:

- Restoring a group of files can be time consuming, because they may be located on several different tapes.

- If you must restore all files, you will need all of the incremental tapes, along with the last full backup tape; if any tape is damaged or missing, you will not have an up-to-date backup of some files.

### Differential Backup

The differential backup strategy is popular because it offers the best of both worlds; it is something of a compromise between the full and incremental strategies. In this system, again, you make a full backup regularly. Between full backups, you make differential backups, which include the information changed since the full backup.

For example, if you make a full backup on Monday, Tuesday's backup includes all files changed since Monday. Wednesday's backup also includes all files changed since Monday, and so on. The advantages of this strategy are clear:

- Backups are reasonably fast because a large amount of data usually remains unchanged.

- To restore a file, or even all files, you need a maximum of two tapes: the last full backup and the last differential backup.

As you might have noticed, each successive differential backup will be larger and more time consuming than the one before. For a successful differential backup strategy, you should schedule full backups frequently enough so that the differential backups don't become inconvenient. This will depend on your users and how often data is changed on your volumes.

### Tape Rotation

With any backup method, you need a number of tapes—a minimum of one for the regular full backup and one for each day of incremental or differential backups. However, you may want to add additional tapes to provide a regularly archived backup.

In deciding on a tape-rotation scheme, realize that backups have two purposes for most companies. While they are obviously useful in case of data loss or system problems, they can also be handy for accounting and auditing purposes.

For example, a company may need to run a report on the data from the end of the previous month or year. The company might have five tapes, labeled MON through FRI. MON is used for a full backup, and TUE through FRI for differential backups. To keep an archive, the company might have four MON tapes and use MON1 one week, MON2 the next week, and so on. This ensures that backups are available for the previous four weeks, along with the current backup.

## NetWare 4 SMS Overview

SMS is divided into several subsystems that handle portions of the backup process. You will work directly with two of these subsystems:

- The *backup engine* is the actual backup application—in this case, Novell's SBACKUP.

- *Target Service Agents* (*TSAs*) are components that allow a particular device—or target—to be backed up.

TSAs are available for a wide variety of systems:

- TSA410.NLM supports backups of NetWare 4 server volumes.

- TSA312.NLM supports NetWare 3.12 server volume backups.

- TSA311.NLM supports NetWare 3.11 server volume backups.

- TSANDS.NLM supports backup and restore of the NDS database.

- TSADOS.NLM is a host TSA that runs on the server and supports backup of DOS workstations. You must also load the TSA executable on the workstation.

- TSAPROXY.NLM is a host TSA that supports backup of OS/2, UNIX, Windows 95, and Macintosh workstations. Again, you must also load a workstation version of the TSA.

When you install client software for DOS, OS/2, Windows 95, or Macintosh, you have the option of installing the workstation TSA component. You can also install it at any time by running the client software installation program.

See Chapter 3 for specific information about DOS and Windows client software and Chapter 16 for information about Macintosh client software.

## Using Novell's SBACKUP

SBACKUP is an application that runs at the NetWare 4 server console. To start this program, type **LOAD SBACKUP** at the console prompt. The SBACKUP menu, shown in Figure 11.6, is displayed. The menu includes options to back up and restore data.

**FIGURE 11.6**

The SBACKUP utility allows you to back up and restore data.

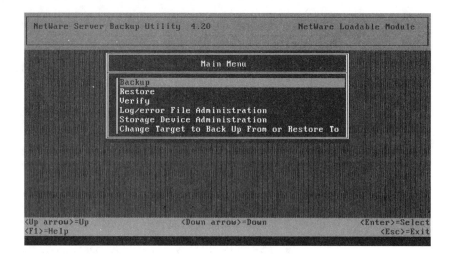

### Backing Up Data

To use SBACKUP to back up data, you must first load the appropriate TSA on the server and/or workstation. Follow these steps to perform the backup:

1. From the SBACKUP main menu, choose Backup.

2. You see a list of servers running TSA software. If you are backing up a server, select the server. If you are backing up a workstation, select the server that is running the host TSA for that workstation.

**3.** If you are backing up a server or the NDS database, you are now prompted for a username and password. This should be a user with full access to the data to be backed up, such as ADMIN.

**4.** After providing the username and password, you see a list of backup devices. Select the device to be used. If you have only one backup device, it is selected automatically.

**5.** You can now, optionally, specify a directory to use for backup logs and other files generated by SBACKUP. Press ↵ to choose a new directory or Ins to use the default directory.

**6.** Choose the type of backup to be made: Full, Differential, Incremental, or Custom.

**7.** Enter a description for the backup session; this is for your own reference and can be any text. Press F10 to continue.

**8.** Specify when to start the backup. Select Start the Backup Now to begin immediately. Select Start the Backup Later to delay the backup; you can enter a date and time for the backup to begin.

When SBACKUP has completed the backup, you see a screen indicating whether the backup was successful. This is useful for unattended backups; you can run the backup at night and check its success the following morning.

*Regardless of when you perform the backup, be sure no users are accessing files you need to back up. For this reason, it's best to schedule backups during off hours.*

### Restoring Data

The process for restoring data using SBACKUP is similar to backing it up. You need to load SBACKUP, as described above, and the appropriate TSAs before you begin the restore process. Follow the steps below to restore a file or group of files.

*These instructions are for restoring a single file or directory. If you are restoring an entire volume or the NDS database after a crash, there are many other considerations; refer to the section "NDS Troubleshooting and Disaster Recovery" in Chapter 12 for details.*

1. From the main SBACKUP menu, choose the Restore option.

2. You see a list of servers running TSA software. If you are restoring a server, select the server. If you are restoring a workstation, select the server that is running the host TSA for that workstation.

3. Choose whether you are restoring NDS or file system data.

4. If you are restoring to a server or the NDS database, you are prompted for a username and password. This should be a user with full access to the data to be overwritten, such as ADMIN.

5. After providing the username and password, you see a list of the session descriptions for backups you have performed. Select the one to restore.

6. You can now optionally change the path to the log file; this is the log that was generated when you ran a backup, and it will be used to verify the success of files you wish to restore. You can press Ins to select a directory or ↵ to accept the default.

7. You see a list of backup devices that are compatible with the backup media; most often, only one device is available, and it is selected by default. Accept the default or, if necessary, choose another device.

8. You see the Restore Options screen, where you specify a file, directory, volume, or portion of the NDS database to be restored. You can also enter a new location for the restored version.

9. Press F10 to accept the options and begin the restore process.

# Summary

N THIS CHAPTER we've looked at various aspects of managing NetWare 4 networks, including bindery services, integration with NetWare 3.1x servers, and backup systems:

- Bindery Services allows a portion of the Directory tree to act as a bindery to support NetWare 3.1x clients and software.

- NetSync allows NetWare 3.1*x* servers to be synchronized with an NDS container and managed with NDS utilities.

- SMS is NetWare 4's built-in architecture for backup software. The SBACKUP utility, included with NetWare 4, allows you to back up server data, workstation data, and NDS information.

In the next chapter we'll look at some more technical aspects of network and server management. We will examine the utilities and techniques you can use to make servers work together, improve server and network efficiency, and prevent or recover from network disasters.

# Optimizing and Troubleshooting the Network

LTHOUGH NETWARE 4 is a very efficient system, there are ways it can be improved. In this chapter we look at the utilities and commands you can use to monitor and optimize the performance of the server and network.

We also look at several of the more complicated issues that arise when working with multiple servers on the network, including adding and removing servers, merging Directory trees, and synchronizing time. Finally, we examine some common problems that can occur with NDS and the network and how you can deal with them.

# Optimizing the Server

N THIS SECTION we examine three functions you can use at the server console to manage its configuration and settings and monitor the performance of the server and network:

- SET commands allow you to configure individual server parameters.

- The SERVMAN utility provides a menu-oriented alternative to the SET command.

- The MONITOR utility allows you to monitor the performance of the server and network.

## Using SET Commands

We looked at the SET command in Chapter 10. You can use this command to change an individual parameter. There are hundreds of available parameters in various categories. As an example, this command turns on file compression:

```
SET File Compression = ON
```

You can use the SERVMAN utility, described below, as an easy way to browse through the various SET commands in categories. For a list of useful SET commands to control network performance, see Appendix D.

## Using the **SERVMAN** Utility

SERVMAN (Server Manager) is an NLM that allows you to view server information and control server settings. Rather than use the SET command to set parameters, you can browse through available parameters with SERVMAN, select one to change, and assign a new value. Changes you make with SERVMAN take effect immediately. You also have the option of saving changes to the AUTOEXEC.NCF or TIMESYNC.CFG file.

To change settings, select Server Parameters from the main SERVMAN screen. The next screen, shown in Figure 12.1, lists several categories of options you can set. After selecting a category, you can review the list of possible settings for the category and their current values.

**F I G U R E 12.I**

The SERVMAN utility allows you to browse server settings by category.

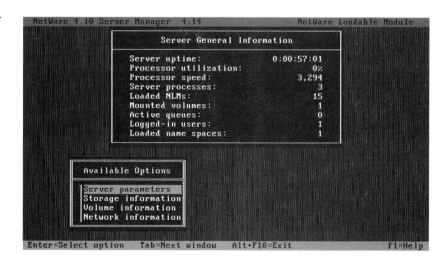

As an example of a category screen, Figure 12.2 shows Directory Services Parameters. Select a setting and press ↵ to change its value. After you change one or more settings with SERVMAN, you are asked whether to save the changes in AUTOEXEC.NCF or TIMESYNC.CFG, whichever is appropriate. If you answer Yes, NetWare sets that option each time the server starts. If you do not wish to save the changes, select No.

**FIGURE 12.2**

SERVMAN lists specific settings in each category, such as these for Directory Services.

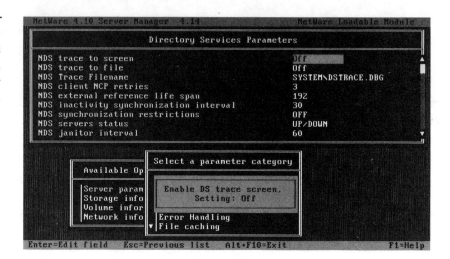

*If you select No, although changes are not written to the file, the setting is in effect until the server is restarted or until you change it again.*

## Using the MONITOR Utility

MONITOR is probably the most widely used NetWare utility. You can start this utility with the LOAD MONITOR command at the server console. The main MONITOR screen, shown in Figure 12.3, provides a dynamic display of information about the server. If you watch these numbers carefully, you can be sure the server and network are running smoothly.

Along with the information displayed at the top of the screen, MONITOR provides a menu you can use to display specific categories of information.

FIGURE 12.3

MONITOR provides
statistics that let you
know how the server
is running.

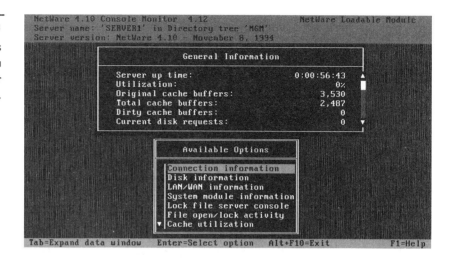

Most of these include running statistics that are updated as server conditions change. MONITOR offers these options:

- **Connection information:** Lets you see who is logged into the server. You can view specific information about a user, such as files the user has open, by selecting the user's login name and pressing ↵. Pressing the Del key when a user's name is highlighted forcefully logs out the user. This is similar to the CLEAR STATION command. Before you do this, be sure the user does not have any data files open; data may be lost if a file is being written to when you disconnect the user.

- **Disk information:** Displays information about disks on the server and the volumes on them.

- **LAN/WAN information:** Displays network numbers, LAN driver information, and statistics for each LAN or WAN network.

- **System module information:** Lists the NLMs loaded on the server.

- **Lock file server console:** Allows you to enter a password to lock the console. Users won't be able to access the console without this password (or the ADMIN password).

- **File open/lock activity:** Displays information about open files on a volume.

- **Cache utilization:** Displays statistics about cache buffers and lets you determine which applications are using them.

- **Processor utilization:** Displays statistics about processor cycles used by each module.

- **Resource utilization:** Displays statistics about resources used by each module.

- **Memory utilization:** Displays the types and quantities of memory used by each module.

- **Scheduling information:** Shows what percentage of the server's time is spent with each module. You can easily determine whether a particular module is slowing down the server (see Figure 12.4).

**FIGURE 12.4**

Scheduling information shows which NLMs are using the server's time.

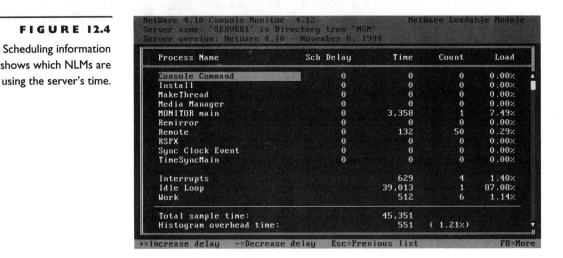

# Working with Multiple Servers

ONE OF NETWARE 4'S strengths is the ability to transparently work with many servers. However, there are considerations you should be aware of when adding or removing a server from the network. In this section we look at the process of adding or removing a server and also at the steps involved in merging NDS Directory trees.

## Adding Servers to the Network

When you install NetWare 4 on a new machine, the installation program analyzes the existing network and servers and attempts to make the server fit in with no trouble. However, there are a few items you should check during and after the installation process:

- Be sure the server is attached to the network when you install it and that all other servers are up, to allow the network to be scanned.

- Be sure the server is set as the proper type of time server. (See the section "Managing Time Synchronization" later in this chapter.) Also be sure to set the correct time zone during the installation.

- Check the external network numbers; be sure they are correct.

- You may need to create replicas of one or more partitions on the server. Only the first four servers in a network receive a replica by default. See Chapter 6 for details about partitioning and replication.

*For an explanation of the actual steps involved in installing NetWare 4 on a new server, see Chapter 13.*

## Removing Servers

In the course of managing a NetWare 4 network, you may need to remove a server from the network. This may be because you are taking down the server for an extended period of time, replacing it with a new machine, or simply eliminating it from the network. Follow these steps to remove a server without causing problems with NDS:

1. Using the PARTMGR or Partition Manager utility, remove any replicas on the server.

2. If any master replicas were stored on the server, change another server's read/write replica to master status.

3. Bring down the server.

4. Delete the Server and Volume NDS objects. You can delete Volume objects within NWADMIN; to delete the Server object, you must use the PARTMGR or Partition Manager utility.

# Merging Directory Trees

If you have created multiple Directory trees for different departments or divisions within your network, you may want to merge them into a single tree for simplified management. When you merge two Directory trees, objects in the [Root] of one tree (the *source* tree) are moved to the [Root] of the second (*target*) tree. You must perform the merge process at the server that contains the master replica of the source tree.

*You use the DSMERGE utility at the server console to merge Directory trees.*

### Merging Considerations

Before you can begin the merge process, check all of the following items:

- All servers that contain a replica of the [Root] partition for either tree must be up and running, and they must be accessible over the network.

- The schema for the trees must be the same. If you have used a product that extends the Directory schema on one tree, you must make the same changes on the other tree.

- The [Root] object of the source tree cannot contain any leaf or Alias objects.

- The trees must have different tree names.

- The servers containing the [Root] partitions of the trees must be running the same version of NetWare.

- You must have the password for an administrator with access to all objects for each Directory tree.

*To protect your data, back up the Directory of both trees before you begin. Most NetWare backup programs include an option to back up NDS information. See Chapter 11 for information about SBACKUP, a backup utility included with NetWare 4.*

### Performing the Merge Process

Directory trees can be merged two at a time. Follow these steps to merge two Directory trees:

**1.** Type **LOAD DSMERGE** at the server console to start the DSMERGE utility. You must do this on the server containing the master replica of the source tree. The main DSMERGE screen is shown in Figure 12.5.

**FIGURE 12.5**

The DSMERGE utility allows you to merge Directory trees.

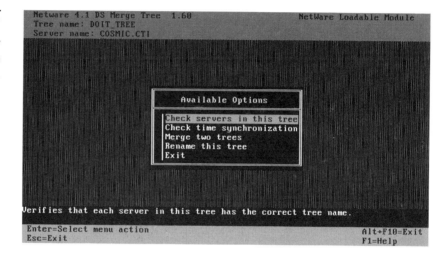

**2.** Select the Check Time Synchronization option. You see a list of servers and their time synchronization status. The difference in times (Time Delta) must be under two seconds for all servers in both trees. You may need to change each server to use the same time source. Time synchronization is explained in the next section.

**3.** Select the Merge Two Trees option. The source tree is set automatically to the server's tree. Fill in the destination tree and provide an administrator name and password for each tree, as shown in Figure 12.6.

**4.** Press F10 to start the merge. The merge process may take quite a while, depending on the speed of your network and the number of existing replicas.

**FIGURE 12.6**

Enter the information to merge two trees.

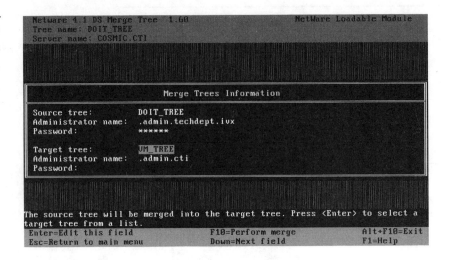

*If you wish to merge several trees into a single destination tree, you must merge them one at a time. Allow one merge process to finish before starting the next one.*

# Managing Time Synchronization

ECAUSE THE NDS database is distributed across multiple servers, all the servers must keep the same time; otherwise, there would be no way to ensure that an update is accurately sent to all replicas. NetWare 4's *time synchronization* feature provides a way to synchronize time between servers.

NDS uses a process called *time stamping* to assign a time to each change in the Directory. Changes can be made to an object in the network from any server at any time. Time stamping ensures that these changes are made in the correct order and that all replicas receive the correct information.

Every activity in NDS is documented with a time stamp. Time stamps use UTC (Universal Coordinated Time), the international standard for accurate time. You may recognize UTC by its old name, GTM (Greenwich Mean Time).

Because the UTC system is independent of time zones, the entire network can have a standard time even if servers are located in different time zones. When you install a server, NetWare 4 asks you for a *time zone offset*. This offset is used to calculate the local time from the network's UTC time. For example, the time offset for Boise, Idaho, is 7:00:00 behind, or seven hours behind UTC. If the time in Boise is 2:00 A.M., UTC time is 9:00 A.M. NetWare also takes Daylight Saving Time into account.

# Types of Time Servers

Because clocks in computers tend to deviate slightly, servers will inevitably end up with different times. To compensate for this problem, NDS's time synchronization feature uses one or more of the servers on the network as *time servers*. Each NetWare 4 server is a time server of one type or another. There are four types of time servers, each with a specific purpose. We examine each of these types in the following sections.

### Single Reference Time Server

A *single reference time server* provides a single, authoritative source of time on the network. The first NetWare 4 server installed on a network defaults to this configuration.

If you use a single reference time server, you must configure all other servers as secondary time servers. Each secondary time server receives the time from the single reference server. This is the typical configuration for small networks; it is set up by default. Figure 12.7 shows an example of a small network using a single reference time server.

*Because the single reference time server never adjusts its clock, you must be sure its time is set correctly.*

### Primary Time Servers

In a larger network, it's often difficult to assign one authoritative time source. *Primary time servers* provide a solution to this problem. Primary time servers negotiate with other primary and reference servers on the network to determine the correct time; they settle on a compromise when they differ.

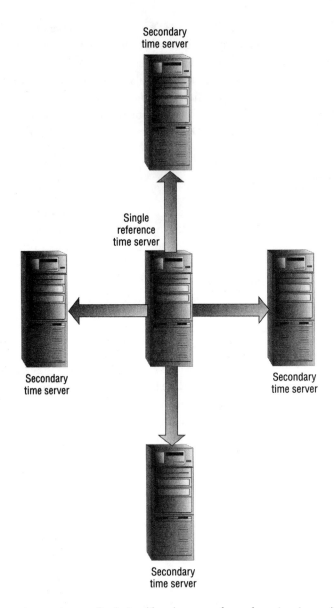

Secondary
time server

Single
reference
time server

Secondary
time server

Secondary
time server

Secondary
time server

If a primary server finds itself to be out of synchronization with the network time, it gradually speeds up or slows down until it is back in synchronization. Because primary time servers work by negotiation, there must be at least one other time source—a reference server or another primary server—on the network.

The negotiation process of primary time servers ensures that the servers agree on a time, but this time is not guaranteed to be accurate. (For NDS, agreement is more important than accuracy.) In situations where accurate time is important, you should use a reference time server along with one or more primary servers. Figure 12.8 shows a typical primary time server arrangement.

**FIGURE 12.8**

Primary time servers negotiate with each other to determine the correct time.

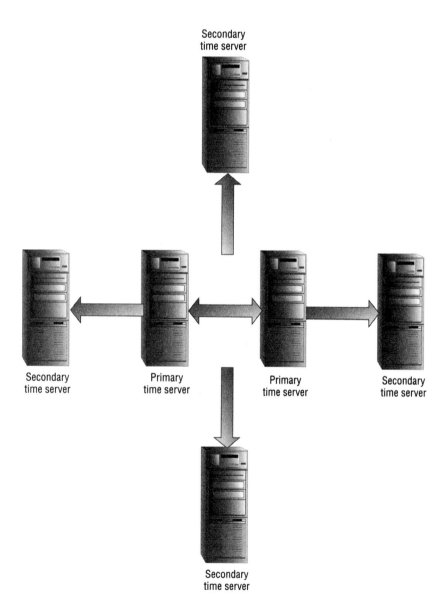

### Secondary Time Servers

A *secondary time server* provides the time to client workstations but not to any other servers. When you install a new server on a network that already has a single reference server, the new server is configured as a secondary time server by default.

Secondary time servers do not negotiate to determine the correct time. They get time information from a single source: a primary or single reference time server. You must define at least one primary server, or a single reference server, before you can configure a secondary time server.

### Reference Time Servers

A *reference time server* is useful when accurate time is important. It is usually attached to an external time source. This could be an accurate hardware clock or a modem or radio link to a reliable time source, such as the clock the U.S. Naval Observatory maintains. Although less accurate, the PC's internal clock can also be used.

The reference time server relies on its external time source for the correct time; it never adjusts its clock in response to other servers. When primary time servers negotiate the network time, the reference server's time is considered an accurate source; the primary servers eventually correct themselves to match that time. If you use a reference server, you must configure at least one primary time server. Figure 12.9 shows a network arrangement using primary and reference time servers.

*Reference, single reference, and primary time servers are called* time sources *or* time providers. *Secondary time servers and client machines are* time consumers.

# Methods of Time Synchronization

You can choose to install time synchronization in either the default configuration or a custom configuration. The default configuration will work well in most single-location networks. For larger networks and networks with multiple locations, a custom configuration will be more efficient.

### Default Configuration

The default time synchronization configuration uses one single reference time server to provide the time to all servers on the network. The first server

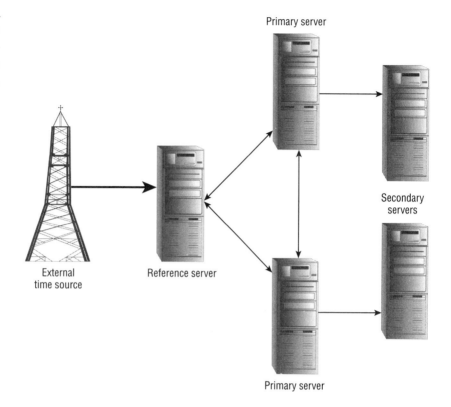

**FIGURE 12.9**

A reference time server
is usually attached to an
external time source.

installed will be the single reference time server. All other servers on the network are configured as secondary time servers when they are installed.

In the default configuration, the single reference server broadcasts time
information using the *Service Advertising Protocol (SAP)*, a standard Net-
Ware communication protocol. Because SAP packets are broadcast to the
entire network, using SAP will increase traffic on your network, particularly
over WAN links.

NetWare 4 provides this default method to simplify installation and to
enable network administrators to set up a network without necessarily understanding the complexities of the time synchronization process. This can be an
effective strategy, but it has the following disadvantages:

- If the single reference time server goes down, all other servers will lose
  their source of accurate time and begin to drift out of synchronization.
  One of the other servers can take over as the single reference server, but
  you must arrange this manually with a SET command at the server.

- All servers in the network will need to contact the single reference server frequently to receive the current time. This activity adds traffic to the network, particularly if servers are at opposite ends of a WAN link. Worse, if a server loses its connection to the single reference server, it will also lose time synchronization.

- Because each server is not given a specific list of time servers to receive time from, any server that claims to be a single reference time server will be used. This means that if a server is accidentally configured as a time provider, the network will end up with conflicting sources of time.

*This is one reason to be sure to attach a new server to the network before installing Net-Ware 4 on it. If you install while disconnected, NetWare will assume that this is the first server and configure it as a single reference server.*

### Custom Configuration

Using a custom configuration, you can optimize time synchronization on your network. You'll need to plan your custom configuration, using the right combination of primary, secondary, and reference time servers to minimize network traffic. Don't use custom configurations unless you really need to; they require careful planning and maintenance. The default configuration is usually sufficient for a small company or department.

Custom configurations require you to create a file, TIMESYNC.CFG, at each server to specify time sources. You will also need to update each of these files each time you add a new time server. NetWare does not provide a centralized method for maintaining these files.

**PLANNING A CUSTOM CONFIGURATION**  When you create a plan for custom time synchronization, the main factors to consider are the physical locations of servers and the speed of the connections between them. Here are some general rules to follow:

- Create primary time servers or reference servers in major locations.

- Configure each server to receive time from the nearest primary server.

- Be sure there are fast network links between each of the primary time servers.

- If you use a reference time server, place it near the network backbone, where it can be reached quickly by each of the primary servers.

Because a custom configuration uses several independent time sources, this strategy does not have a single point of failure. As long as network communication lines remain open, servers will have more than one available source of time. This design ensures that no server will lose time synchronization.

*Avoid using more than five primary and reference time servers on a network; the traffic generated by the voting process can cause an excess of network traffic. For larger networks, you will want to use multiple time provider groups, as described in the next section.*

## Using Time Provider Groups

A *time provider group* usually consists of a reference time server, one or more primary time servers, and a number of secondary time servers. A simple time provider group was shown earlier in Figure 12.9.

In a large network with many servers communicating across WAN links, single time provider groups are not practical. The voting process used by primary servers adds traffic to the WAN link and is likely to create a bottleneck. In this situation you should use multiple time provider groups. An example of a network using multiple time provider groups is shown in Figure 12.10.

If you use multiple time provider groups, it is important to use some form of external time source for synchronization. If each location's reference time server communicates with the same external source (such as a radio time signal), you can keep a consistent time across all locations without adding traffic to the WAN.

## Implementing Time Synchronization

To use time synchronization on your network in a custom configuration, you need to adjust settings on each server. These settings determine several factors, including the type of time server the server will act as and which server it will use as a time source.

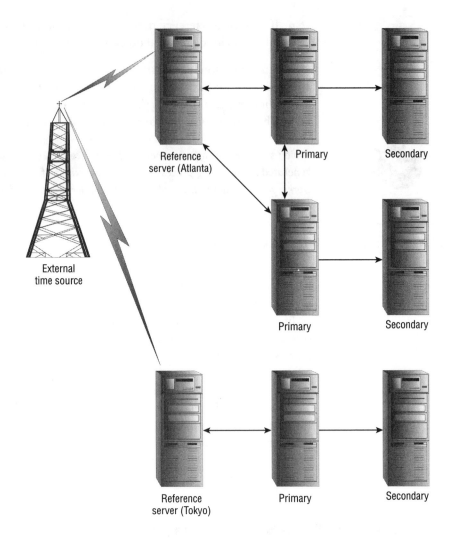

**FIGURE 12.10**

You should use multiple time provider groups on a larger network.

External time source

Reference server (Atlanta)

Primary

Secondary

Primary

Secondary

Reference server (Tokyo)

Primary

Secondary

## Setting Time Synchronization Parameters

You can use several SET parameters to control your network's time synchronization. These SET commands all begin with SET TIMESYNC and are described in Table 12.1. Rather than using the SET command, you can make these changes in the server's TIMESYNC.CFG file. You should use this method unless the change is meant to be temporary.

| **TABLE 12.1**<br>NetWare 4 Time Synchronization SET Parameters | **SET TIMESYNC PARAMETER** | **DESCRIPTION** |
|---|---|---|
| | Configured Sources | Controls which type of time source is used. If set to ON, you must specify a list of time sources in the TIMESYNC.CFG file. If set to OFF, the SAP protocol is used to listen for a time source |
| | Directory Tree Mode | Controls whether SAP packets from other Directory trees are accepted. If set to ON, SAP packets are ignored unless they come from the server's own Directory tree. This parameter prevents time servers on different trees from creating conflicts |
| | Hardware Clock | Controls whether the server's hardware clock will be used for time synchronization. This parameter should be set to OFF only if the server will use an external time source |
| | Polling Count | Controls how many time packets are exchanged when servers are polled. Increasing this number can create unnecessary traffic. The default is three |
| | Polling Interval | Controls how often the server polls other servers. This number defaults to 600 seconds (10 minutes). If you change this, you must use the same setting for all servers on the network |
| | Service Advertising | Controls whether the SAP protocol will be used to broadcast time. If it is turned off, you must create a list of time sources in the TIMESYNC.CFG file of each server |
| | Synchronization Radius | Controls the maximum amount a server's time can be adjusted and still remain in synchronization with other servers. It defaults to 2000 milliseconds. Increasing this parameter may prevent servers from losing synchronization |
| | Type | Determines the type of time server the server is currently acting as: reference, primary, secondary, or single reference |

*An easy way to specify SET parameters and save them in the AUTOEXEC.NCF and TIMESYNC.CFG files is to use the SERVMAN utility, described earlier in this chapter.*

### Creating the TIMESYNC.CFG Files

If you are using a custom configuration, you must create a TIMESYNC.CFG file in each server's SYS:SYSTEM directory. The file consists of two parts:

- **Parameters:** These are the parameters listed in Table 12.1. When they are used in the TIMESYNC.CFG file, you do not need to include the SET TIMESYNC portion of the command.

- **Time Sources:** This is a list of time sources for a custom configuration. The first server in the list will be polled as a time source. If it is unavailable, the other servers in the list will be tried in order.

Here is an example of a TIMESYNC.CFG file. This file is for the server CORP1, which is a primary time server. It negotiates with the servers CORP2 and CORP3 to determine the correct time.

```
#TIMESYNC.CFG for Server CORP1
# (lines beginning with # are comments)
Configured Sources = ON
Directory Tree Mode = ON
Hardware Clock = OFF
Polling Count = 3
Polling Interval = 600
Service Advertising = OFF
Synchronization Radius = 2000
Type = PRIMARY
# Time Sources
Time Source = CORP2
Time Source = CORP3
```

Since time synchronization operates at a lower level than NDS, you can't use NDS utilities to make changes to time synchronization. These changes must be made in the individual TIMESYNC.CFG file for each server.

## Starting and Verifying Time Synchronization

If you have configured time synchronization correctly, the servers should synchronize with each other as soon as they are brought online. You can verify synchronization by typing the **TIME** command at each server's console. Here is the typical output of the TIME command:

```
Time zone string: "MST7MDT"
DST status: ON
DST start: Sunday, April 17, 1998 2:00 am MST
DST end: Sunday, October 29, 1998 2:00 am MDT
Time synchronization is active.
Time is synchronized to the network.
Sunday, July 2, 1998 3:35:14 am UTC
Saturday, July 1, 1998 9:35:14 pm MDT
```

Check that the message "Time is synchronized to the network" is displayed on each server. If the servers are not synchronized, check the time synchronization settings; you may need to bring servers down and back up to synchronize them.

*After time synchronization is established, you should avoid changing the time on any server. If the server is a time consumer, your change will be ignored because time is received from the other servers on the network; if it is a time provider, it will affect the network's time, which could corrupt NDS data.*

# *NDS Troubleshooting and Disaster Recovery*

NDS IS THE most important new feature of NetWare 4. Not surprisingly, it is also the most common source of problems with NetWare 4 servers. In the following sections we discuss how to avoid some of the most common NDS problems and how to correct them when they do happen. We also look at techniques you can use to recover from a network disaster, including restoring the NDS database or a server's SYS: volume.

## Avoiding Common NDS Problems

There is no way to avoid all NDS problems. In fact, if you deal with a NetWare 4 server for any length of time, you will undoubtedly need to handle several problems. However, many of the most common NDS problems can be avoided with a bit of planning. Here are some tips to keep NDS running smoothly:

- Always keep at least three replicas for each partition. If a replica is lost, even if it's the master replica, it can be restored if another replica is available.

- Make frequent backups of the NDS database. The frequency depends on how often changes are made in your network, but you should perform the backup at least once a week. See Chapter 11 for information about backup software and strategies.

- Use a single workstation to manage NDS partitions—when you are splitting partitions, merging partitions, or moving container objects. This will make it easy to keep track of the changes you have made and avoid inconsistencies. Otherwise, different locations in the network can receive conflicting messages, causing NDS corruption.

- Never let any server's SYS: volume run out of space. The NDS database is kept in a hidden directory on the SYS: volume. If the volume runs out of space, no changes can be made to NDS, and replicas on the server lose synchronization. To be safe, keep at least 50MB free at all times. If possible, keep space-consuming data, such as print queues, on a volume other than SYS:.

- Use DSREPAIR (described in the section "Using DSREPAIR to Check Synchronization" later in this chapter) to check synchronization before performing any complicated NDS operation. This includes merging partitions, splitting partitions, moving a container object, and merging Directory trees. It is also a good idea to make a backup copy of NDS immediately before performing any of these operations.

## Managing NDS Inconsistencies

Each change you make to an NDS replica is passed to each of the other servers that contain a replica. Depending on communication delays, network use, and the complexity of the change, it can take anywhere from ten seconds to two hours for all replicas to receive the change.

Fortunately, NDS was designed to deal with this time requirement. The NDS database is *loosely consistent,* which means it remains functional even if replicas do not have exactly the same information. You may occasionally notice these inconsistencies, but they do not necessarily represent a problem with NDS.

The process that NDS uses to send information between replicas is called *synchronization*. Two replicas are synchronized if they contain exactly the same information. In a busy network, the synchronization process is happening constantly to update the latest changes.

The exact process depends on the type of change. Simple changes, such as adding a User object or changing a property, are synchronized quickly. All the server must do is send updates to each server that has a replica of the partition where the object is located. Creating a partition is also a relatively simple task.

Complex changes include joining partitions, moving partitions, and merging Directory trees. These changes require updates to multiple partitions, and each server with a replica of any one of the partitions must be contacted to send updates. These changes can take a long time and cause increased network traffic.

## Symptoms of NDS Problems

Although some inconsistencies between NDS replicas are normal, severe inconsistencies may indicate a corrupt NDS database or another problem. Here are the symptoms you should watch for:

- Changes made to an NDS object or its rights seem to disappear.

- An object or its properties change unexpectedly. For example, a user can no longer log in because the password is incorrect, but the user has not changed the password.

- Errors may be inconsistent. For example, a user may be able to log in after several attempts.

- Unknown objects, shown with a question mark, appear in the Directory tree. It is normal for these objects to show up when a server has been removed or when a partitioning operation is in progress. However, if they appear without an apparent cause, there may be a problem.

If you notice any of these symptoms or if any part of NDS seems to behave inconsistently, follow the instructions in the following sections to narrow down and correct the problem. If a corrupt Directory is left alone, it will gradually become worse. Be sure to follow the troubleshooting advice below as soon as you notice any symptoms.

# Checking NDS Synchronization

If the problems you are having with NDS are not severe, you should let the servers run for a few hours before attempting any repairs. NDS double-checks itself, and it may repair the problem automatically. Do not take down any servers, because this prevents NDS from synchronizing and correcting errors.

If the problem continues or worsens, you should check the synchronization of the server. You can use the DSREPAIR and DSTRACE utilities to accomplish this, as described in the following sections.

## Using DSREPAIR to Check Synchronization

DSREPAIR is a versatile utility you can use to solve many NDS problems. You can use one of the functions of DSREPAIR to check the synchronization of replicas on the network. You should do this if you suspect a problem in NDS. In addition, you should check the synchronization before performing a major operation, such as merging trees, splitting partitions, joining partitions, or moving a container object.

To use this function of DSREPAIR, follow these steps:

1. Start the DSREPAIR utility by typing **LOAD DSREPAIR** at the server console.

2. Select Replica Synchronization.

3. Enter a full distinguished name for the administrator and a password. DSREPAIR will use these to log in to NDS.

4. DSREPAIR checks synchronization for all replicas and displays a log file, as shown in the example in Figure 12.11. Examine this log file. If OK appears next to each server, the server is fully synchronized.

## Using the DSTRACE Parameter

DSTRACE is a special SET parameter you can use to monitor the activities of NDS. Information is displayed each time NDS replicas are synchronized. This information can be helpful when you are diagnosing an NDS problem. The output of DSTRACE will tell you whether synchronization is successful and if any replicas cannot be reached.

FIGURE 12.11

The DSREPAIR
synchronization log
displays synchronization
status for all servers.

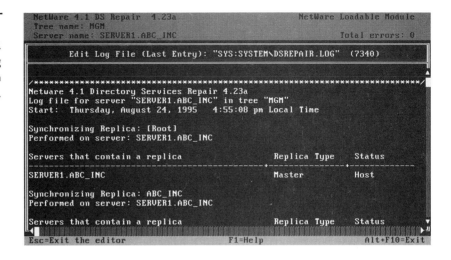

**FIGURE 12.11**

The DSREPAIR
synchronization log
displays synchronization
status for all servers.

To start tracing NDS, type this command at the server console:

```
SET DSTRACE = ON
```

Press Alt+Esc at the server console to switch to the Directory Services
Trace screen, shown in Figure 12.12.

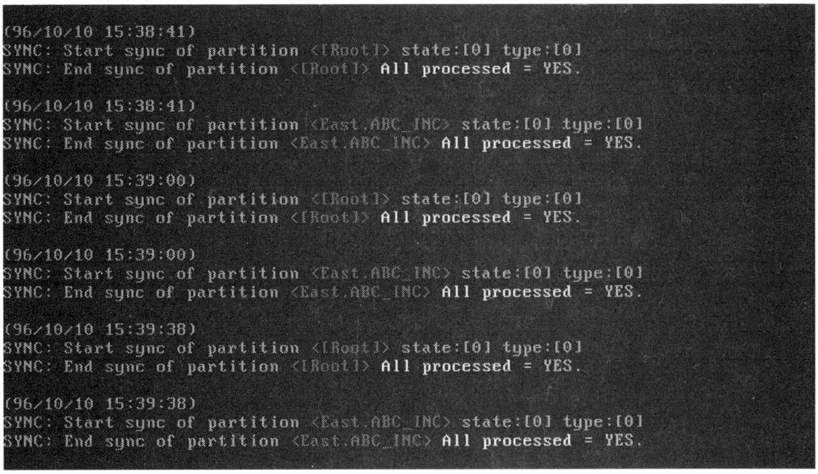

**FIGURE 12.12**

The DSTRACE screen
displays information each
time NDS replicas are
synchronized.

You can leave DSTRACE running and check the screen periodically for problems. One of the most common problems will produce this message:

```
SYNC: End sync of partition name. All processed = NO.
```

If NO is displayed here and the message repeats after each synchronization attempt, NDS has a serious problem. You should run the DSREPAIR utility, as described in the next section.

When you no longer need the DSTRACE screen, at the server console, type:

```
SET DSTRACE = OFF
```

## Checking Synchronization with NDS Manager

If you are using NetWare 4.11 or later, you can also check a replica's synchronization from the NDS Manager utility. Follow these steps under Windows 3.1 or Windows 95:

**1.** Run NDSMGR (NDSMGR16.EXE or NDSMGR32.EXE).

**2.** Highlight the root container object for the partition.

**3.** Select Object ➤ Check Synchronization.

The results are displayed in a dialog.

## Repairing NDS Problems

Once you have determined that there is a problem in the NDS database, you should take action to repair it. The next sections describe three ways to do this. You should try the DSREPAIR utility first. The second option, forcing replica synchronization, is a more drastic action. As a last resort, you can restore an NDS backup.

### Using the DSREPAIR Utility

The DSREPAIR utility provides several options for repairing NDS problems. These are listed on the utility's Available Options menu, shown in Figure 12.13. The most useful of these is Unattended Full Repair. When you select this option, NetWare scans the NDS database for errors and repairs the errors if possible.

The other options allow you to perform specific steps for troubleshooting, which may be useful if the Unattended Full Repair option fails or if you are troubleshooting a specific problem.

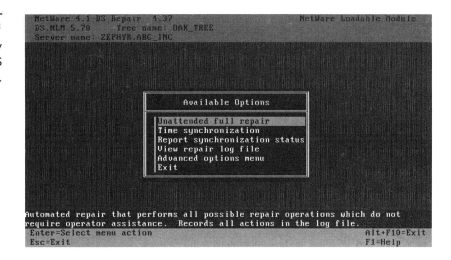

*Before you run DSREPAIR, make a backup copy of NDS using your backup software. If the NDS database becomes corrupted further, you may lose information on all replicas. Since there may be errors in the database, do not overwrite an older backup if you have one.*

After DSREPAIR has finished scanning the database, it displays a log file. This log lists the tasks that were performed and problems that were found and corrected. Examine the log carefully and make sure any errors were repaired.

Although DSREPAIR can repair most NDS corruption, you may lose some information in the process. After DSREPAIR has finished its work, use NWADMIN to look at the Directory tree and verify that all objects are intact; replace any missing objects.

### Repairing NDS with NDS Manager

An alternative to DSREPAIR is the NDS Manager Windows utility. This utility allows you to maintain partitions and replicas and also includes a comprehensive set of NDS repair tools. To access these features, follow these steps:

1. Run NDS Manager (NDSMGR16.EXE or NDSMGR32.EXE).

2. Select the root container object of the partition.

3. Select Object ➤ Partition Continuity.

You are now shown the status for the partition and its replicas. The Repair menu, available from this screen, provides several options for diagnosing and repairing NDS problems. These include the following:

- **Synchronize Immediately:** Forces synchronization for the replica from the master replica. Changes that have been made on other replicas may be lost.

- **Receive Updates:** Checks other replicas for updates and synchronizes them with the master replica.

- **Send Updates:** Sends updates to the other replicas.

- **Verify Remote Server IDs:** Checks the servers containing replicas for the proper identification.

- **Repair Replica:** Attempts to repair any problems with the replica's database.

- **Repair Local Database:** Allows you to run DSREPAIR on the server containing a replica.

- **Assign New Master:** Provides an easy way to assign a read/write replica as the new master replica.

- **Remove Server:** Removes a server's NDS object and any replicas it contains. This is useful when you are removing a server from the network.

- **Repair Volume Objects:** Attempts to fix problems with Volume objects and their security assignments.

- **Abort Operation:** Aborts an operation (such as merge partitions or synchronize) in progress.

Try the appropriate options based on the problems you have noticed. If you are unable to correct the NDS problem using these features, you may have to restore an NDS backup, as described in the next section.

## Restoring an NDS Backup

As a last resort, you can restore NDS from a backup. Assuming the backup was performed before the NDS problems began, this process should permit a full recovery. Note the date of the backup. If you have made changes to NDS (such as creating users or changing rights) since that date, you must reenter them after restoring the backup.

To restore NDS, follow these steps:

**1.** Make a new backup on a separate tape, just in case.

**2.** Use Partition Manager or the PARTMGR utility to delete all replicas for the partition.

**3.** Restore the partition data using your backup software to create a new master replica.

**4.** Re-create the other replicas.

*Be sure all users in the Directory tree are logged out of the network when you back up or restore NDS data. Do not bring down any servers, however.*

## Restoring the SYS: Volume

If a server crashed or has been replaced by a new machine, you may need to restore the SYS: volume from a backup. Because this volume holds the Net-Ware 4 installation and the NDS database, restoring it is a complex process. Follow these steps to restore a SYS: volume:

**1.** Delete the Server object and Volume objects from the NDS tree. You must use the PARTMGR or Partition Manager utility to delete a Server object.

**2.** If the server that crashed contained the master replica, change one of the read/write replicas to master status.

**3.** Fix the hardware problem and reinstall NetWare 4 as though it were a new server. Install the server into the same Directory tree.

**4.** Restore a backup of the data (not NDS) onto the server.

5. Create any replicas that are needed on the server.

6. Check the synchronization of replicas before proceeding further (use DSMERGE, as described in the section "Performing the Merge Process" earlier in this chapter).

7. If the server contained the master replica, reassign it as the master replica if desired. Change the status of the server that you changed in step 2 back to a read/write replica.

# Summary

N THIS CHAPTER we've looked at ways of optimizing the server and network, monitoring performance, and making servers work together:

- You can use SET commands to change server parameters.

- You can use the SERVMAN utility to control SET parameters from a menu.

- The MONITOR utility provides a window into the server's performance.

- You need to use specific techniques when adding or removing servers from the network.

We also looked at the process of merging NDS trees and, finally, at NDS troubleshooting techniques and the process of recovering from a disaster, including restoring backups.

In the next chapter we'll look at the actual process of installing a NetWare 4 server, along with the hardware requirements for a server. We will also present the steps needed to upgrade from NetWare 3.1$x$, 4.$x$, and earlier NetWare versions.

# Installing NetWare 4

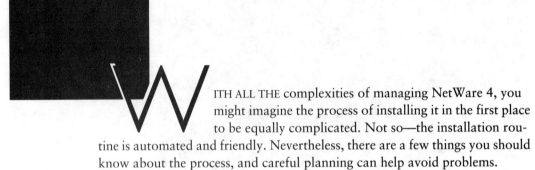

ITH ALL THE complexities of managing NetWare 4, you might imagine the process of installing it in the first place to be equally complicated. Not so—the installation routine is automated and friendly. Nevertheless, there are a few things you should know about the process, and careful planning can help avoid problems.

In this chapter we look at all aspects of NetWare 4 installation. We begin with a guide to determining the type of computer and other hardware you will need for a server. We then look at the installation process itself, including new installations and upgrade installations.

# Evaluating Hardware Requirements

OR A SUCCESSFUL installation, you should carefully consider the hardware you're going to use before you purchase it. While most of the PCs on the market today would function as NetWare 4 servers, some would work better than others—and some aren't worth the added expense.

In this section we look at the various aspects of a PC—memory, disk storage, CPU, and so on—and show what you'll need for a NetWare 4 server. These guidelines will serve as a starting point if you're selecting a machine for use as a server or determining whether an existing machine (possibly running an earlier version of NetWare) will work.

*Novell's "NetWare Tested and Approved" certification program may be helpful in choosing a PC and components that will work with NetWare; however, be sure the product also meets your own needs.*

# Disk Storage

One of the most important uses for a server is to store files, so disk storage is an important consideration. Luckily, disk storage is getting less expensive every day, so you can err on the side of caution without spending too much. Here are NetWare 4's basic requirements for disk storage:

- NetWare 4 itself requires between 100MB and 140MB, depending on the optional components you install. If you keep the online documentation on the server, it will require about 60MB more.

- You'll need a minimum of 15MB for the DOS partition; it never hurts to have 25MB or more, just in case.

- If you're upgrading a NetWare 3.1*x* server, you'll need at least 40MB free to upgrade to NetWare 4.

As you can see, the server's basic requirements don't add up to much. What you need the most storage for is your own data. The amount you need for this will vary greatly depending on the needs of your company and users. Here are some rough guidelines for the total amount of storage:

- For a typical five-to-ten user company, 1GB is a good starting point. You could start with less, but with 1GB drives at less than $300, you might as well be prepared for expansion. Larger companies should start with more space; even 4GB drives are economical.

- If you have an idea of the type of applications you will be using, add together their disk storage requirements. You should also estimate the space required for each application's data files.

- A few types of data tend to require large amounts of space: sound, video, CAD, imaging, and desktop publishing. If you intend to use any of these, be sure to allocate extra space.

In the process of running a network, it can be surprising how fast disk space disappears. A good rule of thumb is to estimate the most storage that you can ever imagine your company using—and double it.

## Memory

Memory (RAM) is another important factor in a server's performance. Adding memory is often all that is needed to speed up a slow server. Since the amount of memory a machine can use depends on the motherboard, you should ensure that you start with an adequate amount—and have room to expand.

Novell recommends a minimum of 20MB of RAM for a NetWare 4 server. This amount should be adequate for a small network (ten or fewer users) with no unusual needs or applications. To be sure you have enough, Novell provides a formula to calculate the storage you need. Follow these steps:

1. Start with the minimum: 20MB.

2. Multiply the amount of disk storage you intend to use, in MB, by .008. Add this number to the minimum. (NetWare uses RAM to store the volume's FAT while it is in use. With inadequate RAM, you may not be able to mount a volume.)

3. Add between 1 and 4MB for cache buffer RAM; this will improve the server's performance. The more, the better—if your network will have heavy traffic, you may wish to add 8MB or more.

For example, suppose you planned to use 2GB of disk storage. You would multiply 2000MB by .008, for a result of 16MB. Adding this number, the 20MB minimum, and 4MB for cache buffers gives a grand total of 40MB.

*At this writing, memory prices are lower than they have been in years. If you can afford more memory, err on the side of caution.*

## Motherboard, Bus, and CPU

You should also consider the basic components of the server PC. Be sure you meet the requirements for NetWare 4. More important, be sure your server will be adequately fast. We will look at each of these components in the sections that follow.

### The Motherboard

Although the type of motherboard used in the server rarely affects speed or compatibility, you should consider two important factors:

- Be sure the board has an adequate number of slots—both high-speed slots (such as PCI) and ISA slots for any older hardware you need to support. Also check the layout of the motherboard; with some models, the CPU and its heat sink or fan actually obstruct two or more slots.

- Be sure the motherboard can support the amount of memory (RAM) you have calculated for your server. You should also have room to add more memory when the need arises.

*Since your server will probably run continuously, heat is another important consideration. Be sure there is adequate ventilation near the CPU and that a proper fan or heat sink is used.*

### The Bus

The bus, which provides a communication link between the CPU, memory, and add-on cards, is an important factor in your server's speed. Be sure the machine has a high-speed bus; currently, this typically means a PCI bus. You can use older standards, such as EISA, MCA, and VESA Local Bus, but you may have difficulty finding up-to-date hardware (such as LAN cards) to support these standards.

### Choosing a CPU

With all the hype surrounding Intel's Pentium processor and its sequel, the Pentium Pro, you might imagine a Pentium to be a good minimum for a NetWare server. Actually, the processor has less effect on the server's performance than you would think—a 486 is adequate for most small networks, assuming it has a fast bus, fast disk drives, and a fast LAN card.

Nevertheless, a Pentium processor will help the server's speed a bit, and 486 machines are practically unavailable today. A 100Mhz Pentium system should be adequate for most networks, even with hundreds of users; the disk speed and network speed usually cause bottlenecks long before the CPU does.

If you really need high speed, systems are now available with two or four processors. NetWare 4 added support for these with the SMP (symmetric multiprocessing) feature. While it's unnecessary for all but the highest-end servers, this is a capability you may need.

*If you do purchase a multiprocessor machine, be sure NetWare 4 supports it. Also make sure a driver for the motherboard has been provided.*

## Disk and CD-ROM Drives

Several types of disk drives and controllers are available for PC systems, and not all of them are appropriate for use in a server. There are two basic choices for a NetWare server:

- SCSI is the tried-and-true standard for NetWare servers and is well supported. The latest revision of the standard, SCSI-3, supports more devices and other features. SCSI is fast and allows you to add drives with a minimum of configuration.

- IDE is the de facto standard for desktop systems. In recent years IDE has also seen use in NetWare servers. The advantage is cost; IDE drives are often half the price of their SCSI counterparts. The disadvantages are speed and a limited number of drives; typical IDE controllers support only two or four drives. SCSI drives are also typically available in larger capacities. A more recent improvement to the IDE standard, enhanced IDE (EIDE), is as fast as SCSI.

If you're upgrading an older machine, you may have an older type of drive, such as MFM, RLL, or ESDI. It is possible to use these in a NetWare server; however, with the low price of IDE drives and controllers, you would be wise to replace any such drives.

You also need to choose an appropriate IDE or SCSI controller to attach to the drives. Be sure it supports the high-speed bus (such as PCI). Many cheap controllers are available, but for a server you should find a high-quality, tested product from a trusted company.

Finally, most servers require a CD-ROM drive to install NetWare 4 and other products. SCSI CD-ROM drives have traditionally been used with NetWare, but NetWare 4 supports IDE CD-ROM drives as well. The speed of the CD-ROM drive is usually not important, and a 2X drive should work fine for most servers. You may wish to purchase a faster drive (6X or 8X) if users will access data on the CD-ROM drive.

*Beware of systems with CD-ROM drives sold as multimedia machines—these often include a sound card, which will only get in the way, and may use a proprietary CD-ROM controller, unsupported by NetWare.*

## Network Cards

Of course, to make the best use of your file server, you must attach it to the network. You need one or more network cards for this purpose. How many and which type will depend on the configuration and wiring of your network; for small networks with 50 or fewer nodes, a single card is usually enough.

Use a high-quality LAN card from a reliable manufacturer; generic cards, while inexpensive, are often slow and prone to problems. If possible, use a card that takes advantage of the server's high-speed bus, such as PCI. Also be sure the card includes an updated driver for NetWare 4.

## Backup Systems

Since you'll be storing important data on the server, you'll want to make backups of the data. We looked at the finer points of backup strategies and software in Chapter 11. When you set up the server, you will need a backup device—usually a tape drive—that is capable of backing up your disk storage.

A wide variety of tapes are available, with as many different capacities, ranging from 120MB to 4GB. High-capacity tape drives can be very expensive; as an alternative, you can back up to multiple tapes, but someone will have to change the tapes.

The majority of server-oriented tape drives are SCSI-compatible. This might affect your choice of SCSI for the disk controller. If you plan to use the tape drive while users are on the network, though, consider using a separate controller; doing so can avoid errors and drops in performance.

# Installing a New NetWare 4 Server

NETWARE 4 INCLUDES an automatic installation utility that makes the installation process simple. In this section we look at the steps involved in using this utility to install a new NetWare 4 server. Before you begin, check the previous section to be sure your server is ready to run NetWare 4.

To begin the installation process, follow these steps:

**1.** Insert the NetWare 4 CD into the drive, either on the new server or on another server on the network.

**2.** Load the drivers to access the CD-ROM drive from DOS. These include a CD-ROM driver if the drive is in the server or a network driver if the CD-ROM is mounted in another server.

**3.** Change to the CD-ROM drive and type **INSTALL** to begin the installation program.

The first screen the installation program presents asks you for a language to use during the installation process; the default is English. Figure 13.1 shows this screen. Note that this is not necessarily the language the server will use after installation; the installation program itself uses it.

**FIGURE 13.1**

Select a language to be used during the installation process.

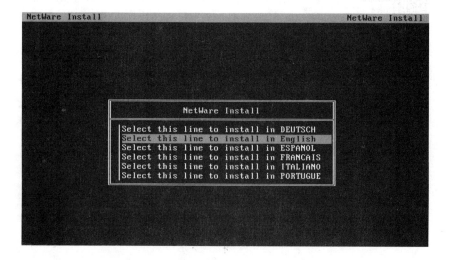

Next, you have the option to install a server or install client software. You also have the option to create disks for installing client software on workstations. This screen is shown in Figure 13.2. Select NetWare Server Installation to install a new server.

**FIGURE 13.2**

The INSTALL utility can install client or server software.

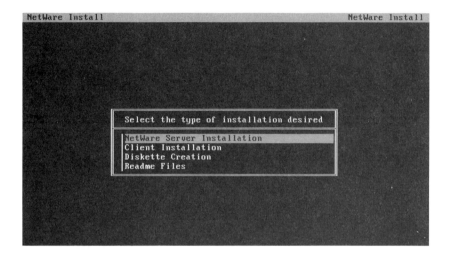

You can now choose to install either the standard version of NetWare 4.11 or the SFT III (redundant servers) option, as shown in Figure 13.3. While SFT III is included with NetWare 4.1, you must purchase a license to use it. See the Novell documentation for more information about SFT III.

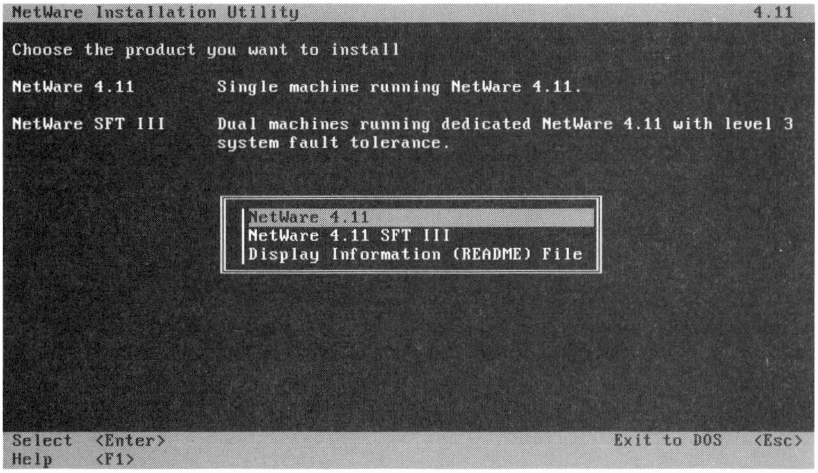

**FIGURE 13.3**

Choose whether to install NetWare 4.11 or SFT III.

After making your selection you see the screen shown in Figure 13.4. You can choose one of the following options:

- **Simple Installation of NetWare 4.11:** Makes many of the decisions for you, such as choosing the size of the NetWare partition

- **Custom Installation of NetWare 4.11:** Allows you to choose all options individually

- **Upgrade NetWare 3.1*x* or 4.*x*:** Allows you to upgrade an earlier version. (See the section "Upgrading from NetWare 2.*x*" later in this chapter for details.)

**FIGURE 13.4**

Choose Simple Installation, Custom Installation, or Upgrade.

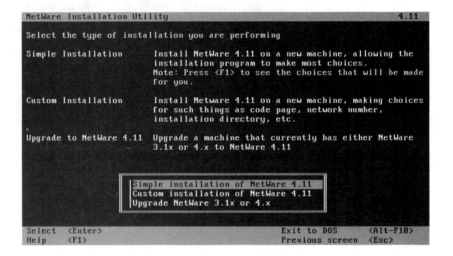

The next step allows you to choose where the NetWare server startup files will be placed on the DOS partition (see Figure 13.5). The default directory is C:\NWSERVER. You can also select a source directory; by default, the CD or remote installation directory is specified.

To acknowledge your directory choice, press F10. The files are then copied from the CD or network to the DOS partition. This may take several minutes. As the files are copied, you are shown a progress indicator. In Figure 13.6 you can see a progress indicator during the process.

After the files are copied, you are presented with a final choice. Here you specify the language and keyboard configuration to be used on the server; the default is English. This screen is shown in Figure 13.7.

**FIGURE 13.5**

Enter the source and destination directories to copy files to the DOS partition.

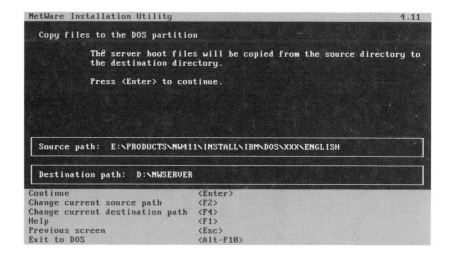

**FIGURE 13.6**

Files are being copied to the NWSERVER directory.

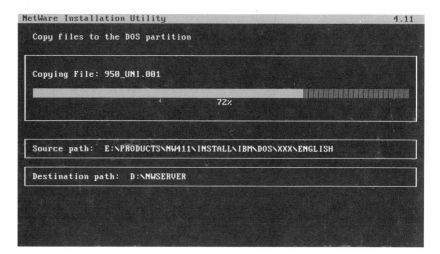

This completes the first phase of the installation process. Until now, the installation program has been running under DOS. At this point, the SERVER.EXE file is executed to start the NetWare server. If it starts up successfully, the INSTALL NLM takes over, displaying the screens you need to complete the following steps:

1. Choose a disk driver to match your system's configuration. For IDE drives, the driver included with NetWare 4 will usually work; for SCSI, use the driver provided with the controller. If you are using an older drive (such as MFM), the ISADISK driver may work.

**FIGURE 13.7**

Select a language and
keyboard configuration
for the new server.

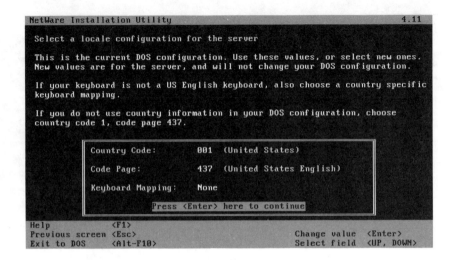

**FIGURE 13.7**

Select a language and
keyboard configuration
for the new server.

**2.** Choose a LAN driver for each of the network cards installed in the
system. If you are installing NetWare version 4.11 or later, NetWare
attempts to detect the network cards automatically.

**3.** By default, the IPX protocol is installed. If you chose the Custom installation option, you can add additional protocols, such as TCP/IP or
AppleTalk.

**4.** For the simple installation, the available space on your disk drive is
automatically used for a NetWare partition. If you chose Custom Installation, you can specify the size of the partition.

**5.** Select a name for the NDS tree and an Organization name to be created
under the [Root] object. In a custom installation you can also specify
additional Organizations or Organizational Units.

**6.** Choose the category of files to be copied to the SYSTEM or PUBLIC
directory. In most cases, you should copy all files. Note that the migration files are not copied by default; if you will be using the MIGRATE
utility, described in the next section, be sure to include these files.

After the installation is complete, you should restart the server. You
can then begin creating users and other NDS objects, as described in
Chapters 5 and 6. If you wish to migrate the users from an older server,
see the next section.

# Upgrading from NetWare 3.1x or 4.x

NETWARE 4.11 OFFERS a variety of options for upgrading older versions. The process can range from very simple to very complicated. In this section we look at the different upgrade schemes you can use and when you should choose each one. The upgrade methods include the following:

- The INSTALL program provides an automatic, and very fast, method of upgrading a server.

- The *across-the-wire migration* method is useful when you are replacing the old server with a new server.

- Use the *same-server migration* method if you need to upgrade or modify the existing server.

## Upgrading with the INSTALL Program

By far the simplest method of upgrading an existing server is with the automatic option the INSTALL program provides. Using this method you can upgrade NetWare 3.1x or 4.x to the latest version in less than an hour.

This method will work only if your machine is adequate to run the latest version. If you are already running a version of NetWare 4, this is not likely to be a problem; if you are running NetWare 3.1x, you may be better off with a new machine. The steps for this method are presented below.

*As with any upgrade method, be sure you have a backup of all data and software on the server before upgrading. While this method rarely has problems, a backup eliminates the chance of error.*

1. Bring down the server.

2. Insert the CD into the drive, either on this server or on another server on the network.

3. Load the drivers to access the CD-ROM drive from DOS. These include a CD-ROM driver if the drive is in the server or a network driver if the CD-ROM is mounted in another server.

**4.** Change to the CD-ROM drive and type **INSTALL**.

**5.** You are presented with a choice of simple installation, custom installation, or upgrade (as shown earlier in Figure 13.4). Choose Upgrade NetWare 3.1*x* or 4.*x*.

After performing these steps, you are guided through the installation process, as with a custom installation (described earlier in this chapter). Where possible, information from your old server will be used as the default in configuring the new server.

## Across-the-Wire Migration

Depending on the capabilities of your original machine, you may elect to replace it with a new machine. NetWare 4 allows you to *migrate* the users, configuration, and data from one server to another across the network. This makes it easy to replace a server with a new machine.

To perform the migration, you must attach both the old and new server to the network. You will also need a workstation on which to run the MIGRATE utility. The steps for this method are presented below.

*You can use this method even if you are using the same version of NetWare on both machines. This method can be useful to replace an old or unreliable machine.*

**1.** Install a new NetWare 4 server on the new server machine, following the instructions provided in the section "Installing a New NetWare 4 Server" earlier in this chapter. When copying files, be sure to check the Copy MIGRATE files option on the Copy SYSTEM and Public Files menu.

**2.** If you require support for the Macintosh or OS/2 name space, install it on the NetWare 4 server now, following the instructions in Chapter 3 (OS/2) or Chapter 16 (Macintosh).

**3.** From the workstation, log in to the NetWare 4 server. Type **LOGIN** *username* **/B** to log in using bindery mode.

**4.** Map a drive to the SYS: volume on the old server. You must also supply the SUPERVISOR or ADMIN password.

**5.** Change to the SYS:MIGRATE directory on the new server.

**6.** 35Type MIGRATE to start the Migration utility, shown in Figure 13.8.

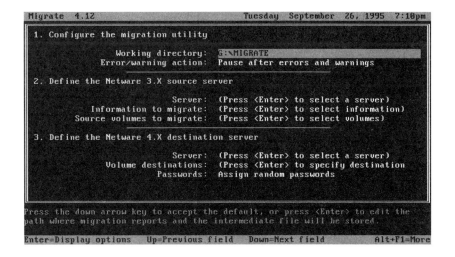

7. Select the type of server to migrate from.

8. Select the type of server to migrate to: NetWare 4.

9. Select the types of data to migrate. Typically you will use the All Information option.

10. Press F10 to view the MIGRATE menu.

11. Press ↵ to begin the migration. Depending on the servers and network speed, this may take several hours.

12. After the migration is complete, test the new NetWare 4 server. If all software works, bring down the old server.

13. Update all clients to use the new client software and to attach to the new server.

## Same-Server Migration

A different migration option is available if you are upgrading or modifying your server machine rather than replacing it. Using the same-server method, you can migrate the configuration information and NDS data to a workstation, and migrate from the workstation to the server after upgrading it.

*This is the riskiest upgrade method; you could easily end up with no server if you run into problems upgrading it. In addition, the NDS data is stored on a workstation, where it could be easily lost in a crash or accidentally deleted. Use this method only as a last resort, and plan carefully.*

Follow these steps to use same-server migration:

1. Back up all data on the old server to a tape.

2. On the workstation, run the MIGRATE utility. You must run this from the NetWare 4 installation CD-ROM, as explained in the previous section.

3. Select the source server.

4. Select the workstation as the destination. (This means the workstation on which you are running the MIGRATE utility.)

5. Select the data to migrate (the bindery or NDS only).

6. Press F10 to view the MIGRATE menu.

7. Press ↵ to begin the migration.

8. After migration is complete, double-check your backup of the server.

9. Perform the upgrades required on the server, or repartition the server's hard disk.

10. Install a new copy of NetWare 4 on the server, using the instructions presented earlier in this chapter.

11. Restore the data to the new server from the backup tape you created in step 1.

12. Run MIGRATE at the workstation.

13. Select the workstation as the source and NetWare 4 as the destination.

14. Press F10 to view the MIGRATE menu.

15. Press ↵ to migrate the bindery or NDS data to the new server.

# Upgrading from NetWare 2.x

OU MAY NEED to upgrade a NetWare 2.*x* server. Since NetWare 2.*x* servers are usually older, it is unlikely that you'll be able to use the same machine. You have three options for upgrading NetWare 2.*x*:

- If your machine is actually capable of running NetWare 4, you can use the in-place upgrade, described below.

- If you replace the server with a new machine, you can use the across-the-wire migration method, described earlier in this chapter.

- If you intend to upgrade the server to make it compatible with Net-Ware 4, you can use the same-server migration method, described earlier in this chapter.

## Using the In-Place Upgrade

If your NetWare 2.*x* server is capable of running NetWare 4, you can upgrade it in place. While this process is more complicated than upgrading NetWare 3.1*x* or 4.*x*, it is not too difficult. Follow the steps below.

*Be sure to back up your entire server before attempting to upgrade in place, and be sure you have your NetWare 2.x disks handy. This will allow you to reinstall NetWare 2.x and restore the data if anything goes wrong.*

1. Create an upgrade disk:

   a. Create a bootable DOS disk with the DOS command SYS A:.

   b. Copy FDISK.COM and FORMAT.COM from the DOS directory onto the disk.

   c. Copy the files in the UPGRADE directory on the NetWare 4.1 installation CD-ROM to the disk.

2. Bring down the NetWare 2.*x* server and boot the machine using the bootable upgrade disk.

3. Type **A:SERVER** to start the server (the NetWare 3.12 version of SERVER.EXE).

4. Enter the server name and IPX internal network number at the prompts. To keep things simple, use the same information the NetWare 2.*x* server used. Your server is now running as a NetWare 3.1*x* server.

5. Load the disk driver from the upgrade disk. Use the type of driver that corresponds with your server hardware. For example, for an IDE disk, use

    ```
    LOAD A:IDE
    ```

6. Load the 2XUPGRDE.NLM file by typing **LOAD A:2XUPGRDE** at the server console prompt. This NLM will upgrade the NetWare 2.*x* file system to NetWare 3.1*x*.

7. After the upgrade to a NetWare 3.1*x* partition is complete, take down the server. You should not bring it up again until you complete the upgrade to NetWare 4.

8. Follow the steps for using the Installation program to upgrade from NetWare 3.1*x* to NetWare 4, presented earlier in this chapter.

# Summary

N THIS CHAPTER we've looked at the process of installing NetWare 4, either on a new server or as an upgrade. We considered these topics:

- The hardware requirements and planning you should consider before installing or upgrading a server

- The Installation program for use on new servers

- Upgrading a NetWare 4.*x* or 3.1*x* server to NetWare 4.11 using the installation utility

- Migrating users and data using the across-the-wire migration method if you are replacing the server with a new machine

- Using the same-server migration method if you are upgrading the existing server

- Upgrading NetWare 2.*x* using the across-the-wire, same-server, and in-place upgrade methods

You should now have a working NetWare 4 server. The next chapter looks at ways you can internetwork, or connect your server with other servers to form a wide area network. It also examines the various options for routing data between networks and servers.

# Internetworking with NetWare 4

14

NETWARE 4 NETWORK can be as simple as a single server and workstation or as complex as a multinational corporation with hundreds of servers. The *internetworking* features of NetWare 4 provide for communication between different types of networks and protocols.

In this chapter we explore the technical details of networking with NetWare 4. This discussion includes the protocols NetWare 4 can use to communicate, the specifications for the various network architectures, and the types of cabling and equipment you need to use them. We will then move on to a discussion of routing, an important part of internetworking.

# Understanding Network Protocols

PROTOCOLS ARE THE languages devices use to communicate on the network. The most common protocols used with NetWare 4 include IPX/SPX, AppleTalk, and TCP/IP, along with two routing protocols, RIP and NLSP. We'll look at each of these in detail later in this section.

## The OSI Reference Model

The OSI reference model illustrates how network communications work. It is divided into seven layers. These range from the application layer—where the network is actually used by clients—to the physical layer, which specifies the cables and connectors used.

### The Physical Layer

The physical layer is where the actual hardware that connects network components is defined. The hardware includes the types of cable used, the connectors and wiring, hubs, and other devices. Ethernet and other network types specify the physical layer along with the data link layer.

### The Data Link Layer

The data link layer defines the way data is transmitted, received, and divided into packets. This layer is the second half of a network specification such as Ethernet; it specifies packet sizes, headers, and other types of information. This layer is actually divided into two sublayers:

- The logical link control sublayer specifies the interface used for network protocols.

- The media access control (MAC) layer specifies the transport method and encoding.

### The Network Layer

The network layer deals with network addresses and hardware and establishes routes for packets. IPX and IP are examples of network layer protocols. NetWare 4 also uses SAP (Service Advertising Protocol), another network layer protocol, to broadcast information about NDS and time synchronization between nodes.

### The Transport Layer

The transport layer deals with reliable transmission of packets. Packets are numbered and checked to ensure that they have been successfully received. Transport layer protocols used by NetWare 4 include SPX and TCP.

### The Session Layer

The session layer is the network connection that is formed between two devices. Once a session is established, data can be reliably transmitted. Security (such as packet signature) is also handled at this layer.

### The Presentation Layer

The presentation layer manages the presentation of data. This layer ensures that the data is presented in a form the application can understand. This layer can provide increased security through encryption.

### The Application Layer

The application layer includes application programs that use the network and client software, which manages applications' access to the network. Network services, such as e-mail, backup, and printing, also operate at this layer.

## Available Protocols in NetWare 4

NetWare supports the IPX and SPX protocols by default. When you install Net-Ware 4 on a server, you also have the option of installing additional protocols, such as AppleTalk, TCP/IP, or NLSP.

### IPX and SPX

IPX (Internetwork Packet Exchange) is the default protocol supported by Net-Ware. This is a connectionless protocol, meaning that data is sent blindly through the cable with the assumption that the appropriate device will receive it. Addressing in IPX is managed with network numbers:

- The *IPX external network number* is set for all servers that share a common network wire, or segment. Multiple servers in the same network segment use the same number.

- The *IPX internal network number* is set at each server. This number is used to locate the server on the network, and it must be unique.

- Each workstation or server has a network address, also called a Media Access Control (MAC) address. This address is used to locate a specific device on the network. Network addresses are usually set in hardware in the network card and usually cannot be changed. Each network card in a server also has a unique network address.

### TCP/IP

TCP/IP is the protocol used by UNIX systems and by the Internet. This is a protocol suite that includes several protocols. It is named after two of them: TCP (Transmission Control Protocol) and IP (Internet Protocol). You can learn more about TCP/IP and the included protocols in Chapter 17.

### AppleTalk

AppleTalk is the protocol supported by Macintosh systems. You can also use it with NetWare 4. The main use for AppleTalk is to allow communication between NetWare and Macintosh networks; we'll examine AppleTalk in detail in Chapter 16.

### Routing Protocols

Connecting networks that use different protocols together requires routing. *Routing* is the process of communication between different types of networks. A device that performs this function is called a *router*. The NetWare 4 server acts as a simple router if connected to multiple networks; you can also use Novell's MPR (Multiprotocol Router) for added features, as described later in this chapter.

RIP (Routing Information Protocol) and NLSP (NetWare Link Services Protocol) are *routing protocols*. Rather than transmit data themselves, these protocols manage the way information is routed in the network. We'll look at the techniques used to manage routing in the section "Managing Network Routing" later in this chapter.

## Managing Protocols with INETCFG

You can use the INETCFG utility at the server console to manage the network boards, drivers, and protocols on the network. To start this utility, type **LOAD INETCFG** at the console prompt.

When you start INETCFG, you see the screen shown in Figure 14.1, which asks if you wish to make modifications to the server's AUTOEXEC.NCF file that are required for routing and using INETCFG options.

If you answer Yes to this question, the LOAD and BIND commands in the AUTOEXEC.NCF file are moved into a new file, INITSYS.NCF. This is the file INETCFG makes changes to. Moving these commands provides a convenient separation of commands and makes the AUTOEXEC.NCF file smaller and easier to manage.

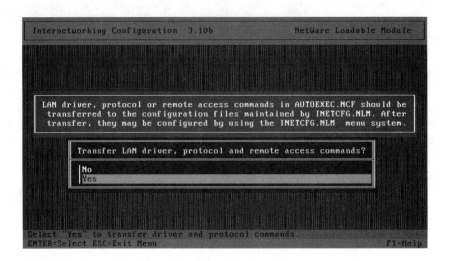

INETCFG also adds the following commands to the AUTOEXEC.NCF file:

| COMMAND | DESCRIPTION |
|---|---|
| LOAD CONLOG | Allows server console messages to be logged to a file to help in debugging |
| INITSYS.NCF | Executes the commands in the INITSYS.NCF file |
| UNLOAD CONLOG | Deactivates console logging. If this is not done, the log file can become quite large. In addition, the file can be lost since changes are written only when CONLOG unloads |

*After you have moved commands to the INITSYS.NCF file using INETCFG, you should not add LOAD or BIND commands to the AUTOEXEC.NCF file or try to modify them in this file. You should make the changes using the INETCFG utility. These changes will be written automatically to the INITSYS.NCF file.*

After the files have been moved and modified, you see the main INETCFG menu, shown in Figure 14.2. This menu provides the following options:

- **Boards:** Allows you to configure network boards. When you configure a network board using this option, the appropriate LOAD command for the network board's driver is added automatically to the server's INITSYS.NCF file.

- **Network Interfaces:** Allows you to configure network boards that provide multiple ports, also called WAN boards. You can set up each port on the board to use a different protocol.

- **WAN Call Directory:** Use this option to define remote servers that will be communicated with using PPP (Point-to-Point Protocol). This is an extension available for the MPR (Multiprotocol Router) to deal with dial-up Internet connections.

- **Protocols:** Allows you to configure the routing protocols supported by the server. Protocols include IPX, TCP/IP, AppleTalk, RIP, and NLSP.

- **Bindings:** Provides the connection between protocols and network boards. This allows you to choose the protocols that will be used for each board. The BIND commands to perform the binding are added to the INITSYS.NCF file.

- **Manage Configuration:** Allows you to configure parameters used in routing and communication, including SNMP (Simple Network Management Protocol), remote access, and the INITSYS.NCF file parameters.

- **View Configuration:** Allows you to view the LOAD and BIND commands that are currently used in the server. You can also view error messages that might have been displayed when the server was started.

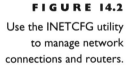

**FIGURE 14.2**

Use the INETCFG utility to manage network connections and routers.

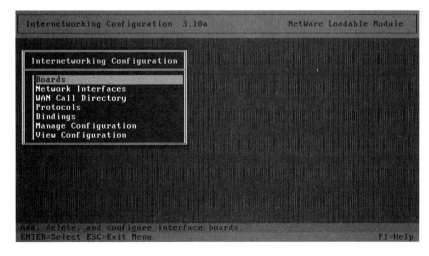

# Managing Network Architectures

C HAPTER 1 INTRODUCED the most common network architectures—
Ethernet, Fast Ethernet, ARCnet, Token Ring, and FDDI. In this
section we take a more technical look at each of these, including the specifications for each architecture, the cabling and other equipment
you can use with it, and the intricacies of configuring NetWare 4 with each
architecture.

## Ethernet

Ethernet is by far the most common type of network in use today. A variety
of types of wiring can be used with Ethernet. These include the original
method—coaxial cable—along with twisted-pair cable. Ethernet is actually
a name for several different and widely used standards. The newest standard,
Fast Ethernet, allows speeds up to 100Mbps. We'll look at each of the Ethernet standards in this section and introduce their specifications and limitations.

### Frame Types

When data is sent across the network, it is divided into packets. Several standards have been developed to specify the size of data packets and the types of
headers they are sent with for Ethernet. These are referred to as *frame types*.
NetWare 4 supports the following frame types:

- Ethernet 802.2

- Ethernet 802.3

- Ethernet SNAP

- Ethernet II

By default, a NetWare 4 server supports only Ethernet 802.2. You can support different frame types in the LOAD command when you configure a network card on the server. You can also modify frame types with the INETCFG
utility, explained earlier in this chapter.

Workstations can also support one or more frame types, and the client software provided with NetWare 4 supports 802.2 by default. You can add frame

types by modifying the NET.CFG file for the DOS Requester or by using the Control Panel for Client32. A workstation and server must have a frame type in common in order to communicate.

**ETHERNET 802.2** Ethernet 802.2 is the frame type used by default in Net-Ware 4 and NetWare 3.12. Previous versions used Ethernet 802.3, which we'll look at next. The 802.2 frame type is an IEEE standard, as well as Novell's standard. (Confusingly, the IEEE standard for this frame type is actually 802.3.) If your network was upgraded from an earlier version or includes older versions of NetWare, you may need to support both 802.2 and 802.3. To configure servers or workstations with this frame type, specify ETHERNET_802.2.

**ETHERNET 802.3** The Ethernet 802.3 frame type is used by default in NetWare 3.11 and earlier. This is not the IEEE 802.3 specification, but Novell's modified version of 802.3. Because NetWare's support for this frame type doesn't fully follow the standard, you should avoid using it in a network with multiple server types or protocols. NetWare 4 can still support this frame type in addition to 802.2 if needed. When specifying this type, use ETHERNET_802.3.

**ETHERNET SNAP** SNAP (Sub-Network Access Protocol) is an extension of the 802.2 format. Its main use is for connection with AppleTalk networks since this is the standard frame type for AppleTalk Phase 2. Support for Ethernet SNAP is provided by the ETHERNET_SNAP frame type in NetWare 4.

**ETHERNET II** Although the numbering may be confusing, this is the earliest of the Ethernet frame types, as far as standards are concerned. For NetWare 4, there are two reasons to support this protocol: you can use it with AppleTalk Phase I networks and for TCP/IP support. Specify this protocol with the text ETHERNET_II.

### Cabling and Equipment

Ethernet typically uses one of four wiring systems:

- Thin Ethernet (10Base2) uses thin coaxial cable and is wired in a bus topology.

- Thick Ethernet (10Base5) uses thick coaxial cable and a bus topology.

- Twisted-pair Ethernet (10BaseT) uses telephone-type cable. It is wired in a star topology with a central hub.

- Fast Ethernet (100BaseT) uses twisted-pair cable in a star topology and is capable of very high speeds.

**THIN ETHERNET (10BASE2)**   Thin Ethernet, or 10Base2, is widely used in many networks today. Its main disadvantage is its bus topology; one bad node or connection can bring down all the workstations and servers on a segment. Its advantages include ease of wiring and low cost for wiring and equipment. It is often referred to simply as thinnet.

One advantage of thin Ethernet is the ease of wiring and low cost of hardware. Here are the cable and other items you can use with this type of network:

- **Cable:** Thin Ethernet requires RG-58 (50-ohm) coaxial cable. This is available in varying grades.

- **Terminators:** Must be placed at the ends of each network segment. At least one terminator per segment should be grounded.

- **BNC T-connectors:** Connect each node to the network. The bus is connected to two of the connections and the node to the third. You should not use a cable between the T-connector and the server or workstation.

- **BNC barrel connectors:** Connect cables to form a segment.

- **Repeaters:** Amplify the signal and allow for greater cable lengths. Each repeater counts as a node on the segment.

- **Network cards:** Used for each node (workstation or server). The T-connector connects directly to the network card.

The specifications for 10Base2 Ethernet are as follows:

| | |
|---|---|
| Maximum length per segment | 607 feet (185 meters) |
| Maximum segments per network | Five; only three of these may contain nodes |
| Maximum nodes per segment | 30 |
| Maximum nodes on the entire network | 90 |
| Minimum cable length between nodes | 1.6 feet (.5 meters) |

**THICK ETHERNET (10BASE5)** Thick Ethernet is the original Ethernet standard. Although used less frequently today, it is still used for backbone connections and in existing networks. Because this type of wiring uses much thicker cable, it can be more reliable—and more expensive.

Sometimes called thicknet, this type of wiring also uses a bus topology. Unlike thinnet, you can use a drop cable to connect a node to the bus. Drop cables can use thick or thin coaxial cable.

The following types of wiring and hardware are used with 10base5:

- **Cable:** Thicknet uses thick coaxial cable, RG-8, 50 ohms.

- **Barrel connectors:** Connects cables together to form a single segment.

- **N-series T-connectors (taps):** Used for each node.

- **N-series terminators:** Terminate each end of a segment; at least one end should be connected to a ground.

- **Repeaters:** Amplify the signal and increase the maximum distance. Each repeater counts as a node.

- **Network cards:** Required for each workstation or server.

- **Transceivers:** Required for each node. These connect the network card and the bus and modify the electrical signals.

- **Drop cables:** Connect the network card to the transceiver.

The specifications of 10Base5 Ethernet are as follows:

| | |
|---|---|
| Maximum length per segment | 1640 feet (500 meters) |
| Maximum segments per network | Five; only three of these may contain nodes |
| Maximum nodes per segment | 100 |
| Maximum nodes on the entire network | 300 |
| Minimum cable length between transceivers | 8 feet (2.5 meters) |
| Maximum drop cable length | 165 feet (50 meters) |

**TWISTED-PAIR (10BASET)** Twisted-pair cabling is the most commonly used type of Ethernet cabling today. It is inexpensive and easy to work with. There are two types of twisted-pair cable: unshielded (UTP) and shielded. Unshielded cable is susceptible to interference but is less expensive. Shielded cable, although more expensive, can be more reliable and is less sensitive to interference.

This type of network is wired in a star topology. All nodes are connected to a central hub. This makes for a reliable network since a problem on one node usually has no effect on the other nodes on the network. The following types of wiring and hardware are used with 10BaseT networks:

- **Cable:** Shielded or unshielded twisted-pair (Category 3 or better)

- **RJ-45 connectors (8-conductor):** Connect to nodes and hubs. Wiring may be connected with other types of connectors or punch-down blocks between nodes and hubs.

- **Punch-down block:** A device that distributes the wires in a multi-wire cable and allows you to easily connect different circuits together. Punch-down blocks require a special tool for use.

- **Hubs:** Available in 4-, 8-, 12-, and 16-port configurations. Some hubs are intelligent and provide diagnostic information.

- **Network cards:** Required for each workstation or server. 10BaseT network cards include an RJ-45 connector.

The specifications for 10BaseT Ethernet are as follows:

| | |
|---|---|
| Maximum distance between node and hub | 330 feet (100 meters) |
| Maximum number of linked hubs | 4 |
| Maximum nodes per network | Depends on hub capability |

**FAST ETHERNET (100BASET)** Fast Ethernet is the latest, and fastest, Ethernet specification. It allows data transfers as fast as 100Mbps. This standard uses unshielded twisted-pair (UTP) cable, like 10baseT. The following hardware is required:

- **Cable:** Fast Ethernet uses Category 3, 4, or 5 unshielded twisted-pair cable.

- **Hubs:** These are similar to 10BaseT hubs but must specifically support the Fast Ethernet standard.

■ **Network cards:** Must also support the Fast Ethernet standard. Some hubs and network cards can support both 100BaseT and 10BaseT.

**SWITCHED ETHERNET** If you have a 10baseT Ethernet network that is running out of bandwidth, a relatively new system called *switched Ethernet* may be the answer. In a normal Ethernet network, all data is sent across the entire network—for example, if one machine requests a file from the server, the entire contents of that file must be processed (and ignored) by other machines.

Switched Ethernet uses packet switching, a technique for sending packets only to the workstation (or group of workstations) they are intended for. Switching capabilities are built into routers and bridges; more recently, switching hubs are available. These provide intelligent packet switching without a dedicated router.

The main advantage of switched Ethernet is the low cost—the existing wire and network cards of a 10baseT Ethernet network can be used with no reconfiguration. The only expense is the cost of switching hubs to replace hubs currently on the network.

# ARCnet

ARCnet, or Attached Resources Computer Network, is one of the oldest network standards. It is inexpensive and easy to work with, although Ethernet is often a better value. ARCnet supports a standard transmission rate of 2.5Mbps, but faster standards—such as ARCnet Plus—support speeds up to 20Mbps.

ARCnet can be wired with coaxial cable or twisted-pair (shielded or unshielded). It can use either a star or bus topology with hubs. More recent ARCnet equipment can also be used with fiber-optic cable.

## Cabling and Equipment

The following types of cable and other equipment are used for ARCnet wiring:

■ **Cable:** ARCnet can use coaxial cable (RG-62, 93-ohm), unshielded twisted-pair cable, or fiber-optic cable.

■ **Terminator:** Used on the last node of the network and to terminate unused ports on active hubs.

■ **Hubs:** Can be either active or passive. Active hubs amplify the signal and allow for greater distances; passive hubs simply relay the signal. You can't connect two passive hubs together; they must be connected with an active hub.

■ **BNC connectors or RJ-11/RJ-45 connectors:** Used to connect cables.

■ **Baluns:** Convert between coaxial and twisted pair formats.

■ **Network cards:** Used for each workstation or server. ARCnet network cards require you to set a unique node number (1–255) for each node.

### Specifications

The following are the specifications and limitations for ARCnet networks:

| | |
|---|---|
| Maximum distance between active hubs | 2000 feet (610 meters) |
| Maximum distance between passive and active hubs | 100 feet (30 meters) |
| Maximum segment length (coaxial) | 2000 feet (600 meters) |
| Maximum segment length (shielded twisted-pair) | 660 feet (200 meters) |
| Maximum segment length (unshielded twisted-pair) | 330 feet (100 meters) |
| Maximum cable segments in series | Three |
| Maximum total network cabling length | 20,000 feet (6000 meters) |

# Token Ring

Token Ring is a reliable standard that is often used for high-traffic networks and backbones. This standard can use twisted-pair or fiber-optic cable. It is wired in a star topology but logically used in a ring topology. Data is sent in packets from node to node.

Although higher priced than Ethernet or ARCnet, Token Ring can be faster and more reliable. The original Token Ring standard was developed by IBM and supported speeds up to 4Mbps. More recent standards support up to 16Mbps.

### Cabling and Equipment

You can use the following types of cable and equipment for Token Ring networks:

- **Cable:** Token Ring can use shielded or unshielded twisted-pair cable or fiber-optic cable. Fiber-optic cable is available in various configurations; see Table 14.1.

- **MAUs (Multistation Access Units):** Used as concentrators or hubs. The logical ring exists inside the MAUs; each node is connected to the MAU via a patch cable.

- **Repeaters:** Amplify the signal and extend the range of a segment.

- **Network cards:** Used for each workstation or server. Token Ring network cards are connected to a port on the MAU.

| **TABLE 14.1**<br><br>Types of Cable for Token Ring Networks | **TYPE** | **DESCRIPTION** |
|---|---|---|
| | Type 1 (shielded twisted-pair) | Two pairs of wire within a shield |
| | Type 2 (hybrid) | Four pairs of unshielded wire combined with two pairs of shielded wire; used mainly for combined voice/data applications |
| | Type 3 (UTP) | Two, three, or four pairs of wire; suitable mainly for voice communications; should not be used for Token Ring networks |
| | Type 5 (fiber-optic) | Two glass or plastic fibers; they support a large distance |
| | Type 6 (shielded twisted-pair) | Two pairs of wire within a shield; a smaller-gauge wire than type 1 |
| | Type 8 | A flat variation of shielded twisted-pair; used for cables that run under carpets or tiles |
| | Type 9 | A plenum version of shielded twisted-pair; suitable for use between floors of a building |

### Specifications

Token Ring has the following specifications and limitations:

| | |
|---|---|
| Maximum MAUs per network | 33 (with type 1 or 2 cable), 12 (type 6 or 9 cable) |
| Maximum node-to-MAU distance | 330 feet (100 meters) for type 1 or 2 cable; 220 feet (66 meters) for type 6 or 9 cable. |
| Minimum node-to-MAU distance | 8 feet (2.5 meters) |
| Maximum MAU-to-MAU distance | 660 feet (200 meters) for type 1 or 2 cable; 140 feet (45 meters) for type 6 cable; 400 feet (120 meters) for type 3; .6 miles (1km) for type 5 |
| Maximum cable segments in series with repeaters | 30 |
| Maximum number of nodes | 260 (cable type 1 or 2); 96 (type 6 or 9); 72 (type 3) |

# FDDI

FDDI is a high-speed standard that uses fiber-optic cable for data transmission. This allows for fast networks with long cable connections. FDDI is often used for high-speed applications and as a network backbone.

### Cabling and Equipment

FDDI uses the following types of cable and equipment:

- **Cable:** Fiber-optic cable is expensive and difficult to work with, but it has its advantages. The cable can be made with glass or plastic fibers; glass cable is generally faster but more expensive.

- **Connectors:** The type of connectors depends on the cable used. Connectors generally require special equipment to attach since the fibers must be carefully prepared before the connection is made.

- **Network cards:** Special fiber-optic network cards are required.

■ **Concentrators (hubs):** Hubs support a set number of connections. FDDI is similar to Token Ring in that it is wired in a star configuration but functions logically as a ring.

### Specifications

The FDDI standard has the following specifications and limitations:

| | |
|---|---|
| Maximum theoretical bandwidth | 250 gigabits per second |
| Data transmission rate | 100Mbps |
| Maximum cable distance (glass) | Approximately 2 kilometers |
| Maximum cable distance (plastic) | 50 meters (165 feet) |

# Managing Network Routing

NETWARE 4 INCLUDES routing capabilities by default. You can use the MPR (Multiprotocol Router) if you require more intelligent routing, including features such as filtering and alternate routing.

## Basic NetWare 4 Routing

Any NetWare 4 server can act as a router, assuming it is connected to at least two different networks or segments. To connect servers and enable routing, you need to be sure you have done the following:

■ Installed network cards in the server to support each of the networks

■ Set the external network numbers in the BIND statements to the same value as other servers on the same segment

Routing does take its toll on a server. You may need to dedicate a server to the purpose or add memory to an existing server. See Chapter 12 for information about optimizing and troubleshooting.

## Configuring the MPR

The MPR can operate as a dedicated router—meaning the server can't be used for other purposes—or as a server-based router, operating along with other network services. You can choose these options when setting up the MPR.

*Not all versions of NetWare 4.1 include a version of the MPR. It can be purchased separately for NetWare 4.1 and NetWare 3.12. Version 3.1 of the MPR is included as part of Novell Internet Access Server (NIAS), part of the Intranetware package. NIAS is explained in Chapter 17.*

The features of the MPR include the following:

- Routing works with IPX, AppleTalk, and TCP/IP protocols

- Support for RIP and NLSP router protocols

- Ability to configure complex filters to allow data based on address or type

- Ability to work with LANs and WANs

- Support for SNMP (Simple Network Management Protocol) for router management

To configure the MPR, you use the INETCFG utility, which we looked at earlier in this chapter. The Manage Configuration option includes options to control the behavior of the MPR.

*Routing is a complex subject, and a complete description of the features of the MPR could fill a book this size. For details about the MPR, consult the NetWare Dynatext online documentation.*

# Summary

N THIS CHAPTER you have learned about the various network protocols and the architectures, wiring, and internetworking features of NetWare 4:

- Network protocols are the languages NetWare 4 uses in communication between servers and workstations. Some of the most commonly used protocols are IPX, SPX, AppleTalk, TCP/IP, NLSP, and RIP.

- The OSI reference model is a way of looking at the various processes involved in network communication.

- Ethernet, ARCnet, and Token Ring are standards of wiring and protocols you can use with NetWare 4 networks.

- Routing is the process of connecting differing networks together; NetWare 4 supports this process with multiple protocols and, more powerfully, through the MPR (Multiprotocol Router).

This book has spent quite a bit of time talking about NetWare 4. In the next chapter we'll take a step back in time and introduce NetWare 3.1*x*, which many networks still use. You will learn how to manage a NetWare 3.1*x* network and what the differences are between NetWare 3.1*x* and 4.

# Managing
# NetWare 3.1x

F YOU'RE LUCKY, you'll find yourself managing a network composed entirely of up-to-date NetWare 4 servers, all using a common NDS tree and networked together. Unfortunately, the real world doesn't always work that way. A typical company's network may include several types of servers.

One of the most common network servers, aside from NetWare 4, is its predecessor, NetWare 3.1*x*. At this writing, although NetWare 4 is becoming more popular, NetWare 3.1*x* is still the most common network operating system. Not every network needs to be upgraded, so NetWare 3.1*x* will likely last a few more years.

In this chapter we take a look at NetWare 3.1*x* and how it compares to NetWare 4. In addition, we look at the basic utilities and techniques for managing NetWare 3.1*x* servers, especially where they differ from NetWare 4.

*If your NetWare 3.1x servers are on the same network as NetWare 4 servers, you may be able to manage them with NDS, using the NETSYNC utility. Chapter 11 looked at this capability.*

# Differences between NetWare 3.1x and NetWare 4

THROUGHOUT THIS BOOK, we've talked about the many features of NetWare 4 and the improvements that have been made over earlier versions. Here we take a step backward to examine some of the most important differences between NetWare 4 and NetWare 3.1*x*.

## NDS and the Bindery

The biggest difference between NetWare 3.1$x$ and NetWare 4 is the way they organize information about users and resources. While NetWare 4 uses NDS, NetWare 3.1$x$ uses a simpler system called the bindery.

The bindery is a simple, flat database. You cannot divide objects into subgroups as you can in NetWare 4. The bindery is also server-centric: if a user needs access to more than one server, you have to create an account individually in each server's bindery.

*On the plus side, the bindery can be much easier to understand. Objects have simple, one-word names, and you don't need to worry about contexts.*

## The File System

The file system in NetWare 3.1$x$ is largely the same as that of NetWare 4. The file-naming scheme and directory structure are the same, and most of the same system directories are used. We'll look at the components of the file system that differ between the two versions in the following sections.

### File System Features

The file system in NetWare 3.1$x$ lacks some of the features that are present in NetWare 4:

- **Block suballocation:** Block sizes in NetWare 3.1$x$ are determined at installation, and entire blocks must be used.

- **File compression:** Not available in NetWare 3.1$x$.

- **Automatic migration:** Not built into NetWare 3.1$x$; however, many third-party utilities provide similar features.

### File Attributes

Like NetWare 4, NetWare 3.1$x$ includes a list of attributes that can be applied to files or directories or are set automatically by the system. The list of attributes is similar to that of NetWare 4 but lacks attributes for features specific to NetWare 4, such as file compression. Table 15.1 shows the attributes supported in NetWare 3.1*x*.

| TABLE 15.1 | ATTRIBUTE NAME | DESCRIPTION |
|---|---|---|
| Attributes Supported in NetWare 3.1*x* | A (Archive Needed) | NetWare sets this flag automatically when a file is changed. Backup programs use this attribute to indicate which files need to be backed up |
| | Ci (Copy Inhibit) | Stops users from copying the file (Macintosh files only) |
| | Di (Delete Inhibit) | Prevents a file or directory from being deleted |
| | H (Hidden) | Prevents a file or directory from being shown in the directory listing. This affects DOS programs only. The NetWare NDIR utility shows hidden files if the user has the File Scan right |
| | I (Indexed) | Activates the turbo FAT indexing feature on the file |
| | N (Normal) | This is not an actual file attribute, but the FLAG command uses it to assign a default set of attributes (Shareable, Read/Write) |
| | P (Purge) | Causes the file to be purged (erased) immediately when deleted. The file cannot be recovered using the SALVAGE utility |
| | Ri (Rename Inhibit) | Prevents users from renaming the file or directory |
| | Ro (Read Only) | Prevents users from writing to, renaming, or erasing the file. This automatically sets the Ri (Rename Inhibit) and Di (Delete Inhibit) attributes |
| | Rw (Read/Write) | Allows both reading and writing to the file. This flag is set when the Ro (Read Only) flag is cleared |
| | S (Shareable) | Allows multiple users to access the file at the same time |
| | Sy (System) | Indicates files used by the system; a combination of the Read Only and Hidden attributes |
| | T (Transactional) | Indicates that the file is a TTS (Transaction Tracking System) file and will be protected by the TTS. You can use this feature only with applications that support TTS |
| | X (Execute Only) | Prevents the file from being modified, erased, renamed, or copied. Once set, this attribute cannot be removed |

### CD-ROM support

The CD-ROM module, CDROM.NLM, is not provided with NetWare 3.11. It is included with NetWare 3.12, but it isn't quite as easy to use as its Net-Ware 4 counterpart. In addition, IDE CD-ROM drives are not supported in NetWare 3.1x, although you can add support by downloading a driver from Novell.

# Printing

NetWare 3.1x supports most of the printing-related features of NetWare 4. The main difference is that printing is managed strictly with the PCONSOLE utility, and information is stored in the bindery and on disk volumes. We look at the printing features of NetWare 3.1x, and how to manage them, in the section "Managing Printing in NetWare 3.1x" later in this chapter.

# Security

NetWare 3.1x has a much simpler security system than NetWare 4. While file system security works in much the same way, there is no NDS security; instead, users can be assigned as managers over users or groups, or as supervisor-equivalent. We'll look at NetWare 3.1x security in detail in the section "Managing NetWare 3.1x Security" later in this chapter.

# Client Software

NetWare 3.1x typically uses a different type of client software than Net-Ware 4, although the latest clients will work with NetWare 3.1x servers. The following types of client software are typically used:

- The NetWare shell is the oldest client software for NetWare. This shell typically includes two TSR programs, IPX (the protocol stack) and NETX (the shell). The IPX program must be generated for each particular network card and settings using the WSGEN utility.

- You can also use the NetWare shell with the ODI architecture, described in Chapter 3. In this case, you use the link support layer (LSL), along with a driver for the network card, the IPXODI protocol stack, and the

NetWare shell (NETX). The NetWare shell is no longer supported by Novell.

■ The NetWare DOS Requester, which Chapter 3 examined, is also included with NetWare 3.12. This substitutes VLM.EXE and its accompanying modules for the shell, still using the ODI architecture. The DOS Requester can also attach to servers running earlier versions of NetWare.

■ Although the latest client (Client32) is not included with NetWare 3.1x (or even NetWare 4.10), you can use it to attach to servers running older versions.

*The types of client software in NetWare 4 and the techniques for configuring them are explained in Chapter 3.*

## Miscellaneous Features

Last but not least, here are a few other features that work differently (or not at all) in NetWare 3.1x:

■ Like NetWare 4, NetWare 3.1x can support the TCP/IP and AppleTalk protocols. However, you must install these separately; they are not available as options when you install a server. The NLSP (NetWare Link Services Protocol) routing protocol is not included with NetWare 3.1x but can be added.

■ The Packet Burst and Large Internet Packets (LIP) features are included with NetWare 3.12 and can be downloaded for use with NetWare 3.11. The DOS Requester included with NetWare 3.12 disables these features by default.

■ NetWare Server for OS/2 is not available with NetWare 3.1x. All NetWare 3.1x servers are dedicated servers.

■ The added stability and crash-prevention features of NetWare 4 are not available in NetWare 3.1x.

# NetWare 3.1x Utilities and Commands

S
OME OF THE most noticeably different things about NetWare 3.1*x* are the utilities you use to manage the network. Notably, the NWADMIN (NetWare Administrator) utility is conspicuous by its absence in NetWare 3.1*x*. You perform all the tasks of managing the server and network at the server console or through DOS utilities and commands.

We look at some of the most important commands and utilities in the sections that follow, with a focus on those that are significantly different from NetWare 4. For a complete listing, see the *Utilities* manual provided with NetWare 3.1*x* or the online (DynaText) documentation.

## DOS Full-Screen Utilities

In this section we examine some of the full-screen DOS utilities you can use to manage NetWare 3.1*x*. These can be run from any DOS workstation. Some of them are similar to utilities in NetWare 4, but with slightly different features; others are unique to NetWare 3.1*x*.

### The FILER Utility

We introduced the NetWare 4 version of FILER in Chapter 4. This utility was also included in NetWare 3.1*x,* but with fewer features. For example, the Salvage Deleted Files option in NetWare 4's FILER is not found in the NetWare 3.1*x* version; instead, the SALVAGE utility serves this purpose.

The main FILER menu for NetWare 3.1*x* is shown in Figure 15.1. It includes the following options:

- **Current Directory Information:** Shows the attributes and trustees of the current directory and allows you to change them if you have the necessary rights.

- **Directory Contents:** Displays a list of files in the current directory. You can browse the list, select a file, and press ↵ to show its list of attributes and trustees and make changes.

- **Select Current Directory:** Allows you to select a directory for browsing. The directory you were in when you typed the FILER command is used by default.

- **Set Filer Options:** Allows you to set options for the FILER utility. For example, you can specify which attributes are retained when a file is copied and whether you are asked for confirmation when deleting files.

- **Volume Information:** Allows you to choose a volume from a list and shows information about the volume. This includes the volume's name, block size, and available space.

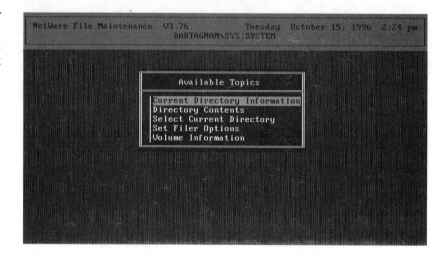

The **SALVAGE** Utility

Like NetWare 4, NetWare 3.1x saves files when they are deleted, as long as disk space is available. The SALVAGE utility allows you to view a list of deleted files in a directory and restore or purge them. The main SALVAGE menu is shown in Figure 15.2.

The SALVAGE utility includes four options for working with deleted files:

- **Salvage From Deleted Directories:** Shows a list of files from directories that were deleted entirely. These are saved in a directory called DELETED.SAV.

- **Select Current Directory:** Allows you to choose a different directory before viewing a list of files. The directory you were in when you typed the SALVAGE command is used by default.

- **Set Salvage Options:** Allows you to set options for the SALVAGE utility.

**FIGURE 15.2**

The NetWare 3.1x
SALVAGE utility
allows you to restore
deleted files.

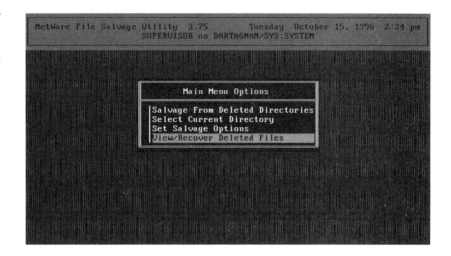

- **View/Recover Deleted Files:** Shows a list of deleted files in the current directory; you can also select subdirectories and view their contents. When you have located the file, press ↵ for a menu that allows you to salvage (restore) or purge (delete) the file.

## The SESSION Utility

Any user on a NetWare 3.1x server can use the SESSION utility. This utility is similar to the NETUSER utility in NetWare 4. It allows you to change drive mappings, printer capturing, and other options:

- **Change Current Server:** Allows you to select from the list of servers you are currently attached to.

- **Drive Mappings:** Allows you to add or delete drive mappings.

- **Group List:** Shows the list of groups for the server. You can then select one or more groups and send a message to their workstations.

- **Search Mappings:** Allows you to add or delete search drive mappings.

- **Select Default Drive:** Allows you to select a default drive, which will be searched first when you type a command.

- **User List:** Shows a list of users who are currently logged in and allows you to send a message to one or more users.

The main SESSION menu is shown in Figure 15.3.

**FIGURE 15.3**

The SESSION utility allows users to change drive mappings and other session-specific settings.

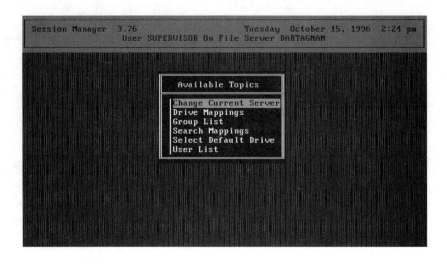

### The SYSCON Utility

SYSCON is the closest thing to NWADMIN in NetWare 3.1x. It allows you to create and manage users, groups, and managers. We examine SYSCON in detail in the section "The SYSCON Utility" later in this chapter.

## DOS Command-Line Utilities

Like NetWare 4, NetWare 3.1x includes a variety of command-line utilities that can be used from a DOS workstation. Many of the utilities, such as NDIR and NCOPY, work just like their NetWare 4 counterparts. The following sections examine the utilities that are not present in NetWare 4 or that work differently.

*There are also several command-line utilities in NetWare 3.1x that relate to security. We'll examine these in the section "Command-Line Utilities for Security" later in this chapter.*

### The BINDFIX and BINDREST Utilities

The BINDFIX utility allows you to repair damage to the bindery and to keep a backup copy for future use. You should run this utility occasionally on Net-Ware 3.1x servers to be sure the bindery is free of corruption. This utility is located in the SYS:SYSTEM directory; type **BINDFIX** to start the utility. You should use it only when no users (except you) are on the system.

The bindery is actually stored in three hidden files in the SYS:SYSTEM directory: NET$OBJ.SYS, NET$PROP.SYS, and NET$VAL.SYS. When BINDFIX runs, it makes copies of the original files and names them NET$OBJ.OLD, NET$PROP.OLD, and NET$VAL.OLD.

If data corruption in the bindery is severe or the fault lies elsewhere, BINDFIX may fail or do more harm than good. If this happens, you can type **BINDREST** to restore the previous bindery files. This copies the backup files back to the original locations, effectively undoing any changes BINDFIX made.

### The FLAG and FLAGDIR Commands

You use the FLAG and FLAGDIR commands to work with file attributes, which we examined earlier in this chapter. The FLAG command works similarly to the NetWare 4 version, which was discussed in Chapter 4. However, the FLAG command works only with files. For directories, use the FLAGDIR command.

### The LOGIN, LOGOUT, and ATTACH Commands

The LOGIN and LOGOUT commands in NetWare 3.1x work much the same as those of NetWare 4. The main difference is that you can log in only to a server since there are no NDS Directory trees. You can also log in to only one server at a time with LOGIN. You can use the ATTACH command after login to attach to another server. LOGIN runs a login script, while ATTACH does not.

### The MAP Utility

The MAP utility in NetWare 3.1x is nearly identical to the NetWare 4 version, and drive mappings on the two systems work in similar ways. The main difference is that NetWare 3.1x does not support Directory Map objects. You can use the MAP command strictly by specifying a volume and directory to map a drive to.

### The PURGE Command

PURGE allows you to access one of the options of the SALVAGE utility—purging a file permanently—from the command line. To use this command, specify the name (with a directory path, if needed) of the file you wish to purge. For example, this command purges all files in the current directory:

```
PURGE *.*
```

An additional option, /ALL, purges all files in the current directory and its subdirectories. If you use the PURGE /ALL command at the root directory of a volume, all deleted files on the volume are purged.

### The RCONSOLE and ACONSOLE Utilities

The RCONSOLE utility is available in NetWare 3.1x and works similarly to the NetWare 4 version. Unlike the NetWare 4 version, this utility does not support asynchronous (modem) connections; a separate utility, ACONSOLE, is provided for this purpose.

One important difference between the two versions is that the NetWare 3.1x version uses a different set of keystrokes. The following keystrokes are available in RCONSOLE for NetWare 3.1x:

| KEYSTROKE | DESCRIPTION |
| --- | --- |
| + (numeric keypad) | Advances to the next screen |
| – (numeric keypad) | Switches to the previous screen |
| * (numeric keypad) | Shows a list of screens and allows you to select one |
| Shift+Esc | Returns to the list of servers and allows you to select another |
| Esc | Exits entirely |

*As with NetWare 4, the REMOTE and RSPX modules must be loaded on each file server to be used with RCONSOLE.*

### The SLIST and USERLIST Utilities

NetWare 4's NLIST utility is not available in NetWare 3.1x. Instead, you can use two specialized commands to list servers or users on the system.

| COMMAND | DESCRIPTION |
|---------|-------------|
| SLIST | Lists the servers on the network. You can specify a server name after this command to view information about a specific server |
| USERLIST | Lists the users who are currently logged in. You can specify a file server or a particular user on the command line. Additionally, you can use the /A command to include network and node addresses for each user in the list |

## Server Commands

The file server console for NetWare 3.1*x* is nearly identical to that of NetWare 4, and most of the commands for managing the server are the same. We examine some of the differences in the sections below.

### The DOWN and EXIT Commands

As with NetWare 4, the DOWN command brings down a NetWare 3.1*x* server. After the server has closed files and dismounted the drives, you are again presented with the colon prompt; the EXIT command allows you to return to DOS.

NetWare 4 includes a command, RESTART SERVER, you can use instead of EXIT to immediately restart the server; this is not available in NetWare 3.1*x*. Instead, you need to type **EXIT** and then type **SERVER** at the DOS prompt to restart the server.

### The SET Command

The SET command is included in NetWare 3.1*x*, and it functions just like NetWare 4. Most of the individual SET commands are the same, but commands specific to NetWare 4 features, such as NDS and file compression, are not included. Consult the NetWare 3.1*x* manuals for a complete list of SET commands.

The SERVMAN utility, which provides a friendly alternative to SET in NetWare 4, is not included with NetWare 3.1*x*. The SET command is the only way to work with server parameters.

## Server Utilities

We now take a look at the two key full-screen server utilities, MONITOR and INSTALL. While these are present in both NetWare 3.1x and NetWare 4, they offer different options. We examine the NetWare 3.1x versions of these utilities in the sections that follow.

### The MONITOR Utility

The NetWare 3.1x MONITOR utility is shown in Figure 15.4. This utility provides fewer options than the NetWare 4 version but is used for much the same purpose. The options include the following:

- **Connection Information:** Shows a list of users and other devices currently logged in to the server. You can select a connection and view detailed information about it or disconnect the user.

- **Disk Information:** Shows a list of disk drives installed in the server and the volumes on them. This list also includes information about disk mirroring or duplexing, if used.

- **LAN Information:** Shows a list of the LAN cards in use on the server and the networks they are bound to. Statistics for LAN activity are also shown.

- **System Module Information:** Lists the modules (NLMs) currently in use on the server and the amount of memory each consumes.

- **Lock File Server Console:** Allows you to lock the console from future access and optionally enter a password. If you don't specify a password, the SUPERVISOR password is used. This password will be required for the next access to the console.

- **File Open/Lock Activity:** Allows you to select a disk file and shows the number of users who have the file open or locked.

- **Processor Utilization:** Shows a list of processes and the amount of CPU processing time each is using. This advanced option is available only if you use the command LOAD MONITOR –P.

- **Resource Utilization:** Shows a list of resources (types of memory) and which NLMs are using them.

- **Exit:** Exits the MONITOR utility. Since this utility uses a minimum of resources, many administrators leave it running for easy access.

**FIGURE 15.4**

The NetWare 3.1x MONITOR utility allows you to track server performance and resource usage.

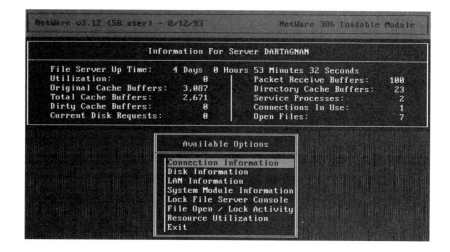

### The INSTALL Utility

The NetWare 3.1*x* INSTALL utility is shown in Figure 15.5. This utility, like its NetWare 4 counterpart, allows you to modify installation options or install additional software and is used in the process of installing a NetWare 3.1*x* server. The INSTALL utility includes the following options:

- **Disk Options:** Allows you to install or remove disk drives and create or manage NetWare partitions.

- **Volume Options:** Allows you to create or remove volumes on NetWare partitions.

- **System Options:** Allows you to edit or create the STARTUP.NCF and AUTOEXEC.NCF files or change the server's name or network number. You also use this option to copy the SYSTEM and PUBLIC files to the SYS: volume during installation.

- **Product Options:** Allows you to install or remove additional products, such as online documentation, e-mail, and backup software.

- **Exit:** Exits the INSTALL utility.

**FIGURE 15.5**

The NetWare 3.1x
INSTALL utility allows
you to install software
or change options.

```
NetWare Server Installation V3.12          NetWare 386 Loadable Module

   Installation Options
  ┌─────────────────────┐
  │ Disk Options        │
  │ Volume Options      │
  │ System Options      │
  │ Product Options     │
  │ Exit                │
  └─────────────────────┘




        ┌───────────────────────────────────────────────────────────┐
        │ Use the arrow keys to highlight an option, then press <ENTER>.│
        └───────────────────────────────────────────────────────────┘
```

# Managing Users in NetWare 3.1x

THIS SECTION TAKES a look at the SYSCON utility, which you use to manage users and groups in NetWare 3.1x. We'll start with a tour of SYSCON's options and then move on to common tasks you will need to perform as an administrator of NetWare 3.1x servers.

## The SYSCON Utility

The main menu of the SYSCON utility is shown in Figure 15.6. This utility allows you to manage users and groups, assign rights, and assign users as administrators. This utility is replaced by the NWADMIN and NETADMIN utilities in NetWare 4.

SYSCON includes the following options:

- **Accounting:** Activates the accounting system. This allows you to monitor each user's use of the network's resources.

- **Change Current Server:** Allows you to manage users on a different server. Servers available on the network are listed; you must have a password (typically SUPERVISOR) for each server you wish to manage.

**FIGURE 15.6**

The SYSCON utility allows you to add, delete, and manage users and groups.

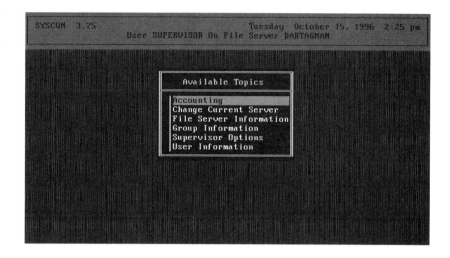

- **File Server Information:** Displays information about a file server, including network numbers, the version of NetWare in use, and licensing information.

- **Group Information:** Allows you to create groups of users, which you can use to assign the same rights or options to a list of users. You can add users to groups and assign rights and options to groups from within the Group Information menu.

- **Supervisor Options:** Allows you to set defaults for new users, change security features, and edit the system login script and the server's AUTOEXEC.NCF file.

- **User Information:** Allows you to create and manage users.

We examine these capabilities of SYSCON in detail in the following sections, according to their use in managing the network.

## Creating and Managing Users

The User Information option in SYSCON shows a list of user names in the server's bindery. Within this list, you can access several functions:

- Select a user's name and press ↵ to view and modify the user's attributes.

- Select a user's name and press Del to delete the user.

- Press Ins to add a new user using the default values.

- Select a user's name and press F3 to change the user's login name.

Figure 15.7 shows the user properties menu, which is displayed when you press Enter to manage the user. This menu allows you to change the various categories of information for the user, such as trustee rights and security restrictions.

**FIGURE 15.7**

SYSCON shows the list of property categories for a user.

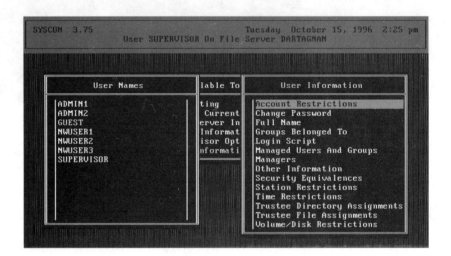

**Creating Groups**

After selecting SYSCON's Group Information option, you see a list of groups. These are similar to the Group object in NetWare 4 and allow you to group together users who will need similar rights or restrictions. A user can be a member of more than one group. By default, all users are members of a group called EVERYONE.

You can perform group-related functions from the list of groups:

- To create a new group, press Ins.

- To delete a group (which does not affect the users in the group), press Del.

- To rename a group, press F3.

- To manage a group, press Enter.

You can assign users as members of a group from the Members option, available from the group's properties screen, or from the user's Group Memberships category. You are shown a list of users in the group. Press Del to remove a user. To add a user, press Ins and select the user from the list of non-member users.

# Managing NetWare 3.1x Security

NETWARE 3.1X SECURITY is much simpler than NetWare 4. There is no NDS security; file system security is the main aspect of security for NetWare 3.1x. In addition, the auditing features of NetWare 4 are not included. We look at the basics of managing security in NetWare 3.1x in the following sections.

## Working with Trustee Rights

As is common with NetWare 4, there is more than one way to assign rights in NetWare 3.1x. If you need to give a user access to a certain file or directory, you can do so in several ways:

- To assign individual rights in SYSCON, select User Information ➤ Trustee Directory Assignments. Press Ins to add an assignment to the list, and select the file or directory.

- To assign rights to an entire group in SYSCON, select Group Information ➤ Trustee Directory Assignments. Press Ins to add it to the list.

- To make a user's rights equivalent to another user in SYSCON, select User Information ➤ Security Equivalence. Press Ins to add a user to the list.

- In FILER, select View Directory Contents. Then select the file or directory you wish to assign rights to. Select the Trustees option and press ↵ to view the list of trustees; press Ins to add to the list.

You can also use the command-line utilities, described in the section "Command-Line Utilities for Security" later in this chapter, to assign trustees to files.

## Using the Inherited Rights Mask

NetWare 3.1*x* supports an Inherited Rights Mask (IRM) for each directory. This is similar to the Inherited Rights Filter (IRF) in NetWare 4 but applies only to the file system. The IRM is also organized differently, in that it lists the rights allowed in a directory rather than those blocked. You can manage the IRM in the following ways:

- In FILER, select Current Directory Information. Select the Inherited Rights option and press ↵ to view the list of rights that can be inherited; press Ins or Del to add or delete from the list.

- The ALLOW command-line utility, described shortly, provides an alternative way of doing this.

## Assigning Administrators

In NetWare 4, you can create as many different types of administrator as you can imagine, assigning each one a specific list of users, properties, or files to manage. NetWare 3.1*x* has a much simpler system for administrators. These are the basic types of administrators for NetWare 3.1*x*:

- A *user account manager* can manage a particular user or the users in a group, change their information, or delete them. This manager cannot create new users. To assign a user as a user account manager, you use the Managers and Managed By options in the user or group information screens.

- A *workgroup manager* can create, manage, and delete users. To assign a user as a workgroup manager, select Supervisor Options ➤ Workgroup Managers. Press Ins to add to the list.

- A *supervisor equivalent* has the same power as the SUPERVISOR account. To assign a user as supervisor equivalent, use the Security Equivalent To option on the User Information screen. Be careful—supervisor-equivalent users can even change the SUPERVISOR account.

- A *print server operator* is given the authority to manage a print server. You can assign users as print server operators from the PCONSOLE utility.

- A *print queue operator* can manage a print queue. Use PCONSOLE to assign this type of operator.

- A *file server console operator* is given access to the FCONSOLE utility, which can be used to send broadcast messages to users, enable or disable logins, and view information about the system and users.

## Command-Line Utilities for Security

NetWare 3.1*x* includes a variety of DOS command-line utilities to manage security. Most of these functions are built into the RIGHTS command in NetWare 4. We look at each of these utilities in the sections below.

### The ALLOW Command

The ALLOW command lets you modify the IRM for a directory. Specify a directory on the command line, along with a list of rights the directory can inherit. For example, this command changes the IRM for the SYS:PUBLIC/TEMP directory to Read and File scan only:

```
ALLOW SYS:PUBLIC/TEMP TO INHERIT R F
```

You can also use the ALL keyword in place of the list of rights or use the ALLOW command without the TO INHERIT option to view the IRM for a file.

### The GRANT Command

The GRANT command allows you to assign a user or group as a trustee for a directory or file. Specify the file or directory, the user or group name, and the rights to be assigned. For example, this command grants all rights for the SYS:PUBLIC directory to user FRED:

```
GRANT R W C E M F FOR SYS:PUBLIC TO FRED
```

### The REMOVE Command

The REMOVE command removes a user or group from a file or directory's trustee list. For example, the following command takes away the assignment for SYS:PUBLIC that we gave to the user FRED above:

```
REMOVE FRED FROM SYS:PUBLIC
```

### The REVOKE Command

REVOKE is less drastic than REMOVE. It revokes one or more rights for a user in a particular directory or file. For example, you could use the following command to take away the user FRED's Erase right in the SYS:PUBLIC directory but leave the other rights intact:

```
REVOKE E FOR FRED FROM SYS:PUBLIC
```

### The RIGHTS Command

The RIGHTS command allows you to view your current effective rights for a file or directory. You can type **RIGHTS** by itself to view your rights to the current directory, or you can specify a path or file name to view your rights for that file or directory. Unlike NetWare 4, the NetWare 3.1x RIGHTS command does not allow you to modify rights.

### The TLIST Command

The TLIST command lists the trustees for the current directory. You can also specify a path or file on the command line to list trustees for that file or directory. In addition, you can add the USERS or GROUPS keyword to the command to list only the users or groups that are trustees.

# *Managing Printing in NetWare 3.1x*

ALTHOUGH PRINTING IN NetWare 3.1x is not managed through NDS, it offers most of the same features as NetWare 4. This section looks at the components involved in printing for Net-Ware 3.1x and the utilities you can use to manage printing.

## Components of the Print Process

In NetWare 4, several components are involved in the process of printing a document, as you learned in Chapter 8. The components for NetWare 3.1x are similar, with the absence of the NPRINTER (port driver), which is not used. The components include the following:

- **Print queues:** Store documents that are to be printed.

- **Printers:** Are configured based on their attachment. Like NetWare 4, printers in NetWare 3.1x can be attached to the server, to a workstation, or directly to the network.

- **Print servers:** Manage the print process and send data from the queue to the printer. In NetWare 3.1x, only 16 printers can be used for each print server. The print server must be run on the server for server-attached printers.

NetWare 3.1x supports one feature NetWare 4 doesn't: dedicated print servers. You can use the PSERVER utility on a workstation to make it act as a print server. Any printers used with this print server must be attached to the workstation. The workstation cannot be used for any other purpose while it is acting as a print server.

Remote (workstation) printers are available in NetWare 3.1x through the RPRINTER utility. This utility is similar to NetWare 4's NPRINTER workstation utility. RPRINTER should be used carefully under Windows, as some versions of RPRINTER are unstable or may conflict with software.

As with NetWare 4, the CAPTURE utility redirects a port to a printer. With the NetWare shell (NETX), only LPT1, LPT2, and LPT3 can be used as logical ports; with the DOS Requester, LPT1 through LPT9 can be used. Most of the CAPTURE options are the same as those for NetWare 4. Use the ENDCAP command to stop capturing to a printer.

## Setting Up and Managing Printers

NetWare 3.1x includes the PCONSOLE utility, which provides options similar to its NetWare 4 counterpart. The main PCONSOLE screen is shown in Figure 15.8. The options available in PCONSOLE for NetWare 3.1x include the following:

- **Change Current File Server:** Allows you to view printer configurations for a different file server, provided you are attached to it.

■ **Print Queue Information:** Allows you to create or manage print queues.

■ **Print Server Information:** Allows you to create and modify print servers. Each print server must also be run at the file server (PSERVER.NLM) or on a dedicated workstation (PSERVER.EXE). This option also allows you to configure up to 16 printers for each file server.

**FIGURE 15.8**

PCONSOLE allows you to manage printers, print servers, and queues.

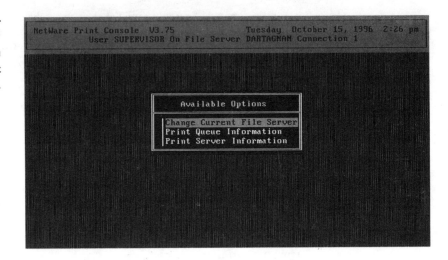

## Print Job Configurations and Forms

NetWare 3.1x includes features to create custom print job configurations and forms, just like NetWare 4. Aside from the lack of NDS support, these function in much the same way. You use two utilities to manage these tasks:

■ **PRINTCON:** Allows you to create print job configurations for use with the CAPTURE command

■ **PRINTDEF:** Allows you to define printer forms

# *Summary*

N THIS CHAPTER we've examined an earlier version of NetWare—
NetWare 3.1*x*. We looked at how it compares with NetWare 4 and
how you can work with it, including these topics:

- The differences between NetWare 3.1*x* and NetWare 4 and the features
  that are missing in the earlier version

- How to manage NetWare 3.1*x* servers and networks using workstation
  commands, utilities, and server commands

- How to manage users in NetWare 3.1*x*, including creating, deleting, and
  assigning rights to users

- How NetWare 3.1*x* security differs from NetWare 4 security, and how
  to manage security and rights

- How to manage printing in NetWare 3.1*x*

In the next chapter we'll look at another type of system commonly found in
networks: Macintosh computers and AppleTalk networks. We'll examine the
process of supporting Macintosh files and Macintosh clients and of integrating AppleTalk with NetWare 4 networks.

# Integrating NetWare and Macintosh Networks

16

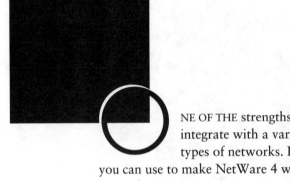

ONE OF THE strengths of NetWare 4 is its ability to seamlessly integrate with a variety of client operating systems and other types of networks. In this chapter we look at the techniques you can use to make NetWare 4 work with Macintosh computers and networks.

Using NetWare for Macintosh, included with NetWare 4, you can configure a server to allow Macintosh file names, allow Macintosh clients on an AppleTalk network to log on, and allow them to share files and printers with users on DOS and Windows systems. We begin with an overview of the AppleTalk networking system and then move on to the specifics of configuring NetWare to work with Macintosh networks.

# Introduction to Macintosh Networking

UNTIL RECENTLY, IT required some effort to form PCs into a network. Now, peer-to-peer network systems such as the one built into Windows 95 allow easy networking. Macintosh users have had this ability for years—one of the first peer-to-peer networking systems was Apple-Talk, which has been built in to most Macintosh computers

Using AppleTalk, all you need to connect Macintosh computers to each other is the proper cable. The required network drivers and software are built in to the operating system. This has made Macintosh computers a popular choice for small networks for many years.

Connecting Macintosh networks to NetWare requires a bit more effort; with previous versions of NetWare, it was not always easy, and advanced features—such as NDS—were not available to Macintosh clients. NetWare 4 has significantly improved the Macintosh connectivity features. Macintosh clients can now access NDS and most other network features.

Before looking at NetWare's Macintosh connectivity features, let's examine the AppleTalk network architecture and the protocols it uses. Knowing the basics of Macintosh networking will help if you need to make NetWare and Macintosh networks work together.

## AppleTalk Network Addresses

AppleTalk networks support two types of addressing: Phase 1 and Phase 2. The first AppleTalk standard was AppleTalk Phase 1. Phase 1 networks are limited to 254 nodes, each with a unique address. The addresses are assigned automatically as devices attach to the network.

AppleTalk Phase 2 is a newer standard, developed in 1989. These networks are also referred to as *extended AppleTalk networks*. An extended network allows many more than 254 nodes—in theory, millions. To use more than 254 nodes, the network uses a range of network numbers rather than a single one.

Like IPX, AppleTalk uses both internal and external network numbers to refer to networks. You can also configure AppleTalk using zones, or named groups of devices. In a small network a single zone is sufficient, but for a larger network it can be useful to create individual zones for various groups of devices.

## Understanding AppleTalk Protocols

AppleTalk networks can use a variety of protocols. These include the following:

- **LocalTalk**: The network protocol built into Macintosh computers. LocalTalk uses unshielded twisted-pair (UTP) cable, connected between computers with DIN or RS-422 connectors.

- **EtherTalk**: Phase 1 AppleTalk networks support Ethernet 2.0 (referred to as ETHERNET_II by NetWare). Phase 2 networks support the ETHERNET_SNAP protocol, which is based on Ethernet 802.3.

- **ARCnet**: Can be used with Phase 1 AppleTalk networks.

- **TokenTalk**: AppleTalk Phase 2 includes support for TokenTalk, an implementation of the Token Ring standard that supports either 4Mbps or 16Mbps communication.

■ **FLAP (FDDITalk Link Access Protocol):** The Macintosh implementation of the FDDI standard, which supports up to 100Mbps communication on fiber-optic cable.

# Adding Macintosh Support to the Server

TO SUPPORT MACINTOSH clients and files, you need to configure the NetWare 4 server. There are several aspects to this configuration:

■ NetWare for Macintosh is a set of NLMs that allow Macintosh clients to access the network and that support file and printer sharing with Macintosh clients.

■ The Macintosh name space must be installed on each volume that will store Macintosh files. Doing so allows you to use the Macintosh naming scheme on that volume. The name space can be added automatically when you install NetWare for Macintosh.

■ The AppleTalk protocol must be installed on the server before Macintosh clients can connect to the server.

We will examine each of these configuration steps in detail in the following sections.

## Installing NetWare for Macintosh

Unlike DOS and OS/2 clients, Macintosh workstations cannot attach to the network unless NetWare for Macintosh is loaded on the file server. Once it is loaded, you can install the client software.

When you install NetWare 4 on a new server, you have the option of installing NetWare for Macintosh. You can also install it on an existing server. The INSTALL utility provides this option. Follow these steps to start the installation for an existing NetWare 4 server:

### Starting Installation

1. Start the INSTALL utility by typing **LOAD INSTALL** at the server console.

2. Select Product Options.

3. Press ↵ to choose an item to install.

4. Select Install NetWare for Macintosh.

5. Specify a path to the installation directory.

The path defaults to the directory you used for your server installation, which may be a CD-ROM or a remote network directory. NetWare for Macintosh will be installed from this directory. The directory is typically \NW411\ INSTALL\ENGLISH on the NetWare 4.11 CD-ROM. If you are using a different language, substitute it for ENGLISH here.

6. Select the Install NW-MAC option to continue.

### Final Installation Options

The files required for NetWare for Macintosh are now copied to the server. These are placed in a directory called NW-MAC under the SYS:SYSTEM directory. When this process is complete, the Final Installation Options window, shown in Figure 16.1, appears. This window offers five options:

- **Volumes for Macintosh name space**: Allows you to select volumes on which to install the Macintosh name space, which provides compatibility with Macintosh file names. You must install the Macintosh name space on the SYS: volume to run NetWare for Macintosh.

- **Start file services**: Adds the command to start Macintosh file services to the server's AUTOEXEC.NCF file. This loads a module called AFP.NLM. (AFP stands for AppleTalk Filing Protocol.) You should choose this option if you wish to share files with Macintosh clients.

- **Start print services:** Adds the command to start Macintosh print services to the AUTOEXEC.NCF file. The module that handles this is ATPS.NLM. (ATPS stands for AppleTalk Print Services.) This module allows Macintosh clients to print to a NetWare printer.

- **Support files:** Lets you install support files for the Macintosh client. These files are installed on the server under the SYS:SYSTEM\NW-MAC directory. (The section "Installing Macintosh Client Software" a little later in this chapter explains how to install the software on the clients.)

- **Continue installation:** Press Enter here to continue the installation.

**FIGURE 16.1**

The Final Installation Options menu allows you to complete tasks needed for Macintosh connectivity.

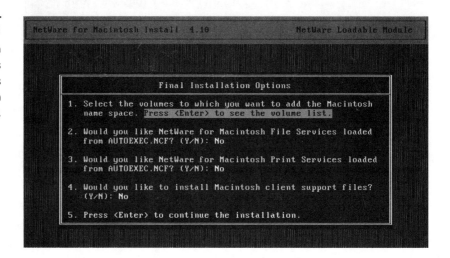

When you continue the installation, you are asked to verify your choice. If you select Yes, the items you selected are installed on the server. Finally, the NetWare for Macintosh Configuration window appears. This gives you a chance to install any options you did not already choose. In addition, four options allow you to configure NetWare for Macintosh features. These options actually run individual NLMs. You can load any of these NLMs yourself if you wish to change the configuration.

- **Configure AppleTalk Stack:** Loads INETCFG.NLM, which sets up the AppleTalk protocol, described in the next section.

- **Configure File Services:** Loads AFPCON.NLM, which allows you to change file-sharing options.

- **Configure Print Services:** Loads ATPSCON.NLM, which allows you to control AppleTalk printing services.

- **Configure CD-ROM Services:** Loads HFSCDCON.NLM, which supports Macintosh CD-ROM drives.

The changes you make will not take effect until you bring the server down and back up. Before you restart the server, you should configure the bindings for the AppleTalk protocol, as described in the next section. If you later need to change NetWare for Macintosh options, you can return to the Configuration window by following these steps:

1. Start the Installation utility by typing **LOAD INSTALL** at the server console.

2. Select Product Options.

3. Select View/Configure/Remove installed products.

4. Select NW-MAC from the product list. You will see the Configuration window, where you can make changes as necessary.

## Configuring the AppleTalk Protocol

To communicate with Macintosh clients, the AppleTalk protocol must be loaded on the server. Follow these steps to install AppleTalk:

1. Load the INETCFG utility by typing **LOAD INETCFG** at the server console.

2. Select Bindings.

3. Press Ins to add a binding to the list. Select AppleTalk.

4. From the list of LAN cards displayed, select the one you will be using to connect to the AppleTalk network.

5. Press Esc to exit and select Yes to save your changes.

These steps add the BIND statement for AppleTalk to the INITSYS.NCF file. You must restart the server for the new binding to take effect. Restarting the server also causes the NetWare for Macintosh modules to load.

# Installing Macintosh Client Software

BECAUSE THE APPLETALK protocol is provided with the Macintosh operating system, you can begin using NetWare for Macintosh services right away, without installing additional software on the Macintosh client. However, you need to install the Macintosh client software, MacNDS, to take advantage of NDS. This software provides access to NDS, much the way the DOS Requester does.

## Enabling Bindery Logins

Until you install the MacNDS software, Macintosh clients will attach to the server using Bindery Services (described in Chapter 11). Before the clients can log in with Bindery Services, you must enable bindery logins for AppleTalk using the AFPCON utility, as follows:

1. Type **LOAD AFPCON** at the server console.

2. From the Configuration Options menu, select Detailed Configuration.

3. Select User Access Information. The options on the User Access Information menu control the types of logins that are allowed.

4. Select the Allow Clear Text Password Login option and change it to Yes to allow bindery attachments.

5. Press Esc to exit and save your changes.

## Installing MacNDS

After you have enabled bindery logins, you can install MacNDS on the Macintosh workstations. Follow these steps for each workstation:

1. Log in to the server. Because the client files are in the PUBLIC directory, you do not need to use the ADMIN user account.

2. Click the NetWare volume's icon and switch to the PUBLIC/MAC folder. Inside this folder are subfolders for each language available. Double-click the appropriate language, such as ENGLISH.

3. Inside the language directory is a file called MacNDS.SEA. (SEA stands for Self-Extracting Archive, and it is a Macintosh standard for compressed files.) Double-click this file.

4. You are asked where to install the files. Click OK to accept the default location, or browse through the folders to select another directory.

The Macintosh client software is installed in a subfolder called MacNDS in the folder you specify. You can open this subfolder to run the client software.

*The Macintosh NDS client requires System 7 or later as the Macintosh operating system. If you are using an older operating system, you can still access the network through Bindery Services.*

# Using Macintosh Utilities

THE LATEST VERSION of NetWare (4.11) includes something new for Macintosh users: a set of utilities that allow you to work with the network. With these utilities you can log in and out of the network, browse objects in the NDS Directory tree, select a network printer for printing, or mount a NetWare volume as a local drive.

In addition to these utilities, a version of the RCONSOLE utility, which allows you to access a file server's console (described in Chapter 10) is included. We will look at each of these in the following sections.

*One utility that's missing here is NWADMIN. There is currently no Macintosh version of the NetWare Administrator utility. You will need to manage the NDS tree from a DOS, Windows 3.1, Windows 95, or OS/2 workstation.*

## Using the NDS Tree Menu

One of the most convenient features for Macintosh users is the NDS tree menu. After you have successfully installed NetWare Client for Macintosh, a small icon resembling a tree appears near the right end of the menu bar.

Clicking this icon allows you to access the NDS Tree drop-down menu shown in Figure 16.2. This menu includes several convenient features:

- **About NetWare Client:** Shows the current version and other information about the client software you have installed

- **Login:** Allows you to enter a username and password to log into the NetWare server or Directory tree

- **Configure:** Allows you to configure options for the Macintosh client

- **Connections:** Allows you to view and manage your current server and Directory tree connections

- **Log Out Completely:** Logs you out of all current servers and Directory trees

We will examine these options in detail in the following sections.

**FIGURE 16.2**

The NDS Tree menu
allows access to
NetWare features from
Macintosh clients.

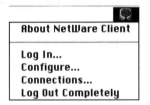

### Logging In and Out

To log in to the network, select Login from the NDS Tree Menu. The login dialog, shown in Figure 16.3, is now displayed. This dialog defaults to the Directory tree you have configured as your default tree. Enter your login name and password in the appropriate spaces and press the Log in button to complete the login.

To log out, simply use the Log Out Completely option from the NDS Tree menu. Selecting this option disconnects you from all current server and Directory tree connections.

*The NDS Tree icon in the menu bar changes to reflect your login status; the tree is empty when you are logged out and has leaves when you are logged in.*

**FIGURE 16.3**

The login dialog allows a Macintosh client to attach to an NDS tree or server.

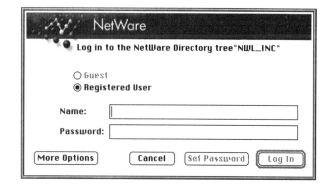

## Setting NetWare Client Preferences

To configure defaults for the NetWare client, select the Configure option from the NDS Tree menu. The NetWare Client Preferences dialog box, shown in Figure 16.4, is displayed. From this dialog you can set the following options:

- In the first section of the dialog, you can select a default Directory tree for logins from this workstation. Select a tree from the pull-down list and click the Set Preferred button to make it the default.

- The second section allows you to configure your default NDS context. Choose the appropriate container object from the pull-down menu and click the Set Default button.

- Finally, you can enter your login name. This name will be used by default when you use the Login option from the NDS Tree menu.

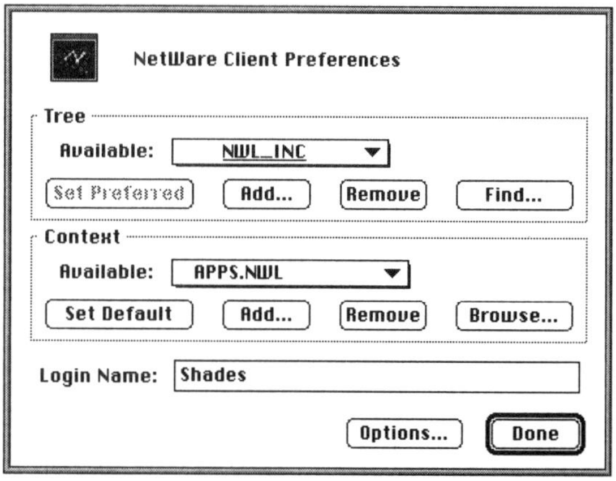

**FIGURE 16.4**

The NetWare Client Preferences dialog allows you to set defaults.

**Managing NetWare Connections**

The Connections option on the NDS Tree menu allows you to view a list of the Directory trees and servers you are currently attached to. From this screen you can log out of any of the connections. The Password button allows you to change your password for a server or tree.

# NetWare Directory Browser

The NetWare Directory Browser is a utility that allows a Macintosh user to browse the Directory tree, examine the objects, and change their settings relating to NetWare printers and volumes. While it's hardly NWADMIN, it is a handy utility for Macintosh users

To activate the Directory Browser, double-click its icon; this icon is installed automatically with the NetWare client software. The Browser window includes a pull-down menu at the top from which you can select a portion of the Directory tree. Below this menu are three sections:

- The Objects section shows a list of objects in the current context.

- The Show Types section allows you to use check boxes to determine which object types are included in the display.

- The Help section shows information about the current option or object.

Aside from browsing the Directory tree, the Directory Browser provides two more useful functions:

- To mount a volume, double-click the Volume object or select Browse ➤ Mount.

- When a Printer or Print Queue object is selected, you can use the Choose Printer or Choose Queue option from the Browse menu to select the printer for print jobs sent from the workstation.

# NetWare Volume Mounter

An icon for the NetWare Volume Mounter utility is also included when you install NetWare Client. Volume Mounter allows you to quickly mount a NetWare volume, making it accessible from the Macintosh desktop.

You use the drag-and-drop method to work with the Volume Mounter icon:

■ Drag a Volume object from the desktop or the Directory Browser to the Volume Mounter icon to mount the volume.

■ Drag a Server object to the Volume Mounter icon to mount the volumes on that server.

When you drag one or more volumes to the Volume Mounter icon, you see the Volume Mounter window, shown in Figure 16.5. Be sure the volume or volumes you wish to mount are highlighted; then click the Mount button to complete the mount operation.

**FIGURE 16.5**

The NetWare Volume Mounter allows you to configure access to server volumes.

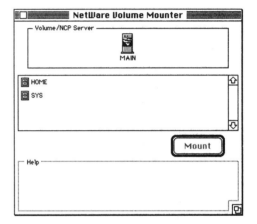

## NetWare Print Chooser

The NetWare Print Chooser application doesn't have an icon. Instead, you access it by double-clicking a Printer or Print Queue icon within the Directory Browser or selecting the Choose Printer or Choose Queue option. The Print Chooser window is shown in Figure 16.6.

Within the Print Chooser window, you can select the Setup button to configure the default capture settings for the printer or queue.

*You can also drag a Printer or Print Queue object to the desktop and double-click the desktop icon when you wish to choose that printer or queue.*

**FIGURE 16.6**

The NetWare Print Chooser allows a Macintosh workstation to send files to a network printer.

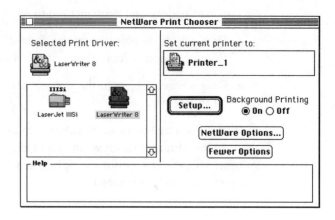

# Remote Console

The final Macintosh utility, Remote Console, is one many administrators have wished for: it allows you to view and control a file server console remotely. It works mich like the RCONSOLE utility for DOS workstations, which Chapter 10 examines in detail.

*To use the remote console (on either Macintosh or DOS) you will need to load the REMOTE and RSPX modules on the server, as described in Chapter 10.*

### Installing Remote Console

The Remote Console utility is not installed by default. You can follow these steps to install it, using the same utility you used to install the NetWare client:

1. Run the NetWare Client Install utility.

2. Select Custom Install to see the Custom Installation dialog, shown in Figure 16.7.

3. Select the Remote Console Install option.

4. Click the Install button.

**FIGURE 16.7**

The Custom Installation dialog allows you to install additional Macintosh client options.

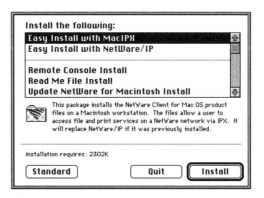

## Using Remote Console

After the installation process is complete, a Remote Console icon is created. Double-click this icon to open a remote console session. You can then select a server to connect to, enter the password, and view the server's screen.

The main difference in the Macintosh version of Remote Console is the keyboard configuration. Because Macintosh and PC keyboards are different, allowances were made in this version. Keystrokes also vary depending on the type of Macintosh keyboard. Table 16.1 shows the keystrokes for Macintosh Remote Console.

**TABLE 16.1**

Keystrokes for Macintosh Remote Console

| KEY (EXTENDED KEYBOARD) | KEY (STANDARD KEYBOARD) | DESCRIPTION |
| --- | --- | --- |
| Option-F2 | Option-Command-2 | Exits the current server and allows you to choose another |
| Option-F3 | Option-Command-3 | Switches to the previous screen |
| Option-F4 | Option-Command-4 | Switches to the next screen |
| Option-F5 | Option-Command-5 | Shows your current network address |
| Ins | Option-Command-I | Use when the Ins (PC) key is needed |
| Del | Option-Command-d | Use when the Del (PC) key is needed |

If you are using a standard Macintosh keyboard, you will also notice that many NetWare utilities and NLMs expect you to use the F1 through F12 keys, not present on your keyboard. You can get around this by turning on the function key palette. To use it, select Edit ➤ Show Function Keys.

Choosing this option opens a window with buttons for each key, which you can access with the mouse. Other commonly needed keys, such as Ins and Del, are also included. The function key palette is shown in Figure 16.8.

**FIGURE 16.8**

The function key palette allows you to access keys found only on extended keyboards.

# *Summary*

N THIS CHAPTER you've learned how to use NetWare 4 with Macintosh clients and networks. We covered the following topics:

- The basics of Macintosh networking, including the AppleTalk standard and its protocols

- NetWare for Macintosh, which allows Macintosh clients to attach to the server and access NDS

- Installing and managing the AppleTalk protocol

- The NetWare Client for Macintosh software, which is installed on the Macintosh client

- The utilities you can use from a Macintosh workstation, including the NDS Tree menu, Directory Browser, Volume Mounter, Printer Chooser, and Remote Console

In the next chapter we'll explore another way of connecting NetWare to non-PC machines and networks. We will look at TCP/IP, the protocol used by UNIX systems and by the Internet, and examine the ways NetWare 4 can work with this and other Internet features.

# Using NetWare 4 with Intranets and the Internet

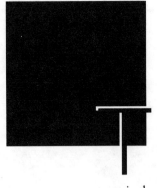

THE INTERNET HAS grown in popularity over the past few years. This is a global network that allows companies and individuals to exchange, present and share information. A more recent development is the concept of intranets—company-wide networks that serve a similar, but local, purpose.

One of the most important improvements in NetWare 4.11 is improved support for the Internet and intranets. Novell's IntranetWare is a product that provides NetWare 4.11 along with several Internet features, including the NetWare Web Server, Novell Internet Access Server, and Novell FTP Services.

In this chapter we look at NetWare 4's Internet-related features and explain how to use NetWare 4 with the Internet and intranets. We start with a look at the TCP/IP protocol suite, which is used by most of the Internet and supported by NetWare 4.

# Understanding TCP/IP

The TCP/IP *protocol suite,* or set of protocols, is widely used on the Internet and with UNIX machines. TCP/IP is named for its two most important protocols, TCP (Transport Control Protocol) and IP (Internet Protocol). The TCP/IP suite also uses several other protocols.

## Protocols in TCP/IP

The OSI reference model, introduced in Chapter 14, divides the processes involved in a NetWare network into seven layers.  The TCP/IP suite is organized using a different model, the DOD networking model. This model is divided into four layers:

- The network access layer specifies protocols for basic network connectivity.

- The Internet layer includes protocols used for internetworking and routing.

- The host-to-host layer includes protocols for communication between hosts.

- The process/application layer is used by actual applications.

We take a brief look at the protocols involved in each of these layers in the following sections.

### Protocols in the Network Access Layer

The network access layer is the lowest layer in the DOD model; it deals with physical connections. This layer is similar to the network layer of the OSI reference model. The protocols in this layer include the network protocols you're probably familiar with already, such as Ethernet, ARCnet, and Token Ring. In addition, Internet-specific protocols are supported, such as the following:

- **SLIP (Single Line Interface Protocol):** Used for Internet dial-up connections

- **PPP (Point-to-Point Protocol):** An improved dial-up protocol

- **X.25:** Used for dedicated-line networks and some dial-up networks

- **Frame relay:** Another type of dedicated line available to businesses

- **ISDN:** A relatively new protocol that allows high-speed access using ordinary phone lines, provided the phone company supports it

- **ATM (Asynchronous Transfer Mode):** A new standard for high-speed local networking

### Protocols in the Internet Layer

The Internet layer includes protocols that allow for routing between networks and protocols that simplify access for the upper-layer protocols. These include the following:

- **IP (Internet Protocol):** Sends data between machines, attaching the IP address for the destination. Other Internet layer protocols use IP.

- **ARP (Address Resolution Protocol):** Translates between IP addresses and hardware addresses.

- **RARP (Reverse Address Resolution Protocol):** Translates between hardware addresses and IP addresses.

- **ICMP (Internet Control Message Protocol):** Manages IP and sends warning messages when problems occur.

### Protocols in the Host-to-Host Layer

The host-to-host layer includes two protocols: TCP (Transport Control Protocol) and UDP (User Datagram Protocol). TCP is a connection-oriented protocol, which means it establishes a connection, or *virtual circuit,* before sending data. This provides for reliable transport of information, much like NetWare's SPX protocol.

UDP, on the other hand, is a connectionless protocol; data is addressed and sent through the network without establishing a connection, and no acknowledgment is received. This function is similar to NetWare's IPX protocol. UDP uses less network bandwidth than TCP but is not as reliable. Both TCP and UDP have their uses.

### Protocols in the Application Layer

The application layer contains protocols for actual applications. These protocols are used for Internet applications and services. Since this layer is isolated from the other layers, applications are platform independent; as long as the protocols are supported correctly, any platforms can communicate. The protocols in the application layer include the following:

- **FTP (File Transfer Protocol):** Copies files between hosts

- **TELNET:** Allows a client machine to act as a terminal to a host machine

- **HTTP (Hypertext Transfer Protocol):** Transfers documents for the World Wide Web, explained in the section "Using NetWare Web Server" later in this chapter

- **SMTP: (Simple Mail Transport Protocol):** Transfers e-mail messages between systems

- **NNTP (Network News Transport Protocol):** Used for USENET news, a global bulletin board–type system that operates within the Internet

*This is just a sampling of the most commonly used protocols supported by the Internet and the application layer of the DOD model. There are many other protocols in use across the Internet.*

## Understanding IP Addresses and DNS

TCP/IP uses an address scheme called *IP addressing*. This scheme assigns a 32-bit address to each node on a network or on the Internet. Each host (node) on the network matches a specific IP address.

### IP Addressing

Nodes on the Internet are addressed using hierarchical IP addresses. Each address is composed of 32 bits; these are organized into four 1-byte numbers (also called octets), ranging from 0 to 255. Thus, the following are valid IP addresses:

- 128.0.0.0

- 204.91.164.152

- 128.110.121.6

In general, the first number in an IP address is the most significant, referring to a large organization or network; the last number refers to a single machine. More specifically, the use of the 4 bytes varies depending on the class of network; the following sections describe the three possible classes.

IP addresses for the Internet are maintained by the InterNIC, a nonprofit organization assigned the task by the U.S. government, which originally funded it. It is now independently operated and funded through domain registration fees.

**CLASS A NETWORK ADDRESSES** Class A addresses are intended for very large networks. In this type of address, the first byte of the IP address refers to the network, and the remaining 3 bytes specify a node number within a network. This allows for a large number of nodes in a class A network—16,777,214, to be exact. The problem is that there can be only 127 separate class A networks globally. Needless to say, given the current size of the Internet, all of these are taken; most companies have class B or C addresses.

**CLASS B NETWORK ADDRESSES** Class B addresses use 2 bytes for the network number and 2 bytes for the node number. This allows for 16,384 separate networks and 65,534 nodes per network. Once again, all of the Class B addresses are currently used in the Internet.

**CLASS C NETWORK ADDRESSES** Class C networks use 3 bytes of the IP address for the network number and 1 byte for the node number. This allows for a great number of networks—over two million—but only 254 nodes per network. Since the vast majority of companies on the Internet have fewer than 254 machines, class C addresses are the most common.

**USING SUBNETS** Class C network addresses for the Internet are still available but are running out. Several schemes are currently being discussed to expand the IP addressing scheme, but in the meantime there is a solution that works in most cases. *Subnet masking* is a technique for using part of the IP address to subdivide the network into smaller networks.

This technique involves assigning a subnet address, or mask, to each machine on the network. This mask extracts the machine address from the IP address. While subnet masking does not allow more than 254 machines in a class C network to be used on the Internet, it does allow a greater number to be used within a network.

## Host and Domain Names

You may have noticed that IP addresses aren't very friendly. The Internet also uses a system of friendly names for sites. These are referred to as host names and domain names:

- A *host name* is the name of a machine on the Internet; this corresponds to the node portion of an IP address.

- Companies and organizations on the Internet are assigned *subdomain names*.

- A *domain name* specifies the type of organization or country. These include: *com* for company names, *org* for nonprofit organizations, *net* for network providers, *mil* for the US military, *gov* for the U.S. government, and *edu* for educational institutions. International domains specify the two-letter country code, as discussed in Chapter 5. International domains are sometimes divided into subdomains based on their function.

Here are a few examples with descriptions, ranging from simple to complex:

| SUBDOMAIN | REFERS TO |
| --- | --- |
| sybex.com | The main machine in the subdomain named sybex in the com (company) domain |
| ftp.novell.com | A machine named ftp in the novell subdomain, and the com (company) domain |
| www.starlingtech.com | A machine called www in the starlingtech subdomain, and the com (company) domain |

## Address Resolution

Each host name corresponds with an IP address. Because the IP address is required to make a connection, the host name must be *resolved,* or converted to an IP address. This is a service performed by *name servers.* These servers use a system called DNS (Domain Name System) to return information about a host name. Name servers exist for each domain and subdomain.

In a local TCP/IP network, DNS is unnecessary. You can simply use a *host table* to define IP addresses for hosts. The host table for a NetWare server is located at SYS:ETC\HOSTS by default.

## Using TCP/IP with NetWare 4

You can optionally install TCP/IP in the process of installing NetWare 4. If you haven't done so, follow the instructions in this section to add the TCP/IP protocols to your server.

You use the INETCFG utility to configure the TCP/IP protocol. This is a general-purpose utility for configuring network protocols and LAN cards. To start this utility, type **LOAD INETCFG** at the server console. Follow these steps to install the TCP/IP protocol:

1. If you have not run INETCFG before, you are presented with the warning and prompt shown in Figure 17.1. For INETCFG to work, it must move the LOAD and BIND statements for network adapters and protocols from the AUTOEXEC.NCF file to the INITSYS.NCF file. This is done automatically if you select Yes from the prompt.

**FIGURE 17.1**

The INETCFG utility moves LOAD and BIND statements for network cards to the INITSYS.NCF file.

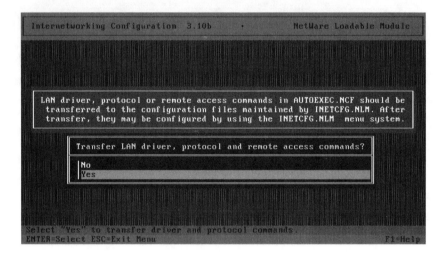

2. The main INETCFG menu is shown in Figure 17.2. It includes options to configure protocols, network cards, and bindings. Select Protocol Configuration from the INETCFG menu to begin configuring the TCP/IP protocol.

3. You are now shown a list of protocols that can be configured on the system (Figure 17.3). If TCP/IP is already configured, the word *Enabled* appears to the right of *TCP/IP*; if it doesn't, select the TCP/IP option and press ↵ to configure it.

4. The TCP/IP Protocol Configuration screen is now displayed, as shown in Figure 17.4. This screen allows you to enable the TCP/IP protocol and specify various options. If you are unsure of the settings you need, the default settings will work in most cases.

**FIGURE 17.2**

The INETCFG utility allows you to configure TCP/IP and other protocols.

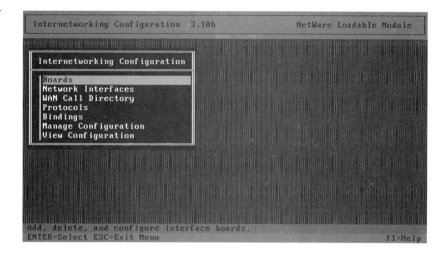

**FIGURE 17.3**

Select TCP/IP from the list of installable protocols.

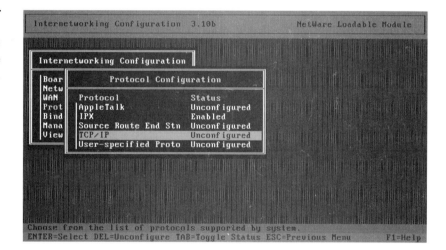

**5.** Press Esc to return to the main INETCFG menu.

**6.** Select Bindings from the main menu. You see a list of current protocol bindings for your server, as shown in Figure 17.5. Most likely, the list includes only IPX.

**7.** Press Ins to add a binding. You see a list of protocols that have been enabled, as shown in Figure 17.6. Select TCP/IP from this list.

**FIGURE 17.4**

Configure the TCP/IP protocol.

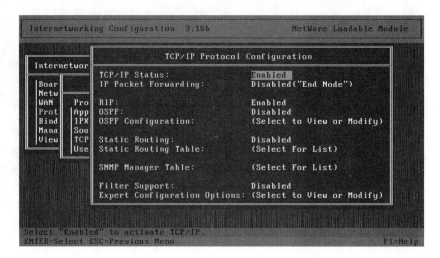

**FIGURE 17.5**

Add TCP/IP to the list of network card bindings.

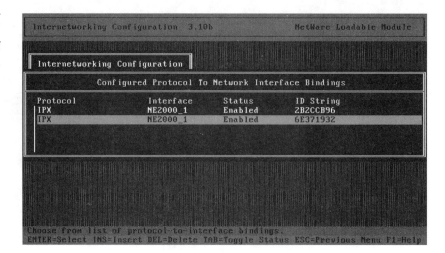

**8.** You now see a list of options for binding the TCP/IP protocol, as shown in Figure 17.7. Specify the IP address and subnet mask for your network, and change the other options as desired.

**9.** Press Esc to return to the main menu, and answer Yes to save the changes to the network card bindings.

**10.** Exit INETCFG.

FIGURE 17.6

Select TCP/IP as the protocol to bind.

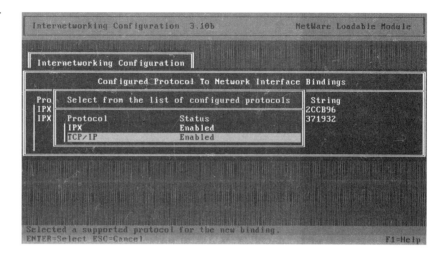

**FIGURE 17.6**

Select TCP/IP as the protocol to bind.

**FIGURE 17.7**

Enter options for binding the TCP/IP protocol.

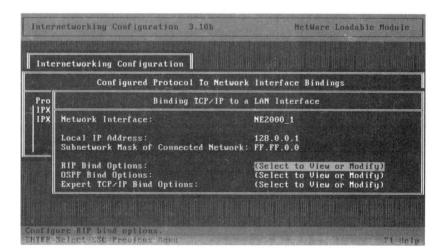

You have now completed the installation of the TCP/IP protocol.

*Before you use the TCP/IP protocol or install additional software, such as the NetWare Web Server, you must restart the server. The NLMs required for the TCP/IP protocol are loaded automatically when you start the server.*

# Using the NetWare Web Server

THE WORLD WIDE Web is one of the most popular areas of the Internet. Internet users can use Web documents to publish hypertext information. This is accomplished through Web servers, which use the HTTP protocol. If you have an Internet connection, you can access Web documents on servers throughout the world.

The client you use to read Web documents is called a *Web browser*. The most popular Web browser, Netscape Navigator, is included as part of Novell Internet Access Server, described in the section "Using Novell Internet Access Server" later in this chapter. Documents on the Web are usually written in HTML, a text markup language designed for the purpose.

A Web server does not have to be a specialized machine. Currently, the majority of servers on the Web run under UNIX. Novell has made it possible to run a Web server on a NetWare 4 server via the NetWare Web Server software. We look at NetWare Web Server in detail in the sections that follow.

*You can use the NetWare Web Server on any server for local (intranet) Web services. If you wish to make documents available through the Internet, your network must have a continuous connection to the Internet.*

## Installing the Web Server

The NetWare Web Server software is normally included on the same CD you installed NetWare 4 from. Before you install this Web server, you must install the TCP/IP protocol, as explained earlier in this chapter. After TCP/IP has been installed, restart the server. You can then proceed with the following steps to install the Web server:

1. Insert the CD into the server's CD-ROM drive. You can optionally use a different server's drive if you mount the CD as a NetWare volume.

2. From the server console, type **LOAD INSTALL** to start the installation utility. The main INSTALL menu is shown in Figure 17.8.

3. Select Product Options from the main INSTALL menu.

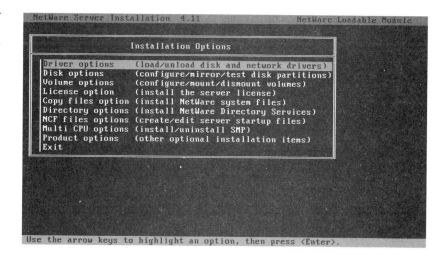

**FIGURE 17.8**

Use the INSTALL utility to install the Web server.

4. A list of products that can be installed is now displayed, as shown in Figure 17.9. Select Install NetWare WEB Server to proceed with the installation.

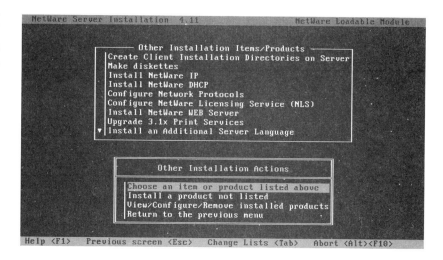

**FIGURE 17.9**

Select Install NetWare WEB Server from the product options.

5. Specify the drive and directory to install the Web server from. The default setting is usually correct.

6. The installation program now copies files into a temporary directory for installation. This takes between five and ten minutes. A progress display is shown while copying, as shown in Figure 17.10.

**FIGURE 17.10**

The NetWare Web Server installation is now in progress.

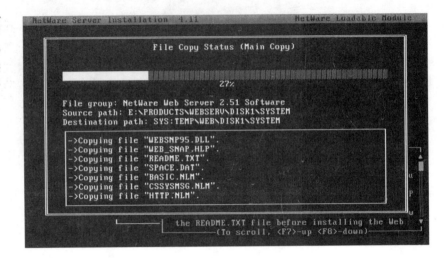

7. After the copy process completes, you are asked for a host name for the Web server. This is the local machine name that will be advertised by the Web server. By default, the server's name is used. This prompt is shown in Figure 17.11.

**FIGURE 17.11**

Enter a host name for the Web server.

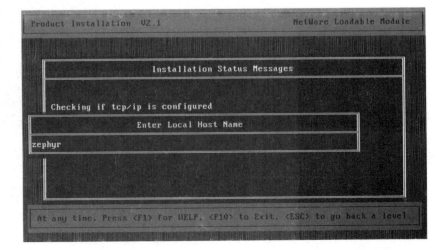

**8.** Next you are asked for an administration password for the Web server (see Figure 17.12). This password will be required to change the Web server's configuration.

**FIGURE 17.12**

Enter an administration password for the Web server.

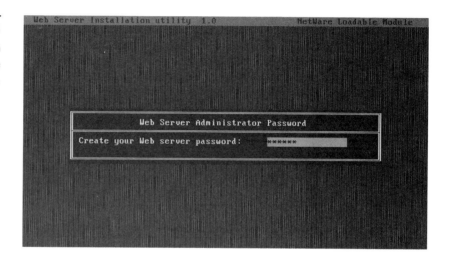

**9.** The installation program now copies files into their final directories. If the Web server installation finishes properly, you will see the final status of the installation, as shown in Figure 17.13.

**FIGURE 17.13**

The Web server installation is now complete.

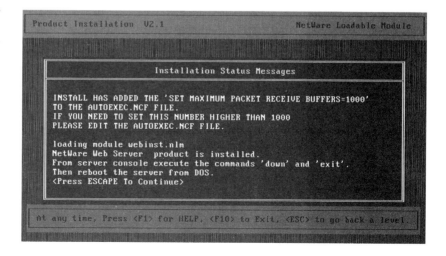

You have now successfully installed the NetWare Web Server. Before it can be used, you must restart the server. The NLMs the Web server uses will be loaded automatically the next time the server starts.

When the Web server is running, it occupies a screen on the server console. Switch to this screen to see the current status of the Web server, including the number of requests currently being handled, the Web server name, and the location of the served documents. This status screen is shown in Figure 17.14.

**FIGURE 17.14**

Status screen for the NetWare Web Server

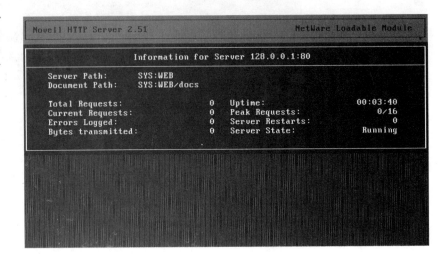

## Creating Web Pages

The Web documents for the NetWare Web Server are stored in a directory on the server. By default, the directory is SYS:WEB\DOCS. You can store files under this directory to make them accessible as Web documents.

Although any type of document can be stored on the Web server, the most common type is HTML, or Hypertext Markup Language. This language was developed for the Web; it allows you to specify formatting for text and create links between documents.

An HTML document is essentially a text file, with special codes (called *HTML tags*) inserted to assign certain attributes to parts of the text. Here is a simple example of an HTML document:

```
<HTML>

<HEAD>

    <TITLE>Test Web Page</TITLE>
```

```
<BODY>

<H1>Test Web Page</H1>

This is the text of the page. It can include <B>bold</
    B>, <I>italic</I>, and <U>underlined</U> text, among
    other things. <P>This is a second paragraph.

</BODY>

</HTML>
```

HTML is a complex language, and beyond the scope of this book. To learn more about it, consult one of the many books available on the subject. You can also use some software packages to create Web pages using a word processor–like interface without the need to understand HTML. One such product, HoTMetaL Lite, is included with IntranetWare.

## Adding Interactive Features

HTML documents are static—they can display information, but they can't really act as programs. You can use programs through the Web server, though, by taking advantage of the available interactive features. These include the following:

- An implementation of the Perl language is included with the NetWare Web Server. You can use this language for CGI (Common Gateway Interface) scripts, which are commonly used on the Web to accept data a user enters and to convert database information to HTML output.

- A simple language called NetBasic, based on the BASIC language, is also included. This language allows you to add simple interactive features to a page with a minimum of programming knowledge.

- For professional developers, two interfaces, RCGI (remote CGI) and LCGI (local CGI) allow you to develop NLMs that can interact over the Web.

- Sun's Java programming language, which allows you to create client-side applications for the Web, is also supported by the NetWare Web Server.

# Using Novell Internet Access Server

NOVELL INTERNET ACCESS Server, or NIAS, is an enhancement to NetWare 4 (included as part of the IntranetWare package) that adds several Internet-related features. We explore the components of NIAS and how to install and use it in the following sections.

## Components of NIAS

The Internet Access Server is a combination of several products that make NetWare 4 more readily useful as an Internet or intranet server. These include an enhanced router, an IPX-to-IP gateway, improved WAN support, and a Web browser. These are described in the sections that follow.

### Multiprotocol Router (MPR) 3.1

As discussed in Chapter 14, any NetWare server can act as a simple router—a device that translates and sends data between different types of networks. The NetWare Multiprotocol Router (MPR) allows enhanced filtering and other capabilities. Included with the Internet Access Server is a new version of the MPR, version 3.1.

*For more information about the new MPR, see the Dynatext documentation included with Internet Access Server. For a basic introduction to the MPR, see Chapter 14.*

### The IPX/IP Gateway

Another feature added to NetWare 4 as part of Internet Access Server is an IPX/IP gateway. This service can be configured to automatically translate data between IP and IPX networks. This allows you to run an IP-specific service (such as the NetWare Web Server) on the network and access it with any client, without the need to install TCP/IP on each client machine.

### WAN Extensions 3.1

Also included with the Internet Access Server is a set of extensions that improve WAN support under NetWare 4.11. These extend the support for WANs using IP and also support PPP, frame relay, and ISDN connectivity.

### Netscape Navigator

The final part of the NIAS package is Netscape Navigator, a Web browser produced by Netscape Communications Corp. and licensed by Novell. You can use this browser under Windows 3.1 or Windows 95 to access documents served by the NetWare Web Server. The documentation for the NetWare Web Server and NIAS is also provided in HTML format and can be viewed using Netscape.

*At this writing, the current version of Netscape Navigator is 3.0; however, version 2.0 is currently included with Internet Access Server.*

## Installing NIAS Server Components

The Internet Access Server includes a simple installation program you can access through the NetWare INSTALL utility. NIAS requires a large amount of disk storage (approximately 97MB), so be sure you have adequate space before you begin. Follow these steps to install NIAS:

1. Load the INSTALL utility at the server console by typing **LOAD INSTALL**.

2. Select Product Options from the main INSTALL menu.

3. Select Products ➤ Install a Product not Listed.

4. Press F3 to specify a path for the installation. The path should be *X*:\NIAS\INSTALL, where *X* is the letter of your CD-ROM drive (or NetWare volume name).

5. The Internet Access Server Installation Options menu is now displayed, as shown in Figure 17.15. Select Install Product from this menu.

6. You now see a list of servers on the network. The menu in Figure 17.16 lists a single server. Select the server to install the product to; usually this is the current server.

**FIGURE 17.15**

Installation options for the
NIAS install program

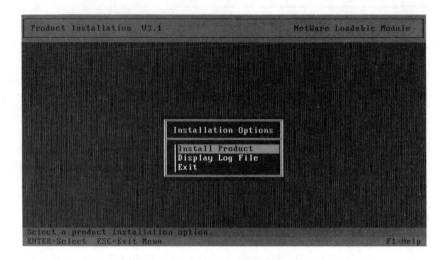

**FIGURE 17.16**

Select the servers
on which to install
Internet Access Server.

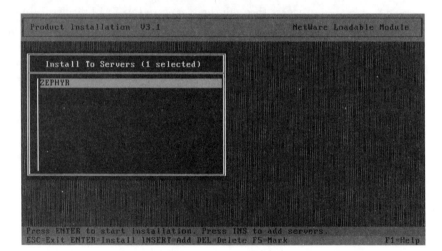

## Configuring the Server

Once you have installed the server components of Internet Access Server, you
can enable the IPX/IP gateway software. You use the INETCFG utility, introduced earlier in this chapter, to do this.

Before you begin, be sure you have installed TCP/IP and moved the LOAD and BIND commands from AUTOEXEC.NCF to the INITSYS.NCF file, as explained in the section "Using TCP/IP with NetWare 4" earlier in this chapter. Follow these steps to configure the gateway:

1. Type **LOAD INETCFG** at the server console to start the utility.

2. Select Protocols from the main INETCFG menu.

3. You are now shown a list of available protocols. Select TCP/IP.

4. From the TCP/IP Configuration menu, select the IPX/IP Gateway Configuration option.

5. Select the Gateway Status option and press ↵ to enable it.

6. If you are running a DNS (Domain Name System) server, specify its address in the space provided.

7. Press Esc to return to the main INETCFG menu and save changes.

## Installing Client Software

To use the IPX/IP gateway, you must install the client software included with the Internet Access Server on each client machine. This is an enhanced version of NetWare Client 32 (described in Chapter 3) that supports the IPX/IP gateway. Versions of the client are available for Windows 3.1 and Windows 95.

*This section is a quick guide to installing Client 32 with support for the IPX/IP gateway. For more detailed information about Client 32, see Chapter 3.*

To install the client software, follow these steps:

1. Determine the appropriate SETUP program to use. For Windows 3.1, use SYS:PUBLIC\CLIENT\WIN31\SETUP.EXE; for Windows 95, use SYS:PUBLIC\CLIENT\WIN95\SETUP.EXE.

2. Select Run from Program Manager's File menu or from Windows 95's Start menu. Enter the path to the SETUP program.

3. You are shown an introductory dialog. Click the Continue button to continue the installation.

4. You are shown a software license agreement. Accept the license agreement for Client 32 by selecting Yes.

5. Select a directory to install the client software to, and specify your Windows directory.

6. You are now shown a list of settings for your current hardware. Select Next to continue.

7. You see the Additional Options dialog. Check the box labeled NetWare IPX/IP Gateway and click Next to continue.

8. After the installation completes, select OK to restart the computer. Client 32 will load automatically when the computer restarts.

# Using FTP and UNIX Services

THE THIRD COMPONENT of IntranetWare is Novell FTP Services. FTP (File Transfer Protocol) was introduced in the section "Understanding TCP/IP" earlier in this chapter. Novell FTP Services allows you to run an FTP server on the NetWare server, along with other UNIX-related features. We look at these features in the sections that follow.

*Novell FTP Services is also referred to as Novell UNIX Print Services; although unrelated to FTP, this is a capability provided by the same program.*

## Installing Novell FTP Services

The FTP server requires TCP/IP to run. If you have already installed and configured the TCP/IP protocol, you can install the FTP server. If you have not yet configured TCP, do so as described earlier in this chapter. To install the FTP server, follow these steps:

1. Insert the Novell FTP Services CD-ROM in the server's CD-ROM drive.

2. Type **LOAD CDROM** at the console prompt to load CD-ROM support and type **CD MOUNT NWUXPS** to mount the CD-ROM.

3. Load the INSTALL utility by typing **LOAD INSTALL**.

4. From the Install menu, select Product Options.

5. From the Product Options menu, select Install a Product Not Listed.

6. Press F3 to choose the installation path and type the path to the NWUXPS directory on the CD-ROM. Typically this is NWUXPS:\NWUXPS.

7. The FTP Services installation program now asks for the path to your server boot files. This is the directory on the DOS partition where SERVER.EXE is stored, usually C:\NWSERVER.

8. Next you are asked whether to install the FTP Services online documentation. Choose Yes or No.

9. The UNICON utility is now loaded; here you can choose the services to be run. This utility is explained in detail in the next section.

## Configuring FTP and UNIX Services

There is a wide variety of options for Novell FTP Services and the other UNIX services. You can configure these options from the UNICON utility. To start this utility, follow these steps:

1. Type **LOAD UNICON** at the server console.

2. You are now prompted for the username and password for the Admin account, as shown in Figure 17.17. Enter the password to continue.

You are now presented with a menu of options. We discuss the features of this utility in the next sections.

### UNICON Options

The UNICON main menu (shown in Figure 17.18) includes the following options:

- **Change Current Server:** Allows you to manage FTP and other services for a different server.

**FIGURE 17.17**

Enter the administrator username and password.

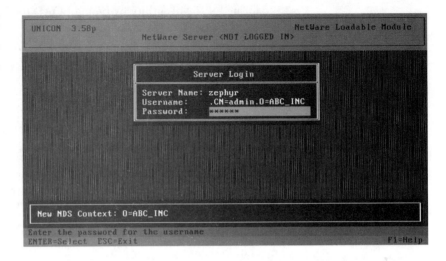

**FIGURE 17.18**

The UNICON utility allows you to configure the FTP server.

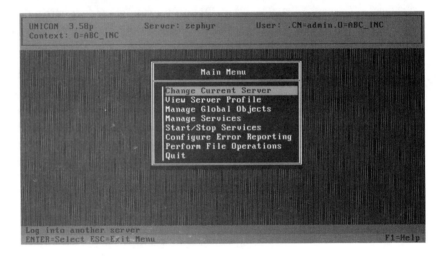

- **View Server Profile:** Displays a list of information about the server and the services running on it, as shown in Figure 17.19.

- **Manage Global Objects:** Allows you to manage NDS users and groups for the FTP server.

- **Manage Services:** Displays a list of services currently running, as shown in Figure 17.20. You can select each service to access a menu of options specific to that service.

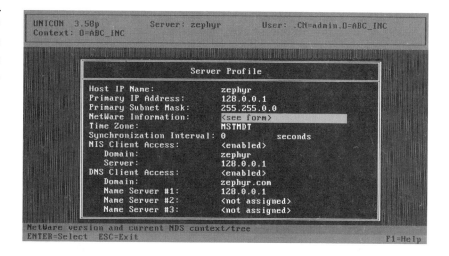

**FIGURE 17.19**

The Server Profile option displays information about the server.

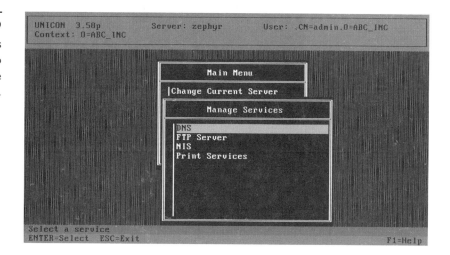

**FIGURE 17.20**

The Manage Services menu allows you to choose a service to manage.

- **Start/Stop Services:** Allows you to start and stop services. This option is explained in detail in the next section.

- **Configure Error Reporting:** Allows you to choose a log file that will store error messages relating to the services.

- **Perform File Operations:** Allows you to perform simple file maintenance operations.

### Starting or Stopping Services

The Start/Stop Services option displays a list of services that are currently running, as shown in Figure 17.21. By default, only DNS or NIS is running. The available services include the following:

**FIGURE 17.21**

The Start/Stop Services
option displays a list of
currently running services.

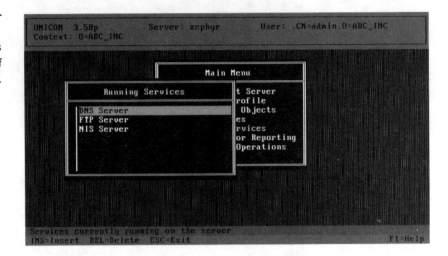

- **DNS Server (Domain Name Service):** Provides identification for domain names

- **NIS Server (Network Information Service):** An alternative to DNS

- **FTP Server (File Transfer Protocol):** Allows network users to transfer files via TCP/IP

- **NetWare-to-UNIX Print Gateway:** Allows clients on the NetWare network to print to UNIX machines

- **UNIX-to-NetWare Print Server:** Allows clients on the UNIX network to print to NetWare printers

To stop a currently running service, highlight its entry and press Del. To start a service that is not currently running, press Ins and choose the service from the list.

### Managing the FTP Server

The most important capability you can manage through the UNICON utility is the FTP Server. You can use Novell FTP Services along with a Web server to allow users of the Web site to download files or browse directories on the network.

To manage the FTP Server, choose FTP Server from the Manage Services menu in UNICON. The FTP Administration menu, shown in Figure 17.22, is now displayed.

**FIGURE 17.22**

The FTP Administration menu allows you to manage the FTP server.

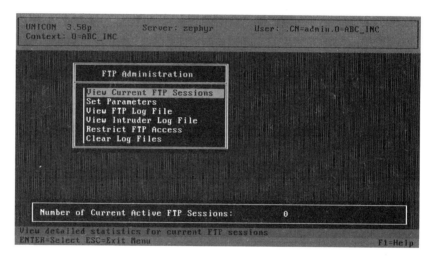

Select from the following options to manage the FTP server:

- **View Current FTP Sessions:** Displays a list of users who are currently accessing FTP services and the files they are accessing

- **Set Parameters:** Allows you to set various parameters for the FTP server, as shown in Figure 17.23

- **View FTP Log File:** Displays the log file, which logs all FTP accesses

- **View Intruder Log File:** Displays a list of attempted logins that failed

- **Restrict FTP Access:** Allows you to edit a file that can restrict access to certain users or domains

- **Clear Log Files:** Resets both of the log files

**FIGURE 17.23**

The FTP Server Parameters option allows you to configure the FTP server.

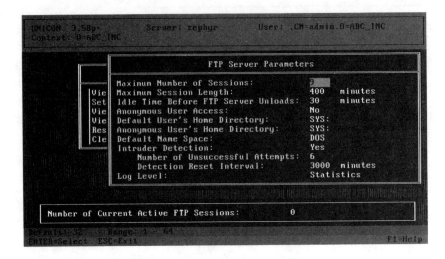

```
UNICON 3.58p+          Server: zephyr        User: .CN=admin.O=ABC_INC
Context: O=ABC_INC

                          FTP Server Parameters
          Maximum Number of Sessions:                9
      Vie Maximum Session Length:                    400   minutes
      Set Idle Time Before FTP Server Unloads:       30    minutes
      Vie Anonymous User Access:                     No
      Vie Default User's Home Directory:             SYS:
      Res Anonymous User's Home Directory:           SYS:
      Cle Default Name Space:                        DOS
          Intruder Detection:                        Yes
             Number of Unsuccessful Attempts:        6
             Detection Reset Interval:               3000  minutes
          Log Level:                                 Statistics


     Number of Current Active FTP Sessions:              0

Default: 32    Range: 1 - 64
ENTER=Select  ESC=Exit                                             F1=Help
```

## Configuring Anonymous FTP

If you wish to make files available to the general public over the Internet, you need to configure the FTP Server to support Anonymous FTP. This is the default mode used by Web browsers. Follow these steps to configure anonymous FTP:

**1.** Select Set Parameters from the FTP Administration menu.

**2.** Set the Maximum Number of Sessions to allow concurrent users.

**3.** Set Anonymous User Access to Yes.

**4.** Set Anonymous User's Home Directory to a directory on the server that you will use to store files available by anonymous FTP.

**5.** Set the other parameters as desired; refer to the Novell FTP Services documentation for further details.

# Summary

N THIS CHAPTER you've learned about the Internet and intranets and how to support these networks with a NetWare 4 server. We covered these topics:

- You can use the TCP/IP protocol suite with NetWare 4 to provide Internet connectivity or to internetwork with UNIX machines. This suite includes several protocols widely used on the Internet.

- The NetWare Web Server provides Web server (HTTP) services over the Internet or an intranet. These services can be used through an IPX-to-IP gateway or for clients with the TCP/IP protocol installed.

- Novell Internet Access Server adds capabilities to clients and servers to make it easier to access Internet and intranet services. These capabilities include an IPX-to-IP gateway, which makes it possible to access the Internet without configuring the TCP/IP protocol on the client machines.

# Quick Reference: Command-Line Utilities

APPENDIX

A

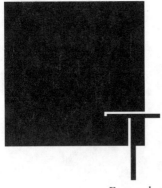

THIS APPENDIX IS intended as a quick reference for command-line utilities. You can use these utilities from a DOS workstation. They are listed in alphabetical order in the sections below. Examples of each command are included where practical, and the most common options are listed. In addition, cross-references to chapters in this book with more information are provided where appropriate. For more detailed information on these commands, refer to the NetWare manuals or online documentation.

## CAPTURE

The CAPTURE command redirects a printer port on the workstation to a print queue or printer on the NetWare 4 server. The following example redirects the LPT1 port to the CHECKS print queue:

```
CAPTURE L=1 Q=CHECKS
```

The following example redirects LPT2 to the LASER1 printer:

```
CAPTURE LPT2 P=LASER1
```

*Refer to Chapter 8 for a complete list of CAPTURE options.*

## CX

Use the CX command to change your current NDS context. This is the NDS container object that will be used by default when searching for objects. For example, this command sets the current context to .O=ADMIN:

```
CX .O=ADMIN
```

*Refer to Chapters 5 and 6 for further information about NDS and the Directory tree.*

## FLAG

The FLAG command displays the attributes for an existing file or directory, or allows you to manage file and directory attributes. The command is followed by a path or file name and options to specify attributes to be added or removed. FLAG by itself displays the attributes of all files in the current directory. Following are several examples of the FLAG command.

This command adds the Hidden attribute to the SYS:ETC\DATA directory:

```
FLAG SYS:ETC\DATA +H
```

This command sets all files in the current directory to Normal (Read/Write):

```
FLAG *.* N
```

This command gives the FILER.EXE file the Read Only attribute:

```
FLAG SYS:PUBLIC\FILER.EXE +RO
```

*File attributes are listed and explained in detail in Chapter 4.*

## LOGIN

The LOGIN command logs you in to a NetWare 4 server or NDS tree. If not specified, the server or tree listed as the default in the workstation's NET.CFG file is used. You can add the /NS switch to attach to a server without logging out of the current server or tree. This command logs in the user HENRY on the default tree or server:

```
LOGIN HENRY
```

This command logs in the user TED on the tree CHERRY_TREE:

```
LOGIN CHERRY_TREE/TED
```

## LOGOUT

The LOGOUT command ends your current login session and allows another user to log in at the workstation. By default, you are logged out of all servers. You can also log out of just one server, keeping your connection to the others, by specifying the server name:

```
LOGOUT SERVER1
```

## MAP

Use the MAP command to map a network drive letter to a volume and directory on the server. You can also use this command with Directory Map objects. For example:

```
MAP J:=SYS:APPS\PROGRAM
```

maps the network drive J to the APPS\PROGRAM directory on the SYS: volume.

```
MAP S3:=SYS:PUBLIC
```

maps the third search drive to the PUBLIC directory.

```
MAP K:=WP
```

maps network drive K to the volume and directory specified by the Directory Map object WP.

*The MAP command and the file system are explained in Chapter 4.*

## NCOPY

The NCOPY command copies files from one directory to another. You can use this command with both local and network directories, and it can copy entire directory structures. However, at least one of the directories must be on a network server. Here are several examples:

```
NCOPY C:\DOS\*.* F:\PUBLIC\DOS
```

copies all files in the DOS directory on local drive C to the PUBLIC\DOS directory on network drive F.

```
NCOPY C:\*.* /S
```

copies all files on drive C, including subdirectories, to the current directory.

```
NCOPY F:\BACKUP\*.* C:\ /S/E/V
```

copies all the files from the BACKUP directory, including subdirectories, to drive C, including empty directories, and verifies each file.

## NDIR

The NDIR command lists the files in a directory. This command is similar to the DIR command in DOS, but it also displays NetWare file attributes and ownership information. NDIR has a wide variety of available options, which you can use to search for files or list specific types of information. Here are some examples:

```
NDIR
```

lists all files in the current directory, using the default format.

```
NDIR * /R
```

displays a list of rights for each file in the current directory.

```
NDIR F:\*.TMP /SUB
```

lists all files with a TMP extension on drive F, including those in subdirectories.

```
NDIR F:\* /SUB /OW EQ SUE.ACCT.STECH
```

lists all files owned by the user SUE on the network drive F. If the user is in the current context, the full distinguished name is not necessary.

```
NDIR F:\PUBLIC\* /CR BEF 03-22-97
```

lists all files in the PUBLIC directory created before March 22, 1997.

# NLIST

NLIST is a general-purpose utility for listing NDS objects. You can use it to list users, servers, or any other type of NDS object, or to look for objects with a certain property. Here are several examples:

```
NLIST USER /A
```

lists all users in the current context.

```
NLIST SERVER /B
```

lists all bindery servers.

```
NLIST USER WHERE "GROUP MEMBERSHIP" = ACCTG
```

lists all users who are members of the ACCTG group.

```
NLIST USER SHOW "TELEPHONE NUMBER"
```

lists all user names and their telephone numbers (if defined).

```
NLIST GROUP /S
```

lists all groups defined in the Directory tree.

```
NLIST *
```

lists all objects in the current context.

# NPRINT

The NPRINT command allows you to quickly send a text file to a network print queue. For example, the following command sends all files with the .TXT extension in the current directory to the LASER1 print queue:

```
NPRINT *.TXT Q=LASER1
```

*This command, and NetWare 4 printing in general, are explained in Chapter 8.*

## NPRINTER

NPRINTER starts the driver for a workstation (remote) printer. This program remains in memory to drive the printer until you unload it. The following command sets up the LASER1 printer attached to the current workstation:

```
NPRINTER LASER1
```

*You can also use the NPRINTER manager to run a workstation printer under Windows 95; see Chapter 8 for details.*

## NVER

The NVER command displays NetWare version information, such as the server you are attached to and the revision of client software. This can be useful if you are testing a workstation's current connection or analyzing a network you are unfamiliar with.

## PURGE

The PURGE command purges deleted files from the current directory, preventing them from being salvaged with the FILER or NWADMIN utility. You can add the /A switch to purge all files on the server. For example:

```
PURGE *.*
```

purges all deleted files in the current directory.

```
PURGE \*.* /A
```

purges all deleted files on the volume.

## RENDIR

RENDIR renames a directory. You can use this command on local directories or on the NetWare server. The following command renames the BACKUP directory on the SYS: volume, giving it the new name TEMP:

```
RENDIR SYS:BACKUP TEMP
```

The following command renames the C:\DOS directory to DOS_OLD:

```
RENDIR C:\DOS DOS_OLD
```

# RIGHTS

The RIGHTS command displays your current rights in a directory of the file system. This command also allows you to grant or revoke rights to a user or maintain the IRF. Here are several examples:

```
RIGHTS VOL1:USERS R W C F /NAME=KRISTEN
```

gives the user KRISTEN the Read, Write, Create, and File scan rights for the VOL1:USERS directory.

```
RIGHTS SYS:DATA REM /NAME=JohnS
```

removes all rights that user JohnS had in the SYS:DATA directory.

```
RIGHTS SYS:APPS\WP /T
```

lists all trustees of the SYS:APPS\WP directory.

```
RIGHTS . R F /F
```

sets the IRF for the current directory (referred to with a single period) to Read and File Scan only.

*The RIGHTS command is used for file system security, which is explained in detail in Chapter 7.*

# SEND

The SEND command sends a message to a user or group. This is similar to the BROADCAST server console command. For example, to ask the users TED and ALICE to log out, use this command:

```
SEND "Please log out immediately" TED, ALICE
```

To send a message to the EVERYONE group, use this command:

```
SEND "System going down at 3:00" EVERYONE
```

To set your workstation to receive messages only from the console or the system, use this command:

```
SEND /A=C
```

# WHOAMI

WHOAMI displays information about your current login session and the server or servers you are attached to. This command is useful as a diagnostic tool or simply to see whether you're the one logged in.

# Quick Reference: DOS and Windows Full-Screen Utilities

HIS APPENDIX IS intended as a quick reference for full-screen and graphical utilities. You can use these utilities from a DOS or Windows workstation. They are listed in alphabetical order in the sections below. Each utility is summarized, and a reference to a chapter where it is discussed in detail is included.

## FILER

The FILER utility allows you to manage files and directories in the NetWare 4 file system. You can use FILER for these tasks:

- To copy, rename, or delete files

- To manage rights to files and directories

- To view and control file attributes

- To list, purge, or salvage deleted files

*FILER and the file system are explained in detail in Chapter 4.*

## NETADMIN

NETADMIN is a DOS utility for managing users and other NDS objects on the network. You can use it for these tasks:

- To create, rename, or delete NDS objects

- To grant NDS trustee rights

- To manage property values

You cannot use NETADMIN to manage the file system; use NWADMIN or FILER.

*NETADMIN is explained in detail in Chapter 5.*

## NETUSER

The NETUSER utility is similar to the SESSION utility in earlier versions of NetWare. It allows you to:

- Map network and search drives
- Redirect printers, as with CAPTURE
- Send messages to users or groups

## NMENU

The NMENU command executes a menu and allows the user to interact with it. You can create menus as source files and compile them with the MAKE-MENU utility. NAL (NetWare Application Launcher) is a Windows-based system similar to this.

*The menu system and NAL are described in Chapter 9.*

## NWADMIN

Also known as NetWare Administrator, NWADMIN is a Windows-based utility for managing NDS objects. You can use it under Windows 3.1, Windows 95, or OS/2 to perform the following tasks:

- Create, rename, or delete NDS objects
- Manage rights to objects
- Control property values
- Copy, rename, or delete files and directories in the file system
- Manage file system security
- Control NDS partitioning and replication

*NWADMIN is described in Chapters 4 through 6.*

## PARTMGR

PARTMGR is a DOS-based utility for managing partitions and replicas in NDS. A Windows alternative, Partition Manager, is available as part of the NWADMIN utility.

*PARTMGR and its alternatives are described in Chapter 6.*

## PCONSOLE

The PCONSOLE utility allows you to manage printers, print queues, and other printing features. Its capabilities include

- Creating and managing printers, print queues, and print servers as objects in NDS

- Managing printer configurations

- A Quick Setup option that allows you to quickly configure a printer and the associated queue and server

*The printing features of NetWare 4 are explained in Chapter 8.*

## PRINTCON

PRINTCON allows you to manage print job configurations—specific sets of parameters that can be referenced with a quick CAPTURE command. You can also manage print job configurations as a property of User objects in the NWADMIN utility.

# PRINTDEF

The PRINTDEF utility allows you to define printer commands and forms, which you can use to send special codes to the printer to control print modes when needed. You can also manage print forms as properties of User and container objects in the NWADMIN utility.

# RCONSOLE

RCONSOLE allows you to establish a connection to the server and access the server console from a DOS workstation. Once you have connected to a server, you can use the following keystrokes to control the connection:

| KEYSTROKE | DESCRIPTION |
| --- | --- |
| Alt+F1 | Activates the RCONSOLE Available Options menu. This menu allows you to navigate between screens, view files and directories on the server, and transfer files to the server |
| Alt+F2 | Exits the RCONSOLE utility. You are asked to confirm your selection |
| Alt+F3 | Moves to the next server screen; similar to Alt+Esc at the server console |
| Alt+F4 | Moves to the previous server screen |
| Alt+F5 | Shows the network address of your workstation |

*See Chapter 10 for details about managing the server and for information about NLMs you must load before using RCONSOLE. A Macintosh version of RCONSOLE is also available, but it uses a different set of keystrokes; see Chapter 16 for details.*

# Quick Reference: Server Commands and Utilities

THIS APPENDIX IS intended as a quick reference for NetWare 4 server commands and utilities. You can use these utilities from the server console. This appendix is divided into two sections; the first deals with console commands and the second with NLM utilities.

# Console Commands

THIS SECTION LISTS console commands for NetWare 4. Examples of each command are included where practical, along with the most common options.

*For more information about many of these commands, see Chapter 10.*

## ADD NAME SPACE

The Add Name Space command adds a name space to a volume. Name spaces allow non-DOS file names to be supported on the volume. The most common name spaces are LONG, which supports OS/2 and Windows 95, and MAC, which supports Macintosh file names. For example, the following command adds Macintosh support to the SYS: volume:

```
ADD NAME SPACE MAC TO SYS
```

# BIND

The BIND command connects a network protocol, such as IPX, to a network adapter driver you have loaded. For example, to bind the IPX protocol to the NE2000 driver, use this command:

```
BIND IPX TO NE2000 NET=1
```

# BROADCAST

BROADCAST sends a message to all users on the system or to a specific user or group. It is similar to the SEND workstation utility, and its syntax is identical. For example, this command sends a message to the user BOB:

```
BROADCAST "Happy birthday" to BOB
```

*You can use the SEND command as a synonym for BROADCAST.*

# CONFIG

The CONFIG command displays a summary of the configuration of the server. This includes the server's name, internal and external network numbers, LAN drivers currently loaded, hardware settings, and the server's Directory tree and context.

# DISABLE LOGIN

The DISABLE LOGIN command prevents users from logging in to the network. It does not affect those who are already logged in. To allow users to log in again, use ENABLE LOGIN.

# DISMOUNT

DISMOUNT dismounts a NetWare volume. This is necessary if you are removing the volume, changing its parameters, or maintaining it with the

VREPAIR utility. For example, to dismount the SYS: volume, use this command:

```
DISMOUNT SYS
```

## DISPLAY NETWORKS

The DISPLAY NETWORKS command displays a list of external network numbers in use on the network, as detected by the server. This list is useful for determining whether a particular server is on the same network or whether the network is functioning properly.

## DISPLAY SERVERS

The DISPLAY SERVERS command displays a list of servers that exist on the same network as the current server. You can use this list to verify that two servers are configured correctly to network with each other.

## DOWN

The DOWN command brings down the server. You can follow this command with the EXIT command to return to DOS or the RESTART SERVER command to restart the server.

## ENABLE LOGIN

The ENABLE LOGIN command allows login to the server after the DISABLE LOGIN command has been used. It also resets accounts that have been locked by the intruder detection feature.

## EXIT

EXIT exits the server and returns to DOS. You can use this command only after the DOWN command.

## LOAD

The LOAD command loads a NetWare Loadable Module (NLM) into the server's memory. NLMs serve as device drivers, add additional functions to the system, or allow you to manage the server. For example, this command starts the MONITOR utility:

```
LOAD MONITOR
```

## MODULES

The MODULES command displays a list of the modules (NLMs) that are currently loaded.

## MOUNT

MOUNT mounts a volume so it can be used. For example, this command mounts the VOL1 volume:

```
MOUNT VOL1
```

Using this command is usually necessary only if you have dismounted a volume or created a new volume; all volumes are mounted automatically when the NetWare 4 server starts.

## SEARCH

The SEARCH command allows you to control which directories are searched for NLMs or command files. The SEARCH command by itself displays the current list of search directories. You can use two variations, SEARCH ADD and SEARCH DEL, to add or delete a directory. For example, the following command adds the SYS:ETC directory to the search path:

```
SEARCH ADD SYS:ETC
```

## SECURE CONSOLE

The SECURE CONSOLE command changes several options to increase the security of the server console. These include disallowing NLMs from directories other than SYS:SYSTEM, disabling NetWare 4's built-in debugger, and preventing the server's date and time from being changed.

## SET

The SET command sets a parameter for server performance. Typing **SET** by itself lists the available commands. The SERVMAN utility allows a friendlier way of managing these parameters.

*See Appendix D for a list of the most useful SET commands.*

## UNLOAD

The UNLOAD command removes an NLM from memory. For example, to unload the MONITOR utility, use this:

```
UNLOAD MONITOR
```

## VERSION

VERSION displays information about the version of NetWare that is running and about the network drivers that are loaded. This command is similar to the NVER command at the workstation.

# Console Utilities (NLMs)

THE FOLLOWING UTILITIES are NLMs (NetWare Loadable Modules); you can use them with the LOAD command at the server console.

*See Chapter 10 for more information about many of these utilities; other chapters are indicated by cross-references in the items below.*

## CDROM

The CDROM utility allows a CD-ROM disk in the server to be mounted as a NetWare volume. After the CDROM module is loaded, you can use the following CD commands to control the CD-ROM drive:

| COMMAND | DESCRIPTION |
|---------|-------------|
| CD HELP | Displays a list of options |
| CD DEVICE LIST | Lists the currently available CD-ROM devices |
| CD MOUNT | Mounts a CD-ROM. Specify the volume or device number |
| CD VOLUME LIST | Lists the currently mounted CD-ROM volumes |
| CD DISMOUNT | Dismounts a CD-ROM volume. Specify the volume name or device number |
| CD CHANGE | Rescans the CD-ROM drive after you have inserted a different disk |
| CD RENAME | Specifies an alternate name for a mounted volume |
| CD GROUP | Allows you to give a group of users access to a CD-ROM volume |
| CD PURGE | Removes index files that were created to use a CD-ROM |
| CD IMAGE | Allows you to mount a CD-ROM image on disk as though it were a CD-ROM. This is useful if you are creating your own CD-ROMs |

## CONLOG

After the CONLOG module is loaded, all the messages displayed at the server console are logged to a file. By default, this file is SYS:\ETC\CONSOLE.LOG. This log is useful for viewing error messages that may have scrolled off the screen.

## DSMERGE

DSMERGE is a utility for merging NDS Directory trees. You can also use it to check synchronization between replicas.

*Chapter 12 explores the uses of the DSMERGE utility.*

## DSREPAIR

DSREPAIR is a general-purpose utility for repairing problems with the NDS Directory. DSREPAIR diagnoses and advises you of problems and fixes them if possible.

*See Chapter 12 for information about the DSREPAIR utility.*

## EDIT

The EDIT utility allows you to edit a file on a NetWare volume. This utility is useful for editing AUTOEXEC.NCF, TIMESYNC.CFG, and other server configuration files. For example, to edit the AUTOEXEC.NCF file, use this command:

```
LOAD EDIT SYS:SYSTEM\AUTOEXEC.NCF
```

# INETCFG

The INETCFG utility allows you to change several settings that affect internetworking between servers and networks.

*Internetworking and this utility are explained in Chapter 14.*

# INSTALL

The INSTALL utility allows you to install features of NetWare that are not installed or to manage the server's configuration.

*See Chapter 13 for details about the INSTALL utility.*

# MONITOR

MONITOR displays information about the server's memory, processor, disks, and many other components. It is useful for fine-tuning the server's performance.

*The MONITOR utility is explained in Chapter 10; its use for troubleshooting is explained in Chapter 12.*

# NETSYNC

The NETSYNC utility allows you to manage a NetWare 3.1*x* server from NetWare 4's NDS utilities. NETSYNC is actually two NLMs: NETSYNC4, loaded on the NetWare 4 server, and NETSYNC3, which you load on up to 12 NetWare 3.1*x* servers.

*The NETSYNC utilities are explained in detail in Chapter 11.*

# NPRINTER

NPRINTER loads the port driver for a server-attached printer. PSERVER usually loads NPRINTER automatically. A workstation component, NPRINTER.EXE, is used for workstation printers.

*See Chapter 8 for information about printing features of NetWare 4.*

# PSERVER

The PSERVER utility starts a print server, corresponding to a Print Server object in NDS. You can use this utility to control printing in progress and change settings. The following command starts the PS1 print server:

```
LOAD PSERVER PS1
```

# REMOTE

REMOTE allows users to attach to the server using RCONSOLE. The RSPX NLM module must also be loaded before RCONSOLE can be used.

# SBACKUP

SBACKUP provides a basic backup system for files in NetWare volumes and for the NDS database.

*Backup strategies and SBACKUP are explained in Chapter 11.*

# SERVMAN

The SERVMAN utility provides a user-friendly system for changing server parameters. You can also use the SET command for specific parameters.

*This utility is explained in detail in Chapter 12.*

# VREPAIR

The VREPAIR utility analyzes and repairs problems in a disk volume. The volume must be dismounted before VREPAIR is used. If only one volume is currently dismounted, VREPAIR automatically repairs that volume; otherwise, you are asked which volume to repair.

*For information about VREPAIR and other troubleshooting techniques, see Chapter 12.*

# SET Commands

T HIS APPENDIX IS a listing of some of the most useful SET commands. You can use these commands to modify the server's
behavior or optimize its performance.

*Many servers can run efficiently with no change to these parameters. Be sure you under-
stand what the settings mean before changing them. If a setting does not solve your
problem or improve speed, change it back to the default.*

# Disk Performance

T HIS SECTION PRESENTS SET commands that can improve disk performance. These include commands dealing with cache buffers and the
file compression features of NetWare 4.

## Cache Buffers

The simplest solution to cache problems is to add more RAM to the server. You
can also use the SET commands in Table D.1 to optimize the cache process.

| TABLE D.1 | COMMAND | DESCRIPTION |
| --- | --- | --- |
| SET Commands for Optimizing the Cache Process | SET Dirty Disk Cache Delay Time | Specifies how long the server waits after a write request before it is written to the disk. This value can range from .1 to 10 seconds; the default is 3.3 seconds. You can supply a higher value if users frequently write to the disk. This may improve access speed |

| **TABLE D.1** | **COMMAND** | **DESCRIPTION** |
|---|---|---|
| SET Commands for Optimizing the Cache Process (continued) | SET Maximum Concurrent Disk Cache Writes | Specifies the number of write requests the server waits for before beginning to write them to the disk |
| | SET Minimum File Cache Buffers | Controls the minimum number of cache buffers that are available. When NLMs are loaded, they take memory away from cache buffers. You can set this parameter to make sure some buffers are always available. You can set this value as high as 1000; the default is 20 |
| | SET Minimum File Cache Report Threshold | Sets a threshold for warnings about low cache buffers. You can set it between 0 and 1000; the default is 20. When the number of available cache buffers decreases below the set amount, a warning is displayed on the server console |
| | SET Read Ahead Enabled | Can be set to ON or OFF. This parameter controls whether the server reads ahead when reading from the disk. This means that extra blocks are read into the cache, assuming they will be requested next. The default is ON. This improves disk access speed in most cases |
| | SET Read Ahead LRU Sitting Time Threshold | Controls the read-ahead process. Reading ahead writes over the least recently used (LRU) areas of the cache. These areas must be sitting, or unused, for the set amount of seconds before they are overwritten. The sitting time can range from 0 seconds to 1 hour; the default is 10 seconds |

# File Compression

You can use the SET parameters listed in Table D.2 to control file compression.

| **TABLE D.2** | **COMMAND** | **DESCRIPTION** |
|---|---|---|
| SET Commands for Controlling File Compression | SET Compression Daily Check Stop Hour | Specifies an hour in military time when the server stops checking for files that are ready to compress. You can use this setting, along with the Check Starting Hour setting described below, to ensure that the compression process happens when few users are on the network. The default is 6 (6:00 A.M.) |

| | COMMAND | DESCRIPTION |
|---|---|---|
| **TABLE D.2**<br><br>SET Commands for Controlling File Compression (continued) | SET Compression Daily Check Starting Hour | Sets the time when the server begins checking for files to compress. The default is 0 (12:00 midnight) |
| | SET Minimum Compression Percentage Gain | Controls the level of compression that is required to keep the file compressed. For example, if this value is 10 percent, the file must be at least 10 percent smaller; otherwise, the original, uncompressed version of the file is kept |
| | SET Enable File Compression | Can be ON or OFF and controls whether the compression process will occur. The default is ON. If you set this parameter to OFF, there may still be compressed files on the server, but no additional files will be compressed |
| | SET Maximum Concurrent Compressions | Specifies the number of volumes that can be compressing files at the same time. The default is 2. Larger values may slow the server considerably |
| | SET Convert Compressed to Uncompressed Option | Can be set to 0, 1, or 2. This parameter controls what is done with a file after it is accessed and subsequently uncompressed. Option 0 keeps the file compressed, option 1 keeps it compressed after the first access only, and option 2 leaves the file uncompressed. The default is 1 |
| | SET Uncompress Percent Disk Space Free to Allow Commit | Quite possibly the longest SET command available, but understanding its purpose is simple. It specifies the percentage of the volume's space that must be available before a file is uncompressed. This parameter prevents uncompressed files from filling up the volume |
| | SET Uncompress Free Space Warning Interval | Controls how often a warning is displayed when there is not enough free space to uncompress a file. This parameter can be set to a value in minutes or to 0 to disable the warnings |

| TABLE D.2 | COMMAND | DESCRIPTION |
|---|---|---|
| SET Commands for Controlling File Compression (continued) | SET Deleted File Compression Option | Controls whether compression is performed on deleted files. (The files are still available for salvage using the FILER or NWADMIN utility.) The setting can be 0, 1, or 2. Option 0 never compresses deleted files; option 1 compresses them one day after deletion; and option 2 compresses files immediately when deleted |
| | SET Days Untouched Before Compression | Controls how many days a file must remain untouched before it is compressed. The default is seven days |

# Memory Management

THE SET COMMANDS listed in Table D.3 affect the way NetWare 4 manages memory usage.

| TABLE D.3 | COMMAND | DESCRIPTION |
|---|---|---|
| SET Commands Affecting NetWare 4 Memory Usage | SET Garbage Collection Interval | Controls how often garbage is collected in memory. This value is in minutes and can range from 1 to 60; the default is every 15 minutes |
| | SET Number of Frees for Garbage Collection | Allows garbage collection to be automatically performed when an NLM completes a certain number of *free* calls to deallocate memory. This value can range from 100 to 100,000; the default is 5000 |
| | SET Minimum Free Memory for Garbage Collection | Sets the number of bytes that must be in the system memory pool for successful garbage collection. This value ranges from 1000 to 1,000,000; the default is 8000 |

| **TABLE D.3** | **COMMAND** | **DESCRIPTION** |
|---|---|---|
| SET Commands Affecting NetWare 4 Memory Usage (continued) | SET Allow Invalid Pointers | Can be either OFF or ON. This parameter allows an application to define a pointer to an invalid area of memory. The default is OFF. With this parameter ON, the system displays a warning at the console rather than an abend |
| | SET Read Fault Emulation | Defaults to OFF. Usually, when an application attempts to read memory in a nonexistent page, a read fault occurs, and the server abends. If this parameter is set to ON, it causes an error message at the console but does not bring down the server. NetWare emulates the read request and returns a value to the application so it won't crash |
| | SET Read Fault Notification | Can be set to ON or OFF; the default is ON. This command controls whether read faults that are emulated will cause a message to be displayed on the server console and in the error log |
| | SET Write Fault Emulation | Controls whether write faults (attempts to write to invalid areas of memory) are emulated |
| | SET Write Fault Notification | Controls whether write fault messages are logged to the server console and the error log |
| | SET Alloc Memory Check Flag | Set to ON if you wish the server to constantly check for memory corruption. This slows system performance but can be useful for tracking down ill-behaved NLMs |

The two SET commands in Table D.4 cannot be typed at the console but must be in the STARTUP.NCF file.

| **TABLE D.4** | **COMMAND** | **DESCRIPTION** |
|---|---|---|
| SET Commands That Must Be in the STARTUP.NCF File | SET Auto Register Memory Above 16 Megabytes | Defaults to ON. This command allows EISA computers to automatically use memory above 16MB if available. You may need to set this to OFF to provide compatibility with the disk controller |
| | SET Reserved Buffers Below 16 Megabytes | Reserves buffer space in the lower 16MB of memory for device drivers that are limited to that area. You can set this value between 8 and 300; the default is 16 |

# Network Communication

HE SET COMMANDS listed in Table D.5 may improve the speed or reliability of network communication.

| **TABLE D.5** | COMMAND | DESCRIPTION |
|---|---|---|
| SET Commands That May Improve Speed and Reliability | SET Maximum Packet Receive Buffers | Sets the maximum number of buffers that can be allocated. You can set this value between 50 and 4000; the default is 100. If the MONITOR statistics show that the maximum number of buffers is being used, you should increase this number |
| | SET Minimum Packet Receive Buffers | Sets the minimum number of buffers. NetWare allocates this amount when the server is started. This allows the server to run immediately at optimal speeds. The minimum number can range from 10 to 2000; the default is 50. If the server is slow after you start it, you can increase this number |
| | SET Maximum Service Processes | Allows you to control the number of communications that can be processed at the same time. Increasing this value may reduce the need for additional packet receive buffers |
| | SET New Packet Receive Buffer Wait Time | The amount of time NetWare waits when additional buffers are needed without allocating them. Increasing this value may prevent the number of buffers from being increased by a brief period of high usage. This period of time ranges from .1 second to 20 seconds; the default is the minimum |

# Workstation
# Configuration
# Files

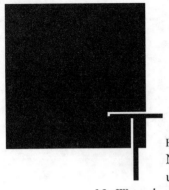

THIS APPENDIX IS a listing of available parameters for the NET.CFG file at a workstation. We have included the most useful commands and categories; for a complete listing, see the NetWare documentation.

The following NET.CFG sections are documented here:

- Link Support

- NetWare DOS Requester

- NetWare DOS TSA

- Protocol IPX

- Protocol SPX

# Link Support Section

THIS SECTION INCLUDES parameters that affect the performance of the Link Support Layer (LSL.COM). You can use the parameters listed in Table E.1 in this section.

| TABLE E.1 | COMMAND | DESCRIPTION |
| --- | --- | --- |
| Parameters Supported in the Link Support Section | Buffers | Indicates the number of communication buffers available to LSL. You can also specify the size for each buffer in brackets [ ] |

| TABLE E.1 | COMMAND | DESCRIPTION |
|---|---|---|
| Parameters Supported in the Link Support Section (continued) | Max boards | Specifies the maximum number of logical network boards supported by LSL. This value ranges from 1 to 16; the default is 4 |
| | Mempool | Specifies a size in bytes for a memory pool that some protocols (not IPX) require |

# NetWare DOS Requester Section

THE NETWARE DOS Requester section is the most commonly used. It includes parameters that affect the performance of the NetWare DOS Requester (VLM.EXE) and its components. The parameters listed in Table E.2 are supported.

| TABLE E.2 | COMMAND | DESCRIPTION |
|---|---|---|
| Parameters Supported in the NetWare DOS Requester Section | Auto large table | Can be set to on or off. This parameter controls whether a small (34 bytes per connection) or large (178 bytes per connection) connection table is used to support bindery reconnects. The default is off |
| | Auto reconnect | Indicates whether the DOS Requester will attempt to reconnect after losing a connection. The default is on |
| | Auto retry | Can be set to a number between 0 and 3640; this parameter is the time before a reconnect is attempted |
| | Average name length | The length used in a table of server names. The default is 48 characters, but you can set it as low as 2 if your servers use smaller names |
| | Bind reconnect | Can be set to on or off. This parameter determines whether bindery connections will automatically reconnect |

| **TABLE E.2** | **COMMAND** | **DESCRIPTION** |
| --- | --- | --- |
| Parameters Supported in the NetWare DOS Requester Section (continued) | Broadcast retries | The number of times a "get nearest server" request is broadcast. This setting can range from 1 to 255; the default is 3 |
| | Broadcast send delay | The delay between broadcasts. This value ranges from 0 to 255 ticks; the default is 0 |
| | Broadcast timeout | Specifies the delay between broadcast retries. This setting can range from 0 to 255; the default is 2 |
| | Cache buffers size | Sets the size of the cache buffers. This value ranges from 64 to 4096 bytes; the default depends on the network topology |
| | Cache writes | Can be set to on or off. This setting indicates whether the cache is used for writes. The default is on |
| | Checksum | The level for NCP packet validation: a value of 0 disables packet validation; 1 enables it; 2 makes it the default; 3 requires it |
| | Confirm critical error action | Specifies whether Windows displays an error dialog when a connection problem occurs |
| | Connections | The maximum number of server connections. This setting ranges from 2 to 50; the default is 8 |
| | DOS name | Specifies the name of the DOS version on the computer. MSDOS is the default |
| | EOJ | Indicates whether files are automatically closed at the end of a job; this setting defaults to on |
| | Exclude VLM | Specifies the path or name of a VLM and indicates that it will not be loaded |
| | First network drive | Specifies the first drive letter to be used for network drives. The default is F |
| | Force first network drive | Can be set to on to remap the first network drive to the SYS:LOGIN directory after a user logs out. Otherwise, the drive the user was on when logging out is used |

| TABLE E.2 | COMMAND | DESCRIPTION |
|---|---|---|
| Parameters Supported in the NetWare DOS Requester Section (continued) | Handle net errors | Specifies whether an interrupt (24) is used to handle errors. The default is on |
| | Large internet packets | Specifies whether packets are passed through a router full size. The default is on |
| | LIP start size | Sets the initial packet size for large internet packets. This value can range from 576 to 65535 bytes; the default is 0 |
| | Load conn table low | Specifies whether low memory or high memory is used for the connection table. The default is off |
| | Load low conn | Specifies whether CONN.VLM is loaded in low memory. The default is on. Turning this value off can save memory but affects performance |
| | Load low ipxncp | Specifies whether IPXNCP.VLM is loaded in low memory. The default is on. Turning this value off can save memory but may affect performance |
| | Load low redir | Specifies whether REDIR.VLM is loaded in low memory. The default is on. Turning this value off can save memory but may affect performance |
| | Local printers | Specifies the maximum number of local printers that can be redirected. The default is 3. Setting this parameter to 9, the maximum, allows you to redirect printers LPT1 through LPT9 |
| | Lock delay | Specifies the amount of time the DOS Requester waits for a file lock. This setting can range from 0 to 255; the default is 1 |
| | Lock retries | Sets the number of retries for file locks. The range is from 0 to 255; the default is 1 |
| | Long machine type | Sets the type of the workstation computer. This parameter defaults to IBM_PC. This value is reflected in the MACHINE variable in login scripts |
| | Max tasks | The maximum number of concurrent tasks. This setting ranges from 5 to 254; the default is 31 |

| **TABLE E.2** | **COMMAND** | **DESCRIPTION** |
| --- | --- | --- |
| Parameters Supported in the NetWare DOS Requester Section (continued) | Message level | Sets the number of messages displayed while VLMs are loading, from 0 to 4. Higher levels include more detail |
| | Message timeout | Sets the length of time messages sent with the SEND or BROADCAST command stay on the screen. This value ranges from 0 to 10,000 ticks (9 minutes). The default, 0, means no timeout; the message is displayed until the user acknowledges it |
| | Name context | Sets the default context for the username. [Root] is the default |
| | NetWare protocol | A list of NetWare protocols; this is the order in which they will be tried. The default is NDS, BIND, PNW |
| | Network printers | Specifies the number of LPT ports that can be captured. This setting can range from 0 to 9; the default is 3. |
| | Pb buffers | Controls the packet burst feature. This value can range from 0 to 10 but is used strictly as a switch; positive values enable packet burst, and a value of 0 turns off the packet burst feature. The default is 3 |
| | Pburst read windows size | Specifies the size of the read buffer for packet burst. This setting ranges from 3 to 128 bytes; the default is 16 |
| | Pburst write windows size | Specifies the size of the write buffer for packet burst. This setting ranges from 3 to 128 bytes; the default is 10 |
| | Preferred server | Specifies a default server to attach to for logins |
| | Preferred tree | Specifies a default Directory tree to attach to for logins |
| | Print buffer size | Specifies the size of the buffer for printing. This value ranges from 0 to 256 bytes; the default is 64 |
| | Print header | Specifies the size of the header buffer for printing. The range is from 0 to 1024 bytes; the default is 64 |

| **TABLE E.2**<br><br>Parameters Supported in<br>the NetWare DOS<br>Requester Section<br>(continued) | **COMMAND** | **DESCRIPTION** |
| --- | --- | --- |
| | Print tail | Specifies the size of the buffer for final print job information. This setting ranges from 0 to 1024 bytes; the default is 16 |
| | Read only compatibility | Can be set to on to allow read-only files to be accessed as read/write files, as long as no write operations are used. The default depends on the client software version |
| | Responder | Indicates whether the workstation responds to broadcasts and server diagnostics. The defaults is on |
| | Search mode | Specifies the default search mode for finding files. This setting can range from 0 to 7; the default is 1 |
| | Set station time | Indicates whether the workstation's time is set to server time when it attaches to a server. The default is on |
| | Short machine type | An abbreviated name for the type of machine. The default is IBM |
| | Show dots | Specifies whether current (.) and parent (..) directory entries are included in a network directory listing. This may be required for compatibility with some DOS utilities. The default is off |
| | Signature level | Specifies the level of NCP packet signature security. Values are 0 for no signatures; 1 for signatures if the server requests them; 2 for signatures if the server allows them; 3 requires signatures |
| | Use defaults | Can be set to off to override the default list of VLMs to load. The default is on |
| | VLM | Loads a specified VLM file. You can use multiple VLM entries to specify the list of VLMs if Use defaults is off |

# NetWare DOS TSA Section

THIS SECTION INCLUDES information used by the DOS TSA (Target Service Agent), which you use to back up workstations using an SMS-compliant backup engine such as Novell's SBACKUP. Backup services are explained in Chapter 11. You can use the parameters listed in Table E.3.

| **TABLE E.3**<br><br>Parameters Supported by the NetWare DOS TSA Section | **COMMAND** | **DESCRIPTION** |
|---|---|---|
| | Disk buffers | The number of bytes used for disk buffers. The range is from 1 to 30; the default is 1 byte |
| | Drives | Specifies the DOS drives that can be backed up. The default is C. If you specify multiple drives, separate the letters with spaces |
| | Password | Sets a password for the workstation; this password will be required at the server when a backup is performed. No password is required by default |
| | Stack size | Specifies the size of a stack used for backup data. The range is from 512 to 4096 bytes; the default is 2048 bytes |
| | TSA server name | Specifies the server that will perform backups |
| | Workstation name | Specifies a unique name for this workstation |

# Protocol IPX Section

OU USE THE parameters in this section to control the IPX protocol. The parameters listed in Table E.4 are supported.

| **TABLE E.4**<br><br>Parameters Supported by<br>the Protocol IPX Section | **COMMAND** | **DESCRIPTION** |
|---|---|---|
| | Bind | Specifies the name of a driver to bind the IPX protocol to |
| | Int64 | Can be set to on or off; this parameter specifies whether IPX uses the 64h interrupt; if off, other applications can use it. The default is on |
| | Int7a | Can be set to on or off; this parameter specifies whether IPX uses the 7Ah interrupt. The default is on |
| | Ipatch | Specifies an offset and value to patch the IPX.COM file. This parameter is used for correcting errors |
| | IPX packet size limit | Sets the maximum size of IPX packets. This setting can range from 576 to 6500 bytes; the default is 4160 |
| | IPX retry count | Specifies the number of times a packet will be re-sent after an error. The default is 20 |
| | IPX sockets | Sets the maximum number of concurrently open IPX sockets. The default is 20 |

# Protocol SPX Section

THIS SECTION SPECIFIES parameters for the SPX protocol. The available parameters are listed in Table E.5.

| **TABLE E.5**<br><br>Parameters Supported by<br>the Protocol SPX Section | **COMMAND** | **DESCRIPTION** |
|---|---|---|
| | Minimum SPX retries | Specifies the number of times an SPX transmission will be retried. This setting can range from 0 to 255; the default is 20 |

| | COMMAND | DESCRIPTION |
|---|---|---|
| | SPX abort timeout | Specifies the amount of time SPX will wait for a response before an error occurs. The default is 540 ticks (30 seconds) |
| | SPX connections | Sets the maximum number of concurrent connections for SPX. The default is 15 |
| | SPX listen timeout | Specifies the time SPX will wait for a packet before re-requesting it. The default is 108 ticks (6 seconds) |
| | SPX verify timeout | The amount of time between verify packets, which SPX sends to make sure the connection is intact. The default is 54 ticks (3 seconds) |

# Worksheets for Network Management

HIS APPENDIX INCLUDES several worksheets you may find useful in the process of documenting your network. Keeping detailed documentation makes the tasks of network management much easier; you can copy these worksheets from the book for this purpose.

Consider these a starting point. Your company may have different priorities or may use features we haven't included here, so you may wish to create your own customized versions.

*Rather than use these or your own worksheets to keep track of data on paper, consider tracking this information in a database program. It can be easier to manage and maintain data this way, and you can print it if needed.*

## Server Installation Worksheet

Server name: _____

Manufacturer and model number: _____

Location: _____

Directory tree name and context: _____

Time server type: _____ Time zone: _____

Protocols: IPX/SPX ___ AppleTalk ___ TCP/IP___

Disk size and type: _____

Disk partitions: _____

Volume name: _____ Size: _____ Mirrored: ____ Duplex: ____

Volume name: _____ Size: _____ Mirrored: ____ Duplex: ____

Volume name: _____ Size: _____ Mirrored: ____ Duplex: ____

Network boards and bindings: _____

_____

_____

Other hardware: _____

_____

Notes: _____

# Workstation Installation Worksheet

Location: _____ Username: _____

Manufacturer and model: _____

Hard disk size: _____ Memory (RAM): _____

Drives: 3.5" floppy ___ 5.25" floppy ___ CD-ROM ___ Tape _____

DOS and Windows versions: _____

Network board: _____

Client software version: _____

Notes: _____

# Printer Configuration Worksheet

Printer name and context: _____

Make/model: _____

Location: _____

Attached to: Server: _____ Workstation: _____ Direct _____

Print queue(s): _____

Print server: _____

Printer type: Parallel ___ Serial ___ AppleTalk ___ Other ____

Administrator(s): _____

Notes: _____

_____

# Time Synchronization Worksheet

Directory tree: _____

Single reference server: _____

Reference server: _____

External time source (if used): _____

Primary servers: _____

_____

_____

Secondary servers: _____

_____

Notes: _____

_____

# Backup Schedule

Backup server: _____

Backup device: _____

Media type: _____

Target server(s): _____

_____

Workstations: _____

_____

Directory trees: _____

Backup administrator: _____

Schedule: Full backup: _____

        Incremental backup: _____

        Differential backup: _____

        Other: _____

Tape rotation scheme: _____

_____

Notes: _____

_____

# Glossary

GLOSSARY

**10base2 Ethernet**   A popular cabling scheme for Ethernet networks. This system uses coaxial cable in a bus configuration.

**10baseT Ethernet**   A common cabling scheme for Ethernet networks. This system uses twisted-pair cable in a star configuration, and all devices are attached to a central hub.

**abend**   NetWare's term for a server crash (short for abnormal end). An application (NLM) writing to an area of memory that belongs to the operating system frequently causes an abend.

**Access Control List (ACL)**   The property of an NDS object that contains the list of *trustees* or other objects that have rights to the object.

**across-the-wire migration**   One of the two possible migration strategies from NetWare 3.1*x* to NetWare 4. In the across-the-wire strategy, a new NetWare 4 server is connected to the same network as the NetWare 3.1*x* server, and data is copied over the network.

**alias object**   An object that represents, or points to, another object in the NDS tree. Alias objects can be created to make a resource in a different context available in the local context. NetWare can create aliases automatically when an object or container is moved.

**AppleTalk**   A networking system developed by Apple for use with Macintosh computers. The software for AppleTalk connectivity is built in to the Macintosh operating system. NetWare for Macintosh allows connectivity between AppleTalk and NetWare networks by emulating AppleTalk services on the NetWare server.

**attributes**   Attributes are stored for each file and directory on a server's file system. File attributes are used for security purposes and for status information for the file. For example, the Read Only attribute prevents a file from being written to or erased, and the Can't Compress attribute indicates that NetWare was unable to compress the file.

   NDS objects also have attributes. For clarity, these attributes are usually referred to as *properties*.

**auditing**   A NetWare 4 service that allows a user, or auditor, to monitor activities on the network. The auditor can monitor the file system or an NDS container. You use the AUDITCON menu utility to monitor activities.

**auditor's password**   A password that is set when you begin an audit on a volume or NDS container. The auditor should change this password when the audit begins. The password is required for all auditing activities, including ending the audit.

**backbone**   A portion of a network that connects network segments together, often between buildings. High-speed networking systems such as FDDI and ATM are ideally suited for backbones.

**backup engine**   An application, such as Novell's SBACKUP, that provides backup services under the SMS (Storage Management Services) system.

**bandwidth**   A general term for the amount of traffic that can be carried over a network, measured in Mbps (millions of bits per second).

**banner**   In NetWare 4 printing, a page that is printed at the beginning of a print job to identify the job and the user who sent it. Banners can be turned on or off with options of the CAPTURE command.

**base schema**   The NDS base schema defines the structure of NDS—which objects are possible, which properties an object can have, and so forth. The NDS base schema is written to the server when NDS is installed. Third-party applications can extend, or add to, this schema using the NetWare API.

**batch file**   A file containing a list of commands to be executed. DOS batch files have the extension .BAT. Examples include AUTOEXEC.BAT, which executes when the workstation is booted, and STARTNET.BAT, which is used to attach to the network. NetWare command files (NCFs) provide a similar feature for server commands.

**bindery**   The database used to store information about users, printers, and other network objects in NetWare 3.1*x* and earlier versions. The bindery is a simple, flat database that is stored separately on each server. NetWare 4 replaces the bindery with NDS.

**bindery context**   The context that will be provided as a simulated bindery by *Bindery Services.* You can set up to 16 separate contexts to serve as bindery contexts; these will be combined into a "bindery" that bindery-based clients can access.

**Bindery Services** NetWare 4's service that allows the simulation of a bindery. This enables clients using older client software, such as the NetWare *DOS Shell,* to access the network. A branch of the NDS tree, the bindery context, is used as a simulated bindery.

**binding** A link between a protocol, such as *TCP/IP* or *IPX,* and a network card. You can create a binding with the BIND command at the server or via the NET.CFG file at a workstation.

**browsing** The process of navigating the Directory tree, usually using the NetWare Administrator (NWADMIN) utility.

**bus** One of the types of network topology. In a bus topology, all nodes are connected to portions of a continuous bus. A break anywhere in the bus can disrupt the entire network.

**cache buffer** NetWare sets aside a portion of the server's memory as cache buffers. These buffers cache information for the file system. The number of cache buffers depends on the available memory.

**caching** A technique NetWare servers use to increase disk performance. Data read from the disk drive is stored in a block of RAM memory, or *cache buffer.* When clients request this data, it can be read directly from the cache, avoiding the use of the disk. NetWare provides both read and write caching.

**child object** In NDS, an object that is under a *container object.* The container object is referred to as the *parent object.*

**client** Any device that attaches to the network server. A workstation is the most common type of client. Clients run client software to provide network access. A piece of software that accesses data on a server can also be called a client.

**client-server network** A server-centric network in which some network resources are stored on a file server, while processing power is distributed among workstations and the file server.

**colon prompt** The prompt at the server console where you can enter server commands. The prompt displays the server's name followed by a colon. This is also referred to as the console prompt.

**common name**   In NDS, the least significant portion of an object's name. This is the name given to the object when it is created. The common name is abbreviated CN in typeful naming.

**compile**   In the NetWare 4 menu system, the process of converting a *menu source file* into a *menu data file* that the NMENU program can use. You use the MENUMAKE program to compile menus.

**concentrator**   A device, also called a hub, that is used at the center of a network with a star topology. All nodes in the network connect to a port on the concentrator.

**container administrator**   An administrator who is given rights to a *container object* and all the objects under it. A container administrator can be *exclusive,* meaning that no other administrator has access to the container.

**container object**   In NDS, an object that contains other objects. Container objects include Organization, Organizational Unit, and Country objects. The [Root] object is a specialized kind of container object. Objects within a container can be other container objects, or *leaf objects*, which represent network resources.

**container security equivalence**   See *implied security equivalence.*

**context**   In NDS, an object's position within the Directory tree. The context is the full path to the *container object* in which the object resides.

**current context**   The current position in the Directory tree, maintained for a workstation connection. By default, objects are assumed to be in this context unless you specify the full *distinguished name.* The current context is also called the *default context.*

**data migration**   A system where infrequently used data is moved to a high-capacity storage device, such as a jukebox. The *High-Capacity Storage System (HCSS)* is the NetWare 4 service that handles data migration.

**de-migrate**   The process of moving data back from a high-capacity storage system to which it was migrated. This occurs when a user attempts to access the file that was migrated.

**dedicated server**    A server that serves no other purpose—it cannot be used as a workstation. All NetWare 3.1*x* servers and most NetWare 4 servers are dedicated. NetWare 4 provides a non-dedicated option through NetWare Server for OS/2.

**default context**    See *current context*.

**Directory**    In NDS, the database that contains information about each of the objects on the network. The Directory is organized into a tree-like structure, the Directory tree, with a *[Root] object* on top and *leaf objects* at the bottom. To distinguish it from disk directories, the NDS Directory always starts with a capital *D*.

**directory map**    A special NDS object you use to map directories in the file system. The MAP command can specify the name of the Directory Map object rather than the exact directory name. The directory name is contained in a property of the Directory Map object.

**Directory tree**    See *Directory*.

**disk partition**    See *Partition (disk)*.

**distinguished name**    In NDS, the full name of an NDS object, which includes the object's *common name* and its *context*, or location in the *Directory* tree. Also referred to as the *full distinguished name*.

**distributed database**    A database that is contained in multiple locations. NDS is a distributed database that is contained on multiple NetWare 4 servers.

**divisional implementation**    One of the methods of implementing NDS in a network. Each division is moved to NDS separately, with its own Directory tree. This is similar to the *departmental implementation*.

**divisional organization**    A type of NDS organization that divides the Directory tree into branches for each division or department within an organization. This is often a practical way to organize since members of a department or division often require access to the same set of resources.

**drive mappings**  Client software uses drive mappings to link DOS drive letters to directories on network volumes. The MAP command is used for this feature.

**DynaText**  The online documentation system included on CD-ROM with NetWare 4. You can use this system from the CD-ROM drive or install it on the network or a workstation. You use the DynaText Viewer to read and search the documentation. DynaText replaces Electrotext, used by NetWare 3.1*x* and earlier versions.

**effective rights**  The rights a user (or other *trustee*) has in a file system directory or NDS object after all factors—*explicit rights, inherited rights,* the *Inherited Rights Filter (IRF),* and *security equivalences*—are considered.

**environmental variable**  In DOS, a named value that can be set and used by software. The SET command sets environmental variables in DOS; these can also be set with the DOS SET command within a login script.

**exclusive container administrator**  A special type of *container administrator* who is given rights to a container and the objects within it. The *Inherited Rights Filter (IRF)* prevents other administrators from having rights in the container.

**explicit rights**  In NDS or the file system, any rights that are given directly to a user for a directory or NDS object. Explicit rights override *inherited rights.*

**explicit security equivalence**  In NDS, a method of giving one *trustee* the same rights as another. Explicit security equivalence can be assigned with group membership, an Organizational Role, or the trustee's Security Equal To property.

**extension**  In DOS, OS/2, Windows 95, and NetWare file systems, a three-letter section at the end of a file name that denotes the file's type.

**file**  An individual unit of storage on a disk, usually corresponding to a single document. The file system in NetWare supports file storage.

**file attributes**  See *attributes.*

**file name**   In DOS, NetWare, and other file systems, a name given to a file. The name may include an *extension* to denote the type of file.

**file server**   A NetWare server. This name is used because file storage is one of the primary purposes of the server.

**file system**   The NetWare file system defines how files can be stored on disk volumes. Files are stored in a hierarchy of directories and subdirectories. NetWare's file system is similar to that of DOS.

**frame types**   Specifications for the method in which data is transmitted over the network. Clients and servers must support the same frame type in order to communicate.

**full distinguished name**   See *distinguished name.*

**Greenwich Mean Time (GTM)**   See *Universal Coordinated Time* (UTC).

**hybrid organization**   An NDS organization strategy that combines two or more of the other methods—*locational, divisional,* and *workgroup.* Hybrid organizations are most useful for larger companies.

**implied security equivalence**   In NDS, an object is security equivalent to (receives the rights of) the object's parent object and its parents, leading up to the [Root] object. This is also called *container security equivalence.* The *Inherited Rights Filter* (IRF) does not affect this process.

**in-place migration**   A method for migrating NetWare 2.*x* to NetWare 4. This involves converting the file system to the NetWare 3.1*x* format and upgrading to NetWare 4 with the installation program.

**inherited rights**   In NDS or the file system, inherited rights are rights a *trustee* receives for an object because of rights to the object's parent (a *directory* in the file system or a parent object in NDS). Inherited rights can be blocked by an explicit assignment or by the *Inherited Rights Filter* (IRF).

**Inherited Rights Filter (IRF)**   In the file system, the IRF is the list of rights a user can inherit for a Directory from Directories above it. An IRF also exists for each NDS object and lists the rights a *trustee* can inherit from the object's parents. In NetWare 3.1*x*, the IRF was called the Inherited Rights Mask (IRM) and applied only to the file system.

**internetworking**   The process of connecting multiple *local area networks* (*LANs*) to form a *wide area network* (*WAN*). Internetworking between different types of networks is handled by a *router*.

**IPX (Internetwork Packet Exchange)**   The principal protocol used in NetWare 4. This is a connectionless protocol that sends data along the network until the appropriate device receives it.

**IPX external network number**   A number that represents an entire network. All servers on the network must use the same external network number.

**IPX internal network number**   A number that uniquely identifies a server to the network. Each server must have a different internal network number.

**LAN**   See *local area network*.

**leaf object**   An object that cannot contain other objects and that represents a network resource. Leaf objects include User, Group, Printer, Server, Volume, and many others.

**local area network (LAN)**   A network that is restricted to a local area—a single building, group of buildings, or even a single room. A LAN often has only one server but can have many.

**locational organization**   A method of organizing the Directory tree that divides it into Organizational Units for each geographical location of the organization. This strategy is often the best for network communication.

**logging in**   The process of entering a username and password to gain access to the network. NetWare 4 allows you to log in to a Directory tree rather than a single server.

**logical ports**   Ports the CAPTURE command uses to redirect a workstation printer port to a network print queue. The logical port has no relation to the port to which the printer is actually attached, or *physical port*.

**login script**   A set of commands that are automatically executed when a user logs in. NetWare 4 includes Container, Profile, User, and Default login scripts. Up to three of these can be executed for each user.

**login script commands**   Special commands that make up the *login script*.

**login security**   The most basic form of network security. A username and password are required in order to log in to the network and access resources.

**master replica**   The main replica for a *partition*. The master replica must be available when major changes, such as partition merging and splitting, are performed. Another replica can be assigned as the master if the original master replica is lost.

**memory allocation**   The system NetWare 4 uses to provide memory for use by applications (NLMs) on the server. Memory is allocated from an allocation pool.

**menu data file**   A file used to run a menu, using the NMENU program. The data file is the result of *compiling* the menu source file using the MENU-MAKE utility. Menu data files have the .DAT extension.

**menu source file**   The file you write, using menu commands, to create a user menu. This file must be compiled into a *menu data file* using the MENUMAKE utility before it can be used. Source files typically have an .SRC extension.

**merging Directory trees**   The process of combining two Directory trees into a single tree. The objects in the source tree are combined into the destination or target tree. You use the DSMERGE utility to merge trees.

**merging partitions**   The process of combining an NDS partition with its parent partition, resulting in a single partition. The master replica of the partition must be available for this process.

**message file**   A file that provides prompts and messages for a NetWare workstation or server utility. Message files are provided for each supported language (English, French, Italian, German, and Spanish).

**multi-valued property**   In NDS, a property that can have multiple values. For example, a User object's Telephone Number property can store multiple telephone numbers.

**Multiprotocol Router (MPR)**   The software that provides *routing* capabilities for a NetWare 4 server. This allows communication between different types of networks.

**name conflict**  A situation in which names conflict with each other. This typically happens in *Bindery Services* or when using *NetSync*. All users in the *bindery context* must have unique common names.

**name space**  A service you can install on a NetWare 4 server volume to allow different types of file names to be used. Name spaces are available for OS/2 NFS and Macintosh naming. The default NetWare 4 name space supports DOS file names only.

**NDS**  See *NetWare Directory Services*.

**NDS schema**  See *base schema*.

**NetSync**  The software that allows NetWare 3.1*x* servers to be managed through NDS utilities. You accomplish this by using the NETSYNC3 NLM at the NetWare 3.1*x* servers and the NETSYNC4 NLM at the NetWare 4 server.

**NetSync cluster**  A NetWare 4 server and a group of NetWare 3.1*x* servers it can manage using NetSync. Each NetWare 4 server can manage up to 16 NetWare 3.1*x* servers.

**NetWare Directory Services (NDS)**  The system NetWare 4 uses to catalog objects on the network—users, printers, volumes, and others. NDS uses a *Directory tree* to store this information. All of the NetWare 4 network's resources can be managed through NDS.

**NetWare DOS Requester**  The client software that is used on a DOS workstation to access the NetWare 4 network and NDS. The DOS Requester replaces the *DOS Shell* in previous NetWare versions. Use the VLM.EXE program to load the DOS Requester.

**NetWare Loadable Module (NLM)**  An application or program that executes on the NetWare server. NLMs are used for device drivers, *local area network (LAN)* drivers, and applications such as backup software. A variety of utility NLMs are provided with NetWare 4, and others are available from third parties.

**NetWare OS/2 Requester**  The client software used to access a NetWare 4 server and NDS from an OS/2 workstation. The OS/2 Requester provides the same benefits as the DOS requester.

**network address**   A unique address that identifies each node, or device, on the network. The network address is generally hardcoded into the network card on both the workstation and the server. Some network cards allow you to change this address, but there is seldom a reason to do so.

**network-centric**   The architecture used in a NetWare 4 network, in which objects are created for the entire network rather than for a single server. This feature is one of the benefits of NDS.

**network client software**   The software used to interface between a client and a NetWare server. Client software is available for DOS, Windows 3.1, Windows 95, Windows NT, OS/2, and UNIX.

**Network Interface Card (NIC)**   A device that is installed in a computer (either a client or server) to interface between the computer and the network wiring. Network cards are also called LAN cards.

**network nodes**   Devices (clients or servers) that are connected to a network are referred to as network nodes.

**Network Operating System (NOS)**   The software that runs on a file server and offers file, print, and other servers to client workstations. NetWare 4 is a NOS. Other examples include NetWare 3.1x, Banyan VINES, and IBM LAN Server.

**network-aware**   A type of application that directly supports networking. Such applications may support network printing, file sharing and locking, and other features.

**NIC**   See *network interface card.*

**NLMs (NetWare Loadable Modules)**   Programs that run on a NetWare server. These may be drivers for devices or system utilities. You can run these by typing **LOAD** followed by the name of the module at the server prompt.

**non-dedicated server**   A server that can also act as a workstation. NetWare 2.2 provided this capability, and NetWare 4 provides it through NetWare Server for OS/2. This is not possible under NetWare 3.1x.

**object**   In NDS, any resource on the network. Users, printers, and groups are examples of *leaf objects*. Another type, *container objects*, is used to organize other objects.

**object trustee**   See *trustee*.

**occupant**   A user who has been assigned to an Organizational Role object. Each Organizational Role can have multiple occupants, stored in the Occupants property of the object.

**Organization object**   Usually the highest-level container object used. Organizations are created under the [Root], or under the Country object if it is used. This object usually represents an entire organization or company. You can use multiple Organization objects in the same Directory tree.

**Organizational Role object**   An object that represents a role—an administrator or other specialized user who requires access to certain NDS objects or files. This object is often used for container administrators. See also *occupant*.

**Organizational Unit object**   The lowest-level container object. You can use Organizational Units to divide locations, divisions, workgroups, or smaller portions of the Directory tree. You can further subdivide Organizational Units with additional Organizational Units.

**packet**   A unit of data transmitted over the network. Different network types use different packet configurations. A packet includes data along with a header that refers to the network address of the destination node.

**Packet Burst protocol**   A streamlined protocol available in NetWare 4 and as an addition to NetWare 3.1*x*. In this protocol, several packets (a burst) are sent, and a single acknowledgment is sent back. If there is an error, only the packets that were not received correctly need to be re-sent. This eliminates most of the process of sending acknowledgments back and forth.

**packet receive buffers**   Areas of memory that NetWare sets aside for receiving packets over the network. Packets are stored in *buffers* until the server is able to process them.

**parent object**   In NDS, an object that *contains* another object—a container object. This is a relative term; a parent object also has parent objects of its own and is considered a child object from that perspective.

**partition (disk)**    NetWare uses disk partitions to divide a hard disk. A disk can contain a single NetWare partition, which you use to hold one or more NetWare volumes. In addition, a disk can have a DOS partition, used to boot the server and hold the SERVER.EXE program.

**partition (NDS)**    A branch of the NDS tree that can be replicated onto multiple servers. The partition includes a container object and the objects under it and is named according to the name of that object. By default, a single partition—the [Root] partition—exists.

**path**    In DOS, the list of directories that are searched to find an executable program or command. NetWare expands this through the use of search drives.

**peripherals**    Non-computer devices, such as printers and storage devices, that are attached to the network, to a server, or to a workstation.

**physical port**    In NetWare 4 printing, the port to which a printer is actually attached. This differs from the *logical ports* used in the CAPTURE command for printer redirection.

**port driver**    A component of NetWare 4 printing. The port driver accepts data from the print server and sends it to the printer. The port driver can be NPRINTER.EXE on a workstation, NPRINTER.NLM on a server, or a hardware device.

**primary time server**    One of the four types of time servers. A primary server communicates with other primary servers and reference servers and negotiates or "votes" to determine the correct time.

**print job**    A file that has been sent by a client for printing. See also *print queue*.

**print job configuration**    A set of parameters for network printing. These are similar to the parameters in the CAPTURE command. Print job configurations can be set for User and *container objects*.

**print queue**    The area that holds the list of print jobs that are waiting to print. The print queue is managed through the Print Queue object in NDS. Print jobs are sent from the print queue to the *print server* one at a time.

**print server**  A device that is used to manage printing. The Print Server NDS object is used to configure the print server. The print server itself can run on a NetWare 4 server (PSERVER.NLM) or in a hardware device. NetWare 3.1*x* included PSERVER.EXE, which ran on a DOS workstation; this is not supported in NetWare 4.

**printer forms**  Configurations that allow you to use specific paper types or send special codes to a printer. These are defined with the PRINTDEF utility.

**printer redirection**  The process of mapping a logical printer port in the workstation to a network printer. The user can then print to the port as though it were an actual printer, and the print job will be sent to the print queue. You use the CAPTURE utility to start redirection.

**printer sharing**  NetWare's feature that allows multiple users to send data to a printer. A print queue is used to store each print job, and they are sent to the printer one at a time.

**Profile object**  A special NDS object for assigning the same *login script* to a group of users. The Profile login script is executed after the container login script and before the user login script.

**properties**  In NDS, all the possible information that can be entered for an object. The properties of a User object include login name, full name, and telephone number. See also *values*.

**protocol**  A method of communicating between NetWare servers and clients. The protocol is the "language" used for sending data. Data is divided into *packets* specified by the protocol. IPX is the typical protocol for NetWare networks.

**[Public] trustee**  A special NDS trustee you can use to assign rights to all users in the network, including those that are not logged in. This allows users to browse the Directory tree before logging in. You should avoid assigning rights to this trustee.

**reference time server**  One of the four types of *time server*. The reference server provides an authoritative source of time. It is often attached to an external clock or a modem or radio link to a time source. One or more *primary time servers* must be used.

**registry**   In Windows 95, a special file that stores configuration information for the operating system and installed applications. You use the REGEDIT utility to manage the registry.

**relative distinguished name (RDN)**   A shortened version of an object's full *distinguished name* that specifies the path to the object from the current context. Relative distinguished names do not begin with a period. You can use periods at the end of the RDN to move up the Directory tree.

**remote printer**   See *workstation printer.*

**repeater**   A device that connects segments of a network together, allowing greater distances. This device amplifies the signal and outputs it.

**replica**   In NDS, a copy of a partition stored on a server. At least one replica, the master replica, is required for each partition. Other replicas include read/write and read-only replicas.

**replication**   The process of keeping copies of the NDS information on separate servers. Each *partition* in NDS has a set of replicas. These include the master replica (the original *partition*) and optionally read/write and read-only replicas.

**root directory**   In the DOS or NetWare file system, the highest location in the directory hierarchy. Files can be stored in the root directory or in subdirectories underneath it.

**[Root] object**   The ultimate NDS container object. The [Root] object is created when NDS is installed and contains all other objects. You cannot delete, rename, or move this object.

**router**   A device that connects two dissimilar networks and allows packets to be transmitted and received between them.

**routing protocols**   Protocols that send information to manage routing. The routing protocols supported by NetWare 4 are RIP (Routing Information Protocol) and NLSP (NetWare Link Services Protocol).

**same-server migration**   One of the methods for upgrading NetWare 2.*x* to NetWare 4. This requires that the server running NetWare 2.*x* be capable of running NetWare 4. The process involves upgrading the file system to NetWare 3.1*x* format and then upgrading to NetWare 4.

**search drives**  A list of paths that will be searched when you type a command on a workstation attached to the network. These are managed with the MAP command. This is similar to the *path* in the DOS file system.

**secondary time server**  One of the four types of time servers. Secondary time servers are strictly time consumers; they do not provide time to any servers. They receive time from a *primary* or *single reference server* and provide the time to clients.

**security equivalence**  In NDS, any situation in which an object or *trustee* receives the same rights given to another *object*. See also *implied equivalence* and *explicit equivalence*.

**segment**  A portion of a network containing devices that use the same network protocols and are connected by similar wiring. Devices in a segment also use the same external network number.

**server**  A machine running NetWare acts as a server. The server provides file, printer, and other services to clients.

**server-centric**  The type of network organization used in NetWare 3.1*x* networks. In this organization, each server keeps its own catalog of users and other resources (the *bindery*). A user who requires access to more than one server must be added to the bindery of each one. NetWare 4 provides a *network-centric* alternative.

**server commands**  Commands that execute on the server console. For example, the LOAD command is used to load an NLM.

**server printer**  One of the methods of attaching a printer to the network, and probably the most common. The printer is attached to a printer port on the NetWare server. The port driver, NPRINTER.NLM, drives the printer.

**Service Advertising Protocol (SAP)**  The *protocol* used for various NetWare 4, as well as 2.*x* and 3.*x*, services. *Single reference time servers* use this protocol to broadcast time information to the entire network at once.

**single reference time server**  One of the four types of *time servers*. If it's used, the single reference server is the only time provider on the network. All other servers must be configured as secondary time servers. This is the default configuration when NetWare 4 servers are installed.

**splitting partitions**   The process of creating a new NDS partition. A container object within a current partition is specified, and that object and all objects under it are moved (split) to a new partition.

**standards document**   A document that describes the naming standards, properties, and values to be used for a network. This is a vital part of NDS planning.

**Storage Management Services (SMS)**   The NetWare 4 service that allows for backup services. SMS consists of several components, ranging from the *device driver* that handles access to the backup device to the front end.

**synchronization**   The process NDS uses to ensure that all replicas of a partition contain the same data. Synchronization is handled through replica rings.

**Target Service Agent (TSA)**   One of the components of the NetWare 4 *Storage Management Services* (SMS). The TSA provides an interface to the device that will be backed up. Devices include servers, workstations, and the NDS database. A separate TSA is used for each one.

**TCP/IP**   A suite of protocols, including Transport Control Protocol (TCP) and Internet Protocol (IP). TCP/IP is supported by NetWare 4 and is typically used for connectivity with UNIX systems and the Internet.

**time consumer**   A machine that receives time information but does not send time information to any other server. Secondary time servers are time consumers, as are network workstations.

**time provider**   A type of *time server* that provides the time to other time servers.

**time provider group**   A group of time servers, usually including a *reference server* and one or more *primary servers*. In a *wide area network* (WAN), you can use separate time provider groups for each location.

**time server**   A server that performs time synchronization. All NetWare 4 servers are time servers of one type or another. The types of servers include *primary, reference, single reference,* and *secondary*.

**time source**   See *time provider*.

**time synchronization** The process NetWare 4 uses to ensure that all servers are provided with the correct time. Time synchronization is managed through *time servers.*

**topology** A type of network connection or cabling system. The term refers to the placement of nodes and wiring on the network. Common topologies include bus, ring, and star.

**trustee** Any object that has been given rights to an NDS object or file. Trustee rights can include *explicit, inherited,* and *effective rights.*

**trustee rights** Rights given to a trustee (such as a user) for a file in the file system, or for an object in NDS.

**typeful naming** The formal method of naming NDS objects, including name types for each portion of the name—for example, .CN=Terry.OU= Mktg.O=QAZ_CO.

**typeless naming** The more common method of NDS object naming, which does not include name types—for example, .Terry.Mktg.QAZ.CO. Typeless naming is adequate for most uses within NDS utilities.

**Universal Coordinated Time (UTC)** The standard time system NetWare 4 supports. The abbreviation is from the French. UTC was formerly known as GMT (Greenwich Mean Time). The time zone for a NetWare server is defined in terms of difference from UTC; for example, the Mountain time zone is UTC minus seven hours.

**User object** In NDS, an object that represents a user on the network. The User object includes properties that identify the user and assign rights to NDS and the file system. You can use a *user template* to create a number of users with similar properties.

**user template** In NDS, a special User object that assigns defaults when a new user is created. You can create a user template for each NDS container, and you can change the property values of this object to provide defaults for new users in the container. The user template does not affect existing users.

**values** The data that is stored in the *properties* of an NDS object. Properties can have one or more values. Some are required and others are optional.

**Virtual Loadable Module (VLM)** One of the components of the *DOS Requester*. The VLM.EXE program loads various VLMs, each for a certain purpose. For example, PRINT.VLM allows redirection of printers. VLMs that are not needed can be unloaded to increase available memory.

**volume** A portion of a disk set aside for NetWare files. Volumes can be created within a NetWare partition on the hard disk. The SYS: volume is the first volume created, and it is required for all NetWare 4 servers.

**wide area network (WAN)** A network that extends across multiple locations. Each location typically has a *local area network* (*LAN*), and the LANs are connected together in a WAN. These networks are typically used for enterprise networking.

**wildcard** In the DOS file system, a character that can substitute for one or more unknown characters when you type a command. The DOS wildcards are ?, which represents one character, and *, which represents any number of characters.

**workgroup organization** One of the methods of organizing the NDS tree. In this method, workgroups (users who perform similar functions or are participating in the same project) are used to divide the Directory tree. This method is best used in a *hybrid* organization.

**workstation** A computer that is connected to the network and has access to a NetWare 4 server. Workstations can be running DOS, Windows, Windows 95, Windows NT, OS/2, or UNIX operating systems. Workstations are also called clients.

**workstation printer** A printer that is attached to a workstation on the network. In NetWare 3.1*x*, these were referred to as remote printers and were handled by the RPRINTER.EXE program. In NetWare 4, the NPRINTER.EXE program handles them.

# Index

**Note to the Reader:**

First level entries are in **bold**. Page numbers in **bold** indicate the principal discussion of a topic or the definition of a term. Page numbers in *italic* indicate illustrations.

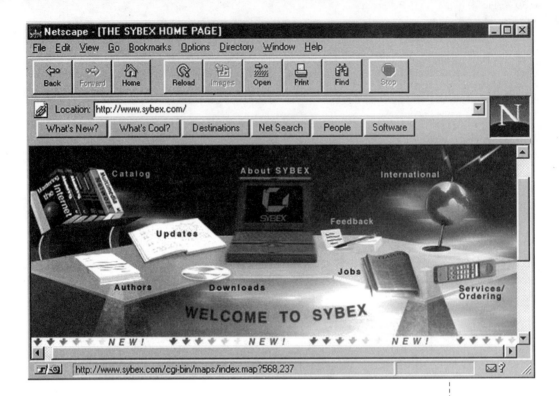